UNDERSTANDING AND APPLYING THE SCRIPTURES

UNDERSTANDING AND APPLYING THE SCRIPTURES

Danny McCain and Craig Keener

Africa Christian Textbooks

2013

UNDERSTANDING AND APPLYING THE SCRIPTURES

Copyright © 2003 and 2008 by Danny McCain and Craig Keener
This Edition © 2008 by Danny McCain and Craig Keener
Reprinted 2008, 2013
All rights reserved.

No part of this publication may be reproduced, stored in a retrieval system or transmitted, in any form by any means electronic, mechanical, photocopying, recording or otherwise, without prior permission in writing from the author and the publisher except for brief quotations embodied in articles and reviews.

Unless otherwise stated, all scriptures are taken with permission from the HOLY BIBLE, NEW INTERNATIONAL VERSION © 1984 by the International Bible Society.

ISBN: 978-905-061-5

Published by: **Africa Christian Textbooks (ACTS)**

ACTS Bookshop, International HQ, TCNN,
PMB 2020, Bukuru 930008, Plateau State, Nigeria.
GSM: +234 (0) 803-589-5328; E-mail: acts.jos@gmail.com
Website: www.acts-ng.com

ACTS Branches:
- Garki Ultra-Modern Market (International Market), No. 143, Umar Bahago Block, "A" Courtyard, Abuja, FCT.
- West Africa Theological Seminary (WATS), 36 Olukunle Akinola Street, Ipaja, Lagos.
- 14 Oba Akran Avenue, Ikeja, Under Bridge Bus Stop, Lagos.
- Theological College of Northern Nigeria (TCNN), PMB 2020, Bukuru 930008, Plateau State.
- ECWA Theological Seminary, Jos (JETS), PO Box 5398, Zaria Road, Jos, Plateau State.
- Nigerian Baptist Theological Seminary (NBTS), PMB 4008, Ogbomoso, Oyo State.
- ECWA Theological Seminary Kagoro, PMB 35, Kagoro, Kaduna State.
- Theological Seminary of Northern Nigeria, Saminaka, Kaduna State.
- No. 23 Obio Imo Street, Uyo, Akwa Ibom State.
- UMCA Theological College, Offa Garage Road, Murtala Mohammed Way, Ilorin, Kwara State.
- Nairobi Evangelical Graduate School of Theology (NEGST), Kenya. E-mail: acts.kenya@gmail.com

Table of Contents

Chapters

Preface vii
Introduction to Hermeneutics 1
Introduction to the Bible 11
Inspiration 27
Canonization 43
Textual Criticism 53
English Translations 69
Tools of Bible Study 93
Rule 1. The Rule of Spiritual Truth 127
Rule 2. The Rule of Selectivity 135
Rule 3. The Rule of Simplicity 141
Rule 4. The Rule of Context 147
Rule 5. The Rule of Words 175
Rule 6. The Rule of Grammar 191
Rule 7. The Rule of Figurative Language 207
Rule 8. The Rule of Progressive Revelation 227
Symbolism in the Bible 251
Interpreting Narrative 261
Interpreting Poetic Literature 273
Interpreting Psalms 285
Interpreting Proverbs 291
Interpreting Prophecy 299
Interpreting Jesus 311
Interpreting the Apostles 319
Application in the Bible 329
Application in the Narratives 349
Application in the Epistles 359

Appendices

Paragraph Context Examples 369
Whole Book Context Examples 386
Background Context Examples 403
Examination of Jesus' Teaching Methods 423
"The Theology of the Blood of Jesus" 427
"Prosperity: A Biblical Perspective" 447

Selected Bibliography 465
General Index 467

Preface

I taught my first class in hermeneutics in 1976. The course was entitled "Principles of Bible Study and Interpretation." Since I was teaching in the USA at that time, where all our students had access to good textbooks, I basically used a textbook and did not prepare any extensive personal notes. By the second time I taught the course, I started developing my own notes on interpreting the Bible. When I came to Nigeria in 1988 and found out that the average student did not have access to a textbook, I expanded my notes and started making them available to my students in a mimeographed form. I have continued to upgrade and hopefully improve these notes every time I go through them.

In 1999, while my good friend Prof. Craig Keener was staying in my house in Jos and lecturing at the University of Jos, we discussed the need for a hermeneutics textbook that would be tailored especially for Africa. Prof. Keener and I eventually agreed to co-author a book on hermeneutics. Prof. Keener, who is a prolific writer, immediately went to work and completed his part of the book within four months. However, it took me over three years before I was able to get my part of the book in a publishable condition.

Co-authoring a book is tricky because both authors have their own personalities and styles of writing and theological convictions. Because of this, it is hard to "marry" two parts of a book that have been written by different people. We have worked hard at it but we are very aware that it is not a perfect union.

In fact, it should be noted that we deliberately left some of the first person singular pronouns in the book like "I" and "me." These are usually found in sections where we are giving examples from our teaching. To make the project very personal and easy to read, we have chosen to keep those personal pronouns in the text as we would use them in our oral lecturing. With the explanations given below about who wrote what sections and through careful observation, it should not be too difficult for the careful reader to figure out which of us is the "I" in these sections.

One thing that we try to keep in mind in teaching here in Africa is that the average pastor and Bible teacher does not have access to all the Bible study resources we have in the Western World. Therefore, in this book I have tried to give enough background information and the appropriate principles that will help the sincere Bible student to extract from the Bible the messages that were intended by the original authors. In other words, this book is written with the assumption that the reader will have very few Bible study materials.

This book can be divided into four general divisions. In the first part, I attempt to give a general overview of the Bible. It is my conviction that we cannot understand the parts of the Bible without having a reasonable understanding of the whole. Therefore, I have described the Bible from the time it was in the mind of God to the Bibles we read every day. This includes a general introduction to the Bible in which I discuss everything from the name of the Bible to the chapter and verse divisions. In this section, I use the educational principle of going from the "known to the unknown" and from the "general to the specific." After that, I talk about the topics of inspiration, canonicity, textual criticism and translation.

The second part of the book is the "tools and rules" section. I wrote all of this material except the chapter on context. When Prof. Keener teaches hermeneutics, he spends more than half his time simply studying problems associated with context. That is why the chapter on context is one of the longest in the book. In addition, there are three appendices that contain additional examples related to the chapter on context.

In this section I spend a couple of chapters explaining what I see to be the most important tools of Bible study. After that I focus on eight different rules of interpretation. Certainly there are more than eight rules related to interpreting the Bible. I have created eight general categories related to interpretation. These enable me to discuss the many principles related to interpreting the Bible. For example, one of these rules is the "Rule of Grammar." Even primary school students know that there are many different rules of grammar. That means that there are many different ways knowing and using the rules of grammar will influence our study of the Bible. In this book, however, I have lumped all those principles together in that one rule called the "Rule of Grammar."

The third part of the book is what theologians call "special interpretation." Most of the eight rules referred to above relate to interpreting any kind of written document, whether in the Bible or not. However, the Bible also contains some genres that are not commonly found in other literature such as psalms, proverbs, prophecy and parables. Prof. Keener prepared most of the material in this section.

The final part of this book focuses on application. One of the most common mistakes my students make is to confuse interpretation and application. We cannot do appropriate application until we have done proper interpretation. However, once we have done our interpretation, we need some guidelines on the best way to apply these truths into our contemporary lives. Prof. Keener and I have tried to supply some of those guidelines in the last three chapters of this book. I wrote the general chapter on application and Prof. Keener wrote the chapters on interpreting and applying narratives and epistles.

Because I live in Nigeria and am more familiar with the communication patterns of African students, Prof. Keener has allowed me to be responsible for the general layout and design and to edit his own material freely. Therefore, any mistakes found in the text are entirely my responsibility. I have also been granted the responsibility of writing the preface on behalf of the writing team and publishers.

We are most grateful to all those who have assisted us in the creation of this book. This includes hundreds of students, at all levels—from diploma students to post-graduate students in universities, seminaries, Bible colleges and seminars, whose questions and observations have helped to shape the book into what it is now. We are also grateful to my colleague at the University of Jos, Dr. Gwamna Dogara, who has not only read this manuscript but has taught hermeneutics using these materials. To my colleagues in Africa Christian Textbooks, Rev. Dr. Scott Cunningham and Rev. Dr. Sid Garland, who have both read the manuscript and made most helpful suggestions, we are most grateful. My daughter, Carmen, has proofread the manuscript and my wife, Mary, has worked many, many hours proofreading, checking references, creating the index, doing visual editing and all the other tedious things that have to be done before a book can be published. To both of them, I am most grateful. I am also grateful to Africa Christian Textbooks for agreeing to publish this book. I must express my personal appreciation to Prof. Craig Keener for his hard work on this book and also for agreeing to work with me on this project.

Finally, we must give thanks to God who has given us the rich privilege of not only teaching the Bible but also teaching others how to study it.

It is my prayer that all who interact with this book will experience what the people in Jerusalem did when Ezra read the law to them: *"They read from the Book of the Law of God, making it clear and giving the meaning so that the people could understand what was being read"* (Nehemiah 8:8).

Prof. Danny McCain
May 2008

Chapter One

Introduction to Hermeneutics

Introduction

Hermeneutics is a big theological word that sounds impressive because the average person does not know what it means. However, it is not really that difficult to grasp. Hermeneutics is the study of the principles and methods of interpretation, and in our case, understanding and applying the Bible properly. Since one important objective of properly understanding the Bible is to communicate the Bible accurately, the study of hermeneutics has a very practical purpose.

We will begin with a look at the Bible. After that we will explore techniques of communication. Finally we will try to understand hermeneutics in light of these things.

What is the Bible?

A well-known education principle says the best way to learn is to go from the general to the specific—from the known to the unknown. We will not be able to understand the specifics of hermeneutics without a good overall understanding of the Bible itself. The more we understand about the Bible in a general way, the better we are going to be able to understand its specific parts.

Starting on September 7, 2001, we experienced a serious crisis in Jos, Nigeria. In the international media, this was reported as a conflict between Muslims and Christians. However, to truly understand the complex roots behind the crisis, we must go back at least 150 years earlier to the jihad of Uthman Dan Fodio. As the Hausa Fulanis moved south and occupied the middle belt region, they came into conflict with the smaller tribes. This conflict has continued for many generations. The crisis in Jos was, in part, a reaction to that. If you do not understand the general history of Nigeria, you will not understand the Jos crisis.

Likewise, there are at least four different processes that have brought the Bible from its conception in the mind of God, to the written Bible that we use today. These processes include Inspiration, Canonization, Textual Criticism, and Translations. We will later examine each of these and see how they relate to understanding the whole Bible.

Key Words Related to Hermeneutics

Hermeneutics is the science of interpreting the Bible.

We call Hermeneutics a science because it follows certain predictable rules. A presupposition of hermeneutics is that the original communicator was intending to communicate a certain message and was doing so in the most simple, straightforward manner possible. However, hermeneutics is not an exact science like mathematics and physics, which have predictable formulas that always work exactly the same way in every situation. Hermeneutics is not an exact science because hermeneutics works with human beings, and humans do not always respond the same way in every situation. The way one person communicates is often different from the way another one communicates. The way one person uses a certain word is often very different from the way another person uses that word.

One of the mistakes young interpreters make is to think that once they have done a word study and understand what a particular word means, it will always mean that. Jesus talks about the *"leaven of the Pharisees,"* meaning their influence is like yeast in the society. Since the Pharisees' influence was not good, yeast must be a negative figure of speech. Therefore when Jesus says the kingdom of heaven is like a woman who puts yeast in a lump of dough and the yeast expands throughout the whole lump (Matthew 13:33), the temptation is to think that yeast must still refer to something negative.

How many different ways is "death" used in the Bible? It means physical death; people actually die physically (Matthew 22:27). It means spiritual death; Adam and Eve "died" on the day they ate the fruit (Genesis 2:17). It means eternal death; those who die without Christ will be eternally without him (Romans 6:23). It means to have dead spirits; Ephesians 2:1

talks about being *"dead in trespasses and sins."* However, death also is used positively in Romans 6:2: we are described as being *"dead to sin."*

Exegesis is extracting from any document the communication intended by the original author.

The exegesis of the Bible is done just as one would interpret any other document. If you received a note from a teacher, you would determine the meaning by the words used. For example, I once received this email from Dr. Mike Blyth related to a visiting lecture I was to give:

> The classes are 45 minutes long, and the first one starts at 1:45. The second ends at 3:20. Both periods are in Room 15. The class is on ethics. We have progressed from an overview of worldviews and ethical theories to the Bible. --Mike

What was the message of that email? How long were the classes to last? How do you know that? You can know these things because you did exegesis. You extracted from the text the intended message of the author.

Interpretation is correctly understanding the message intended by the communicator.

In my opinion, interpretation is simpler than most people think. I frequently ask my students, "What percentage of the Bible do you think you understand?" Some estimate they understand 50 percent. Some estimate they understand 90 percent. Over the years I have demonstrated how much we understand the Bible by picking a passage at random and reading it orally in class. As a general rule, the students will understand everything that was said. My estimation is that master's level students have the ability to understand perhaps 95+ percent of the Bible. Even diploma level students are capable of understanding more than 90 percent of the Bible. The objective of a hermeneutics course is to increase one's ability to understand one or two more percentage points.

Remember this: The people who heard Jesus speak were semi-literate people who heard Jesus speak one time, orally, and understood His communication. None of the people Jesus preached to, taught, or counseled, ever saw any of the words of Jesus in writing. They had not studied Greek grammar or learned all of the fine nuances of some of Jesus' words. They simply heard what He said and understood easily and naturally.

Also, the people in Philippi heard Paul's letter read once, orally, and got the point. We can assume that the author is doing his best to communicate in the simplest form possible. He is not trying to conceal truth. He is trying to make truth clear and plain.

Application is making the truths of the Bible relevant in the contemporary world.

Interpretation is relatively straightforward. It is simply trying to understand the communication that was intended by the author. However, application of the Bible is taking those truths that were presented in another culture, in another time period, in another language, and demonstrating how they should apply to us today.

For example, Ephesians 5:18 says, *"Do not get drunk on wine."* What does that mean? We know what the various words mean. "Wine" is the juice from grapes that has been allowed to ferment to the point that it has alcohol in it. "Drunk" means to have ingested enough alcohol to affect the mental and physical functions of the body. Therefore the prohibition of "getting drunk with wine" means that one should not drink enough wine to affect one's physical and mental functions. That is the correct interpretation of this passage. A literalist might say, "OK, I will not drink wine. I will drink beer or whisky or vodka or rum or champagne or *burukutu* (homemade alcohol). If I drink these things and get drunk, I am not disobeying what the scripture says." The principle being taught here is that one should not take alcohol or drugs or Indian hemp or anything else that would alter a person's physical and mental functions. Whenever a person preaches against smoking marijuana, he is applying the scripture based upon his interpretation of scripture.

Things that Affect Interpretation

Our ability to interpret the Bible is seriously affected by two things:

The Bible was written in a different language.

Words do not always mean the same thing when they are translated. All who speak more than one language understand this very well. Some years ago, I had a man from America visit me in Port Harcourt. I arranged for him to preach in a local church. His sermon was translated into Pidgin English. He was telling a story about a person who was a poor employee. The employee kept doing bad things. The American preacher said, "Finally, his boss could take it no longer, so he fired the man." The man translating into Pidgin English looked a bit shocked but faithfully translated, "His ogah vexed too much so he take de man and shoot um." In American English, "Fire" means to terminate a person's employment, but in Nigerian English, it means, "to shoot." Therefore, in the Pidgin translation, the employee got shot instead of getting sacked.

The Bible was written in a different culture.

We do not always understand the idioms in the Bible. We do not always understand the cultural practices. We do not always understand the social norms and standards. Because of these things, we often miss the communication. Although we may understand most of the words, words in a certain context may mean something different than we are accustomed to. I might describe a certain event this way.

> The quarterback lines up in the shotgun. The center hikes the ball to him. He rolls out to the right five yards from the line of scrimmage. He is being rushed by the middle linebacker. However, he fires to his tight end who is hit at the twenty but not before he gets a first down.

The above paragraph illustrates the way a radio announcer would describe a typical play in American football. You probably understand most of the words, but you do not understand the specialized use of these words or the way they are used in this context.

Problems with Interpretation

There are three ways that we often fail to understand communications, including communications in the Bible.

Misinterpretation

To misinterpret is to read something in the Bible and think it says one thing when it actually says something else.

Once I was conducting a prayer meeting and I read Psalm 91:4 (KJV) which says, *"He shall cover thee with his feathers, and under his wings shalt thou trust: his truth shall be thy shield and buckler."* A buckler is a small shield. However, one of the ladies in the church thought I said *"shield and butler."* She then gave a wonderful exhortation about the Lord being our "butler." She explained about how a butler was a person who answered the door when someone knocked. She was happy that when the devil came knocking on her door, Butler Jesus was there to answer the door. She mentioned that a butler was the one who prepared the bath water for a person. She was happy that Butler Jesus prepared the water that washed all her sins away. She actually got a great blessing from the passage, but she misinterpreted it. She simply misunderstood what it said.

I am convinced that one of the things that contributes to our misunderstanding the Bible is that we continue to use the King James Bible. The King James Bible is almost 400 years old. We no longer speak the kind of English that was used in the King James Bible. Many of the words found in the King James Bible are no longer used. Some of them mean something totally different from what they meant before.

About twenty years ago, I became convinced that I should read a modern language Bible. To continue to read a Bible that used old English and also did not have access to the older and better manuscripts that have been made available during the last four hundred years, was to deliberately deprive myself of the truth. About ten years ago, I became convinced that I should no longer use the King James Bible in my teaching and preaching, because every time I used in publicly, I encouraged other people to do the same and when they did so they also limited their ability to understand the Word of God.

I would encourage pastors and Bible teachers to persuade their constituents and students to get a modern language Bible that they can understand. One of the things that will help is if you regularly use a modern language Bible in the pulpit and in the classroom. When your people see a person they respect using a modern language Bible, this will give them courage to make the change themselves.

We must try our best not to be guilty of misinterpretation.

Under-Interpretation

To under-interpret is to have more in the passage than we actually see. It is to fail to get everything from the passage that is there. This also happens often. Because we do not understand the culture or a particular idiom or even geographical information, we fail to really understand the significance of a passage.

For example, in Matthew 16:18, Jesus said, *"And I tell you that you are Peter, and on this rock I will build my church, and the gates of Hades will not overcome it."* When Jesus made this statement, he was near Caesarea Philippi. In fact, he was sitting near a little river that flowed out of a wall of rock that was almost perpendicular. The pagans in that area had carved a pagan temple out of the stone immediately above where the river flowed out of the rock. Pagan worshippers would go there every day to worship their pagan gods. The Jews in this area of course hated paganism. They had an interesting name for this pagan temple. It was the "Gates of Hell." So when Jesus mentioned that the "Gates of Hell" would not be able to prevail against the growing church, he was saying that neither pagan gods nor any other religion would be able to stand in the way of the onward march of the church. If we do not understand that the local people called that particular place the "Gates of Hell," we will not really fully understand the significance of the statement Jesus made.

Over-Interpretation

To over-interpret is to see more in a passage than was intended by the original author. This is a particular danger when we are interpreting proverbs and parables. For example, the story of the Ten Virgins takes up thirteen verses in Matthew. We often get all involved in the meaning of the five wise virgins and the five foolish virgins, the oil and the lamps, and the bride and the bridegroom. What do all these things represent? They do not represent anything. The point of the story is in its entirety not in the individual details. In fact, Jesus himself gave us the interpretation of this passage. It is simply that we must watch. As certainly as the ten virgins needed to be watching for the coming of the bridegroom and his party, we need to be watching for the return of Jesus. In my opinion, perhaps the way we misunderstand the Bible the most is through over-interpretation. I want to expand on this a bit more.

Why Do We Tend to Over-Interpret the Bible?

Because we have a magical view of the Bible.

There is a little bit of pagan in all of us. Many of us view the Bible as if it were some kind of magical book. For example, one of my relatives used to place the King James Bible on the dashboard of his vehicle when he was making a long trip. He thought that surely if he had the Bible there, the Lord would protect him.

The Bible is not a book of magic. We Christians do not have the same view toward the Bible as Muslims have towards the Qur'an. We do not believe that the paper and ink and cover are sacred. It is the truth in the Bible that is sacred. However, when we have a magical view of the Bible, we tend to think that it is filled with all kinds of magical formulas that only the spiritual can understand. Let us have proper respect for the Bible, but let us not treat it like a book of magic.

Because we assume that the Bible is for spiritual giants or experts.

We must not forget about the doctrine we call the "priesthood of the believers." The Reformers rejected the concept that only the priest or the well-educated could understand the Bible and clearly taught that the common person can understand the truths of the Bible. There is an old theological word that describes what we believe about the Bible—the "perspicuity of Scripture." This word basically means "clarity." The term means that the Bible is clear enough for everyone to understand all they need to know to receive God's salvation and do the work God has called them to do.

We often develop a mental block about the Bible. We tend to think that surely I, a very ordinary person, cannot really understand the Bible. Please remember that the Bible was written in simple language to simple people. It was written to be easily understood not to conceal truth and confuse people.

Because we tend to look for "spiritual" truths.

The secularism of the western world has penetrated our Christianity. We have divided the Bible up into the sacred parts and the regular parts. Therefore, we tend to read the Bible to find the "spiritual parts." We get bored when we read through the Book of Numbers because it contains so much uninteresting material. We like the Psalms, which we perceive to be more spiritual. However, we must remind ourselves that all of the Bible is spiritual. The next point is closely connected with this.

Because we look for nuggets of truths rather than whole truth.

Many of our pastors preach "textual sermons." These are sermons that are taken from one brief text. Preachers find some small phrase that is easily remembered, remove it from its context and use it as the foundation for a sermon. Actually, all preachers do this occasionally. I like to preach a sermon on "Come Unto Me." I build my whole sermon around that phrase. However, because we are exposed to this kind of preaching, we tend to read the Bible in such a way as to look for those small nuggets of truth rather than looking for the truth found in the whole passage.

There is an old proverb in my country that says, "Sometimes we cannot see the forest for the trees." Another version of this is "We cannot see the city for the buildings." In the Bible, we tend to lose the Story in the stories. In other words, we get so bogged down looking at the individual components that we fail to see the big picture. I am convinced that we get so interested in the small details of the Bible, we often fail to understand the big central truths that we would get from normal reading.

Because we read the Bible in chapters rather than whole segments.

We read the Bible differently than we read any other document in the world. If you traveled to the USA and while there you received a ten-page letter from your wife, would you read one page per day until you finished the whole letter? No, we would not do that. However, that is the way we often read the Bible.

The people who divided the Bible into chapters and verses did us a big favor by making it easier to find various parts of the Bible. However, they also did us a disfavor by encouraging us to read the Bible in segments rather than reading it like we do other written documents.

Conclusion

Interpreting and applying the Bible is one of the most important tasks that the Christian believer has. The outcome of one's interpretation and application affects not only his or her life now but for all eternity as well. It is the goal of this book to help all of us understand the teachings of the Bible better and apply them more carefully in our contemporary world.

Study Questions

1. How does having a general understanding of the Bible affect the interpretation of the whole?
2. Give an illustration about how understanding the big picture helps one understand the individual parts.
3. Write out definitions and give illustrations of the following words: hermeneutics; exegesis; interpretation; application.
4. What is the difference between exegesis and interpretation?
5. What is the difference between interpretation and application?
6. What are the major things that affect interpretation?
7. Write a paragraph explaining how we can avoid a "magical view"
8. Why are we often guilty of over-interpretation?
9. Write a paragraph interacting with the statements in this chapter about the need for the use of a modern language Bible.
10. Write a paragraph explaining how we can avoid a "magical" view of the Bible.

Chapter Two

Introduction to the Bible

Of all the ways God had at his disposal to communicate truth and transfer it from one generation to the next, he chose written communication. If God thought that it was important enough to write truth for his creatures to understand, we should try to find out as much about that written revelation as possible. We believe that the Bible is God's collection of truth for humanity. It is the foundation stone upon which all Christian doctrine is built. It is that which God has given to us to help us understand Himself, His world, and our relationship to Him. It is God's primary communication to the human race.

Never before has there been a generation who has available such an abundant amount of information about the Bible. The Bible has been on the bestseller list ever since the invention of printing. In the last fifty years alone, there have been at least eighty English translations of the Bible. The average Christian home has over three Bibles in it. The Bible is read over the radio. Many different translations of the Bible are available on cassette tapes. The Bible and thousands of Bible study aids have been placed on CD's and made available on the Internet.

In spite of that, it is amazing that there is still so much ignorance about the Bible. Though there is an abundance of publications about Biblical themes, there is a huge gap between those who prepare this material and those for whom it is intended.

The Name "Bible"

The word "Bible" is a great-grandson of the Greek word *biblos* or *biblia*, which meant a "writing" or "books." During the New Testament days, this was one of the names given to the Old Testament, and by about the fifth century AD it had become firmly attached to the whole collection of sacred writings. The Greek word *biblos* gave birth to the Latin word *biblia*, which was transliterated into the French word, *Biblia*. Our English word, "Bible," comes from the French with a slightly different ending and pronunciation. Before the word "Bible" became the official title to God's word, St. Jerome, in the fourth century, called it *Bibliotheca Divina* or "the Divine Library."

Biblical Divisions

The Bible is a collection of sixty-six separate books divided into two sections known as the Old and New Testaments. The word *testament* could really be better translated *covenant*. It refers to the covenant that God has between himself and his people. The Old Testament is actually more than just a covenant. It includes the covenant, but it also includes the history of God's people, the prophecies related to the future of God's people, and the songs, poems and other meditations written by God's people in that period.

The New Testament contains a record of the covenant that God established between himself and his new people, the church. It also contains details of the events surrounding the beginning of the new covenant. There are practical instructions about how the covenant relates to our lives. There are also prophecies about the future of God's relationship with His people. Although the terms "Old Testament" and "New Testament" are not all-inclusive terms, they are well-established titles of these divisions of the Bible.

The sixty-six books of the Bible were written over a period of sixteen hundred years by over thirty different authors. They were mostly written in Palestine, but a few were written in Greece, Turkey, and Italy.

The Old Testament has been divided in different ways. The most ancient division was simply "the law and the prophets." This is the most common way in which the New Testament refers to the Old Testament.

The ancient and modern Hebrew Bibles are divided into three parts.

Introduction to the Bible

1. The Law (*Torah*); containing the Pentateuch
2. The Prophets (*Nebhiim*)
    a. The Former Prophets: Joshua, Judges, Samuel, Kings
    b. The Latter Prophets: Isaiah, Jeremiah, Ezekiel, The Twelve

    The Writings (Kethubim)

    c. Poetical Books (Psalms, Proverbs, Job)
    d. Five Rolls (*Megilloth*) (Song of Songs, Ruth, Lamentations, Esther, Ecclesiastes)
    e. Historical Books (Daniel, Ezra-Nehemiah, Chronicles)

The Septuagint divided the Old Testament into four divisions:

1. The Law (five books)
2. Poetry (five books)
3. History (twelve books—Joshua through Esther)
4. Prophets (seventeen books)
    a. Major Prophets (five books)
    b. Minor Prophets (twelve books)

The New Testament is divided into three general divisions:

1. History
    a. Four Gospels: brief biographies of Jesus
    b. Acts: the first thirty years of church history
    c. Instructions/Epistles
    d. Prophecy/Revelation[1]

---

[1] Not everyone agrees that the Book of Revelation is primarily a book of prophecy. Some view it as the apocalyptic style of writing about contemporary events.

Another division is:

1. Manifestation of Christ (Gospels)
2. Propagation of Christ (Acts)
3. Interpretation and Application of Christ (Epistles)
4. Consummation in Christ (Revelation)

Biblical Languages

Hebrew

The Bible was written in three different languages. Almost all of the Old Testament was written in Hebrew, an interesting language made up of 22 different letters. The language was originally written from right to left in square blocky letters with no vowels in the words and no breaks or spaces between the words. Even today, if one wanted to read a modern Hebrew Bible he would open it to what we think of as the back and read from the back to the front.

THLRDSMSHPRD (or DRPHSMSDRLHT—reading right to left) is an illustration of the Hebrew way of writing the phrase *"The Lord is my shepherd."* Fortunately, modern Hebrew Bibles separate the words and indicate the proper vowels to be added.

יהוה אלוֹהים

These two words are Yahweh Elohim and mean "the Lord God."

The parts of the Old Testament not written in Hebrew were written in Aramaic, a dialect that grew out of Hebrew. Aramaic was something of a trade language that was spoken in that part of the world by many different Semitic peoples. Aramaic would have been the principle language that Jesus spoke. The Aramaic portions of the Old Testament include parts of about ten chapters from Ezra and Daniel, and one verse in Jeremiah.

Greek

The New Testament was written in Greek. Greek, like practically every language, is a changing language. It existed as a written language several hundred years before the writing of the New Testament. This was known as the Classical period, the time in which Plato, Aristotle, Euripides, and other great Greek philosophers and playwrights wrote. The Greek of this period is very romantic and sophisticated and difficult.

The Greek of the New Testament, however, is much more simple and straightforward. It has been called by the scholars, *Koine* Greek, which simply means "Common" Greek. It is interesting that when God chose to communicate with His people, He did not choose the flowery sophistication of Classical Greek but the common ordinary language that most of the first century people spoke. The sample below is from John 5:24.

>Ἀμὴν ἀμὴν λέγω ὑμι˜ν ὅτι ὁ τὸν λόγον μου ἀκούων
>καὶ πιστεύων τῳ˜ πέμψαντί με ἔχει ζωὴν αἰώνιον

>*I tell you the truth, whoever hears my word*
>*and believes him who sent me has eternal life.*

Most serious Bible scholars study Greek, so they can understand the finer shades of meaning of the words in the Bible. There are some things in the Bible that can only be understood if one has some understanding of the original languages.

Writing Materials

Many years ago, the enemies of Orthodox Christianity tried to prove that the Bible was in error. They pointed out that writing had not been invented by the time of Moses, whom Christian theologians had traditionally believed was responsible for writing the Pentateuch. However, we now know that writing was developed to a rather high degree at least two thousand years prior to the time of Moses.

There were several different writing materials used by the writers of the Bible. At least a portion of the Bible was written in stone. God himself apparently wrote the Ten Commandments in stone (Exodus 24:12; 31:18;

Deuteronomy 4:13; 5:22). Stone was not an uncommon material for writing. Laws or messages or historical records were chiseled into stone in order to provide a permanent record of these things.

Clay shaped into tablets was also used for writing. While the clay was still soft, messages were inscribed in it. These tablets would be baked in an oven or by the sun to preserve a permanent record. This is the method Ezekiel used (Ezekiel 4:1) when God instructed him to get a *"brick"* (KJV) and inscribe the city of Jerusalem upon it. It was probably a soft unbaked tablet.

By far the most important writing material in the Old Testament was animal skin known as vellum or parchment. These skins were of various qualities depending upon their source and their preparation. Skins from all kinds of animals, including cattle, antelopes, sheep and goats, were used. Some of the leather was used on only one side. Some were used on both sides. When Paul said, *"and bring . . . my scrolls, especially the parchments"* (2 Timothy 4:13) he was referring, no doubt, to portions of the Old Testament that had been written on leather.

Leather was a very sturdy writing material, lasting for many years. Since most of the ink did not have the permanent quality of today's ink, frequently, parchments were erased and copied over. These were known as palimpsests. Some of these old leather manuscripts are still available. When the Dead Sea Scrolls were discovered in 1948, a number of these parchment manuscripts were found, including a nearly perfect copy of the Book of Isaiah. It had been written approximately two hundred years before Jesus was born.

The most common writing material during the New Testament times was papyrus. Papyrus was actually a reed that grew near wet damp areas especially in Egypt. This particular plant had long fibers that were used to make up a rough type of writing material. Two layers were pressed and glued together to make the writing material. Individual sheets were joined together to make a scroll. Later individual pages were joined on the edges, much like our modern books, to make what was known as a codex.

A stylus was used to write on soft clay and a chisel was used to write in stone. Pens made of different substances were used to write on the parchment and papyrus. Ink was made from herbs and vegetables.

Authors

There are over thirty different authors in the Bible. They wrote over a period of one thousand five hundred years and represent many different professions and walks of life. Note these examples of the various professions represented among the writers of the Bible:

- Farmer: Amos
- Shepherds: Moses and David
- Government Leaders: Moses and Joshua
- Civil Servants: Daniel and Nehemiah
- Kings: Solomon and David
- Musicians: Asaph and Ethan (they wrote some of the psalms)
- Prophets: Isaiah, Jeremiah and many others
- Professional Scribe: Ezra
- Fisherman: Peter and John
- Tax Collector (Civil Servant): Matthew
- Rabbi: Paul
- Physician: Luke
- Carpenter: Probably James the brother of Jesus

Although the writers of the Bible represent a wide range of backgrounds, amazingly, the Bible is a unified whole. Ultimately, it is the word of God.

Literary Styles

The Bible is a diverse book—different authors writing from different places in different languages and even in different time periods. This amazing diversity is illustrated in the many different styles of writing contained in the Bible.

Most literature falls within one of several easily distinguishable categories. A written document may be a poem, novel, essay or a short story. In English classes, students are often required to produce poems, essays, short stories and be familiar with other types of literature like novels, biographies, and autobiographies. The Bible is an excellent literary textbook because it contains many of these same genres or types of literature.

Prose

The majority of the Bible, and especially the Old Testament, is made up of prose, which is normal straightforward narrative type of writing. All historical narrative in the Bible is prose. For example, Genesis simply tells the beginning events in the history of the world and the history of Abraham's family. The familiar story of David and Goliath is written in this same simple style. By far the majority of the Bible fits into the category of prose.

Hebrew Poetry

A large portion of the Old Testament is written in poetry. There are certain characteristics of poetry that are basic to all languages, such as the use of highly figurative language, and the putting of thoughts in parallel lines—sometimes called couplets. However, in other ways Hebrew poetry differs from English poetry. When we think of poetry, frequently we think of words and phrases that are put together with a certain rhythm and have words in them that rhyme or sound alike. Note this couplet:

> *Mary had a little lamb, his fleece was white as snow;*
> *And everywhere that Mary went, the lamb was sure to go.*

One can easily hear the bounce and rhythm of the words and also recognize that "snow" rhymes with "go." This is not always true in English poetry, especially contemporary poetry, but frequently there is a parallelism of sound.

In Hebrew poetry there is no attempt to make words rhyme. Hebrew poetry does have rhythm sometimes, though this is difficult to show in a translation. The main characteristic of Hebrew poetry is its parallelism of thought. Instead of the second line having a word that rhymes, the Hebrews attempted to make the second phrase parallel in thought with the first. Sometimes, the second line essentially repeats the first line

Introduction to the Bible

except in different words. For example, David asked the question in Psalm 15, *"Lord, who may dwell in your sanctuary? Who may live on your holy hill?"* The second question essentially repeats the first, though in different words.

Another type of parallelism is contrasting parallelism in which the second line gives the opposite or contrasting truth to the first. Proverbs 15:9 says, *"The Lord detests the way of the wicked but he loves those who pursue righteousness."* Proverbs 13:11 says, *"Dishonest money dwindles away, but he who gathers money little by little makes it grow."*

In a third type of parallelism, the second line completes the thought or adds something to the first line. Psalm 126:1 says, *"When the Lord brought back the captives to Zion, we were like men who dreamed."* The second line in this couplet completes the thought of the first.

Poetic Books

Much of this Hebrew poetry is found in what we call the "Poetic Books," which include Job, Psalms, Proverbs, Ecclesiastes, and the Song of Solomon. These books were written by true poets. They are the expression of the inner life of the Old Testament saint. They tell us about the things that he thought, the prayers that he prayed, the questions that he had in his mind, the things he was afraid of and the things that produced joy and peace in his life. The poetic books are God's inspired record to us of Old Testament wisdom, ethics and devotion.

Poetry in the Prophets

Poetry is not limited to the "poetic books." There is a large segment of Old Testament poetry found in the prophets. The books of the Prophets like Isaiah, Jeremiah, and others do not contain so much of their own thoughts but the words and messages that God gave to them to be expressed to God's people in poetic fashion. It is interesting that God chose to present the message, usually messages of judgment, in poetic fashion. Isaiah 53, the great passage on the suffering Savior, is a good example. Note the parallelism found in verses 4-6a:

*Surely he took up our infirmities
and carried our sorrows,*

*yet we considered him stricken by God,
smitten by him, and afflicted.*

*But he was pierced for our transgressions,
he was crushed for our iniquities,*

*the punishment that brought us peace was upon him,
and by his wounds we are healed.*

*We all, like sheep, have gone astray,
each of us has turned to his own way.*

Biographies

Another Biblical literary device is the biography. A biography is a story written about the life of one person. In the Old Testament we have large biographical sections of Abraham, Moses, and especially David. In the New Testament, we have four examples of biographies in the four Gospels. It may be argued that they are not biographies in the truest or most complete sense of the word, since they skip many details of the life of Jesus. But they are biographies because it is their objective to present the life and work of one person.

Autobiographies

There is no example in the Bible of a pure autobiography. However, we have autobiographical sections in the Bible. Nehemiah is autobiographical in the sense that it was written with first person pronouns. The book begins,

> *The words of Nehemiah the son of Hacaliah: In the month of Kislev in the twentieth year, while I was in the citadel of Susa, Hanani, one of my brothers, came . . . and I questioned them . . . They said to me . . .*

Interestingly, though Moses wrote the first five books of the Bible, including many details about himself, he chose to write in the third person. The "we sections" in the Book of Acts are an example of autobiographical sections written within a larger book because the author was present for those particular events. In Acts 16:610, the passage shifts from third person (they) to first person (we).

Epistles

The epistle was developed more as a true literary device by the New Testament writers than by any of their literary predecessors. God communicated to us the most important New Testament doctrines through epistles. An epistle is simply a letter, much like a letter that you would write. However, this type of letter is more than just a friendly chat. A Bible epistle is hortatory in nature. That means that it gives instructions, exhortations and clarifies doctrines. However, epistles do all this in a warm and friendly manner. The fact that these Bible epistles were actual letters written to real people with real questions and real problems makes them to be even more relevant in meeting our needs today. The epistle is not just a collection of theoretical religious thoughts. It is God's chosen tool to communicate His truth to His people.

Homilies

The term "epistle" was used in a fairly broad sense in the New Testament era. There are two books in the New Testament that are generally recognized as epistles but are probably better characterized as homilies or a series of homilies. A homily is a short sermon or meditation and is less personal than a typical epistle. The Books of Hebrews and James, though containing some epistolary characteristics, appear to be more general exhortations and meditations.

Prophetic Literature

Both the Old and New Testaments contain prophetic literature. The word "prophecy" is used in more than one way in the Bible. However, here I am using it to refer to predictions of the future. All of the prophets give predictions of future events. Though there are prophetic passages in the New Testament, Revelation is the only book that devotes the majority of its space to prophecy (though some theologians would not agree).

Some prophetic writings are known as apocalyptic literature. These are Biblical writings that contain revelations or visions of heavenly, but earth-shaking events, usually in graphic figurative forms. For example, all the visions in Daniel are apocalyptic in nature. The Book of the Revelation is also a clear example.

Chapter and Verse Divisions in the Bible

The modern chapter and verse divisions were not originally in the Bible. When John was writing *"For God so loved the world . . ."* he did not think, "Well, here goes John 3:16." However, there were divisions in the Bible. These were usually indicated by small breaks of space in the text. There was no consistent form of dividing the Bible for hundreds of years.

In approximately 1552, a certain Stephen Langton, a professor at the University of Paris, divided the Bible into the current chapter divisions. The current verse divisions first appeared in a Greek edition of the New Testament in 1551. They were included by Robert Stephanus, a printer who did so to facilitate cross-referencing and public reading. Stephanus was a busy businessman. We are told that he did a lot of his work while riding horseback, a common practice in those days. Some feel that when Stephanus got to certain places in his verse division, the horse must have stumbled because his pen came down in the wrong place. For example, the division between Hebrews 5 and 6 is rather unfortunate. From Hebrews 5:11 through 6:3, the writer of Hebrews is describing spiritual maturity. If one stops reading at the end of Chapter 5, he will stop in the middle of a thought.

The verse divisions first appeared in the English New Testament in 1557. However, there had been a few verse divisions before that time. Psalm 119 is an example. It was divided into twenty-two sections that correspond to the twenty-two letters in the Hebrew alphabet. These twenty-two sections were also divided into eight small "verses" within the main sections. Though they were not necessarily numbered like our modern Bibles, they were divided

I once heard a theologian say, "The first rule in interpreting the Bible is to forget the modern chapter and verse divisions." That statement certainly contains some truth. However, we also must recognize that the chapter and verse divisions have been extremely helpful to the student of the

Bible. Can you imagine the confusion in finding certain passages of Scripture if we did not have the kinds of chapter and verse divisions that are currently in our Bibles? The common practice used by most modern Bibles of reducing the size of the verse numbers and reorganizing the Bible into paragraphs makes reading and interpreting the Bible more natural and understandable.

Illustration of Research into an Old Building

As I have studied the Bible over the years, I have become convinced that the Bible describes a process. Many people view the Bible as some kind of mystical book. However, it is not. It is a collection of many different writings and the entire collection describes an orderly process of events.

If one hundred years from now someone were to do research for a PhD in history on the Faculty of Arts building at the University of Jos, he might collect and compile many different types of information. He would try to find out who originally owned the property and perhaps get a copy of the deed transferring the property to the university. He might find in archives somewhere, the speeches that were given at the groundbreaking ceremony. He would try to find an eyewitness account of how the work progressed. Perhaps a newspaper reporter had visited the site one day and reported that there were laborers from Kano digging the foundation with shovels and diggers. They worked from 7:00 AM to 3:00 PM every day, and they worked without their shirts. Later the researcher finds an account about how the electricians put the wire all throughout the building by putting pipes in the walls and pulling the wire through the pipes. There is another account of the carpenters who hung the doors and separated the buildings into rooms. There is another speech at the dedication of the building in 1997. There are also records of students who attended classes in the building.

When the student finishes writing his project he puts all of this material together in one big book. He has many exhibits. He gets his PhD and a copy of his project goes into a library. Hundreds of years later, after the building has been destroyed and the land has been turned back into a farm, someone picks up the book and sees that it is about the University of Jos Faculty of Arts building. This person knows nothing about the University of Jos or the book so he opens it at random. The book opens to the place where the workers from Kano state are described digging the foundation from 7:00 AM to 3:00 PM every day. The reader closes the book and announces to his friends, "Do you know what that Faculty of Arts Building of the University of Jos was all about? It was about men working without their shirts from 7:00 AM to 3:00 PM." Someone else picks up the book and turns at random to another place where he reads about electricians pulling wire through pipes, so he argues with the first person that the building is all about people pulling wires through pipes. Another argues that those things are not important. What is important is this was a place where big people came and made speeches.

Who is right? All of them are right to a small degree. However, they are wrong if they believe that they understand the building by simply looking at part of the research. The dissertation describes a process and it includes many different documents in order to describe that process. In addition, the Bible also describes a process. It contains many different documents in order to do that. If one reads only part of those documents, he will not understand the process. The message of the book is in the whole. Without going through the entire document, one will never understand the message of the Bible.

Conclusion

The Bible is a diverse book. It was written by many different authors during different time periods, and includes different types of literature. The Bible is a difficult book. In one sense, it is so simple that a fool can understand, but in other ways, it is so profound, the most intelligent man in the world cannot comprehend its wisdom. The Bible is a dangerous book—it is sharper than a two-edged sword, dividing asunder the soul and spirit. The Bible is a divine book. Its subject is God. Its true author is God. Its thoughts are God's thoughts. The Bible is God's gift to us to provide some idea about the God of this universe and His expectations of His creation and creatures.

Study Questions

1. Give a brief overview of the history of the word "Bible."
2. What was St. Jerome's name for the Bible? What did that mean?
3. What are at least four divisions in the Bible?
4. What is one difference between the Hebrew and Greek languages?
5. Define: vellum; parchment; palimpsest; papyrus; codex; stylus
6. List six of the professions represented by the writers of the Bible.
7. Write a paragraph about the diversity in the Bible.
8. What is the primary characteristic of Hebrew poetry?
9. Give some examples of at least three kinds of Hebrew poetry.
10. Give examples of biography and autobiography found in the Bible.
11. Explain how the chapter and verse divisions entered the Bible.
12. Explain some of the advantages and disadvantages of chapter and verse divisions in the Bible.
13. Give examples of biography and autobiography found in the Bible.

Chapter Three

Inspiration

Introduction

While I was attending the university, I heard a sermon entitled, *"If I were the Devil."* In the sermon, the preacher outlined the various steps he would take in trying to pervert and damn the world, if he were the devil. One of the methods he said he would use was to try to destroy or discredit the Bible. Since the Bible is the document from which Christians get all of their information, it would be the primary point of attack. He said he would call into question its inspiration, its accuracy and its ability to meet the needs of modern man. He would further attempt to show that it was just a human book like any other book.

Harold Lindsell, a well-known contemporary Christian theologian wrote a book entitled, *Battle for the Bible.* In this book, he documents Satan's attack on the Bible throughout history. The Bible is the foundation stone upon which Christianity is built. Therefore not only is it the center of attack by the enemy, the Bible also must be the center of any serious study of Christianity.

Perhaps the first place that the enemy attacks the Bible is on the doctrine of inspiration. The doctrine of inspiration relates to how the Bible came from God to the human race. The best defense against attacks on the Bible is to have a very good understanding of the doctrine of inspiration.

Key Scriptures

Christians have always believed that the Bible is "inspired." But what do we mean by saying "the Bible is inspired"? This terminology comes from 2 Timothy 3:16 which reads, *"All scripture is God-breathed"* (KJV *"given by inspiration of God"*). The long expression *"God-breathed"* or *"given by* inspiration of God" is actually one Greek word *theopneustos*.[1] This word is made up of two Greek words which mean literally *"God breathed."* This combination of words creates a word picture that helps us understand the method God used to write the Bible. The idea is that God was so close to the writers of the Bible that the transfer of thoughts and ideas was like breathing. Normally one breathes in oxygen and breathes out carbon dioxide. The picture in this verse suggests that God breathed into the sacred writers his thoughts and they breathed onto the original written documents the ideas God wanted them to communicate. Therefore the Bible is *"God-breathed."*

Another key verse is 2 Peter 1:21: *"For the prophecy never had its origin in the will of man, but men spoke from God as they were carried along (KJV, "moved") by the Holy Spirit."* The key word here is "carried along" or "moved." It is the Greek word *pheromenoi,* a word that was used in sailing. In a sailboat the wind so fills the sails that the vessel is carried or borne along by the wind. The idea is that God was so involved in the lives of the sacred writers, he filled their minds with the truth he wanted them to present. In addition, he carried along the writers as they wrote so that the end product was the message God wanted the writers to communicate.

Extent of Inspiration

We believe that God so overshadowed the writers of the Bible that though they wrote using their own vocabulary and style, they wrote the very words of God and did so without error. We further believe that the Bible is inerrant which means without error. When we speak of the inerrancy of Scripture, we mean that the original writers wrote without error. They were protected by God from making mistakes when they wrote the original documents. Though we believe that we have a very reliable Bible now, we do not extend the doctrine of inerrancy to the translations or

---

[1] The Greek words *theopneustos* and *pheromenoi* illustrate the two common ways that theological words are created. *Theopneustos* is a word that apparently was created to illustrate a theological truth. *Pheromenoi* is a word that was borrowed from another part of society to illustrate a theological truth. It is interesting that both of these words are related to wind or breath.

even the modern Greek and Hebrew versions. Inerrancy only applies to the original manuscripts (or autographs).

We do not believe that there are historical mistakes, scientific mistakes, geographical mistakes, or any other types of mistakes in the Bible.[2] It is certainly well known that the Bible is under attack by many liberal[3] or critical Christians who do not believe in the inspiration of the Bible. For years liberal Biblical scholars have pointed out various inaccuracies which they have supposedly found in the Bible. However, like their claims that Moses could not have written the Pentateuch because writing was not invented at that time, these claims have been discredited one by one. We do not claim that every possible problem of chronology or geography or other questions related to the accuracy of the Bible over the years has an easy answer. However, we are confident that new archaeological discoveries and modern methods of research will continue to confirm the accuracy of the Bible.

Limitations of Inspiration

I must also inject here a word of caution. There is untruth in the Bible. For example, there are some quotations from Satan in the Bible. There are some long quotes from Job's three friends, which represent pious human

---

[2] Although we believe in the inerrancy of the Bible, we do recognize that ancient means of calculating time and distance and measurements are not always consistent with the precision of modern western technology. In addition, as will be described in more detail later in the book, the Bible is filled with idioms and figures of speech, which if interpreted literally will lead to questions and apparent discrepancies.

[3] In theology a conservative theologian is one who believes Christianity as it has traditionally been taught throughout church history—including the supernatural elements of the Bible. In recent years the term "evangelical" has become almost synonymous with the word "conservative." However, an evangelical not only accepts the traditional view of inspiration but also stresses the importance of having a personal relationship with Christ. A theological liberal is one who has been influenced by rationalism. He tends to re-interpret the Bible in light of critical scholarship and, as a general rule, rejects or at least plays down the supernatural parts of the Bible.

reasoning not orthodox truth. God later said these statements were not true (Job 42:7). We believe these passages have been accurately recorded. They are inerrant in that sense, but not inerrant in what they teach. A common way of describing this is to say that Christians believe that the Bible is absolutely true in all that it affirms to be true. Obviously, the Bible quotes various evil men and errors to refute them, but it does not affirm that these are true. Therefore we must read the Bible discerningly. We do not read and apply the Bible without knowing or understanding the context of what we are reading.

We must be very careful with the "promise box" mentality, where we choose a Biblical promise from a box as our word from God for that day. I heard about a man who liked to open the Bible and read the first thing that he saw and use that as God's instructions for him. On one occasion, he was seeking God's will about some matter and opened the Bible and read, *"And Judas went out and hanged himself."* He did not like that verse so he opened the Bible again. This time he read, *"And go thou and do likewise."* He quickly opened to another place in the Bible and read, *"What thou doest, do quickly."* Needless to say, it was not God who was speaking to him that day!

The word *"inspired"* is used in other ways as well. We say, "John Newton was inspired of the Lord when he wrote 'Amazing Grace.'" We talk about having an inspiring service. We talk about other writers or singers or speakers being inspired while performing their ministry or tasks. However, we must remember that when we use the word "inspired" in conjunction with the Bible, we are using it in a technical theological sense. It means something totally different from what it means when used in conjunction with other people. People who are inspired today are simply excited; they are high; they are "up" for their performance. They may even be blessed in a special way by God. Their emotions have gotten involved in their performance or presentation. When the Bible writers were inspired, they were guided and directed by the Holy Spirit in such a way that they wrote the very words of God and did so without error.

Who is the Author of the Bible?

When we are quoting the Bible, we will often say, "The Apostle Paul declared . . ." At other times, we may quote the exact same verse and say,

"God says in His Holy Word . . ." So the question arises, "Who is the real author of the Bible? Is it God or is it man?" The answer is that both are the authors. God is the author in the sense that he inspired the words and overshadowed the writers as they were writing. However, the individual writers are also the authors because they used their minds to formulate the ideas, their vocabularies to create the sentences, and their understanding of grammar to formulate the thoughts into written communication.

Some years ago, I was invited to Port Harcourt to participate in a committee that was planning a certain project for the Rivers State Government. I arrived a day before the committee meeting was going to take place. On the evening before the opening ceremony, someone representing the governor came to my hotel room and said, "The governor wants to make some opening remarks about this project tomorrow. He would like for us to put together a draft of the speech he will make. Would you be willing to help us do that?" I was very happy to do so. I sat down and drafted out what I thought would be appropriate remarks for the governor to make the following day. I was quite pleased the next day when I heard the governor's speech to recognize that that he and his editors had changed very little of what I had written. That evening on Radio Nigeria, I heard a news report about our meeting that day. The reporter said, "The governor of Rivers States, today said . . ." and then he quoted exactly what I had written. Nowhere did the radio reporter indicate that there had been a silent speechwriter for the governor. Once the governor spoke those words publicly, they were no longer my words but the words of the governor. In one sense of the word, they had been coined by me but they had the authority of the governor because he had spoken them publicly.

In a similar way, the various writers of the Bible are the ones who coined the words and phrases that are found in the Bible. However, they have the authority of God upon them because these writers were filled and overshadowed by the Holy Spirit. Therefore, though the various documents within the Bible bear the marks of the individual writers, they all bear the authority of the Holy Spirit.

Testimony of Historical Characters

It has been almost the unanimous testimony of the major church leaders throughout church history that the Bible is inspired by God and entirely accurate and trustworthy. St. Augustine, who lived from AD 354 to 430, wrote:

> Freely do I admit to you, my friend, that I have learnt to ascribe to those books which are of Canonical rank, and only to them, such reverence and honour, that I firmly believe that no single error due to the author is found in any of them.

Martin Luther, the founder of Protestantism, said,

> This I have learned to do: to hold only those books which are called the Holy Scriptures in such honour that I finally believe that not one of the holy writers ever erred.

Later he said, "The scriptures cannot err."

The Westminster Confession says that the Bible is "the only infallible rule of faith and practice." John Wesley declared,

> If there be any mistakes in the Bible, there may as well be a thousand. If there be one falsehood in that book it did not come from the Word of Truth.

Charles Haddon Spurgeon, the well-known British Baptist, stated,

> This is the Word of God. Come, search, ye critics, and find a flaw; examine it from its Genesis to its Revelation and find an error. This is a vein of pure gold, unalloyed by quartz or any earthy substance. This is a star without a speck; a sun without a blot, a light without darkness. . . . This is the book untainted by any error, but is pure, unalloyed, perfect truth.

Many modern theologians have departed from this traditional way of understanding the Bible. However, their critical comments are another indication that the Bible is still a threat to the kingdom of darkness and, therefore, still under attack.

Modern Theories about Inspiration

How did this inspiration take place? Peter partially answers that question in 2 Peter 1:21. He states that the writers of scripture were *"carried along by the Holy Spirit."* However, not everyone understands inspiration that way. There are many theories of inspiration that have been suggested throughout church history, particularly during the last century.

1. **Classical Liberal Position.** This view may be summarized in the expression: *"The Bible contains the word of God."* Liberal theologians sometimes admit that the Bible does contain some words of God along with a whole host of words of men. These theologians say the Bible is not completely the word of God nor is the word of God complete in the Bible. There may be other sources where one may find God speaking just as clearly as in the Bible. God may speak to one through Shakespeare. They admit that God granted to pious men of old a certain amount of deep religious insight into his truth. These pious men recorded these insights but in a very imperfect form. The Bible then is a kind of religious scratch pad of the religious scribes.

   One common way of describing the Bible is that "it is a necklace of pearls strung out at random amid many less valuable and some even undesirable stones." Of course, it is up to us human beings to determine which are the pearls and which are the undesirable stones. That makes us human beings the final authority about what is the word of God and, in some sense, makes us the final authority since we are the ones who determine what God's word is and what it is not.

2. **Neo-Orthodox Position.** This position is represented by men such as Karl Barth and Emil Brunner. They were disturbed by much of the liberalism and attempted to return to a more orthodox approach to Scriptures. The statement that summarizes this position is this: *"The Bible becomes the word of God."* These men thought that the Bible was filled with errors and inconsistencies. However, they felt that God could still use this imperfect tool to speak to us.

   They emphasize the special "encounter" that one might have with the Bible. For example, someone might be reading in the Bible. All of a sudden, a passage speaks very directly to the reader. It almost leaps off the page at him. At that point, the neo-orthodox theologian would say that that part of the Bible has *become* the word of God. To another person reading the same passage, it was not the word of God because it did not speak to him. They say that just as one might recognize the voice of a musician on an old scratched and warped record, so we can detect the word of God through the imperfect instrument—the Bible.

3. **Dynamic View.** This position maintains that it is not the words of the Bible that are inspired but the thoughts. Theologians holding this position believe that God inspired the thoughts of the Bible writers but allowed them to express these thoughts any way they chose even if that included error. This supposedly explains all of the variations in writing due to personality differences, vocabulary differences, and minor mistakes of geography, history or other incidental things.

   This is closer to the truth than the two earlier positions. God did indeed inspire the thoughts of Biblical writers but orthodox Christianity believes he also supervised their selection of words so that they accurately wrote what God wanted them to write. The end product then can be said to be the very words of God.

4. **Partial Inspiration View.** This position maintains that only portions of the Bible are inspired. The parts of the Bible that deal with theological issues are inspired and inerrant. However, those parts that deal with history, science or geography are not necessarily inerrant. One theologian affirms the "full certitude of the spiritual part of Scripture," and adds, "there is a high degree of certainty for the rest."

   One of the problems with this theory is that one of the theological truths of the Bible is that it is inerrant. If one of the theological doctrines of the Bible is that the Bible is inerrant and if all of the doctrinal portions of the Bible are correct, then it logically follows that the Bible must be inerrant. This kind of reasoning undermines the very theory itself.

   Another problem with this position is that it is not easy to separate the theological parts of the Bible from the non-theological parts. For example, is the resurrection of Jesus an historical doctrine or a theological doctrine? One of the unique things about Christianity is that it is rooted very firmly in history. One cannot separate the theological part of Christianity from any other part.

5. **Dictation View.** This view teaches that God literally dictated the contents of the Bible to the various Bible writers. This is a minority opinion sometimes held by very conservative Christians. There is some truth to this theory because portions of the Bible were dictated. Jeremiah 30:1-2 says,

> This is the word that came to Jeremiah from the Lord: 'This is what the Lord, the God of Israel, says: "Write in a book all the words I have spoken to you."

However, this view does not account for all the data in the Bible. If God dictated everything, why all the stylistic variations? Some writers prefer certain words and certain styles. Why is John's Greek simple and Paul's complicated? Why did the writers not say that they had received these words directly from God? Why would God send greetings to certain Christians like those in Romans 16? The dictation view does not fit the data of the Bible. And it is not necessary. There is a better explanation.

6. **Orthodox View.**[4] We believe that God so overshadowed and superintended the writers of the Bible, that though they used their own vocabulary and style in the actual construction of the sentences (just like they used their own characteristic style of handwriting) they were protected from writing error and the final product was stamped with God's authority as Absolute Truth, the word of God.

Proofs of Inspiration

The most positive proof of inspiration is the teachings of the Bible. (We will discuss the Scriptural proof later.) There is no way to prove scientifically that the Bible is inspired of God. However, there are things about the Bible that suggest that there is something supernatural about it. These include the following:

1. **Its Unity.** Though it was written by dozens of different authors over a period of 1600 years, the Bible does not contradict itself. There are still things that we find hard to reconcile because of our limited

---

[4] The term "orthodox" has a variety of meanings in the church world. "Orthodox" in theology refers to that which is authentic or original. In Nigeria, the "orthodox" churches are thought of as the original churches planted by missionaries such as the Catholic, Anglican and Methodist Church. The term "orthodox" is also used to describe what basically became the eastern part of Christianity, including churches in Eastern Europe and Russia. However, in this book, orthodox Christians are those who believe in the traditional tenets of the faith such as the virgin birth, the resurrection and second coming of Jesus.

knowledge, but as a general rule every statement harmonizes with every other statement in the Bible. Though the Bible contains sixty-six different books, it is actually one book with one main message. Though certain doctrines introduced earlier in the Bible progressively unfold and are expanded later in the Bible, the Bible presents a comprehensive and united presentation of the basic doctrines and ethical requirements of God's followers.

2. **Its Prophecy.** There are literally dozens of different prophecies in the Bible. Many of the prophecies made in the Old Testament were fulfilled later in the Old Testament. The Babylonian Captivity was prophesied. Isaiah even accurately predicted by name the king who would release the Israelites to go back to their land and rebuild the kingdom (Isaiah 44:28; 45:1). Many prophecies made in the Old Testament were fulfilled in the New Testament. Many of the details of Jesus' life and death were predicted with great accuracy in several portions of the Old Testament. A very accurate description of His sufferings is found in Isaiah 53, eight hundred years before they occurred. The outpouring of the Holy Spirit predicted by Joel was fulfilled on the Day of Pentecost (Joel 2:28-32; Acts 2:17-21). There are Biblical prophecies that have been fulfilled since the close of the Bible and even in our day. The re-establishment of Israel as a nation in 1948 is viewed by some theologians as a major fulfillment of prophecies found in the Scripture. There are many prophecies of the end days that are yet to be fulfilled. But with the accuracy with which others have been fulfilled, one can be confident that all the unfulfilled prophecies will be fulfilled.

3. **Its Accuracy.** Though the Bible has undergone an amazing amount of scrutiny by the most critical scholars, it has developed a record for the most extraordinary accuracy. Even when scientific experts believed that the earth was flat, Isaiah wrote about the *"circle of the earth"* (Isaiah 40:22). Its history, geography, culture and other details have demonstrated a remarkable amount of integrity, even when inundated by unbelieving criticism.

4. **Its Popularity.** The Bible is by far the best seller of all time. It has been said that those documents translated into three or more language are the best of all literature. The Bible has been translated into literally hundreds of languages. The popularity of the Bible

speaks for itself and declares that there is something very special about this book.

5. **Its Ability to Speak to the Basic Needs of Mankind.** The Bible is a book for all occasions. It is read at weddings and funerals. Its words and principles apply equally to the rich and poor, to the sinner and saint, to the educated and illiterate. It is the book of all occasions, for all people and all time periods. Thousands of people have testified how the Bible has ministered to them in one way or another and given them the exact information they needed at specific periods in their lives.

These evidences do not prove in any scientific way that the Bible is inspired by God. God is a God who is pleased when we exercise faith, and it takes faith to believe that the Bible is the inspired word of God. However, these evidences are significant enough to cause the honest inquirer to seek more information about the Bible, and the one who hungers and thirsts after truth and righteousness will be filled. The honest person will look at these "proofs" and attempt to determine what the Bible itself says about its own authorship and authority. It is that issue we will now address.

Scriptural Proof of the Inspiration

God instructed Moses to write down the words that he spoke to him (Exodus 34:27); "The Lord said to Moses, 'Write down these words, for in accordance with these words I have made a covenant with you and with Israel.'" Isaiah claims that the Bible is God's word (34:16); "Look in the scroll of the Lord and read . . ." The Psalmist claims that the Bible is perfect (19:7-9).

> *The law of the Lord is perfect, reviving the soul. The statutes of the Lord are trustworthy, making wise the simple. The precepts of the Lord are right, giving joy to the heart. The commands of the Lord are radiant, giving light to the eyes . . . The ordinances of the Lord are sure and altogether righteous.*

Similar things could be cited from other Psalms, especially Psalm 119.

The New Testament continues the theme that the word of God is inspired and inerrant. God's words are true (John 17:17): *"Sanctify them by the truth; your word is truth."* God's word is a unity (John 10:35b): *"If he called them*

'gods,' to whom the word of God came—and the Scripture cannot be broken . . ."
What applies to part of the Bible applies to the whole. If part of it is true, then the whole is true. The writers of the Bible were assisted by the Holy Spirit (2 Peter 1:20-21):

> No prophecy of Scripture came about by the prophet's own interpretation. For prophecy never had its origin in the will of man, but men spoke from God as they were carried along by the Holy Spirit.

There are at least two things stressed by this passage. First, this passage gives us a hint as to the source of scriptures. They did not come from the *"will of man."* If that is true, then the scriptures must have originated with God. This passage also gives us a hint about the nature of inspiration. As earlier indicated, these holy men were *"carried along"* by the Holy Spirit. The word *"carried along"* is the same word used of a sailboat that is borne along by the wind as it sails through the water. This implies supernatural involvement.

The Bible teaches the extent of inspiration (2 Timothy 3:16):

> All Scripture is God-breathed and is useful for teaching, rebuking, correcting and training in righteousness, so that the man of God may be thoroughly equipped for every good work.

Note three key words in this section: The word "God-breathed" is the word translated "inspired" in the KJV. It is as if God literally breathed truth into these men and they breathed out truth through the words they wrote. The word "Scripture" suggests that it is Scripture and only Scripture that is inspired. No man is, has, or ever will be "inspired" in the same sense as the Bible was inspired. We love and revere good godly saints, our pastors and elders, but these men are all fallible. What they say is important but it is not final and authoritative like the scriptures. The Bible only is the final rule for measuring our behavior and character and integrity.

No historical movement of Christianity is inspired in the same sense as God's word. The Wesleyan revival was a tremendous move of the Spirit in the eighteenth century. However, not everything that came out of this movement was "inspired" and infallible like the Bible. Pentecostalism has added to the Christianity of Africa in many ways, but it is not infallible. Not everything that goes on in the Pentecostal and Charismatic churches is inspired of God or even approved by God.

No church manual or rulebook is inspired. No manual or discipline or constitution of any church or denomination is infallible regardless how they try to be Biblical in their wording. The only group, which has an infallible inspired manual, is the one that uses the Bible alone for its manual. Obviously all churches and organizations that are officially registered with the government have constitutions and most churches have some written document that guides the affairs of the organization. These are certainly good and useful documents. However, they must never be viewed as having the same authority as the Bible.

No music or song is inspired in the same sense that God's word is inspired. We rejoice in such great songs as "Amazing Grace" and "And Can it Be" and "How Firm a Foundation" but the words and music are not inspired like the sacred Scriptures. The only songs that are inspired are those that are taken directly from the Scripture.

We must recognize that the Bible is the only and final authority on everything it addresses. What I say, or what your bishop says, or what Billy Graham says, is not as important as what the word of God says. I have friends who believe that if a man who is really sanctified spends enough time in prayer before his sermons, what he says from the pulpit is just as authoritative as the Bible. Unfortunately, that is not true. In certain charismatic circles, one of the common phenomena in church services is prophecy. This is a time when a person gets a prophetic word—that is, his spirit is so lifted up that he gives a direct word from God. Whereas I am happy that God can speak through a human being today, no sermon or prophecy in your church is inspired in the same way the Bible is. We human beings can be mistaken in what we think we hear from God. However, the Bible writers were not mistaken. They perfectly wrote what they received from God.

The word *"all"* in the passage suggests to us the breadth of inspiration. We enjoy some scriptures but take great pain to avoid others. We pay lip service to the total authority of all Scripture but will do exegetical gymnastics to avoid the plain teachings of other clear scriptures. We enjoy using the scriptures that teach about healing but we ignore verses like James 4:11: *"Brothers, do not slander one another. Anyone who speaks against his brother or judges him speaks against the law and judges it."*

We like the verses on power, but we do not like the verses on humility. We love the verses on dancing and hand clapping but we ignore the verses about conducting our church services decently and in order (or *vice versa*). We love the verses on the gifts of the Spirit, but we overlook those on the fruit of the Spirit. We like what Jesus said about laying hands on the sick but we do not like Jesus' teachings in Matthew 6:19-20 about not storing up for ourselves treasures on earth where moth and rust corrupt but instead laying up treasures in heaven.

Remember all Scripture is inspired. It is not all equal in importance, but if there is a plain teaching in God's word, no matter how important or unimportant it might seem to us, it is true. God's word is the final authority.

The Bible places New Testament writings on the same level as the Old Testament writings. 2 Peter 3:15-16 declares:

> *Bear in mind that our Lord's patience means salvation, just as our dear brother Paul also wrote you with the wisdom that God gave him. He writes the same in all his letters, speaking in them of these matters. His letters contain some things that are hard to understand, which ignorant and unstable people distort, as they do the other Scriptures, to their own destruction.*

The statement about the *"other Scriptures"* implies that Paul's writings were on the same level as the *"other Scriptures,"* which of course refers to the Old Testament.

Conclusion

The Bible clearly teaches the doctrine of inspiration and inerrancy. There are only two ways these doctrines can be destroyed. First, one can maintain they are not doctrines of the Bible. I think that it has been satisfactorily demonstrated that inspiration and inerrancy are doctrines of the Bible. Second, one can maintain that the Biblical writers cannot be trusted in doctrine. If the Bible teaches the doctrine of inerrancy and there are indeed errors in the Bible, then the Bible is untrustworthy. The doctrine of inerrancy has never been seriously challenged throughout church history until recently. The inspiration and inerrancy of Scripture is the historical doctrine of the church.

We believe that we have a fully authoritative, divinely inspired, totally inerrant Bible.

Study Questions

1. Why is the doctrine of inspiration a likely target for Satan to attack?
2. What are the two most important scriptures related to the doctrine of inspiration, and what do they teach?
3. What does the word "inerrant" mean? How does it relate to the doctrine of inspiration?
4. Define the following words: conservative; liberal; orthodox. Explain which of these words relates to your particular church denomination and why.
5. What do the testimonies of the major church leaders throughout church history teach about the Bible?
6. Give a one-sentence description of each of these theories of inspiration: classical liberal theory; neo-orthodox theory; dynamic theory; partial inspiration theory; dictation theory. Explain which of these you think is the most accurate and why.
7. Write a paragraph on the dangers of rejecting the traditional understanding of inspiration.
8. List at least five external evidences that support the belief that the Bible is inspired by God.
9. List six key verses related to the doctrine of inspiration and explain the main thing that each one teaches.
10. Describe how a modern preacher is different from the ancient prophets when speaking on behalf of God?

Chapter Four

Canonization

Introduction

How did the Bible come together as the Bible? Who made the decision that certain things would be included in the Bible and certain things would not? Is it possible that something today could ever be included in the Bible? How do we know that God is not still speaking in such a way that something should be included in the Bible? All of these are fairly common questions that I have been asked about the Bible over the years. They all relate to the subject of the canonization of the Bible.

The subject of the canonization of Scripture is normally studied in a fairly advanced course in theology. For obvious reasons, it is normally not a subject often shared with laymen. However, God wants us to know as much about the Bible as possible. The information contained in this chapter is something one needs to know in order to understand the Bible better. We also need to know these things to properly answer questions when they arise.

Meaning of Canon

Canonization is the name given to the process God used to determine which books should be considered Scripture. For our purposes, though pronounced the same way, the word "canon" does not mean the big gun that is used to shoot big shells in war. Rather canon is a theological word used to describe those books which were accepted as authoritative—those that should be included in the Bible.

The word canon comes from a Greek word *kanon,* which literally meant a straight rod or bar, like a ruler used by masons or carpenters. In ancient construction there was often not an objective standard, such as is found in the metric system, by which to measure a building. Therefore, the builder and the customer would agree on a stick or a rod that would be the standard of measurement. Because the *kanon* was used as a ruler, it developed the meaning of keeping something straight and then as a testing of that which was straight. Theologically, it came to mean that which serves to measure, a rule, norm, or standard. For example, the ancient Greek writers were considered "canons." Every other writer measured his writing by the standard laid down by the ancient writer.

As used in reference to the Scripture, the word canon came to be associated with those sixty-six books that measured up to the standard. In other words, it refers to those books that should be a part of the Bible.

Canonization of the Old Testament

It should be pointed out that the canonization of the Old Testament has never been seriously doubted. The Old Testament as it is now constituted was accepted as authoritative by the Jews even before the days of Jesus. There were other ancient Jewish writings such as the Apocrypha. However, the Jews never really accepted these books as God's Word though they did respect it as history and good devotional reading. Because Jesus quoted from the Old Testament as authoritative we have little doubt about its authority and authenticity. It should further be pointed out that the early church used the Old Testament freely. Peter preached the sermon on the Day of Pentecost based on a text from the Old Testament. Stephen reviewed the history of the Old Testament in his speech before the Sanhedrin. Philip preached Christ to the Ethiopian eunuch from Isaiah 53. Paul frequently used the Old Testament when preaching in the synagogues. Therefore, the recognition of the Old Testament as sacred Scriptures by Jesus and the apostles, settles the question for Christians.

My objective in this section will be to point out the process whereby certain books were included in the New Testament and others were rejected.

The Problem

There were three major problems that encouraged the early church fathers to establish the Holy Canon.

Other Writings

The apostles were not the only ones writing during the early days of the church. Writing was more difficult than it is now, but still there were many documents being written. The question was: Which of these books should be in the "canon"—that is, which books should be accepted as authoritative in the lives of the Christians? Some of the books were obviously false. Some were fictional accounts of Jesus' life. Others borrowed one of the apostles' names to give credibility to their writings.

There are a number of "infancy stories" which supposedly tell about things Jesus did when he was a child. For example, one story tells about a time when Jesus was a young child, he was playing hide and seek with some other little children. Jesus was the one who was to go seek the children while they all hid from him. When Jesus went to find them, he asked some women if they had seen the children. They denied that they had. He then asked them what it was which had gone into a big oven, apparently one that was not being used at the time. The woman replied that it was three kids (goats) that had gone in the furnace. Jesus then replied, *"Come out hither, O ye kids, to your shepherd."* At that time, the boys came out but they had been changed into young goats, which frolicked around. After being begged by the women for a while, Jesus turned the little goats back into children in front of the eyes of the women.[1] One can see from this story the mythical nature of these writings. It was not hard to determine that these books were fictional and had no place in the canon.

These books are sometimes described as pseudepigraphal writings or false writings. However, not all of the books written during this time period were false writings. Some of the books were good books either claiming to have been written by an apostle or a close associate of an apostle. Some early Christians considered one or more of these to be inspired.

---

[1] *The Apocryphal Books of the New Testament* (Philadelphia, PA USA: David McKay Publishers, 1901), p. 54. Another story tells about Jesus forcing a snake that had bitten a little child to go up to the child and suck all the poison from the child. He then caused the snake to burst asunder and die. *Ibid.*, p. 55.

The following is a list of books considered inspired and authoritative by at least some Christians.

1. **I Clement.** Clement was a leader in the church at Rome. He wrote to the Corinthians about AD 96. There is nothing wrong with this document. In fact, it contains much good truth. This book was still being read in the church services in Corinth about AD 170. However, it was not eventually selected to be a part of the Bible. Since it is probably the oldest surviving non-Biblical Christian document it provides valuable insights into the development of Christian doctrine at the end of the first century. The following is a small sample from the book:

   > Let us, therefore, humble ourselves, brethren, laying aside all pride and boasting, and foolishness, and anger: And let us do as it is written. For thus saith the Holy Spirit; Let not the wise man glory in his wisdom, nor the strong man in his strength, nor the rich man in his riches; but let him that glorieth, glory in the Lord, to seek him and to do judgment and justice. Above all, remembering the words of the Lord Jesus, which he spake concerning equity and long suffering, Be ye merciful and ye shall obtain mercy; forgive, and ye shall be forgiven; as ye do, so shall it be done unto you; as ye give, so shall it be given unto you; as ye judge, so shall ye be judged; as ye are kind to others so shall God be kind to you; with what measure ye mete, with the same shall it be measured to you again" (I Clement 7:1-4).[2]

   One can see that Clement depended very heavily upon other apostolic writers. Although there is no error in it, there is nothing original either. In other words, there is nothing in the book that is not found in other canonical books. That is probably one of the main reasons it was not eventually accepted into the Holy Canon.

2. **II Clement.** This book was a forgery, written much later than I Clement perhaps in Syria. It is actually a long sermon, which touches on several doctrines including repentance and the church. It was probably written about AD 140-150. Apparently someone used Clement's name in hopes of getting a wider circulation. II Clement was never widely accepted.

---

[2] *Ibid.*, p. 118.

3. **The Didache.** The full title is *The Teaching of the Lord to the Gentiles through the Twelve Apostles.* This document contains various things supposedly taught and said by the apostles. Though it reflects a much earlier oral tradition, it was compiled and written down about AD 120. These writings contain various type of advice: a) Advice about how to treat traveling prophets. One specific piece of advice declared that if a prophet came asking for money, he was a false prophet. b) Advice about baptism. The Didache directed that baptismal candidates should be dipped in *"living water"* three times, in the name of the Father, the Son and the Holy Spirit. If they were sick or there was a scarcity of water, they could have water poured on their heads instead of being dipped.

4. **The Epistle of Barnabas.** This document was written about AD 130. It is obviously another attempt to use the name of a popular Bible character to get wider circulation. It quotes Matthew and seems also to know Paul's writings. There is little error in this book.

5. **Shepherd of Hermas.** This is a rather long work consisting of five visions, twelve mandates and ten parables. It was quite popular among the early Christians, particularly in the East up until about the third century. The shepherd was a guardian angel who took care of Hermas. It is rather fanciful and probably a good illustration of how much inspiration helped the Bible writers. The major themes of the work are purity and repentance.

6. **Apocalypse of Peter.** This book was written about AD150. It deals with what is supposed to take place in the last days. It contains a vision of both heaven and hell.

7. **Acts of Paul.** This document describes the additional travels and ministry of Paul. It also talks about a lady named Thecla whom Paul was instrumental in converting. Later she met Paul again and he commissioned her to preach the word of God. She had several amazing experiences including fighting with wild beasts in the amphitheater in Antioch where a lioness supposedly died defending her. The book was probably written about AD 170. It is likely that some seeds of historical truth are contained in it, but most of the book is probably fictional.

Some of the books that did get accepted into the Bible were debated at first, mainly because there was debate about the authorship; the following were called *antilogomena*—that is books that were spoken against: Hebrews, James, 2 Peter, 2 & 3 John, Jude, and Revelation.

Marcion's Canon

A second reason it became necessary to establish the canon was because of other canons being developed. A man named Marcion had developed a canon of his own about AD 140. This was a list of books he considered to be inspired. Marcion was a heretic who taught Gnosticism (which believes that everything material is evil). Therefore, he omitted some of Paul's Epistles that conflicted with his doctrine. In order to refute the canon of Marcion, it became necessary for the orthodox Christians to come up with a canon of their own.

Severe Persecution

Another thing that encouraged the official recognition of the canon was persecution. There were periods of time in the early church when there was severe persecution. In fact, the Edict of Diocletian in 303 declared that all religious books were to be destroyed. Frequently, Christians would be put to death if they were caught with these illegal books. Christians needed to know which books they were willing to die for. By the time of the Edict of Diocletian, most Christians recognized that there were sacred books for Christians as well. If these books were from God, they would die for them. However, should one die for The Didache or the Acts of Paul? Were they really of the same status as the Gospel of St. Matthew? For example, today most of us would be willing to die for the Bible, but we would hardly die for *Pilgrim's Progress* though it is a good book.

These are the main reasons it became essential for the orthodox Christians to come up with a recognized list of books that would be fully authoritative for all Christians.

The Solution

Four key tests were placed upon each book to determine whether or not it should be included in the collection of Holy Scriptures.

Tests of Inspiration

1. **Apostolicity.** Was the document written by an apostle or a close associate of an apostle? The reason books like Hebrews and James were debated is because there was some question about their authorship. Luke and Mark are examples of close associates of an apostle. The early church fathers knew Mark was Peter's traveling companion and interpreter. The stories he heard Peter tell are the stories he wrote down. Therefore, the facts about Jesus in the Gospel of St. Mark contain the authority of Peter. Luke was Paul's traveling companion and it is assumed that the things Luke wrote would have been reviewed and approved by the Apostle Paul. Therefore, they had apostolic authority as well.

2. **Contents.** The contents of each of the books presented for canonization were scrutinized according to several criteria.

    - Was the content of the book of such a spiritual character as to entitle it to the rank of scripture? One can easily see why most of the apocryphal books were omitted.

    - Did the books add significant spiritual information to the existing body of sacred literature? There was no particular reason to needlessly add to the bulk of the canon. If the issue of circumcision was sufficiently covered in one of the undisputed canonical books, there was no reason to add a book that primarily covered the doctrine of circumcision.

    - Were the teachings of the book consistent with the known doctrines of Jesus and the apostles? The document under consideration had to be consistent with the oral teachings, which were recognized at that time, and with the teachings of the books that were not disputed. The document might add something, but it could not contradict that which was accepted.

3. **Universality.** Did the book have universal appeal? Was it accepted in all parts of the church? Did it have only regional application? A book did not have to have unanimous approval but it did have to be accepted by the majority in all parts of the Christian church. This is the main reason why books like I Clement and the Barnabas and some of the others were not included. They were accepted in certain parts of the church but not in all parts.

4. **Inspiration.** Did the book give evidence of being divinely inspired? Actually this was what the other three tests were supposed to determine. If a book passed the other three tests, it was considered inspired and if it were considered inspired, it was included in the canon.

Church Councils

There were a number of church councils that discussed the canonization of the New Testament, including the Councils of Nicaea (325), Laodicea (363) and Carthage (397). Though the twenty-seven books we now accept were accepted by various individuals many years earlier, there was little or no debate about these after the Council of Carthage in 397.

Conclusion

We sincerely believe that the Holy Spirit guided these men in the selection of the books that became a part of our New Testament. One church historian has stated,

> The Holy Spirit, given to the Church, quickened holy instincts, aided discernment between the genuine and the spurious, and thus led to gradual, harmonious, and in the end unanimous conclusions. There was in the Church what a modern divine has happily termed an 'inspiration of selection.'

Study Questions

1. Where did the word canonization come from?
2. What is the primary evidence for the canonization of the Old Testament?
3. Give a brief description of each of the books that were considered for canonization but did not eventually make it into the Holy Canon.
4. Why did it become necessary for the early church to establish the canon?
5. Define these words: antilegomena; pseudepigraphal.
6. Who was Thecla?
7. How did Marcion's canon encourage the canonization process?
8. Explain how persecution encouraged the development of the canon.
9. Explain briefly the tests that were placed upon each of the documents to determine whether or not it would be included in the canon?
10. What part did various councils have in determining the canonization of the New Testament?
11. What is the meaning of "inspiration of selection?"
12. Write a paragraph explain why you believe or why you not believe that inspiration is still possible today.

Chapter Five

Textual Criticism

Introduction

In the NIV Study Bible, between Mark 16:8 and 16:9, we read these words, "The most reliable early manuscripts and other ancient witnesses do not have Mark 16:9-20." Occasionally you see similar comments in commentaries or theological literature. Have you ever wondered what statements like that mean? It will be the objective of this section to try to help answer that question.

How did the Bible come to us? The individual parts of the Bibles were originally written by hand in Hebrew and Greek on leather and papyrus scrolls. We now read the Bible in English on good clear paper in a clean printed type. I will now try to explain what intervened between the original writing and now, why there are different types of manuscripts, and why some are more accurate than others.

The technical name for this study is textual criticism. It is also called lower criticism.

Scholars do not recommend that preachers or Bible teachers talk to laymen about this subject. This recommendation is not made because it is a subject that one is embarrassed about or something that scholars are trying to hide from laymen. It is a rather technical field. It is somewhat difficult to explain and also difficult to understand without having a lot of time to explain. It can create confusion among laymen because they do not have the necessary background to understand the issues involved. However, most people who study hermeneutics are not true laymen. They are or become leaders in their churches. This is one of those areas of Biblical scholarship that we study for our own personal and professional knowledge. It is not a subject we must share with the average layman.

A farmer once bought a big tractor. He parked the tractor in a shed all throughout the week and only used it to drive to church. He wanted everyone at the church to know he had a new tractor. However, a tractor is not designed to be driven to church. A person buys a tractor to use in the field to prepare, cultivate and harvest his crops. A tractor should not be an object to demonstrate one's wealth; it should be an instrument of work. A theological education is like that also. It is not designed to demonstrate that the person is a theologian but rather it is designed to prepare ministers and teachers to dig into the Bible to produce excellent sermons and lessons. Therefore, we do not take our theological tools to the pulpit to demonstrate that we are highly educated people. We use this information in our quiet place of study to dig out practical truth for God's people.

Writing Period

The Original Manuscripts

The original manuscripts were the actual documents upon which the Bible writers first wrote their words. The technical name for these manuscripts is autographs.

Many of the writers used an amanuensis. This person was something like a professional secretary who would take dictation and write out the communication the author intended. This means that sometimes the Biblical writers dictated their letters and other documents and someone else wrote them down. Who wrote the Book of Romans? The obvious answer is the Apostle Paul. However, Romans 16:22 says, *"I, Tertius, who write down this letter, greet you in the Lord."* Tertius was the amanuensis. He was not the author of the epistle but the secretary who wrote it down.

The Original Readers

When the recipients received the letters sent to them by the apostles they greatly appreciated and cherished them. Probably the pastor of the local church kept the original copy of any letter received from an apostle. Some letters were written to individual churches such as 1 and 2 Thessalonians and 1 and 2 Corinthians, some were written to individuals such as 1 and 2 Timothy and Titus, and some were designed to be shared among the different churches. We are quite sure that Ephesians was designed as a circular type letter. It was written to a general reading audience in the Asia Minor area. If there were good information about Jesus and the Christian church available, even though the document was not written directly to a particular person, it would still be cherished.

The Earliest Copyists

Here is a typical scenario in the early church: Someone hears the epistle of Philippians read in a church service and decides that he would like a copy of it. When we hear or read something that we like, we frequently rush off to find a photocopy machine to make a copy. There were no copy machines available in those days, so those interested in getting a copy for their own personal use were forced to make a copy of the original by copying it by hand. In this way, the various documents of the New Testament were reproduced and spread from one church and one individual to another.

The Hebrew Copyists

Before I continue with the way the New Testament documents were preserved, I need to say a word or two about the copying of the Old Testament scriptures. The Hebrew Scriptures were greatly prized and cherished by the Jews. There were two things that helped to insure that they preserved these ancient documents with the greatest possible accuracy. First, the Old Testament people recognized the documents as God's word. Therefore, when they were hand-copying them, they did not copy them carelessly or casually like they might copy other documents. They recognized that they were copying the very word of God.

Second, only professional scribes could copy the ancient Hebrew manuscripts in those days. They took great care in copying them. For example at the end of every ancient manuscript was a little box in which technical information about that particular manuscript was contained. That section would give the actual number of letters in the manuscript and the middle letter. Once the scribes had completed the copying of a certain manuscript, they would count the letters to make sure they had copied correctly. If the new document had exactly the same number as the one from which they were copying, they could be reassured that they had a good copy. However, just to make sure, they would find the central letter in a document and then count both ways to make sure that was still the central letter in the new copy. They would frequently stop and pick up a fresh pen when writing the sacred name of Yahweh. The care, which the ancient scribes took in accurately copying the Old Testament, cannot be overstated.

Because of this there are few textual problems in the Old Testament. The discovery of the Dead Sea Scrolls has demonstrated the great accuracy of the Old Testament manuscripts. When Isaiah 53 in the Isaiah Scroll of the Dead Sea Scrolls was compared with the previous earliest Old Testament manuscript we had, dated about AD 900, there were only three small deviations and they were all insignificant. The reason we did not have a lot of ancient Hebrew manuscripts before that time is because when they got old and worn they were destroyed properly. They were too precious to be allowed to rot away somewhere or perhaps used for some less than honorable purpose.

More About the New Testament Copyists

Unfortunately, the earliest New Testament copyists did not have the same professionalism as did the Old Testament copyists. In the early days, they did not fully realize that they were copying the Bible—the word of God. For example, it is doubtful that the first person who copied the letter of Philippians understood that he was copying the word of God as the Old Testament scribe understood when copying the scroll of Isaiah. In addition, the earliest copyist of New Testament documents did not have the formal training that his Old Testament counterparts had. Few of the early copyists were professional scribes. They viewed these writings as so important they were willing to hand copy them, but they did so in an informal atmosphere.

The problem is that few people can hand copy the Book of Philippians without making a mistake. When one hand copies a document, he makes a number of different kinds of mistakes. All of these kinds of mistakes were also made in the early copies of the New Testament documents. These include:

1. Misspelled words
2. Words that were reversed.
3. Words that were omitted.
4. Words that were copied twice.
5. Lines that were omitted. One's eye went from the end of one line to another and skipped the line in between.
6. Seeing one word but interpreting it as another. For example, one might see the word James but thinks he saw Jacob.
7. Many other types of transcription problems.

Another problem develops. Udoh makes a personal copy of the Book of Philippians. In so doing he makes a few minor copyist errors along the way. Next, Danjuma wants a copy of the Book of Philippians. However the original copy that is being kept at the pastor's house is not available, so Danjuma finds Udoh and asks to make his own copy of Philippians and does. Since he does not know that Udoh made a few mistakes as he copied, he includes all of Udoh's mistakes, plus makes a few more of his own.

Amadi has also made a copy from the original book of Philippians and made a few copyist's errors of his own, but they are not the same ones that Udoh made. Yomi makes a copy of Amadi's copy. Now we have four copies of the Book of Philippians and all vary slightly from the original. Now each time someone makes a copy, he makes all of the same mistakes that all of the copyists ahead of him has made, plus a few more of his own.

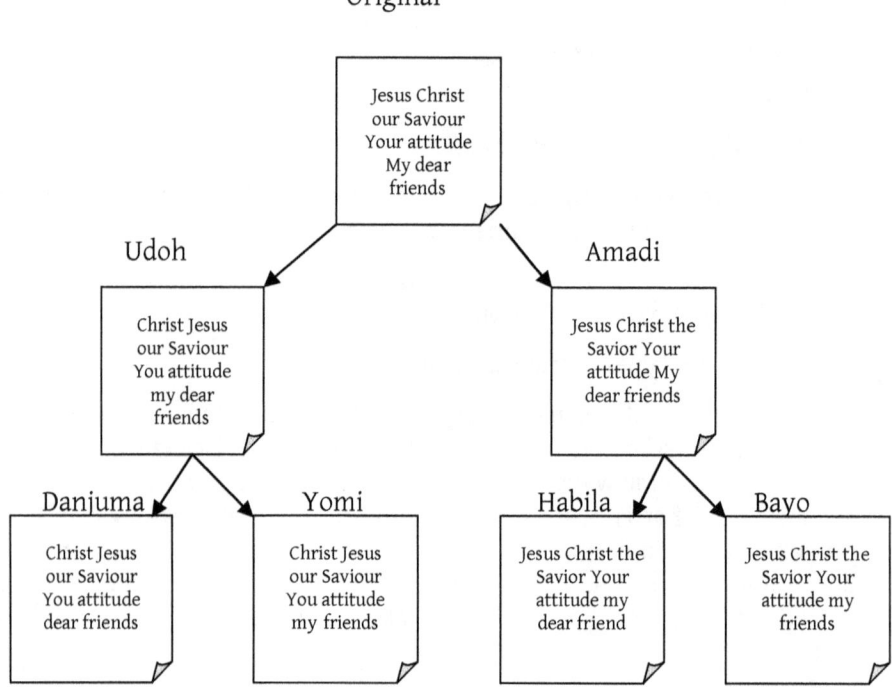

Another problem develops. As one of the copyists reads over his finished copy, he discovers that he has left out a word or a line or sentence. What would you do in that situation? He did what most of us would do. He wrote the missing word or sentence in the margin. However, ancient Christians also did another thing we do today. They made notes in the margins of their Bibles. So here is a pastor copying a handwritten manuscript. He comes upon a few words in the margin. He does not know whether this is something that was added by the original copier, because it had been omitted from the copy, or whether this is just additional preacher's notes.

As a general rule, the ancient copyists tended to include those marginal readings rather than omitting them, because they might indeed be a part of God's word. It would be better to include something that might not have been part of the original rather than run the risk of leaving out part of God's word. Besides many of the earliest copyists did not fully realize they were copying the word of God. Since the note in the margin was

Textual Criticism 59

good anyway, there was no reason to omit it. This is how some things crept into the Bible that were not part of the original.

A clear example of this is in 1 John 5:6-8 (especially verse 7) sometimes known as *Comma Johanneum*. The KJV reads,

> *This is he that came by water and blood, even Jesus Christ; not by water only, but by water and blood. And it is the Spirit that beareth witness, because the Spirit is truth. For there are three that bear record in heaven, the Father, the Word, and the Holy Ghost: and these three are one. And there are three that bear witness in earth, the spirit, and the water, and the blood: and these three agree in one.*

The NIV of verses 7-8 reads, *"For there are three that testify (8) the Spirit, the water and the blood . . ."* Verse 7 is omitted in practically all of the ancient Greek manuscripts. It is found in the margin of one minor Greek minuscule manuscript (635),[1] which comes from the eleventh century. As far as I know, this is the oldest Greek manuscript in which this verse is found. It is found in an old Latin manuscript, which comes from the fourth to the ninth century. It is also found in the Clementine version of the Latin Vulgate from about the fourth century.

If this were not in the original manuscript John wrote, how did it creep into the text? No one knows for sure, but it probably happened something like this: During the third and fourth century there was a great controversy over Christology and the Trinity. Probably some Bible scholar was reading this portion one day and he noted the expression in verse 8 about the three that bear witness on earth, the Spirit, the water and the blood. As he meditated on these, a thought occurred to him, "If there are three that bear witness on earth, there are also three that bear witness in heaven, the Father, the Son, and the Holy Spirit." Therefore, like millions of Bible scholars after him, he jotted down this thought in the margin of the text he was working with.

Sometime later, a friend borrowed his copy of 1 John to make a copy of it. When he got to this place, he has a question: "Is this a sentence that was left out by the last copyist and then added into the margin when it was

---

[1] The miniscule is a manuscript written with smaller Greek letters, which were used in later copies of the New Testament. These letters were much smaller than the large capital letters, called uncials, in which the New Testament was originally written.

discovered that it was missing? Or is this simply a marginal note that someone has added?" Since the average person would rather add something that was not originally a part of the text than to run a risk of omitting any part of the writings of an apostle, and since the marginal comment made sense and certainly contained no error, he decided to add it to his copy of 1 John. When the next person made a copy of this version of 1 John, because the sentence had been inserted into the text, he did not even know that there was a problem and therefore, copied it straight into his text. From that time forward, the verse was inserted into that family or generation of manuscripts.[2]

It is much easier to see how things like spelling variations or word omissions or similar things crept into the text. However, it is also understandable how additions crept into the text as well.

Textual Variations

Although there are literally hundreds of textual variations in the manuscripts of the New Testament that we have at our disposal, ninety-nine percent of them are very minor and of no consequence. B. F. Westcott and J. A. F. Hort, the two most important textual scholars of the nineteenth century, state that of all the textual problems in the New Testament, those where there is any real question about the actual reading could fit onto one half page of a Greek New Testament. In other words, they are less than one thousandth of the whole Greek New Testament.

I should also point out that the textual variations in the New Testament in no way alter any doctrine in the Bible. The textual variations are purely random in nature and demonstrate no bias for or against any particular doctrine or denominational perspective.

The following is a sample of the most important textual problems:

---

[2] The reconstructed events described above all took place in the Latin Bible not in the Greek. There is no evidence of the Trinitarian statement in any major Greek manuscript before about the fifteenth century, and there is good evidence that it was copied into the Greek manuscript from the Latin.

John 7:53-8:11

This is the story of the woman caught in adultery. The NIV says at this point, *"The earliest and most reliable manuscripts do not have 7:53-8:11"* though the NIV does include it. The edition of the Greek New Testament that I use most often, omits the story at the point it normally appears but includes it at the end of the Gospel of John. Several ancient manuscripts do the same thing. Though most textual scholars do not believe this story should be included in John, most of them believe that it is indeed an authentic story.

The Ending of Mark

After Mark 16:8, the NIV reads, *"The two most reliable early manuscripts do not have Mark 16:9-20."* However, again the NIV does add the section. Although most textual scholars agree that the present ending of Mark is not the original ending Mark gave to the document, they do not know what the genuine ending should be. For Mark to conclude with 16:8 would leave a very abrupt ending. Therefore some think the real ending of Mark was lost. Perhaps it was the last page on a codex and got torn off. Some scholars believe that the longer ending is an attempt by someone to reconstruct the original ending. Perhaps someone tried to write it from memory or to add what would be considered an appropriate ending.

There are other reasons to doubt its authenticity. In addition to doubtful textual evidence, there is internal evidence that confirms these doubts. For example, there are words and expressions found in this section that are not found anywhere else in Mark. Also the grammatical style seems to be different. There is nothing unorthodox or heretical in this section. Therefore, there is not a problem with it. However, when one reads and studies it, he must be aware that scholars have serious questions about whether it was originally a part of Mark's writing in the form it is now.

This information is not presented to cause believers to have doubts about the authenticity and credibility of the Bible, but for these reasons:

1. To know what writers and preachers mean when they talk about the "best manuscripts."
2. To be able to discuss this subject intelligently when it arises in theological circles.

3. To help appreciate the efforts which have gone into providing us with a reliable Bible.
4. To show that God has gone to a lot of trouble to preserve a trustworthy text.
5. To help Christians understand and defend against the attacks made by some people on the "corruption" of the Biblical text.

Here is one more thought: One does not have to believe or accept what I have said about the passages with doubtful textual support. Many Christians "accept them by faith" as we do many other things that we do not understand. However, once a person begins to advance a bit in his or her understanding of the Bible, it is important to understand something about this whole area of textual criticism.

Transmission Period

Later Copyists

After these books of the New Testament became recognized as a part of God's Word, they were treated with greater care and copied more carefully. "Publishing companies" were developed to get out copies of the Bible. Remember all written documents were still hand copied at this time. The factories that produced Bibles were called scriptoriums. A reader would stand up and slowly read the Bible. Dozens of copiers would listen and write down what they heard. Although these were professional copyists, problems still arose. Sometime the copier would hear a word that could be confused with another word. English examples include such words as hear and here; bare and bear; write and right. Words often sound similar to other words. A student responding to one of my questions once said "soldier" and I thought he said "surgeon." Therefore, even in these scriptoriums, minor problems continued to creep into the text, even though great care was taken to avoid them.

Families of Manuscripts

As one can see, a great many variations developed among the manuscripts. These eventually developed into what were called "families." Certain manuscripts had certain common variations. It can be assumed that they all came from a common source. These families have been divided up different ways. Westcott and Hort organized them into four main families of manuscripts, all of which have different characteristics:[3]

1. **Syrian.** This was a revision of the various manuscripts available in the fourth century; it was widely disseminated in the Byzantine Empire.
2. **Western Text.** This family was been preserved in a manuscript called *Bezae* of Gospels and Acts. It comes from a very early date. Many of the early church fathers used this text. It omits a lot, changes much, and tends to paraphrase.
3. **Alexandrian.** This family was preserved largely in Egypt. It attempts to smooth and polish the text.
4. **Neutral.** This text is preserved in *Vaticanus* and *Sinaiticus*. These are the two oldest and most complete Greek manuscripts we have available today. Where these two manuscripts agree, they are nearly always accepted.

Early Printed Manuscripts

Ximenes and Complutension's Polyglot

A polyglot is something like today's parallel versions of the Bible. It contained the Hebrew, Aramaic, Greek, and Latin texts. A polyglot was planned by a certain Spanish cardinal named Ximenes de Cisneros. The

---

[3] Bruce Metzger, *The Text of the New Testament* (Oxford, England: Oxford University Press, 1968), p. 131. Another division of the family of manuscripts is the following: Alexandrian (almost the same as Westcott and Hort's "Neutral Text"), Caesarean (a text based in Palestine combining elements of both Western and Alexandrian readings), Western (the same as Westcott and Hort's Western text), and Byzantine (corresponding with Westcott and Hort's Syrian text). See Henry Thiessen, *Introduction to the New Testament* (Grand Rapids, MI USA: Wm. B. Eerdman's Publishing Company, 1976), pp. 72-74.

New Testament part of this work was eventually printed in 1514 and the entire project was published in 1522. The Greek manuscripts behind the Greek text used in the Polyglot have never been satisfactorily ascertained

Erasmus and the First Printed Greek New Testament

Desiderius Erasmus was a brilliant New Testament scholar who had sympathies with the Protestant reformation but never formally broke with the Catholic Church. He was requested by a Swiss printer, Johann Froben, to prepare a Greek text for publication before the Polyglot got onto the market. Erasmus went to work and completed the first edition on March 1, 1516 after only six months of work. Although the New Testament Version of Complutension's Polyglot was technically the first Greek New Testament printed, Erasmus is usually given credit for the first Greek New Testament to be published and distributed to the public. This first edition was based upon about six manuscripts, all minuscules (a manuscript written in a later form of smaller Greek letter unlike the large capital letters in which the New Testament was written), the oldest dating from about the tenth century. Erasmus had only one manuscript of Revelation and part of it was missing. Consequently in his first edition, Erasmus translated several verses of Revelation back into Greek from his Latin Bible.

This edition was filled with hundreds of typographical errors. Erasmus' second edition became the basis for Luther's German translation of the Bible. In the third edition, Erasmus included the controversial Trinitarian statement in 1 John 5. Apparently he came under a lot of pressure from certain church officials and the printer to include that statement. He made a hasty promise that if he could find one single Greek manuscript with that statement in it, he would add it to the text. A few months later, the church officials brought him a Greek manuscript with the verse in it. The manuscript now called, *Comma Johanneum,* was obviously of recent origin having probably been produced for that purpose. Erasmus himself wrote a lengthy footnote stating his belief that that manuscript had been prepared to force him to change the reading.[4]

---

[4] Metzger, p. 101.

The fourth edition of Erasmus' Greek New Testament was the definitive one. For this edition, he had access to Complutension's Polyglot and took advantage of it to correct some of his mistakes. He altered his text of Revelation in 90 places. This edition was published along with the Latin Vulgate and Erasmus' own Latin translation, all in parallel columns. The fifth edition differs little from the fourth, except Erasmus discarded the Vulgate in this edition.

Robert Estienne (latinized Stephanus)

Robert Estienne issued four editions of the Greek New Testament. The first three came from Paris; the last one came from Geneva (1546 - 1551). The first and second editions were a combination of Erasmus and the Polyglot. The third followed closely Erasmus' fourth and fifth editions; this became the standard Greek text of the time, especially in England. The fourth edition contained the first verse divisions.

Theodore Beze (or Beza)

Theodore Beze succeeded John Calvin is the leader of Reformed Protestantism in Geneva. He published nine editions of the Greek New Testament and had a tenth published after his death. However there were really only four distinct editions. His editions followed very closely the fourth edition of Stephanus. His editions popularized what later became known as the *Textus Receptus* (Anglicized to the "Received Text"). The King James translators made large use of his 1588-89 and 1598 editions to translate the Authorized Version.

Bonaventure and Abraham Elzevir

These were two Dutch printers who became famous for their elegant and correct style of printing. They helped to further popularized what became known as the Received Text. They followed closely Beza's 1565 edition. In their second edition published in 1633, the preface contained a little note that stated that they were publishing *"the text which is now received by all, in which we give nothing changed or corrupted."* The little phrase *"text which is now received"* is the Latin phrase *textum receptum*. This phrase caught on as something of the nickname for that particular Greek text. From that time on, this Greek text of the New Testament was known as the *Textus Receptus* or the "Received Text."

Later Developments

B. F. Westcott and F. J. A. Hort (1825-1901; 1828-1892)

B. F. Westcott and F. J. A. Hort were the two most important textual scholars of the nineteenth century and perhaps the two most important textual scholars or all time. They developed new techniques for getting back to the original manuscripts. Some of their principles are

1. The oldest manuscript is probably the most accurate rather than majority text.[5] (The majority refers to the greatest number of manuscripts.)
2. The most difficult text (theologically) is most likely to be the most accurate. When faced with two possible choices, copyists tended to choose the variation that would make better theological sense. However, it is more likely that a person would deliberately change a passage to make it easier to understand than more difficult.
3. The shorter reading[6] is to be preferred. Copyist tended to expand rather than reduce passages.
4. The reading that best explains the variants is to be preferred.
5. The reading that has the widest geographical support is to be preferred.

---

[5] Prior to this time the prevailing philosophy of textual criticism was that the majority text was followed. In other words, scholars would basically count up the number of manuscripts and the reading that was found in the largest number of manuscripts was accepted as the correct one. However, Westcott and Hort demonstrated that the majority is not always correct. In fact, multiple identical readings constitute only one testimony because all of these copied from the same source.

[6] The word "reading" refers to a difference in the text of the manuscript.

6. The reading that most conforms to the style and diction of the author is to be preferred.
7. The reading that reflects no doctrinal bias is to be preferred.
8. The simplest reading (grammatically) is to be preferred. Scribes tended to explain, add pronouns, and try to make things more clear.

Profile of Westcott and Hort

B. F. Westcott was the Regius Professor of Divinity at the Trinity College, Cambridge from 1870 onwards. In addition to pioneering new techniques in textual criticism, he wrote outstanding critical commentaries on John, Johannine Epistles, and Hebrews. He was eventually called from academic work to become the Anglican Bishop of Durham where he served very effectively. F. J. A. Hort was also a fellow at Trinity College, Cambridge. In addition, though he was a very scholarly type of person, he was also an Anglican parish priest. Though he was also gifted in classical languages, he was more of a philosopher than an exegete.

Westcott and Hort were warm-hearted, Bible-believing men. They were deeply committed to the incarnation of Christ, the fact that God had become man. They have been attacked in recent years by those who prefer the *Textus Receptus*, as being compromisers who were heavily influenced by critical scholarship. However, that was not the case. They were honest and professional scholars. We owe a great debt of gratitude to these men who have given their lives and health to providing us with an accurate copy of the Bible.

Conclusion

As a result of the tireless sacrificial effort of committed Bible scholars we now have an accurate and reliable Bible.

Study Questions

1. Write out a brief explanation of how you would explain textual criticism to a layman.
2. Define the following terms: lower criticism; autograph; amanuensis.
3. What were some of the kinds of variations that crept into the Greek texts?
4. What were the main reasons why the Old Testament texts are more accurately preserved than the New Testament texts?
5. Explain how the Trinitarian statement may have crept into the text of 1 John 5:7-8.
6. List some reasons why the ending of Mark is usually considered by most New Testament scholars to not be the original ending.
7. List and briefly explain the various families of manuscripts.
8. What contribution did Erasmus make to textual criticism?
9. What is the Textus Receptus?
10. What contributions did Westcott and Hort make to textual criticism?
11. Why is textual criticism important to the study of the Bible?
12. Describe some of the potential dangers in failing to understand textual criticism?

Chapter Six

English Translations

Introduction

Very few of us can read the Bible in the languages in which it was originally written. I studied Hebrew two years. At the end of the class, I had to pass a comprehensive exam by translating 500 words in two hours with an eighty percent accuracy. I was able to do that successfully. However, can you imagine taking two hours to read 500 words? Though I am still able to use my Hebrew to do word studies and check out things, I would find it difficult having my quiet time in Hebrew at the present time. I have studied Greek for about six years. I have also taught Greek for several years. I am much more familiar with the Greek New Testament than I am the Hebrew Old Testament. If I had to I could sit down and translate the Greek with a reasonable bit of accuracy. However, it would be difficult for me if I had to stand up in church next Sunday morning and read the New Testament in Greek. God has blessed me with the opportunity of studying the languages in which the Bible was written. I am grateful for what I have learned from them and continue to use these tools on a regular basis. However, the vast majority of Christians have never had the opportunity of studying the original languages.

Throughout much of the history of the church, if one could not read Hebrew, Greek, or Latin, he really could not read the Bible. Few people have made one great contribution to the world-wide church. However, Martin Luther has contributed two very significant things. First, he rediscovered and redefined the doctrine of justification by faith. Second, he recognized the importance of placing the Bible into the hands of the common man and supported the growing Bible translation movements. He himself translated the Bible into German—the common vernacular of his people. After Luther translated the Bible into German, others became interested in translating the Bible into many other languages including English.

Giving the common person the ability to read the Bible in his own language has not always been a popular idea with the clergy. There was a deliberate attempt, at least throughout certain periods of church history, to keep the Bible in Latin and other scholarly languages that the common man could not understand. It was thought that only those skilled in such languages could properly interpret the Bible.

When God selected a language in which the New Testament should be written, he did not select Classical Greek, the language of the scholars. He selected *Koine* Greek or "common" Greek, the language of the masses. I think that simple fact in itself suggests to us that God would want the Bible translated into the languages of the common man. It is interesting that the Protestant Reformation came at the same time that the Bible was translated into the common language of the people. Modern missionary strategy is not complete until the Bible has been translated into the mother tongue of the new converts.

Survey of English Translations

Vernacular Translations

Amazingly, within the first four hundred years of the birth of Christianity, the Bible or portions of the Bible had been translated into over 500 languages. However, by AD 600 the Bible had basically been reduced to one translation—Latin. Whether it was a deliberate conspiracy to keep the Bible out of the hands of the common man or whether it was a genuine attempt to preserve the integrity of the Bible by making sure it was read and interpreted only by professionals, the end result was the same. All throughout the Middle Ages, the Bible was only available to those who could read Greek, Hebrew, and Latin.

There are a few examples of portions of the Bible being informally translated into Saxon even prior to AD 1000. One of the early portions is a part of the Psaltery that was translated by the Bishop of Sherborne. This is thought to have been translated in about AD 709.[1] The first complete

---

[1] Paul D. Wegner, *The Journey from Texts to Translations* (Grand Rapids, MI USA: Baker Academic, 1999), p. 275.

French Bible appeared in the thirteenth century. It was translated in Paris. It had an uneven quality about it. There were other vernacular translations that appeared shortly after the development of the printing press, but there was not one in English.

John Wycliff,[2] who lived from 1329 to 1384, was the president of Balliol colleges at Oxford and later a very popular pastor. He translated the Bible into the common English vernacular of that time and attempted to circulate it. Perhaps it is more accurate to say that he was responsible for the translation. He did not personally translate it all himself. The Wycliff Bible follows the Latin Vulgate very closely. The first version of the New Testament was published in 1380 with the Old Testament following in 1382. The Wycliff Bible was intended for the common man not the scholar. Since these Bibles were all hand-copied they were of tremendous value. It is said that the rent of one of these Bibles for only one hour was a load of hay. In 1408, the pope banned Wycliff's Bible and all other vernacular Bibles. In fact, he was so unhappy with Wycliff that in 1428, almost forty-five years after Wycliff had died, the pope ordered that Wycliff's bones be dug up and publicly burned. The following is a copy of the Lord's Prayer from Wycliff's translation:

> Oure fadir that art in hevenes, halowid be thi name. Thi kyngdom come to. Be thi wille don in erthe as in hevene. Geve to us this day oure breed ovir other substaunce. And forgeve to us oure dettis, as we forgeven to our dettouris. And lede us not in temptacioun, but delyver us fro yvel. Amen.[3]

The First Printed English Edition: The Tyndale Version

William Tyndale attended both Oxford and Cambridge. He was a brilliant scholar who spoke eight languages as fluently as his mother tongue. While at Cambridge he was influenced by a lecturer, John Colet, who was using a new method of education. Rather than simply quoting from the scholars and authorities in the field, he started going back to the original sources in both the classics and the Bible. He attracted great attention by

---

[2] The name of this man has been spelled several ways throughout church history including Wycliff, Wycliffe and Wicliff.

[3] Quoted in Wegner, p. 283.

just reading the Greek New Testament publicly and then giving a vernacular translation of it. This methodology apparently greatly impressed Tyndale and gave him a desire to go back to the original sources. Tyndale was full of enthusiasm for translating the Bible. His stated objective was to translate the Bible so that the plowboy would know the Bible better than the priests.

However, in 1408, there had been a convention at Oxford forbidding any man under the penalty of "greater excommunication" from translating the Bible. Tyndale went to Germany where he met Martin Luther and later began the translation and printing process. In 1524, he printed 6000 copies of the Bible and attempted to smuggle them back to England. Tyndale's translation of the New Testament became the first copy of the Bible to be printed in English. In 1526, a copy of Tyndale's Bible was publicly burned and an attempt was made to buy up all the copies so that they could be destroyed. This process continued. A certain Augustine Packington became the middleman between the bishop of London and Tyndale. The Bibles would be smuggled into England. The bishop would buy them up and destroy them. This really satisfied everyone. The bishop was happy to be able to stop these translations from getting to the common man. Packington loved the arrangement because he was making a profit. Tyndale did not even mind because the bishop's purchases gave him money to print more, and it also made the bishop look bad as a Bible burner.

Tyndale's translation was based upon the original Greek rather than Latin and as a general rule was a very good one. Its influence still lives today because it greatly influenced the King James Version. It is estimated that of the portions on which Tyndale worked, ninety percent of his translation is found in the King James Version and eighty percent of his translation is still reflected in modern English translations we read today. In 1530, Tyndale published the Pentateuch. He continually revised his translation from that time until his death. The following is a sample of Tyndale's translation of 1 Corinthians 13:

> Though I spake with the tonges of men and angels, and yet had no love, I were even as soundinge brasse: or as a tynklynge Cymball. And though I coulde prophesy, and vnderstode all secretes, and all knowledge: yee, yf I had all fayth so that I coulde move mountayns oute of ther places, and yet had no love, I were nothynge . . . Love suffreth longe, and is corteous. Love envieth not. Love doth nott frowardly, swelleth not dealeth not

English Translations

dishonestly, seketh not her awne, is not provoked to anger, thynketh not evyll, reioyseth not in iniquite ... When I was a chylde, I spake as a chylde, I understode as a childe, I ymagened as a chylde: but assone as I was a man I put awaye childesshnes. Now we se in a glasse even in a darke speakynge: but then shall we se face to face ... Now abideth fayth, hope, and love, even these thre: but the chefe of these is love.[4]

Tyndale was eventually betrayed by Henry Philips, a supposed "colleague." He was taken to a prison where he suffered greatly for the next eighteen months. However, even in prison it is believed he was able to continue his work of translation. On October 6, 1536, he was taken out of the prison, strangled and publicly burned at the stake. His last words were a brief prayer, "Lord, open the King of England's eyes."

The Coverdale Bible: October 1535

The man responsible for this edition was Miles Coverdale who lived from 1488-1568. The political climate was somewhat more favourable for him. Anne Boleyn had just become the second wife of Henry the VIII and she was interested in an English Bible. Later she was beheaded, but her influence had had a positive influence on an English translation. Coverdale admitted freely that he was not a Greek or Hebrew Scholar. In his translation he depended heavily upon Tyndale's version in the New Testament and the Pentateuch. In the other portions, he translated from the Latin Vulgate and Luther's German translation. This Bible was first printed on the continent, either in Switzerland or France. It was printed in October 1535 while Tyndale was in prison, about a year before his death. The first Bible to be printed in England was Coverdale's second edition in 1537. To insure its acceptability it was dedicated to Henry VIII, describing him as a "Defender of the Faith."

The Matthew Bible: 1537

The Matthew Bible was supposedly translated by a certain Thomas Matthew. However there was no such person. This was actually the work

---

[4] Quoted in Geddes MacGregor, *A Literary History of the Bible* (Nashville, TN USA: Abingdon Press, 1968), p. 115.

of John Rogers, a friend and colleague of William Tyndale. He apparently used the name Thomas Matthew to conceal his identity. John Rogers had helped Tyndale smuggle Bibles back into England and later became Tyndale's literary executor. Hence his translation basically reflects Tyndale's translation. Where Tyndale was incomplete he followed the Coverdale Bible.

The Matthew Bible was granted a royal license, perhaps because it also included an elaborate dedication to King Henry VIII. This license did not grant the Bible the authorization of being read publicly in churches, but it did protect the private reader. These early Bibles frequently included marginal notes from the editors or translators. One of the editorial notes in a later edition of the Matthew Bible is a note of I Peter 3 where husbands are instructed about how to treat their wives. *"And if she be not obedient and healpfull unto hy (he) endeoureth to beate the feare of God into her heade, that therby she may be compelled to learne her dutie, and to do it."* Interestingly, John Rogers, like his mentor, William Tyndale, was eventually burned at the stake as a "heretic."

The Taverner Bible: 1539

The Taverner Bible was translated by a lawyer named Richard Taverner. It was a revision of the Matthew Bible. It no doubt would have been a more influential Bible if it had not been published the same year as the Great Bible.

The Great Bible: 1539

There was a great need to get an "English" edition of the Bible that would be officially recognized as the translation for England. Coverdale was officially appointed by Thomas Cromwell, the vicar-general under Henry VIII to head up this project. Coverdale and others worked on this project and the translation was completed in 1539. It was the first Bible authorized for public use in churches in England. All of the controversial marginal notes from the Matthew Bible were omitted. Twenty thousand copies were printed, enough for every church in England to have a copy. It was printed on very large paper and was indeed a splendid book, filled with pictures. The name "Great Bible" is a worthy name.

Geneva Bible: 1560

Many people had fled the oppressive environment in England to live in Geneva, Switzerland. In 1560 the first edition of the Geneva Bible was printed. William Whittingham, the brother-in-law of John Calvin, was primarily responsible for the New Testament and assisted in the Old Testament. The Geneva Bible was really a revision of the Great Bible and became very popular. It was dedicated to Queen Elizabeth I who was sympathetic to the Protestant Reformation. This Bible was quoted by Shakespeare 5000 times. A copy of the Geneva Bible also went across the Atlantic on the Mayflower[5] and was used by the Pilgrims, one of the first groups of settlers in America. It was the most popular Bible in the English-speaking world for the next 250 years.

The Geneva Bible also had many marginal notes in it, perhaps more than any of the other translations. In fact, one scholar has said that it was like the curriculum of a Bible college because it gave pastors many of the kinds of help they needed to properly expound the Bible. These marginal notes were very Calvinistic in doctrine and very anti-Catholic in tone. They had a profound impact upon Scotland and England, even though the Bible was never appointed to be read in the churches in England.

The Bishop's Bible: 1568

Up until this time, there was no official Bible of the Church of England. Matthew Parker, the Archbishop of Canterbury was responsible for overseeing this translation, which was actually a revision of the Great Bible. The Bishop's Bible became the official translation of the Church of England. It was called the Bishop's Bible because there were a large number of bishops on the translation board.

---

[5] The Mayflower was a small ship that took one of the first groups of pilgrims, religious refugees and other settlers to North America.

Douai-Reims Version: New Testament, 1582; Old Testament, 1609

All of the Bibles described so far were translated and sponsored by those who were sympathetic to the Reformation in one way or another. Though the Roman Catholic Church was totally committed to the authority of the word of God, there were different attitudes within the church about translating the Bible into the vernacular. However, as vernacular translations and particularly English translations proliferated, the Catholic church felt it was important to have an English translation that was officially approved by the Roman church.

Another fact that influenced this decision was the evangelistic zeal of the Roman church. Most churchmen were very interested in winning back those who had strayed from the church. Hence colleges were started on the continent with the purpose of training missionaries to the English. One of those colleges was at Douai in France. It was from this place that a steady stream of Catholic writings flowed. One of these "missionary" projects was the translation of the English Bible. It was started at the Douai College.

Later the college at Douai was closed, so the translation of the English Bible was completed at Reims, the place many Catholic scholars went after the close of Douai. Therefore, the translation became known as the Douai-Reims Version. Interestingly, this Bible was not well received in England. It was confiscated and destroyed by church officials. However, it was the official English translation of the Bible for the Roman Catholic Church for over three hundred years.

The Authorized Version (King James Version): 1611

King James was the son of Mary, Queen of the Scots. He was a rather vain effeminate man but had a great interest in the Bible. For some time the Puritans had been requesting a new translation of the Bible. In addition, a certain John Reynolds, president of Corpus Christi College in Oxford "moved His majesty that there might be a new translation of the Bible." This suggestion struck the fancy of King James, and he authorized that such a translation be undertaken. The only condition he placed upon the

Bible was that it could have no marginal notes. At first there was an appeal made to the bishops and churches for funds to support the translation. However, this failed and the royal treasury eventually paid for the translation.

The preparation for the King James Version was the most ambitious ever. Fifty-four men were appointed in 1604 to do the translation work. However, it was not until 1607 that the main body assembled and the work began. By that time, the number had been reduced to 47 and before the project was completed, several of the translators had died. The translation team was divided into six committees. Two met at Oxford; two met at Cambridge; two met at Westminster. There was also a committee of twelve consisting of two members from each of the six teams, which served as the revision committee.

The committee worked under fifteen different rules.[6] Written, of course, in Old English, they were as follows:

1. The ordinary Bible read in the Church, commonly called the Bishops' Bible, to be followed, and as little altered as the truth of the original will admit.

2. The names of the prophets and the holy writers, with the other names of the text, to be retained as nigh as may be, accordingly as they were vulgarly used.

3. The old ecclesiastical words to be kept, viz., the word church not to be translated congregation, etc.

4. When a word hath divers significations, that to be kept which hath been most commonly used by the most of the ancient fathers, being agreeable to the propriety of the place and the analogy of the faith.

5. The division of the chapters to be altered either not at all, or as little as may be, if necessity so require.

6. No marginal notes at all to be affixed, but only for the explanation of the Hebrew or Greek words which cannot, without some circum-locution, so briefly and fitly be expressed in the text.

7. Such quotations of places to be marginally set down as shall serve for the fit reference of one Scripture to another.

---

[6] Quoted from MacGregor, pp. 184-185.

8. Every particular man of each company to take the same chapter or chapters; and having translated or amended them severally by himself where he thinketh good, all to meet together, confer what they have done, and agree for their parts what shall stand.

9. As any one company hath dispatched any one book in this manner, they shall send it to the rest to be considered of seriously and judiciously, for his Majesty is very careful in this point.

10. If any company, upon the review of the book so sent, doubt or differ upon any place, to send them word thereof, note the place, and withal send the reasons; to which if they consent not, the difference to be compounded at the general meeting, which is to be of the chief persons of each company at the end of the work.

11. When any place of special obscurity is doubted of, letters to be directed by authority to send to any learned man in the land for his judgment of such a place.

12. Letters to be sent from every bishop to the rest of his clergy, admonishing them of this translation in hand, and to move and charge as many as being skilful in the tongues, and having taken pains in that kind, to send his particular observations to the company either at Westminster, Cambridge, or Oxford.

13. The directors in each company to be the Deans of Westminster and Chester for that place, and the king's professors in the Hebrew or Greek in either university.

14. These translations to be used when they agree better with the text than the Bishops' Bible: Tindale's, Matthew's, Coverdale's, Whitchurch's, Geneva.

15. Besides the said directors before mentioned, three or four of the most ancient and grave divines in either of the universities, not employed in translating, to be assigned by the Vice-Chancellor upon conference with the rest of the Heads to be overseers of the translations, as well Hebrew as Greek, for the better observation of the fourth rule above specified.

The following are some interesting facts about the King James Version:

1. Twenty thousand copies of the KJV were produced in the first printing.

2. The King James Version was not universally recognized or praised in its early days. In fact, there were many vociferous attacks on it.

3. There were many typographical errors in the King James Bible. One was found in a later edition, printed in 1631. It was known as the "Wicked Bible." It was so called because the printer left out the word "not" in one of the Ten Commandments so that the edition read, *"Thou shalt commit adultery."* The editors were fined 300 pounds sterling for this error. Another one was called the "Unrighteous Bible" because it read in 1 Corinthians 6:9, *"the unrighteous shall inherit the kingdom of God."* In the expression where Jesus condemned the Pharisees, we read (Matthew 23:24), *"You strain at a gnat and swallow a camel."* it should have read, *"You strain out a gnat and swallow a camel."* This is a typographical error that is still reproduced in our current Bibles.

4. All of the early editions of the Authorized Version included the fourteen books of the Apocrypha. In fact, one of the original translators of the King James Bible wrote a very strong warning to any printer who would dare print the Bible without the Apocrypha, threatening him with a very substantial fine.

5. The King James Version has continued to be edited on a regular basis ever since then. Typographical errors have been corrected. Spelling changes have been updated.

No one can overestimate the importance of the King James Bible. In addition to becoming the standard Bible of the English-speaking world, the King James Bible also helped to standardize the English of the world. It has been greatly used of God.

English Translations since the Authorized Version

The following is a list of the most important translations of the English Bible during the last 125 years:[7]

---

[7] I am deliberately making a distinction between those translations that may be referred to as translations and those that may be called paraphrases. Into the first category are those who followed a more literal translation with some dynamic equivalence influence, especially in the case of the NIV. Into the second category goes those that use a paraphrase or dynamic equivalence philosophy of translation.

Revised Version: 1881, 1885

The *Revised Version* (RV) was the first major revision of the English Bible after the King James Version was completed. The New Testament was completed in 1881 and the Old Testament was completed in 1885. Both British and American scholars translated the project. The British scholars set the rules but the American revisers were not happy about them. The translation took advantage of the textual criticism work of Westcott and Hort and set the direction for most future English translations. The Old Testament translators placed poetic passages in couplets, thus making them appear more poetry-like. Because there were no English language experts on the committee, the final product was a bit stilted and literal and lost some of the beauty of the *Authorized Version*. Because of that, it never really did make a serious challenge to the *King James Version*. The *Revised Version* included the Apocrypha.

American Standard Version; 1901

The American and British scholars who worked on the *Revised Version* often disagreed on procedure and wording. Therefore, this encouraged the American committee to create an American revision of the English Bible called the *American Standard Version* (ASV). The translation took advantage of many of the new discoveries in textual criticism but continued to use much old English. It received a better reception in America than did the *Revised Version* but continued to lag behind the *Authorized Version*.

Revised Standard Version: 1946, 1952

The New Testament of the *Revised Standard Version* (RSV) was completed in 1946 and the Old Testament in 1952. The Apocrypha was later added in 1957. The project was developed by the International Council of Religious Education, which was a part of the National Council of Churches. It changed Old English words to modern English but attempted to preserve some of the majesty and style of the *King James Version*. It added quotation marks for direct quotes. The work became the most widely accepted English Bible next to the *King James Version*. The Nigerian Ministry of Education has accepted the RSV as the official translation to be used in CRK classes. However, the RSV was not accepted by all. Because the owner of the copyright was the National Council of Churches, which was viewed as a theologically liberal organization by some, the RSV was rejected by many branches of the Christian church. An example of the perceived liberal bias was the changing the word "virgin" to "young woman" in Isaiah 7:14.

New American Standard Bible; 1971

The *New American Standard Bible* (NASB) was an attempt to update and revise the American Standard Version. It was developed by the Lockman Foundation, a non-profit organization. The NASB took advantage of all the latest textual criticism discoveries. It continued the tradition of using modern English but tended to follow the same word order as found in the original Hebrew and Greek. The translation is usually recognized as the most literal English translation available which makes it ideal for the student of the Bible. It was accepted and has been used broadly by conservative evangelicals.

New International Version: 1973, 1978

The translation of the *New International Version* (NIV) was sponsored by a coalition of evangelical groups, primarily because of their dissatisfaction with other modern-language English translations of the Bible. The New Testament was completed in 1973 and the Old Testament in 1978. The NIV was partially sponsored by the National Association of Evangelicals and eventually funded by the New York International Bible Society. One hundred and ten scholars from most of the countries that speak English as a first language worked on this project. This was a genuine attempt not only to use modern English but to use international English. The editors also tried to bring together the literal and dynamic equivalent philosophies of translation in this work. This Bible has become the best seller of English Bibles and is likely to become the Bible of choice by the majority of English speaking Christians.

New King James Version: 1979, 1982

The translators of this version saw themselves as not creating a new translation but simply providing an updated version of the *King James Version*, using the same translation principles and the same Greek text, the *Textus Receptus*. The New Testament was completed in 1979 and the Old Testament in 1982. The revision uses modern English language but, in an attempt to preserve as much of the *King James Version* as possible, tends to use ancient phrases and style. It is fair to say that this translation appealed to the more conservative part of the body of Christ.

New Revised Standard Version: 1989

The *New Revised Standard Version* (NRSV) translation was sponsored by the same group that had originally created the *Revised Standard Version*. It was not viewed as a new translation but a revision of the RSV. The one new feature of this translation is that whereas masculine pronouns are used to refer to God and Christ, there is an attempt to use gender-neutral language in other places.

New Living Translation; 1996

The *New Living Translation* (NLT) was an attempt to take advantage of the enormous popularity of the *Living Bible* that had originally been done by Kenneth Taylor. More than 90 revisers attempted to create a more accurate translation that used the dynamic equivalence philosophy of translation rather than the paraphrase technique that had been used in the *Living Bible*. This Bible is a real improvement over the *Living Bible*. It is a very simple straightforward translation that is very readable.

It should be noted that all of the major translations of the English Bible since 1881, except the *New King James Version*, have been translated based upon the Greek text produced by Westcott and Hort and their successors rather than the *Textus Receptus*.

Important Paraphrases and Modern Language Translations

The following is a list of some of the English translations of the Bible that might be considered paraphrases of the Bible. Some of them, like the *Living Bible* and the *Good News Bible,* have surpassed some of the translations in popularity and influence.

Philips Translation: 1958

This was a paraphrase of the New Testament done by J. B. Philips. It clearly uses very contemporary English and at times is brilliant.

New English Bible: 1961

The *New English Bible* (NEB) project was sponsored by a coalition of churches in the United Kingdom. It reflects British English throughout. It was 24 years in preparation and cost more to prepare than any other English Bible prior to this time.[8]

Jerusalem Bible: 1966

The *Jerusalem Bible* was an English translation officially sponsored by the Roman Catholic Church. In fact, it was the first English translation ever sponsored by the Catholic Church that came directly from the original language and was not based upon the Latin Vulgate.

Living Bible: 1971

When Kenneth Taylor read the King James Bible to his children, he found that they got little out of it. Therefore, he used his time commuting from work to home by train every day to paraphrase the Bible into language that his children could understand. This proved so successful he prepared these translations for publication. The first part published was *Living Letters* in 1962. He expanded his translations to eventually include the New Testament in 1967 and the entire Bible in 1971. The *Living Bible* was largely the work of one man though it was reviewed by many Greek and Hebrew scholars and English experts. In the 1970's more copies of the *Living Bible* were sold than any other English translation. Its strength is that it is extremely readable. Its weakness is that it is a paraphrase of the Bible and does not always reflect the fine shades of meaning that a translation does.

Today's English Bible/Good News Bible: 1966, 1976

This project was originally published by the American Bible Society. It was first called *Good News for Modern Man* but was also known as *Today's English Version*. After the Old Testament was completed it was called the *Good News Bible*. It used a dynamic equivalent philosophy of translation. It

---

[8] Wegner, p. 370.

was extremely popular, selling fifty-two million copies of the New Testament by 1976.

The New Living Translation: 1996, 2004

Tyndale Houses Publishers assembled a substantial committee in the mid 90's to revise Kenneth Taylor's monumental work, the *Living Bible*. Well over a hundred theologians and Bible scholars, representing a broad spectrum of evangelical Christianity, worked together to create this substantial revision. The publishers still were not satisfied with the work so a further revision was completed in 2004. This translation of the Bible is written in simple straight-forward English and is likely going to be one of the most popular Bibles in the English world in the future.

Philosophy of Translation

Translation is difficult work. It is more involved than just translating words. You may give a word for word translation and still not communicate. There are two distinct philosophies of translation:

Literal Translation

A literal translation attempts to reflect the exact words in the target language as close to the original language as possible. This is sometimes called a "formal equivalence." The translator tries as much as possible to give a word-for-word translation. He keeps interpretation at a minimum, leaving it up to the reader to interpret any passages that may be ambiguous. Where the original is ambiguous, he attempts to reflect that ambiguity. Where the passage presents a difficult interpretation, he presents the same thing.

Dynamic Equivalent Translation

A dynamic equivalent translation focuses more on transferring the thought into the new language rather than just the words. When doing this type of translation, the translator attempts to reflect the meaning of the passage. He is not concerned about actual words or word order. He is willing to make interpretations and reflect those in the text.

On one occasion, Jesus said, *"I am the bread of life."* What was Jesus saying? To properly understand the passage, we must understand that bread was the basic staple of the Palestinian's diet. A Palestinian Jew of the first century ate bread every day. Therefore for Jesus to say, *"I am the bread of life,"* he was saying that he is essential for life: He is that which makes us live and gives us strength. However, in the African culture, bread does not have that connotation. Bread is a luxury—a special treat in most homes. The real staple of the diet here is gari or pounded yam or guinea corn. Therefore, to really translate this passage and give the real sense, one would translate, *"I am the gari (or yam or guinea corn) of life."* That would be a dynamic equivalent translation. It gives the real meaning of the passage, even if it has to sacrifice a word for word translation.

Observations about Translations

A dynamic equivalent translation is preferable for the vast majority of Christians and perfectly appropriate for public reading.

Paraphrases are extremely valuable tools. In many places they serve as small commentaries. Often they reflect the meaning of the passage even better than a literal translation. Bibles using a dynamic equivalent translation are almost always much more simple and easy to read. This kind of Bible is ideal for most of our Biblical reading and studying. These kinds of Bibles are especially helpful in reading historical passages because they tend to make the sections much more understandable. In light of the fact that getting the word of God into our hearts is perhaps our highest priority and the dynamic equivalent translations tend to do this better than literal translations, most Christians should regularly use the dynamic equivalent translations. In addition, to encourage people to use these Bibles more, pastors and worship leaders should use such Bibles in public worship.

Advanced students of the Bible should also use a literal translation for their personal study.

For several years, I have personally read the New Living Translation in my personal quiet time. I have found this a fascinating translation because it presents the truth of the Bible in a new and memorable manner. However, I continue to do my personal study for lectures and sermons out of the New International Version. As a general rule, I recommend this practice for other preachers and teachers and advanced students of the Bible. I make this recommendation for several reasons: We believe that the Holy Spirit inspired the very words that the Bible writers used. Although we do not see those original words in our English translations, the most ideal form of Bible interpretation is to attempt to get as close to the original words as possible. That is easier to do with a translation than with a paraphrase. When one paraphrases, he is interpreting. I would prefer that those who reach an advanced level of Bible study be given the right to interpret the Bible themselves, rather than have the interpretation presented to them without them knowing it.

Conclusion

I love and appreciate the King James Version. It is the queen and mother of all translations. It was the translation that I heard preached from and memorized all throughout my childhood and early adult life. Even at the beginning of the twenty-first century, it is still the Bible of choice for millions of people. However, I am convinced that for our own personal study of the Scriptures and even for public reading, we should use a modern language translation. I am convinced that the English Bible of the future church in Africa is going to be either the *New International Version* or the *New Living Translation*. Therefore, I encourage all my students to buy and start using one of those translations. May God give us a thankful heart for those who have made it possible for us to read and study the Bible in our own language.[9]

Study Questions

1. Explain why it is important to be able to have the Bible in the common language of people.
2. How did Martin Luther encourage the translation of the Bible into the common language of people?
3. Who was responsible for the first English translation of the Bible? What else do we know about this man?
4. How was William Tyndale persecuted for translating the Bible into English?
5. What did each of the following men contribute to the English Bible? Miles Coverdale; John Rogers; William Taverner.
6. Why was the "Great Bible" given such a name?
7. List five facts about the Geneva Bible.
8. Briefly summarize the history of the Douai-Reims Bible.
9. What do we know about the translators of the Authorized Version or King James Version of the Bible?
10. List five unique rules under which the King James translators worked.
11. What is different about all of the English Bibles translated since 1881?
12. Explain the difference between a literal translation and a dynamic equivalent translation?

---

[9] Much of the information in this chapter has been adapted from Geddes MacGregor, *A Literary History of the Bible* (Nashville, TN USA: Abington Press).

Chapter Seven

What is Communication?

Communication is transferring what is in the mind of one person into the mind of other persons. If we were all computers, this would be relatively easy. We could plug one cord into the mind of one person and the other cord into the mind of the other person, press the button and the communication would transfer quickly and completely with no error. However, God has not chosen for man to learn that way. God has a much better plan. In fact, God has designed learning to be one of the most enjoyable experiences in life.

Have you ever noticed, that in the proportion certain things are necessary to sustain life, God has made them enjoyable? It is necessary for us to eat to have strength, so God has made eating very enjoyable. It is necessary for us to have rest to renew the strength of our bodies. Therefore, God has made rest very enjoyable. In order for the human race to continue from one generation to the next, there must be procreation. In order for there to be procreation, there must be sexual relations between a man and a woman. I am sure you have noticed that God has made sexual relations enjoyable.

In a similar way God has made learning very enjoyable. Proverbs 25:2; *"It is the glory of God to conceal a matter; to search out a matter is the glory of kings."* What does this passage mean? It means that there is nothing more glorious or enjoyable or pleasurable that one can do than learn. God cannot learn because he knows everything. Therefore, God gets pleasure out of concealing truth. He hides truth from us and then gets a certain amount of pleasure out of watching us, his creatures, search out and discover truth.

The point is that God has not only created communication, but he has created it to be enjoyable. It is a joy and pleasure to learn.

Components in Communication

There are three essential components in communication.

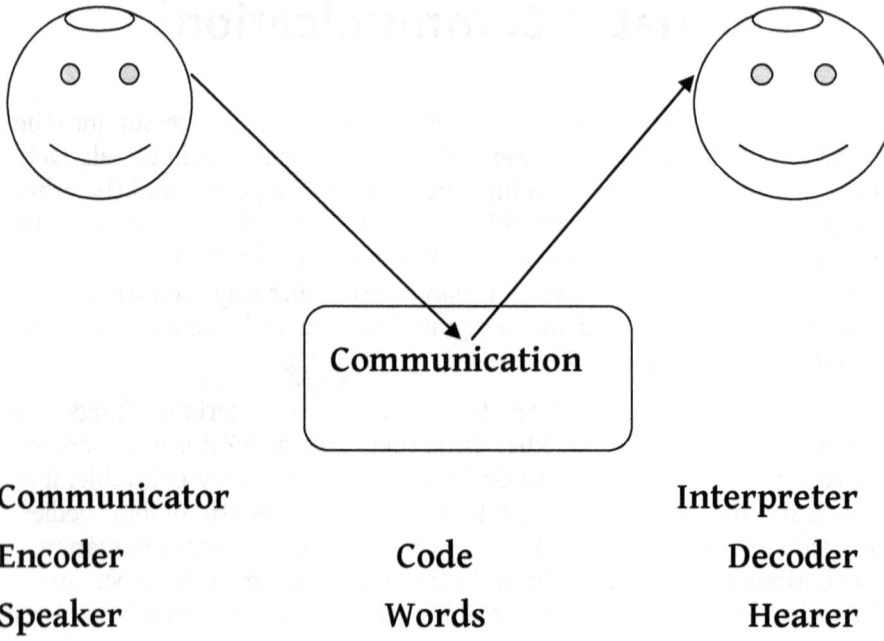

Communicator		Interpreter
Encoder	**Code**	**Decoder**
Speaker	**Words**	**Hearer**
Writer	**Document**	**Reader**

The three essential components of communication are the communicator, the interpreter and the communication. It is the responsibility of the communicator to reduce his thoughts into some form of communication. Since the interpreter cannot see into the brain of the communicator, the interpreter must see and hear the communication that the communicator has created and interpret that in order to discern what is in the mind of the communicator. The interpreter assumes that the words and actions, which the communicator is using, mean the same thing as he understands them to mean.

Problems with Communication

1. **Communication breaks down when the communicator is transferring his thoughts into the communication.** There is no perfect communicator. All of us have thoughts that are difficult for us to express. It is even sometimes difficult to express ourselves to God. That is why we are told that the Holy Spirit helps us with our prayers, expressing things that we do not know how to express. Therefore, regardless of how skillful a person is as a communicator, he is never quite able to express everything.

2. **Communication breaks down when the interpreter is interpreting the communication.** Seldom can one concentrate well enough to really get everything another person is saying, either in oral or written communication. Even if one understands all of the words of the communication, it is still difficult to understand everything because the nuances of the words change from one person to the other.

If a person is a pretty good communicator and is able to transfer ninety percent of what is in his mind into his communication, and a person is a pretty good interpreter and is able to interpret ninety percent of the communication from the communicator, how much communication has taken place? The correct answer is eighty-one percent.

The task of the interpreter is to try to reduce the percentage of misunderstanding and improve the ability to understand the communication. In the case of the Bible, the communication is perfect in the original languages. The Holy Spirit has inspired the writings so that they contain the correct communication. Our job is to understand the communication.

Does that mean that the Bibles we have on the tables in front of us are one hundred percent of the communication from God? No, we have lost some of the original communication through textual corruption. We do not have the exact original manuscripts today, therefore, we cannot be sure that we have the exact words God originally gave us. Also, we study the Bible in a translation. When one translates from one language to the other, we seldom get a one hundred percent perfect translation. Perhaps we lose up to one percent of the communication due to textual problems and translation. Do you know why people study Greek and Hebrew? They do so to get that one percent back.

Conclusion

Communication is one of the most important activities that we as human beings do every day. God has made us to be creatures who are constantly creating and interpreting communication.

In addition, God has made us as creatures who can communicate with Him. One of the ways that God communicates with us is through His written word. Therefore, we must make every effort to learn how to interpret those words as carefully and accurately as we can.

Study Questions

1. Give a definition of communication.
2. What does Proverbs 25:2 teach about learning?
3. What are the three components of communication?
4. Where are the places that communication is likely to break down?
5. What are some of the problems with interpreting the Bible?
6. Write a paragraph explaining how communicate fails and the consequences of failed communication.

Chapter Eight

Tools of Bible Study

Introduction

When I was a final year student in secondary school, I learned the roofing trade. In the USA, one of the most common roofing materials is an asphalt shingle, a strip of material about one meter long and about a third of a meter wide. It is quite flexible. Each shingle has to be lined up in a certain way and nailed in place with four nails. Installing this kind of roofing is very hard work, and usually, very hot work. However, it is a skill that one can acquire relatively quickly, and it pays quite well.

A few months later, I enrolled in a seminary. I needed to make some money to pay my school fees. Therefore, I looked for opportunities to get a roofing job. One day, I met a friend who was also a roofer. He said to me, "Danny, I am getting out of the roofing business. Would you like to buy my tools?" I paid him ten dollars and he gave me all of the tools he used to put shingles on a roof. I received a hammer, a roofing hatchet, a tape measure, a chalk box, two knives for cutting the roofing material, a pair of tin cutters, and a nail apron for holding nails. All of these tools were essential for putting on asphalt shingles. I needed every one of those tools in order to do my work.

A few days later I went to a roofing contractor. I told him I was a roofer and wanted to put the roof on the house he was building. I assured him that I knew how to do the work and had the necessary tools. Therefore, he gave me a job to do. Once I did the first job, I then had many jobs. At first, I did not even have a ladder to get up on the roof. I would have to borrow one from the carpenters. However, gradually, I acquired more and more tools. Eventually I bought a van to carry all my tools in. I had three ladders that I carried on the top of the van. Later, I bought an air compressor and an air hammer to do my work. Soon I had thousands of dollars worth of tools.

When I first got in the roofing business, my colleagues at the seminary who were also working on the side to make a living, were working for the minimum wage of $1.65 per hour. However, because I had a trade and the tools, I could make up to $5.00 per hour. Later, as I got more tools and developed more skills, I continued to make more money so that eventually I could make at least $25 per hour and sometimes much more. What made the difference? It was having the right tools and knowing how to use them.

Every profession has its tools. Those who are involved in Christian ministry, such as pastors, evangelists, missionaries and teachers of the Bible, have tools. Their primary tools are books. There are some books that are absolutely necessary for us to do our work. There are other books that are not quite as necessary, but if we acquire them and learn how to use them, they will make us more efficient with our time and make us more productive in our ministry. However, having books without using them or without knowing how to use them is like having tools that one never uses. It would have done me no good to spend a lot of money on sophisticated roofing tools if I did not know how to use them or refused to use them. In a similar way, there is no particular reason to buy a lot of books that one will not or does not know how to use.

What are the most important tools that we use in the Christian ministry? In the following pages, I will outline what I consider to be the most important tools and give a few suggestions about the best way to use them.

Bible Dictionary

If a pastor could have only one other book besides his Bible, probably he or she should get a Bible dictionary.[1] A dictionary is a book that contains words and their meanings arranged in alphabetical order. It is a valuable

---

[1] If I could have only one book besides the Bible, I personally would choose a complete concordance of the Bible. However, a Bible dictionary gives a great variety of background information to the pastor and that probably tips the scales toward a Bible dictionary as the first supplemental book in one's personal theological library.

tool for someone learning another language. But it is also helpful to those who speak only one language, because the dictionary helps explain the precise meanings of words. A Bible dictionary is very similar. It is a book that contains words with their meanings and explanations arranged in alphabetical order. A good Bible dictionary will provide at least a few sentences about practically every person, place, or thing in the Bible. For example, if one wanted to know about wine or cattle or the Ark of the Covenant or practically anything else associated with the Bible, he would simply look up that word in the Bible dictionary.

Bible dictionaries vary in the amount and quality of material that they give. Most Bible dictionaries will give what they consider to be the most important material. Some Bible dictionaries like the *International Standard Bible Encyclopedia* (*ISBE*) will give almost everything the Bible has to say about a given topic. As a general rule, the Bible dictionary article will contain multiple scriptural references so that the researcher can go directly to the Bible and check out the observations presented in the dictionary.

Therefore, if a pastor is preparing a sermon on a baptism, he can look up the word "baptism" in the Bible dictionary. Nearly all Bible dictionaries will give the basic information about baptism found in the Bible. They will include the kind of baptism practiced by John the Baptist, as well as, the figurative usage of the word in such experiences as the "baptism of the Holy Spirit." More comprehensive Bible dictionaries will have additional information about how the various Christian traditions have interpreted and practiced baptism. For example, in *ISBE*, a book described below, the information about baptism is found in Volume I from pages 385 to 401. It has three articles about baptism, one written from the Baptist point of view by A. T. Robertson, one written from the non-immersionist point of view by T. M. Lindsay, and one written from the Lutheran point of view by W. H. T. Dau. *ISBE* also has additional articles entitled "Baptismal Regeneration," "Baptism for the Dead," "Baptism of Fire," and "Baptism of the Holy Spirit." The dictionary directs the reader to two more articles in other parts of the book entitled, "Infant Baptism" and "John the Baptist." *ISBE* is a five-volume work that is more comprehensive than most Bible dictionaries. In these pages, one could find just about everything he needed to know about baptism.

On the other hand, the *Bridge Bible Dictionary* is a book about the same size as one volume of *ISBE*. It only has about one and a half pages in the article entitled "Baptism." It is primarily limited to what the Bible says about baptism and refers to at least sixty different scriptural references. This Bible dictionary also has a half-page article on the "Baptism of the Holy Spirit." The following is a list of standard Bible Dictionaries[2] that can be found in Africa:

International Standard Bible Encyclopedia (*ISBE*), Geoffrey W. Bromiley, editor (Grand Rapids, MI USA: William B. Eerdmans Publishing Company, 1979). The original version was published in five volumes. The revised version has been published in four volumes. This is a very comprehensive set of books that is invaluable for the serious student of the Bible. ISBE represents those very large comprehensive Bible dictionaries that are nearly always written by multiple authors under the guidance of a general editor.

Zondervan Pictorial Encyclopedia of the Bible (*ZPED*),[3] Merrill C. Tenney, editor. (Grand Rapids, MI USA: Regency Reference Library). This is another five-volume set and is similar in many ways to ISBE. The book has 241 contributors, involving many of the most outstanding evangelical Biblical scholars and theologians of the latter part of the twentieth century. It contains far more maps and pictures than ISBE. It is a treasure of information, a tool that any minister or Biblical scholar would be proud to own and use.

Bridge Bible Dictionary, by Don Fleming. (Brisbane, Australia: Bridgeway Publications). This Bible dictionary is at the opposite end of the scale from *ISBE* and *ZPED*. It is one volume of 473 pages and was all written by one person. It is an excellent work. It focuses primarily on Biblical information related to the words it contains. It is not as comprehensive as the larger Bible dictionaries, but it is probably all that most pastors and

---

[2] Some reference works use the term "encyclopedia." There is no basic difference between books that use that name and those that use the name "dictionary," except the encyclopedia tends to be a bit longer.

[3] Both *ISBE* and *ZPED* are very expensive and probably beyond the reach of most pastors. However, they are found in many theological libraries.

Bible teachers would ever need. It is a book that is available in Africa and one that I heartily recommend.

New Bible Dictionary (3rd edition) edited by I. H. Marshall, A. R. Millard, J. I. Packer and D. J. Wiseman. (Leister, England and Downers Grove, IL USA: Intervarsity Press). This is a 1298 page work. It is an excellent Bible dictionary and perhaps the one most available in Nigeria.

In addition to Bible dictionaries, there are several other tools that fall under this same genre of writing. For example, a handbook of the Bible contains many of the same kinds of information that a Bible dictionary does. The difference is that in a handbook, the material is arranged in the order those topics would naturally arise in the Bible. Therefore, articles related to the inspiration of the Bible would be at the front of the book and articles related to the resurrection of Jesus would be toward the back of the book. There are many other kinds of dictionaries, including dictionaries of Biblical words, theology, church history, and other themes.

The following list contains works closely related to Bible dictionaries.

The Lion Handbook to the Bible, David and Pat Alexander, editors. (Oxford, England: Lion Publishing).[4] This is a beautiful book of 680 pages, filled with over 500 color pictures, maps, charts and documents that are useful to the Bible interpreter. The first article is entitled "The Bible in its Environment," and the last article is "Apocalyptic Literature." Like a commentary, it gives brief descriptions of all the sections of the Bible. It is an outstanding Bible study aid and should be in the library of every serious student of the Bible.

Evangelical Dictionary of Theology, Walter A. Elwell, editor. (Grand Rapids, MI USA: Baker Book House). This book is well named. It is a dictionary of doctrines, theological terms, and key theologians. It has articles in it from 286 theologians. Though it is written in the same format as a Bible dictionary, it focuses on theological concepts rather than Biblical concepts.

New Dictionary of Theology, Sinclair Ferguson and David Wright, editors. (Leicester, England and Downers Grove, IL USA: Intervarsity Press). This

---

[4] This book has recently been revised and expanded and is now called *The New Lion Handbook to the Bible.* The revised version contains 816 pages.

book is similar to the *Evangelical Dictionary of Theology*. It contains excellent bibliographical material related to every article so is an excellent tool for research. It contains 300 articles written by 210 contributors.

New Dictionary of Biblical Theology, T. D. Alexander and Brian Rosner, editors (Leicester, England and Downers Grove, IL USA: Intervarsity Press). This is similar to the two theological dictionaries mentioned above but approaches doctrine from a Biblical theological methodology rather than a systematic theological methodology. This book also contains extensive bibliographies. The book was written by 125 scholars from 5 continents.

The New International Dictionary of the Christian Church, J. D. Douglas, editor. (Grand Rapids, MI USA: Zondervan Publishing House). It contains 1074 pages and articles from 182 writers. The primary focus of this book is on persons, places, and events related to church history. Anything one would like to know about church history would most likely be treated in this book.

Other reference books that follow the "dictionary" format include: *Evangelical Dictionary of World Missions,* A. Scott Moreau, editor (Grand Rapids, MI USA: Baker Books); *Dictionary of Paul and His Letters,* Gerald F. Hawthorn, Ralph P. Martin and Daniel G. Reid, editors. (Leicester, England and Downers Grove, IL USA: Intervarsity Press); *Dictionary of Biblical Imagery,* Leland Ryken, James C. Wilhoit, and Tremper Longman III, editors. (Leicester, England and Downers Grove, IL, USA: Intervarsity Press).

Commentary

A commentary is a book that makes comments about various texts of the Bible and arranges those comments in the order in which the verses appear in the Bible. A commentary is one of the simplest forms of communicating the Bible. The writer will take a verse and make whatever appropriate comments he thinks needs to be made about that verse. He will then move to the next verse or next section and do the same thing. The typical commentary has observations and comments about the words, grammar, culture, history, geography, doctrine and any other details that relate to that passage. There are many kinds of commentaries, from those that are extremely technical to those that are little more than paraphrases of the Bible. There are several ways that we divide commentaries. I will list only two.

Technical Commentaries

A technical commentary is one that freely uses information from the original Hebrew or Greek languages. Therefore, a person unfamiliar with the original languages will not get much out of these kinds of commentaries. For example, one of the most comprehensive works on the Old Testament is the *Commentary on the Old Testament in Ten Volumes* written by C. F. Keil and F. Delitzsch. These books were originally written in German. They contain very detailed grammatical and linguistic information. They are extremely valuable for the person who has some knowledge of Hebrew. However, to someone without a working knowledge of Hebrew, they would have only limited usefulness. A New Testament example would be *The Expositor's Greek New Testament,* edited by W. Robertson Nicoll. This commentary contains much information related to Greek grammar and linguistics and is helpful to theologians and Biblical scholars, but not very helpful to the person who does not know Greek.

Non-Technical Commentaries

On the other hand, there are many very fine commentators who have used their Greek and Hebrew skills to extract useful material but have written their observations and comments in language that the average person can understand and appreciate. The objective of this kind of commentary is to give readers the necessary background information so that they can properly interpret the passage under consideration. Focus is given to the meaning of words, the cultural and historical context, various theological considerations and varying ways others have interpreted this passage. This kind of commentary is sometimes called a homiletical commentary because it is primarily used by preachers in preparing sermons.

Older commentators like Adam Clarke and Matthew Henry were not afraid to use their Greek and Hebrew, but wrote in such a way that their material was understandable to most believers and especially preachers and Bible teachers.

One of the best commentators I have ever read is D. Edmond Hiebert who has written major commentaries on Mark, Thessalonians and James. Hiebert's primary interest is to help the reader interpret what the original writers wanted to communicate. In my opinion, that is exactly what a commentator, preacher, or Bible teacher should be doing.

A very contemporary writer who is producing outstanding commentaries is Craig Keener. His commentary entitled *The New Testament Background Commentary* was ranked as the best Bible study aid in 1996. This book is not a "commentary" in the sense that it gives a verse-by-verse exposition of the meaning of the passage. Rather it focuses on various kinds of background information that will help interpret the passage. His recent *Commentary on the Gospel of Matthew,* published by William B. Eerdmans Publishing Company, Grand Rapids, MI in 1999, contains many references to technical material but is very user friendly.

One of the most brilliant contemporary writers and expositors is John Stott. His works always have the right balance of linguistic, cultural and theological foundation and practical application. I have used his commentary on Acts, *The Message of Acts,* extensively. I would recommend any commentary or other book he publishes.

A sub-division of the non-technical commentary is what is sometimes called the "devotional commentary." These kinds of commentaries do not focus so much on interpretation as application. They are actually more like sermons, which start from a Biblical text, but focus more on how the scripture relates to the contemporary world. These books are very useful for one's personal growth and development but are not as useful in studying and interpreting the Bible. The old commentary of Matthew Henry and the more recent commentaries of J. C. Ryle fit into this category.

Sets and Individual Commentaries

There are hundreds of sets of commentaries and probably thousands of individual commentaries on the various books of the Bible. As a general rule, Biblical scholars tend to specialize in one area. Therefore, a commentary written by a person in his own specialty is likely to be more comprehensive and more useful than a commentary written on that same book by a generalist who has written commentaries over the whole Bible. For that reason, pastors and Bible teachers should attempt to fill their library with those individual commentaries where the authors are specialists.

There are also many very good sets of commentaries. I have earlier referred to Matthew Henry and Adam Clarke who lived over 250 years ago. Both of these men were brilliant scholars who wrote commentaries over the entire Bible. Many contemporary Bible students scoff at these old works and wonder what they could offer to our modern world. However, we must remember that interpretation is primarily putting ourselves back into the ancient world and extracting from them what they were saying. People two hundred years ago could do that as well as we can today, if not better, because they were closer to the events than we are. It is true that there have been many archaeological discoveries and other developments in Biblical studies that they did not have access to. Nevertheless, I have found that these older commentaries still contain valuable information.

One of the most valuable sets of commentaries that I have used over the years is William Barclay's *Daily Bible Study Series.* William Barclay was a brilliant theologian who published at least sixty books in his life. His main flaw was that he was much more influenced by the rationalistic approach to Scripture than I like and this permeates his writings. For instance, he tended to provide natural explanations for as many of Jesus' miracles as he could. However, he provides outstanding background information. His understanding of the original Greek is equally as good, and his word studies are superb. The amazing thing about these commentaries is that they are written in the most non-technical fashion possible and are actually designed for laymen to read devotionally every day. Once one understands his theological weaknesses— related to issues that evangelicals believe strongly—and is able to navigate around those, his observations can be very helpful. I think it would be fair to say that I have used William Barclay in my study over the years more than any other single commentator. I would encourage the mature pastor or teacher of the Bible who has opportunity to purchase a set of Barclay's commentaries to do so.

One of the tools that is now available in Africa is several one-volume commentaries. A one-volume commentary can be a useful tool for general study of the Bible. However, because the comments have to be so brief and so general, I have not personally found one-volume commentaries overly helpful. They do provide introductions to books and give certain general overviews, so if you do not have other tools that will provide this information, such as a good Study Bible, then a one-volume commentary can be very helpful. However, as a general rule, I believe that one-volume commentaries are not as useful as the more expanded versions. My friend and colleague, Rev. Luka Vandi,[5] whose opinion I value very highly in these matters, says that the best one-volume commentary available in Nigeria is the *New Bible Commentary,* edited by D. A. Carson, R. T. France, J. A. Motyer and G. J. Wenham, (Leicester, England and Downers Grove, IL, USA: Intervarsity Press).

For any serious student of the Bible, commentaries are essential. It would be irresponsible to preach or teach the Word of God without attempting to learn what great Bible scholars have said about various passages of Scripture. It is my conviction that when we study Bible, we should do our own research first. However, after having learned all we can on our own, turning to the commentaries can and should be a rich and rewarding experience. Often we can find summarized in just a few words the exact explanation of a passage we have been struggling to find for years.

Concordances

I studied under a theologian named S. I. Emery. He once made this statement: "If I could have only one other book beside my Bible, I would

---

[5] Rev. Luka Vandi is the General Manager of Africa Christian Textbooks (ACTS). In this capacity he knows more about theological reference books than almost anyone else in Nigeria.

want to have a copy of *Strong's Exhaustive Concordance*." I think I would personally prefer *Young's Analytical Concordance,* but I would certainly agree with him that if I could have only one other book beside my Bible, I would want a good complete concordance. I frequently tell my students that I do not like to loan out my books. However, if they are nice people I will sometimes loan out my theology books, my Greek books, or other Bible study aids. If they really beg, I might even loan out some of the books of which I have the only copy I know of in Nigeria. However, nobody need ever come to me and ask to borrow my concordance. It is a book I use nearly every day.

A concordance arranges all the words found in the Bible in alphabetical order. Every concordance is translation specific.[6] In other words, every translation has its own concordance since the words in the concordance come from the words of the translation. Under each word is a list of scripture phrases, which contain that word. A complete concordance will have every word in the Bible and every reference where that word is found in the Bible. Because a concordance has all of these words listed in alphabetical order and then all the references to that word arranged in the order in which they are found in the Bible, the concordance is the primary tool used to look up references. The most typical way that a concordance is used is when a person remembers some phrase from the Bible but cannot remember where it is found. He would like the exact quotation and the exact reference. Therefore, he selects one of the words that he can remember and looks it up. He then looks through all of the

---

[6] In this book, I have primarily used *Young's Analytical Concordance* and *Strong's Exhaustive Concordance* as illustrations. Both of these are concordances for the King James Version of the Bible. Although I recommend that we use a modern language Bible for our study of the Bible, I have used Young's and Strong's as examples for at least two reasons. First, there are many of these available in Africa right now and very few of the newer concordances. Second, since both of these are complete concordances, having original word information in them, one can do the same kinds of word studies with a complete concordance for the King James Version as he can with a modern language concordance, since the focus is on the original words and not the English translation. If a person has access to a modern language concordance, that is ideal. However, if he has only Strong's or Young's, he can still do excellent word studies.

references given by the concordance to see if he can spot the particular reference he is looking for.

For example, if we remember the phrase *"her long hair is given to her for a covering"* and decide to try to find that reference, what we want to do is to find the word that is used the fewest number of times in the Bible and look up that reference. Of course, we could choose to look up any one of the words. However, it would not be very wise to look up the words "her" or "is" or "for" because these are such common words and there would be hundreds of references to look through. So the natural choice would be to look up either "hair" or "covering." We decide to look up "hair." We turn to *Young's Analytical Concordance,* page 442, and discover that there are over 60 references to hair in the Bible translated from at least eight different Hebrew and Greek words. We think that we remember that phrase probably comes from the New Testament so we concentrate our search on the places where the word "hair" is found in the New Testament. There are only about fifteen references to "hair" in the New Testament. We quickly spot a phrase in 1 Corinthians 11:15 which says, *"a glory . . . for . . . hair is given her for a covering."* This seems to match what we are looking for. We look it up in our Bibles and we do indeed find that this is the passage we are looking for.

The best use of a concordance is for doing word studies. A complete concordance lists, not only all of the words in the Bible, but it also contains the Hebrew or Greek words behind that particular English word. There are several ways that these original words are given. In the *Young's Analytical Concordance,* all of the Hebrew and Greek words are given right in the context. The original words are also transliterated, which means that they are reduced to English letters. Each of the different Hebrew or Greek words then gives all of the references to that word in one section. For example, when we looked up "hair" earlier, we would have noticed that there were two Greek words for hair. The first is *thrix* and the second is *kome.* One can then go to the back of the concordance and look up the transliterated word to find out additional ways that particular word may have been translated.

We can get nearly the same information from *Strong's Exhaustive Concordance.* However, we will have to go about it in a different manner. Strong's assigns a number to every Hebrew or Greek word. It then lists all of the references to a particular English word in the order in which that

Tools of Bible Study

English word appears in the Bible, regardless of what original word it came from. However, beside every reference is a number indicating which original Hebrew or Greek word was used in that instance. Again, one can go to the back of the concordance and look up that number and find additional information, including other ways the original word is translated into English.

Modern language concordances usually follow one or the other of these ways of organizing their concordances. For example, the *Zondervan NIV Exhaustive Concordance,* edited by Edward W. Goodrick and John R. Kohlenberger III (Grand Rapids, MI USA: Zondervan Publishing House) follows the Strong's pattern with a numbering system. Regardless of the method used to organize a complete concordance, it allows one to do is to do extensive word studies. This is further discussed in the chapter on words.

Technical Word Study Aids

For the advanced Bible student who has some understanding of the original languages, there are many outstanding works available. They are very technical and usually expensive. Unfortunately, unless one has an advanced theological education, they are of limited value. The following are examples:

Theological Dictionary of the New Testament, Gerhard Kittel, editor. This is a set of ten books that gives very thorough information about all of the words in the New Testament. Because Gerhard Kittel was the editor, this set is often referred to as "Kittel." The articles are arranged in alphabetical order according to the Greek alphabet because it is the Greek words being analyzed.

To give an example of the extensive nature of this book, I will summarize some of the details about one of the ἅγιος family of words—words related to holiness. The entire article, found in Volume I, extends from page 88 to 115:

ἄγιος

A. In Greek and Hellenistic Writings
B. The Use of the Term Holiness in the OT
C. The History of the Term in the OT.
1. The Pre-prophetic Period
2. Prophetic Theology
3. The Post-exilic Period
4. Philo and Josephus
D. The Concept of Holiness in Rabbinic Judaism
E. ἅγιος in the NT
   1. The Holiness of God
   2. Jesus Christ as ἅγιος
   3. The Holy Spirit
   4. The Holiness of the ἐκκλησία
   5. The Holy Life of Christians
   6. The Ecclesia triumphans

ἁγιάζω

ἁγιασμό"

ἁγιότη"

ἁγιωσύνῃ

Two similar works, which are a bit more recent though not quite as detailed, are *Theological Wordbook of the Old Testament* (two volumes) whose editor is R. Laird Harris and *The New International Dictionary of New Testament Theology* (three volumes) whose editor is Colin Brown. Bible scholars use these books the same way they would use Kittel. However, since these books are a little newer, they tend to be more user-friendly. These are all expensive books, but they contain outstanding scholarly material. I do not use these books much for sermon preparation but use them a lot when I am preparing lectures or doing other serious academic theological work.

Study Bible

One of the most helpful tools in Bible study and one that nearly every pastor and Bible teacher can afford is a good study Bible. A study Bible contains useful background information and many helpful notes. All study Bibles will have general introductions to each of the books of the Bible. Most study Bibles have notes at the bottom of the page to explain words, phrases, and other details in the text. These notes actually become a very brief and selective commentary. All study Bibles have good maps that help one understand the geography of the Bible. In addition, most study Bibles have some kind of cross-reference system. Some of these are quite simple and simply contain cross-references in the margin. Others have a sophisticated numbering system that enables the student to do extensive thematic and word studies. The following is a list of study Bibles that are available in Africa:

The NIV Study Bible. This Bible begins with a very good chronology chart that helps one understand how the various major events of the Bible fit together chronologically. It contains good introductions to each book of the Bible plus a very good essay about the inter-testamental period. There are 20,000 notes in this study Bible with an average of one fourth of the page being taken up in notes. In addition to the notes, it has small event maps, charts and other details found in the text near to where these issues are mentioned. In the middle of each page, it has a good cross-reference system with over 100,000 cross references noted. In addition, it contains one of the most extensive concordances that is found in a Bible. This concordance has over 35,000 entries and contains a very helpful index of various subjects in the Bible. Of course, it has the traditional colour maps at the end of the Bible.

This is the Bible that I use every day in my personal quiet time as well as my teaching and preaching. I travel a lot, and often the only research tool I take with me is my NIV Study Bible. Having only the NIV Study Bible with me enables me to prepare sermons and sometimes lectures. It is the single tool that I use the most in my Bible study.

Thompson Chain Reference Bible. This is a Bible that is organized specifically for comparing and doing research about various Bible themes. It is an outstanding tool. It contains a very sophisticated numbering system, which relates to the various themes in the Bible. Each theme and sub-theme is reduced to a number. In the margin, beside most every verse of the Bible will be one to five numbers and themes. By going to the number in the back of the Bible, one can find additional references to that particular theme. It contains maps and other details, but its greatest contribution is the extensive thematic organization.

The *Thompson Chain Reference Bible* has been adapted to several translations. I used the Thompson Chain Reference Bible for probably fifteen years, wearing out two copies. For a person with limited Bible study tools, it is an invaluable resource. Even though I have many very expensive and technical tools, I still use my old worn-out King James *Thompson Chain Reference Bible* when I am wanting to find key verses on certain themes.

Life Application Study Bible. This is a good study Bible whose name accurately describes it. The focus of the Bible is on application more than interpretation. It contains many of the same features as the NIV Study Bible including introductions to books, extensive notes, charts, maps and other details. It is available in all of the major English translations of the Bible.

Other Study Bibles

Perhaps one of the earliest Bibles that may be considered a study Bible was the old *Scofield Reference Bible.* This was a Bible produced by C. I. Scofield with brief notes at the bottom of the page primarily focusing on eschatological passages. It reflects a dispensational point of view of eschatology and is very highly respected in some circles. A Bible, which follows that theological tradition but is produced in a much more modern format, is the *Criswell Study Bible.* This study Bible was developed by W. A. Criswell, who was trained as a theologian but served as the pastor of First Baptist Church of Dallas, Texas, for most of his illustrious career. I have found that his notes touch on most of the problem passages in the Bible. A third Bible that fits into the same mold was produced by Charles Ryrie who for many years was the chairman of the Department of Systematic

Theology at Dallas Theological Seminary. His study Bible is known as *The Ryrie Study Bible.*

There are several other study Bibles available in Africa. For example the *Full Life Study Bible* has been produced by Pentecostals and reflects a Pentecostal perspective in its notes. Those from a Wesleyan background have produced the *Wesley Study Bible.* The *New Geneva Study Bible* caters to the Reformed part of the body of Christ. Chuck Swindoll, one of the leading expositors in the USA today, and currently the president of Dallas Theological Seminary, has produced the *Living Insights Study Bible.* More and more of these study Bibles continue to come out. They all tend to reflect the theological point of view of their editors.

In Nigeria, I am asked more about the *Amplified Bible* than any other Bible. The *Amplified New Testament* was first produced in 1958 and the Old Testament part was completed in 1964. The purpose of this Bible is "to reveal, together with the single word English equivalent to each key Hebrew and Greek word, any other clarifying shades of meaning that may be concealed by the traditional word-for-word method of translation."[7] Various additional words or phrases are given to further explain or clarify the original text. The one difference between this Bible and most modern Bibles is that the Amplified Bible is based upon the *Textus Receptus* family of Greek manuscripts rather than upon the Westcott-Hort family of manuscripts. However, it does note textual variations by putting them in italics. The following is the translation of John 3:16 from the *Amplified Bible:*

> *For God so greatly loved and dearly prized the world that He [even] gave up His only-begotten (unique) Son, so that whoever believes (trusts, clings to, relies on) Him shall not perish—come to destruction, be lost—but have eternal (everlasting) life.*

Bible Atlas

A Bible atlas is a book that focuses on the geography of the Bible lands. There are several on the market, and they are all helpful. One of the most

---

[7] From "Publishers Foreword" in *The Amplified Bible,* (Grand Rapids, MI USA: Zondervan Publishing House, 1971).

recent, which includes the latest scholarship available in the area of the Bible lands, is the *New Bible Atlas*, edited by John J. Bimson, John P. Kane, John H. Paterson and Donald J. Wiseman (Leicester, England and Downers Grove, IL, USA: Intervarsity Press). As a general rule, a good study Bible has the essential maps of the Bible lands. A Bible atlas just goes into more detail. It is helpful to have at least one Bible atlas in one's personal library.

Harmony of Gospels

A harmony of the gospels is a book that places all of the events in the life of Christ in parallel columns in the chronological order in which they occurred. A. T. Robertson's *Harmony of the Gospel* is perhaps the standard in the industry. Some study Bibles create harmonies by putting together only the references rather than writing the text out completely. A harmony of the gospel is an ideal tool for studying the life of Christ.

Topical Study Books

Introductions to the Bible

One of the standard courses that a seminary student takes in the early part of his theological education is a course introducing the Old and New Testaments. These courses are designed to give students the big picture of the two parts of the Bible. There are two general approaches to these courses. Some courses are known as "surveys" and tend to simply review the basic content of the Bible. Others are known as "introductions." These focus more on the background materials to each of the books of the Bible, such as the author, the readers, the circumstances of writing, and problem passages, and not so much on the verse-by-verse presentation that a commentary takes. Naturally there have been many textbooks written to support these kinds of classes and to provide this kind of material to those who are not fortunate enough to formally study the Bible.

One of the old standard works on the Old Testament is S. R. Driver's *An Introduction to the Literature of the Old Testament*. A more recent contribution is R. K. Harrison's *Introduction to the Old Testament*. This work focuses more on the historicity of Scripture and less on the literary and theological aspects. A standard in the industry for the last twenty years or so has been *Old Testament Survey* by William Lasor, David Hubbard and Frederic Bush (Eerdmans). It is very readable and interacts with recent scholarship from an evangelical perspective. Another recent contribution is *An Introduction of the Old Testament* by Raymond B. Dillard and Tremper Longman III (Apollos), which attempts to provide a balance between historical background, literary analysis and theological perspectives. Luka Vandi at ACTS bookstore says "This is undoubtedly the best, and it is available—but not cheap."

There have been many very good surveys and introductions to the New Testament. Merrill C. Tenney's *New Testament Survey* has been distributed very widely in Africa. I must include here Henry Thiessen's *Introduction to the New Testament* (Eerdmans), though it is getting a bit old and I am not sure how available it is in Africa. This is the classic Introduction that is appropriate for post-graduate level work. Other recent additions to this body of literature includes: *An Introduction to the New Testament* by D. A. Carson, Douglas J. Moo, and Leon Morris; and *Encountering the New Testament* by Walter A. Elwell and Robert W. Yarbrough (Baker Books). *Encountering the New Testament* is filled with beautiful color pictures, maps, charts and other helpful visual aids and has the feel of the *Lion Handbook to the Bible*. Since most of these books are not widely available in Nigeria, I have also had the privilege of putting together two introduction books entitled *Notes on Old Testament Introduction* and *Notes on New Testament Introduction*.

Books of Theology

Books of theology can largely be divided into two general categories: systematic theology and Biblical theology.

Books of systematic theology are normally arranged according to basic doctrines. These often follow a fairly consistent pattern including discussions of Bibliology, Theology Proper, Christology, Pneumatology, Angelology, Anthropology, Soteriology, Ecclesiology and Eschatology. Some of the standard systematic theology books that have been used during the last generation or two, include books entitled *Systematic*

Theology by Louis Berkhof, Augustus H. Strong, Charles Hodge, and one entitled *Christian Theology* by H. Orton Wiley. One of the best recent systematic theology books was published by Wayne Grudem in 1994 and, interestingly, entitled *Systematic Theology*. This book is written in clear simple language and provides a strong Biblical foundation for each doctrine. One of its most helpful features is a cross-reference scheme to 34 other systematic theologies.

Bruce Milne's *Know the Truth* (Intervarsity) is a small but very useful theology. Wilbur O'Donovan has produced a work called *Biblical Christianity in African Perspective.* In this book he explains most of the standard doctrines of systematic theology against an African worldview. This is a very unique and helpful approach to theology. I have also made a small contribution in this field with a two-volume set of doctrinal books called *We Believe I* and *II.*

A second approach to the study of Christian doctrine is Biblical theology. Biblical theology focuses more on exegesis and the historical development of theology in the Biblical era and less on logic and the opinions of theologians throughout church history. One of the smallest, but most brilliant, examples of Biblical theology is A. M. Hunter's book, *Introducing New Testament Theology*. Other helpful books on New Testament theology include those written by George Eldon Ladd, Donald Guthrie and Charles Ryrie. W. T. Purkiser, Richard Taylor and William Taylor have cooperated together to produce *God, Man and Salvation,* a book of Biblical theology from a Wesleyan point of view. A work that covers both the Old and New Testament is *Biblical Theology: Old and New Testament* by Geehardus Vos. J. Baryon Payne has written one of the standard works of Biblical theology in the Old Testament, entitled *Theology of the Older Testament.* A more recent contribution to Old Testament theology is Paul R. House's book, *Old Testament Theology* (Intervarsity).

Of course, thousands of books have been written on specific doctrines of the Bible from both the systematic and Biblical theology perspectives.

Hermeneutics

One of the problems we struggle with in Africa is finding appropriate books on hermeneutics. Most of those produced in the West assume that the reader has all the basic tools for Bible study that are available in the

West. However, several are still worth noting. I must begin with a book that I have probably used more than any other, *Understanding and Applying the Bible,* by my former professor, Robertson McQuilkin. I have always viewed this as something of an ideal hermeneutics textbook. Anything John Stott writes is outstanding. His little book, *Understanding the Bible,* and Gordon Fee and Stuart's book *How to Read the Bible for All Its Worth* are both classics.

Books of Church History

Every pastor and Bible teacher should have a good understanding of church history. Some of the standard sets, which cover church history in general, include Kenneth Scott Latourette's *A History of the Expansion of Christianity,* and a multiple volume set by Philip Schaff entitled *History of the Christian Church.* A more simple and popular contribution is *The Story of the Church* by A. M. Renwick and A. M. Harman (Intervarsity). Certainly one of the classic seminary textbooks on church history has been *Christianity through the Centuries* by Earle E. Cairnes (Zondervan). This book was originally written in 1954 and the third edition was produced in 1996. The publishers of *The Lion Handbook of the Bible* have also produced *The History of Christianity* using the same format of colorful pictures, charts and other helpful supplementary material. Two books, which give a good survey of the church in Africa, are Jonathan Hildebrandt's *History of the Church in Africa* and Peter Faulk's *The Growth of the Church in Africa.* Of course, there have been hundreds of books written about various periods of church history, as well as, individuals, churches, movements, conflicts and other issues related to the history of the Christian church.

Books on Specialized Topics

There have been thousands of books written on various doctrines and topics. These include theological topics such as baptism, the second coming of Christ and similar subjects. I probably have at least fifty books in my personal library which are related to the doctrine of sanctification. Just briefly looking at one shelf of my personal library I see books on inspiration, election, eternal security, dispensationalism, historical theology, apologetics, prophecy, the Westminster Confession, contemporary theology, practical theology, Protestant theology, and the theology of the early church fathers.

Professional Books

A most helpful group of specialized theological books may be identified as "professional books." They specifically focus on the "profession of the Christian minister." Into this category we place books on personal growth, preaching, counseling, church planting, evangelism, witnessing, writing, leadership, all aspects of pastoral ministries, all aspects of counseling, and contemporary issues such as women's issues, AIDS, and so on.[8] These books are usually written by professionals who have significant experience in the areas about which they are writing. These books provide an invaluable resource to the minister by giving information not only about what to believe but what to do. Ministers or Bible teachers should get advice from senior people on the best professional books to add to their personal library.

Greek and Hebrew Tools

For the person who has had the opportunity of studying the original languages, there are plenty of very helpful tools available. Because the market is not very large, these books tend to be very expensive. This category includes such books as Hebrew and Greek Bibles, lexicons and grammars of Hebrew and Greek. There are also many technical aids available. However, these technical aids are not a wise investment for the typical pastor unless he or she is going to continue to develop his or her understanding of the original languages.

---

[8] To date, I have produced two books on preaching, *Living Messages* and *Millennium Messages*. In addition, I have produced a simple, but practical, book on leadership entitled *Two Models of Leadership for Kingdom Building*.

Electronic Tools

One of the most recent additions to the tools available to study the Bible are tools that are to be used on computers. Computers have greatly enhanced the study of the Bible in several ways. First, the ability to write with a word processor, which makes it so easy to change or edit a document, has encouraged many more people to write. And this phenomenon has also made it possible for their writing to be much better. In addition, various software companies have put together computer programmes which enable a person to do the work in seconds that it would have taken hours to do before. For example, one can easily search through the entire Bible for any word or combination of words in any one of fifty translations. That can be done in a matter of seconds.

Many computer software programmes are now available in Nigeria. One that I use is the Zondervan Reference Software. This is a low-end piece of software, meaning that it is not nearly as sophisticated as some of the others. However, it has several different translations on it including the Greek New Testament, NIV, KJV, New American Standard Bible, the New Revised Standard Version with Apocrypha and Notes on the NRSV, Nave's Topical Bible, NIV Study Bible Notes, NIV Bible Dictionary, Encyclopedia of Bible Difficulties, Expository Dictionary, NIV Bible Commentary, Inspirational Readings, and an extensive collections of colored maps and charts. All of these things are instantly available to me while I am working on the computer.

Conclusion

Some master craftsmen do their work with very simple tools. They get the maximum amount of usefulness from them. However, true craftsmen should continue to grow and develop themselves and be willing to acquire and develop new tools. As people who work with the word of God, we need to make sure that we become master craftsmen who know how to work with the word of God and how to use our tools as efficiently as possible.

Study Questions

1. List the major categories of theological books and give examples of each.
2. Explain the difference between the two kinds of commentaries.
3. What is a harmony of the gospels?
4. What are some of the ways electronic Bible study tools can help us in our research?

Chapter Nine

The Most Important Tool in Bible Study

Introduction

The tool I will tell you about now is the best tool I have ever discovered for studying the Bible. If you faithfully use this tool, I guarantee that you will get twice as much out of your Bible study time and that you will remember it twice as long. This is a very inexpensive tool; this tool can be purchased just about anywhere; it can be used by practically anyone. By using this tool, you will be amazed at what you learn; you will see things in the Bible you never saw before; you will receive blessings that would have escaped you before and you will be able to remember these blessings in order to share them with others. When I discovered this tool, it changed my life; it changed my devotions; it made them much more rich and rewarding; it enabled me to remember these blessings all day and share them with others. In fact, I still have some of those blessings that came to me over fifteen years ago when I first really discovered and learned to use this tool. The tool is a pen and piece of paper. The practice is taking notes as you study.

The Writing Technique

Taking notes as you study is essential to successful Bible study. In fact, it is probably the single most important thing you can do to improve your ability to understand the Bible.

A few years ago, I taught a course on Minor Prophets. It was the first university level class I taught. During the course, every day I read and studied and filled my head with knowledge, using only brief notes. Later I discovered I had lost a lot of that research because that which was in my head was forgotten. At that time, I made a little promise to God that if he would give me the opportunity to do research, even for sermons or lectures, I would go the "second mile" and write this information down. That decision has proven to be a great blessing; I have hundreds of pages of information that I have compiled on all types of different subjects. I have hundreds of pages of lecture notes prepared for college/university classes. I also have hundreds of four-page sermons that I have written over the years. These are all written out in an extended outline format in complete sentences. I have approximately 1500 pages of radio broadcasts written out for a five-minute daily radio broadcast, which I did for three and a half years. These are all entitled "We Believe." They are written about the basic beliefs of Christianity in lay terminology.

Taking notes as one studies needs to be utilized in devotional study as well. When I have used this methodology in my devotions I have found them rich and rewarding; when I have not, I have found my devotions just average. It is easy to get out of the habit and hard to get back into it. In December, 1993, I wrote 39 pages of notes on my devotional study alone.

Reasons for Writing as you Study

1. Writing helps concentration.

Our minds tend to stray when we study; writing helps to stop that. As you study, force yourself to write a note about every verse or paragraph. The concentration of looking for things to write down will force you to learn and that is the reason for studying. A study guide questionnaire works in a similar way. A study guide is a sheet with questions on it which has been prepared in advance about a certain portion of scripture. These study questions not only teach you about the particular subject matter in the question, but they also stimulate many additional thoughts. This is a helpful technique to use in teaching. Preparing questions that will force the student to study the Bible or other study books is always very useful.

Some psychologists tell us that the average person can comprehend about 800 words per minute. The average public speaker speaks about 150 to 200 words a minute. That means that even if a preacher could speak three times faster than the 150 words per minute, we would still be able to understand what he was saying. What that means is that when we are listening to someone speak, we are only using about one fourth of our mental ability. Because there is so much mental ability not being used, our minds tend to wander and we begin thinking about other things. The same thing happens when we read. Many people also read about 200 words per minute. Therefore, while we are reading, we are tempted to think about other things. One of the ways that we stop our mind from wandering is to take notes, either while listening to someone speak or while reading. When we are taking notes, we are using much of our additional mental power to write things down. That means we now have less mental ability to be thinking about other things. The end result is greater concentration.

2. Writing forces you to see truth you would not see otherwise.

If you force yourself to write something about every verse or every paragraph you are studying, you will look until you see something to write. It may be something you have never seen before. Sometimes our minds blank out when we study. However, if you force yourself to write down ten things about a particular verse, it is amazing what you will learn.

The Puritans are known for their ability to see a lot of truth in a little bit of Biblical information. I am convinced that they got all this information because they spent a lot of time meditating upon Biblical passages and then wrote down their thoughts. Thomas Boston was such a man. He wrote an entire book on the verse in Ecclesiastes 7:13 (KJV) that says, *"Consider the work of God: for who can make that straight, which He hath made crooked?"*

3. Writing helps organize your thoughts.

Writing helps you organize your thoughts in at least two ways. First, in order to write something, you have to think about it long enough to organize it. This whole process helps you organize your thoughts. You cannot just write down every tenth word that you read. Presently I do most of my study at a computer. This is a modern version of the pen and paper. As I read and study, I type down thoughts. Many times I will throw away the original file that contains all these miscellaneous thoughts. There is no reason to keep such things. However, doing the work forced me to organize my thoughts. Before the days of computer, for every sermon I preached, I threw away something like a manuscript; it was usually about four or five typewritten pages long; in it I had the outline and most of the sentences written out completely.

Second, writing captures our thoughts and records them. Once thoughts are written down, it is much easier to rearrange and organize them in some kind of logical manner. Some people can simply organize all of their thoughts while thinking about them. However, for me and for most people, it is much easier to organize thoughts once I can look at them on paper.

4. Writing helps to cement facts into your mind.

Writing greatly enhances your memory. The more times and the more different ways that you think about something, the easier you will remember it. There is a theory that everything you learn makes something like a small crease in a certain part of your brain. The more you think about that subject, the deeper the creases or grooves become. By writing, and thinking as you write, you are deepening the groves in your brain and thus helping to firmly affix this information in your mind.

5. Writing preserves a permanent record of what God is teaching you.

Psalm 137:5-6 urges the readers to remember God's blessings.

> If I forget you, O Jerusalem, may my right hand forget its skill. May my tongue cling to the roof of my mouth if I do not remember you, if I do not consider Jerusalem my highest joy.

When God sought for a method to preserve truth so it could be passed down from one generation to another, the best method he found was writing it in a book. None of us has a perfect memory; however, if we write things down, we will always have a record of what we learned and what we saw while it was fresh.

6. Writing gives you a useful tool to help other people.

There are always going to be hurting people who need our help. If you have been faithful to write down the lessons God has taught you, this material can be useful in at least two ways: First, you can refresh your own memory about what God has taught you. Second, you may want to share some of this written information with others by making a photocopy available to them.

After I preach, I frequently have people request a written copy of my sermon. I have shared these with a number of people who have requested them. I have also received many positive reports from those who have read and received some special help from one of my sermons.

One of my church members was going through a deep crisis in her life. I encouraged her to write and she produced literally dozens of pages of thoughts and meditations and poetry about what God was teaching her. The written record is now a useful tool to help her encourage other people.

7. Writing can serve as a foundation for future lectures, sermons, articles, books and other documents.

Nearly every book starts with miscellaneous notes that someone has jotted down. There are very few people who simply sit down and write a book from start to finish. Writing any kind of publishable work nearly always involves taking notes and gradually expanding those notes.

Very often I will jot down notes in my devotions. When I am working on a sermon on that same subject, those notes frequently become the material I use for that sermon. In addition, I am constantly in the process of converting material that was originally written as sermons into some kind of book. That which I originally jotted down for my own meditations has now been written in a permanent form for hundreds of others to benefit from.

8. Writing can serve as a means of getting relief from problems and pressures.

Writing can serve as a catharsis. All of us need to express our feelings and questions to someone. If these emotions stay bottled up inside us, they will eventually cause us trouble. Often we do not feel comfortable sharing our thoughts with others. However, if we cannot talk with someone, the next best thing is to write these problems out in some kind of secret journal.

One of the things that I frequently encourage people who are having problems to do is to write. They should write about their problems; they should write about possible solutions; they should write about their feelings; they should write about their questions and blessings. As I have made this recommendation over the years, a number of people have tried it and I think all of them have benefited from it.

Specific Details

How should one write? What should one write? How should one go about the process of writing things down?

Make Observations

I suggest that we make observations while they study. An observation can be anything that comes to mind while studying: a thought, a question, a cross reference, an illustration, an application, a prayer, or anything else that one thinks of while studying. While writing down observations, do not try to organize them; just write down the thoughts in the order they come to you. As you jot down these ideas, you will be forced to concentrate, and the very act of writing them down will cause you to have more thoughts. You should constantly ask the questions given in the following poem:

> *I have six faithful serving men*
> *Who taught me all I know.*
> *Their names are What, and Where and When*
> *And How and Why and Who.*

The following are some things to note:

1. *Grammatical considerations.* What are the tenses of the verbs? Can you diagram the sentence? Identify the adjectives and adverbs and the prepositional phrases and the particular words that they modify. Are these verses commands, exhortations, promises, etc.?
2. *Parallelism.* In poetic portions, note the type of parallelism. Is it synonymous, contrasting or some other kind?
3. *Key Words.* Find the key word in each verse or each paragraph.

4. *Any word you do not understand.* Jot down any word or idea you do not understand. This can later be looked up in a dictionary. Later, you may also wish to do a word study of this word.
5. *Main Thought.* Determine what is the main thought of the passage under consideration. Try to reduce it to one short sentence.
6. *Doctrines.* List all of the doctrines suggested in a certain passage.
7. *Applications.* Make an effort to convert the interpretation of the passage into a contemporary application.
8. *Prayer.* It is good to write out prayers related to the topics one is studying.

There are four things we need to be doing constantly as we study the Bible.

- *Summarizing.* Reduce a longer passage to something much smaller.
- *Paraphrasing.* Put the words of the Bible into your own words.
- *Amplifying.* Expand a short section of scripture with application.
- *Translating.* For those who can speak another language, it is very good to translate the passage under consideration into another language.

McCain Devotional Journal Entry

The following is one page from my "Devotional Observation Journal" from 20 November, 1976. The passage I meditated on that morning was Proverbs 27:23-27 (KJV), *"Be thou diligent to know the state of thy flocks, and look well to thy herds; (24) For riches are not for ever: and doth the crown endure to every generation? (25) The hay appeareth, and the tender grass showeth itself, and herbs of the mountains are gathered. (26) The lambs are for thy clothing, and the goats are the price of the field. (27) And thou shalt have goats' milk enough for thy food, for the food of thy household, and for the maintenance for thy maidens."* The following observations are exactly as I recorded them that morning.

1. I am not exactly sure what the main message of this verse is. Perhaps he is talking about 1) stewardship 2) watchfulness 3) appreciation 4) provisions 5) preparation.

2. Verse 25 is talking about the time of shearing apparently. When the grass disappears ... you can get wool from the sheep.

3. Verses 26 and 27 are talking about God's provisions through one's labors.

4. Verse 23 is simply saying that one must know and take care of his business.

5. Verse 24 is the explanation why. Wealth and fame are very temporary. There are many examples of both wealth and high government positions being lost. Richard Nixon (former president) of the USA is a good example of the latter. Dennis St. Georges (contractor that I worked for once) is a good example of the former. He made $38,000 in five months (he cleared that amount). I saw him about a year later and he borrowed a dollar from me to have enough money to buy enough petrol to get back home.

6. What is he saying in the whole section? The man that knows and takes care of his business will have his basic needs satisfied. Not only was that true of the keeper of the flocks but that seems to be a principle with God.

7. If one will be diligent about his business, remembering that it could be taken away from him at any minute, that business will produce his basic necessities.

8. Wealth and prestige may come and go, but one who is diligent will always have his basic needs supplied.

9. This should be encouraging to Mr. Smith who lost $40,000 in a business deal last week. I am sure that he must be discouraged, but he can be comforted in the fact that he will always have clothing and food.

10. Father, you have proven this principle true to me many times, May I always be diligent about my work, guarding against any selfish deviation, so that my basic needs will be supplied. Amen.

Project

A good project is to take fifteen minutes to study Psalm 23. This is one of the most well-known psalms in the Bible. Surely, we have learned everything we can learn about that psalm. However, if you sit down for fifteen minutes with a pen and piece of paper, you will observe and discover several things that you have never observed before.

Conclusion

Studying the Bible is not an easy task. However, I believe if one seriously uses the tool described above, he or she will become one who *"rightly divides the word of truth."*

Study Questions

1. How does writing enhance your concentration?
2. List four other advantages of writing as one studies.
3. How can writing help a person who is depressed?
4. What is an "observation"?
5. List some of the things that one would jot down while making observations.
6. List and briefly explain the four things that a person should constantly be doing while studying the Bible.

Chapter Ten

Rule 1
The Rule of Spiritual Truth

The Bible is a paradox. On the one hand, it was written by men who were trying to communicate to their readers in the most simple straightforward manner possible. Interpreting the Bible is like interpreting any other written document. It can be assumed that the writers were wanting to make things clear, not make them obscure. Thus, we read the letters of Paul like we would read a letter from our employer. We assume that the words used in his letters should be understood as those words are normally understood in that language and culture.

On the other hand, the Bible is a divine book. Its true author is God. The thoughts are God's thoughts. The principles taught in the Bible come from God. This creates problems for interpretation. First, God is a spirit. Although man is also a spirit, he is far more conscious of the physical world about him and often never has any contact with the spiritual world. Understanding the spiritual world is as difficult for natural man to understand as for a primitive person to understand how radio waves could be transferred from one city to another by a small box. However, the lack of experience or understanding of the spiritual world does not mean it does not exist. In addition, God is an infinite eternal being. It would be totally impossible to understand God completely unless one were also God. Therefore, it is understandable that the thoughts of God may also be difficult to understand.

Spiritual Truth is Spiritually Discerned

The Apostle Paul declared in 1 Corinthians 2:14,

> *The man without the Spirit does not accept the things that come from the Spirit of God, for they are foolishness to him, and he cannot understand them, because they are spiritually discerned.*

Paul had said in the preceding two verses (2:12-13),

> We have not received the spirit of the world but the Spirit who is from God, that we may understand what God has freely given us. This is what we speak, not in words taught us by human wisdom but in words taught by the Spirit, expressing spiritual truths in spiritual words.

These verses suggest several important truths. First, there is truth that may be considered spiritual truth. Second, this kind of truth cannot be understood by the natural man. Third, the Holy Spirit aids man in understanding these spiritual truths. The conclusion of the matter is that man needs the Holy Spirit to be able to understand truly the spiritual truths that are revealed in the Bible.

Reasons Natural Man Cannot Really Understand the Bible

1. Man has a fallen mind.

Most theologians believe that when God originally created human beings, he created them with enormous mental ability. Adam was able to name and categorize all of the animals in the Garden. He was able even to communicate with God on a daily personal basis. However, when Adam and Eve sinned, not only did it affect their relationship with God, it also marred their ability to think.

God is the one who created reason and logic. Since we are made in the image of God, it can be assumed that God is also a creature who exercises reason and logic. However, when man sinned, his ability to reason was weakened so that he is no longer capable of perfect reasoning. That is why two people can be presented with the exact same facts and honestly come up with two different conclusions.

Our logic cannot explain where God came from. We cannot comprehend eternity. The mind of man can only go so far back into eternity and it stops. However, just because we cannot understand God's eternity that does not discredit it.

Spiritual truth starts with faith. Faith always has some element of the unknown about it. Once something becomes fully known, there is no longer any need to have faith. For reasons, we do not fully comprehend, faith pleases God. The Bible says *"without faith it is impossible to please God"* (Hebrews 11:6). That means that God is pleased to allow man to remain ignorant about certain issues because without that ignorance, there can be no faith. However, faith is not a part of the natural man's life, particularly the modern man. Modern man likes to believe only what he can see or what he can rationally understand.

Two New Testament stories illustrate the difference between man's ways and God's ways. While Jesus was on the cross, the chief priests and the teachers of the law stood around and mocked Jesus. They sarcastically demanded, *"Let this Christ, this King of Israel, come down now from the cross, that we may **see and believe**,"* (Mark 15:32). Several months before that, Jesus stood in front of Lazarus' tomb and instructed his friends to remove the stone that covered the tomb. Martha, the brother of Lazarus objected and said, *"by this time there is a bad odor, for he has been there for four days."* Jesus said, *"Did I not tell you that **if you believed, you would see** the glory of God?"* (John 11:40). Note that the religious leaders wanted to *"see and believe."* However, Jesus said that Martha should *"believe and see."* Fallen man often refuses to believe that which he cannot see. However, the spiritual man is willing to believe what he has not seen so that he can see it in the future.

2. Man has a depraved nature.

When Adam and Eve sinned, they passed on to every human being not only a fallen mind but a sinful nature. This means that natural man has a tendency to sin. Though expressed in different ways, most denominations and theological movements believe that man has a fallen sinful nature. Man does not simply sin because of the immediate temptation in front of him. He sins because there is something within him that draws him toward sin.

If man has a sinful nature, he will have a tendency to interpret the Bible in a way that will excuse the sin about which he is guilty. People often split theological hairs to defend their behaviour. A drunkard knows all about Jesus turning the water into wine and uses that to excuse his drunkenness. One who is guilty of adultery is quick to point out that David was an adulterer and yet God used him. Homosexuals say that the sin of Sodom and Gomorrah was not the sin of homosexuality but the sin of homosexual rape. We tend to interpret the Bible in a way that will excuse our behaviour.

I heard a story about a deacon who was caught stealing chickens. He was invited before the deacon board for questioning. When the fellow deacons demanded to know why he had stolen the chickens, he quoted the Bible but rearranged the punctuation a bit to justify his actions. He said, "Brethren, the Bible says, *"Let him that stole, steal . . . no more working with his hands . . ."* (Ephesians 4:28). His interpretation of this passage was that the one who had stolen should continue to steal and no longer work with his hands.

It is only the presence of the Holy Spirit in the life of the interpreter which will guarantee that man does not become guilty of misinterpreting the Bible in order to justify his actions or beliefs. This is why it is difficult if not impossible for the natural man to properly interpret the Bible.

Observations about Spiritual Truth

1. Spiritual truth is always consistent with the Word of God.

Though we do not believe the Bible is a science textbook or a math textbook, we believe that the Bible is the source of ultimate truth. That which is contrary to the teachings of the Bible, however logical and attractive, is not ultimate truth. Spiritual truth is not contrary to reason or logic nor does it reject obvious facts. However, the spiritual man is willing to believe the Bible, even if it is inconsistent with what is accepted as contemporary knowledge.

For example, only about five hundred years ago did scientists finally have proof that the earth is round. Before that time, many people believed that the earth was flat because one could easily look around him and see that it was flat. Therefore, theologians prior to about AD 1500 had a difficult time explaining Isaiah 40:22, *"He sits enthroned above the circle of the earth."* There were certainly many discussions about what Isaiah meant about God sitting on the circle of the earth. However, in the final analysis, those with faith believed it, even though they did not fully understand it. There are still some unanswered questions in the Bible and things that we do not fully understand. However, the man with the Spirit of God living in him will measure all new knowledge in light of the word of God.

2. Spiritual truth is not understood until applied.

One cannot fully understand or comprehend truth until it is experienced. All Africans know that there is a place called America. However, they do not fully understand America until they go there and visit the place and see and experience the things of America for themselves.

A non-Christian can study the Bible and can understand the various doctrines of Christianity almost in the same way as a Christian. However, the non-Christian cannot understand prayer in the way one understands it who has had his heart warmed by the presence of God. A non-Christian can understand what the Bible teaches about regeneration and could perhaps even teach it to others. However, he cannot understand regeneration like one who *"was dead in his trespasses and sin"* but has become *"alive to God."* He can understand what Christians consider to be sin, but he cannot understand like one who has had his conscience awakened by the Holy Spirit and who has seen his sin through the eyes of God.

The point is that one can have a theoretical understanding of the truths of Christianity, but this is different from an experiential understanding of Christianity.

3. Spiritual truth is sometimes discerned apart from the senses.

Christians believe that God can communicate to man through means other than the five senses. Obviously, when Jesus was on the earth, he taught his disciples through their ears and eyes and senses of feel, taste and smell. However, since Jesus has permanently gone to heaven, he communicates to us today through the Holy Spirit who communicates in a spiritual way. For example, Paul wrote in Romans 8:16, *"The Spirit himself testifies with our spirit that we are God's children."* Paul did not say that the Spirit testifies to our eyes or ears or sense of feeling. He says that the Spirit testifies directly to our "spirit." The spirit of man is the part of human beings that enables us to interact with the spiritual world. It is that part of us which enables us to pray to God and worship God. It is also the part of man which receives direct input from God apart from our five senses.

At times, God gives a person a restless spirit or a sense that something is not right. That person may not be able to explain why he feels bad.

However, his spirit tells him that something is not right. This is another ministry of the Holy Spirit. Most of the time, the Holy Spirit is going to remind Christians of Scriptures which tell him that certain things are right or wrong. However, there are times when the Spirit will communicate directly to one's spirit about a certain truth. This may be a positive encouragement to do or say something, or it may be a negative warning against a certain thing.

Some time ago, we had a very serious religious crisis in Jos. It started on a Friday afternoon and continued very seriously until at least the following Wednesday. I had no way to communicate with friends outside of Jos to ask them to pray for us. My senior daughter, Carmen, who was living in New York City at that time, heard about the crisis and wrote an email to our family members asking them to pray for us. A few days later, I received this email from my brother-in-law:

> We were in tears Sunday morning when I opened my e-mail from Carmen and read her plea to hear from you soon about your safety. I felt a strange feeling come over me as I read about the violence there. I could not believe what I was reading. Just the day before, on Saturday about 2-3 in the afternoon I was sitting in our back porch, listening to soft music and meditating and praying. I looked out over our back yard and into the distance and started feeling a strange feeling. I suddenly felt that you were in danger. I was looking at the university area and down the streets and back to your house. I felt that violence and killing were going on. It was like I was in a trance . . . I was a little terrified at what I was seeing happening to Danny, and I breathed a prayer . . . You can imagine how I felt when I opened that e-mail the next morning since I had heard nothing about anything happening in Africa. At any rate, I believe that you are in God's hands.[1]

How did my brother-in-law know that we were in danger and that he should pray for us at exactly the time when the conflict was going on? He did not learn these things through his physical senses. They were discerned through his spirit which was alive to God.

Bill Gothard is a Bible teacher who has developed an extensive ministry in the USA. He once told a story about a simple child who went to school and was given a book to read. However, she refused to read it because she said

---

[1] Dan Simmons, Email sent to Danny McCain on 14 September 2001.

it was "bad." The teacher read it and thought it was OK. The teacher, being a conscientious person, sent the book home to the girl's parents and the father read it three times before he was able to discern the evil in it. It was a book about a group of rowdy children who got into all kinds of mischief. However, there were never any consequences suffered as a result of their bad behaviour. If a child read the book very well and really got the message, he might be tempted to think he could do bad things without there ever being negative consequences. Though the little girl could not objectively determine what was wrong with the book, her spirit which was sensitive to the Holy Spirit knew that something was wrong.

Conclusion

Though the Bible should be read and interpreted like any other book, we must recognize that it is a spiritual book. Because it is a spiritual book, we need to have the assistance of the Holy Spirit to truly understand it.

Study Questions

1. What is the main theme of 1 Corinthians 2:14, and how does it relate to interpreting the Bible?
2. What are some of the reasons why natural man has a difficult time interpreting the Bible?
3. Explain how the two stories from the life of Jesus demonstrate the difference between the way God looks at life and the way man looks at life.
4. What is the primary ingredient to understanding "spiritual truth?"
5. Give an example of truth being taught in the Bible long before it was understood by science.
6. Besides the five senses, how else is it possible to discern truth?

Chapter Eleven

Rule 2
The Rule of Selectivity

The Bible is a highly selective book. In fact, John said that if all the facts about Jesus were written down, *"even the whole world would not have room for the books that would be written"* (John 21:25). This means that John and the other writers had to carefully select what they would include in the scriptural record and what they would omit. Of all the millions of interesting facts God could have chosen to tell us, He restricted that information to what we have in the Bible.

Since the Bible is a highly selective book, we can assume that whatever is there has been placed there for a purpose. Paul said in reference to what we now call the Old Testament, *"All Scripture is God-breathed and is useful for teaching, rebuking, correcting and training in righteousness"* (2 Timothy 3:16). This verse says that every part of the Old Testament is useful. This underscores the fact that there are no parts of the Bible that are worthless.

Selectivity of Content

Although the Bible is made up of sixty-six different books, it assumes in some parts that the readers are familiar with the other parts of the Bible. In other words, the New Testament writers assume that those who read their books are familiar with Abraham and Moses and David because they do not explain who these people are. In other words, the Bible assumes that the readers know some things.

This is true of all literature and, in fact, it is true of all communication. A preacher preaching a sermon in Nigeria about the importance of turning to God might say, "If you continue to reject God in your life, you may end your life like Okwonkwo." If he chose not to explain who Okwonkwo was, he would be assuming that most of his congregation would understand who Okwonkwo was and what happened to him. Okwonkwo was one of the main characters in Chinua Achebe's book, *Things Fall Apart*. Okwonkwo resisted the change that was coming to his village as a result of the missionaries and the colonial government and eventually hanged himself. If a person were not familiar with Chinua Achebe's book, he would totally miss the point the preacher was trying to make.

The Bible makes certain basic assumptions. For example, whenever it refers to certain individuals or events without explaining who they are, it assumes that the reader knows these people. Hosea 1:1 begins this way:

> *The word of the Lord that came to Hosea son of Beeri during the reigns of Uzziah, Jotham, Ahaz and Hezekiah, kings of Judah, and during the reign of Jeroboam son of Jehoash king of Israel.*

On the other hand, Habakkuk begins his prophesy be simply saying, *"The oracle that Habakkuk the prophet received"* (1:1). Remember, the Bible is a highly selective book. It does not needlessly include unnecessary details. Why did Hosea begin his prophesy by giving us the specific details about when these prophesies were given while Habakkuk did not include those details? Was Hosea simply a better and more precise record keeper than Habakkuk?

The answer to that question lies in the rule of selectivity. Because the Bible is a highly selective book, every word is important. Apparently, Hosea thought that it would be impossible to understand the prophecies contained in his book without understanding something about the historical events related to those prophecies. In other words, if a person does not know what was happening during the days of Uzziah, Jotham, Ahaz and Hezekiah, kings of Judah, he or she is not going to understand the messages in the Book of Hosea.

On the other hand, the converse is also true. If certain background details like the date or the circumstances of the time of writing are not mentioned, then apparently the author did not think those things were essential to properly interpret the book. For example, the message found in Habakkuk is not anchored in one historical moment because the crisis in the book is a crisis in the prophet himself. Understanding the specific historical background is not as relevant to Habakkuk as it is to Hosea.

The point is that as a person studies, he should pay close attention to the details of the scriptures he is studying. God did not include these things just to fill up the space. The details of the Bible are included because they are necessary to understand the message of the Bible.

Selectivity in Quantity

Because the Bible is a highly selective book, when one sees certain events or persons or time periods, being given special attention, he should pay special attention to those things.

Emphasis of Time Periods Covered

Genesis 1-11 covers the first several thousands of years of the history of the world. Genesis 12-50 covers four generations of one family or about 200 years. The fact that thirty-nine chapters cover 200 years, while eleven chapters cover thousands of years of history, would suggest that there is something special about those 200 years that the reader should know. In the Gospels, nearly one half of the content covers the last week of Jesus' life. This suggests that this was the most important week in the life of Jesus. Approximately one half of the Book of John covers the last 24 hours of Jesus' life. Once again, this suggests that the last day of Jesus' life was more important than all the other days.

The principle of selectivity tells us that these time periods, which are stressed in the Bible, have very special meaning, and the Bible assumes that the reader will master those special times. The careful Bible student will pay special attention to those time periods that receive more coverage than others.

Multiplication of Coverage

Because the Bible is a highly selective book, one should especially note whenever one sees certain events or time periods receiving multiple coverage. God does not waste space in his book. Therefore, if an event is repeated or if the life of a person is mentioned in more than one place in the Bible, one can assume that person or event is important.

In a typical daily newspaper, there is normally one article given to one particular subject. Whenever you see two articles or several articles on the same subject in the same newspaper, you know that the editors of the paper thought that was a very significant subject. During the Gulf War, it was typical for the average American or British newspaper to have fifteen or twenty different articles on the war. These would include reports from the front lines, descriptions of the weapons being used, interviews with family members back home, discussions of the political ramifications, and editorials about the purposes of the war. This multiplication of coverage about a single topic suggests that the editors of the newspaper thought this was a very important event.

There are several examples of persons and events receiving multiple coverage in the Bible. 1 and 2 Samuel and 1 and 2 Kings give the history of Judah and Israel starting from Samuel to Babylonian Captivity. I and 2 Chronicles repeat that history, devoting one whole book to the reign of David. In addition, 2 Chronicles gives the history of Judah but ignores Israel. It is interesting to note that the great majority of the poetic literature comes from the time period when David and Solomon were serving as kings of Israel. From the principle of selectivity, one should understand that the reigns of David and Solomon and this time period in the history of Israel apparently has special significance.

The four Gospels give us four independent views of the life and ministry of Jesus. If David was one of the most important persons in the Old Testament period and he received double coverage, how much more important is the person who has four independent accounts of his life inserted in the Bible?

Multiplication of Concepts

Some truths are emphasized over and over again in the Bible. Others are mentioned once or twice. All truth is equally true, but not all truth is equally important. The fact that a truth is mentioned only once or twice in the Bible does not make it any less true. However, it may mean that particular truth is not as important as other truths that are mentioned more often. For example, the Bible tells us one time that a king by the name of Amon died. The Bible tells us many times that Jesus died. The fact that Amon died is just as true as the fact that Jesus died, but it is not nearly as important.

1 Corinthians 11:6-15 describes the importance of women having long hair and men having short hair and women wearing a head covering but

men refraining from wearing head coverings. Interpreted literally this passage seems to say that women should have long hair and wear a head covering and that men should have short hair and should not wear a head covering. This is the only place in the Bible where this truth is emphasized. Though the principle being taught in that section is just as true as the resurrection of Christ, it is certainly not nearly as important.

It is important not only for us to teach the truth of God's word. We must also teach the emphasis of God's word. One of the ways that we discover what God emphasizes is through the rule of selectivity. By looking at the topics that received multiple coverage in the Bible, we find that God emphasized such things as worship, prayer, holiness, justice, and salvation.

This is one of the beautiful things about serial expository preaching. Serial expository preaching is taking one book of the Bible and preaching through it, one paragraph at a time, so that truths are covered in the order they appear in the text. As one preaches from week to week, devoting a sermon to each paragraph or section, he tends to emphasize the things God is emphasizing because he devotes the same amount of time to various truths that God does.

Conclusion

The rule of selectivity helps us to determine what God thought was important in the Bible by observing the amount of space devoted to various themes, persons and time periods. Without understanding the rule of selectivity, one will fail to appreciate the more important parts of the Bible.

Study Questions

1. "The Bible is a highly selective book." Explain that statement.
2. What is meant by the "Selectivity of Content"?
3. How do Hosea 1:1 and Habakkuk 1:1 help us understand the Rule of Selectivity?
4. Why is multiplication of coverage important?
5. Give an example of a person who received multiple coverage in the Bible.
6. Give an example of a concept that receives multiple coverage.

Chapter Twelve

Rule 3
The Rule of Simplicity

The Bible is often viewed, as a mysterious book—one filled with powerful secrets, which only the most well educated and most pious can understand. The truth of the matter is that the Bible, like practically all other literature in the world, was written to communicate truth not conceal truth. Therefore, it can be assumed that the writers of the Bible were trying to communicate the truth in the simplest means known to them.

The rule of simplicity includes three principles of interpretation that apply to interpreting practically all literature.

The simplest interpretation is usually the best interpretation.

Often in interpreting the Bible, or any other document, the reader sees two possible interpretations of a word or phrase. The above rule states that whenever this is the case, one should take the simplest interpretation. In other words, he should follow the interpretation that seems to be the most reasonable and logical in that particular context. The purpose of writing is to communicate. The assumption is that a writer will use words and phrases and idioms that the readers will know, so that they will understand the communication without confusion.

For example, in Genesis 1, there is a description of the events of creation. After each period of God's creativity, we read such statements as *"And there was evening, and there was morning—the second day."* The Hebrew word yom is capable of describing events that are longer than one twenty-four hour period. Therefore, some interpreters have suggested that the days of creation were not twenty-four hour periods but indefinite long periods of time. However, the most simple straightforward interpretation is that God created the earth in six twenty-four hour periods.

Another example is found in Genesis 6:1-2, which reads,

> When men began to increase in number on the earth and daughters were born to them, the sons of God saw that the daughters of men were beautiful, and they married any of them they chose.

There are two fairly common ways of interpreting that passage. Both of them assume that the term "sons of God" and "daughters of men" are not used absolutely literally. The first interpretation believes that the "sons of God" were fallen angels—demonic creatures and the "daughters of men" were human beings. This is used to explain the presence of the giants, "Nephilim," on the earth (6:4). Somehow the ability of spiritual beings to intermarry with normal human beings produced a hybrid race. The second interpretation believes that the expression "sons of God" is a synonym for righteous people and the expression "daughters of men" is a synonym for unrighteous people. The question now arises: Which of these is the most simple interpretation? The answer is that the second interpretation is surely the most simple because one has real theological problems having spiritual beings marrying human beings.

In Judges 11:30-40, we read the troubling story of Jephthah who was a courageous soldier. When he had gone into battle, he had promised the Lord if He would give him victory over the Ammonites, he would offer as a burnt offering the first thing that came out of his house when he returned home. To his great dismay, the first thing that came out of his house was his daughter. He gave the girl two months to mourn her virginity and then he *"did to her as he had vowed"* (11:39). This has created such an ethical dilemma that many have suggested an alternative interpretation. They suggest that Jephthah did not actually offer her as a burnt sacrifice but gave her to the temple to work there for the rest of her life. That is certainly a more attractive interpretation than the more literal one, but it is not the most simple. As horrible and repulsive as it seems to us, the most simple interpretation is that Jephthah actually offered the girl as a burnt offering. This is the most simple grammatical interpretation but it is not the most simple theological interpretation.

Another way of saying this: **If the literal interpretation of a passage makes good sense, do not try to find some other meaning.** We should always attempt to allow the grammar of the sentence and the context determine whether or not a passage should be interpreted literally or in some non-literal sense.

There are certainly exceptions to this rule that the literal and simple meaning of the passage is the best. For example, Jesus declared in Luke 14:26, *"If anyone comes to me and does not hate his father and mother, his wife and children, his brothers and sisters—yes, even his own life—he cannot be my disciple."* This certainly makes good sense grammatically but does not make good sense theologically. In fact, it is totally inconsistent with other statements Jesus made. Therefore, we must assume that the literal interpretation of this passage is not the correct one.

Interpret the obscure passages in light of the clear passages.

There are many passages in the Scripture that are not clear. However, many times passages in other places will clarify these truths. For example, several passages including 1 Thessalonians 4:13-14, 1 Corinthians 15:20, 51 and other passages speak of death as "sleep." This has caused some interpreters to view death as "soul sleep." In other words, when a person dies, not only is the body in a non-living state but the soul is also in an inactive non-conscious state. However, by comparing these verses with 2 Corinthians 5:6-9 and Philippians 1:23, this idea is made clear. The first passage says to be *"away from the body and at home with the Lord . . ."* The second says, *"I desire to depart and be with Christ."* Therefore, when a believer is out of the body, he or she is with the Lord. That suggests that there is life and consciousness and blessing.

The question about the *"sons of God"* marrying the daughters of men in Genesis 6 fits into this category. It is an obscure passage but Jesus gave a clear statement on this in Matthew 22:30: *"At the resurrection people will neither marry nor be given in marriage; they will be like the angels in heaven."* The implication is that angels do not marry. Demons are fallen angels and would not marry as well. Therefore the clear statement that Jesus made here makes the interpretation that these *"sons of God"* were angelic beings impossible.

Jesus makes what appears to be a strange statement in Luke 14:26.

> If anyone comes to me and does not hate his father and mother, his wife and children, his brothers and sisters—yes, even his own life—he cannot be my disciple.

However, this troublesome statement is made clear by Matthew's version of that same truth.

> Anyone who loves his father or mother more than me is not worthy of me; anyone who loves his son or daughter more than me is not worthy of me (10:37).

This statement was likely originally made in Aramaic. Luke probably translates it literally while Matthew translates the meaning. By comparing the two passages, one can see that the Luke passage is not telling us actually to hate anyone but rather to love God more than anyone else.

This rule is not just a rule of Biblical hermeneutics. It is a rule of communication that we use every day. We are constantly evaluating the communications we receive by later or more expanded communications. Those messages, which we hear in part or in brief, are often clarified when we get a later or a more complete communication.

A passage can have only one meaning - one simple meaning.

The Bible is not written in riddles. It says what it means and it means what it says. Some interpreters see a double meaning in various Biblical passages. The Alexandrian school of interpreters, in the early church period, was committed to this kind of interpretation. Some of them taught that any given passage of scripture had three meanings. The first was the literal meaning, which is what the passage appeared to be teaching. The second was the allegorical meaning. This meant that various parts of the Bible, and particularly the stories in the Bible, had parallel deeper meanings. The third interpretation was the spiritual meaning. This meaning was hidden even deeper than the allegorical meaning and only the deeply spiritual could understand it.

It is my understanding that a Biblical passage has only one correct interpretation. That is what the original writer intended to say. Anything beyond that is misinterpretation. It is certainly true that a passage can have many applications. However, it has only one meaning.

1 Thessalonians 4:4 says in the King James Version, *"That every one of you should know how to possess his vessel in sanctification and honour."* The point of interpretation is to determine what the word "vessel" means. There are two possibilities. It could mean his wife or it could mean his body. The NIV selects the latter. Interestingly, the Bible uses the word "vessel" to refer to both the body and the wife. Either interpretation could be correct. However, the point is that both cannot be correct. The passage cannot mean two things.

A similar dilemma exists in 1 Corinthians 7:6-37 where Paul talks about *"keeping his virgin"* (KJV). The question is: Does this refer to an engaged couple who have withstood marriage, or does it refer to a father who has refused to give his daughter in marriage? Either interpretation is possible but both of them cannot be correct.

Most of us have heard pastors and Bible teachers say such things as, "Now, there is a deeper meaning in this passage." If they meant that because of our limited understanding of the culture and language of the Bible, we have failed to understand all that is meant in that passage, that could certainly be true. However, if the preacher or teacher means that there is some deeper or spiritual meaning which is beyond the meaning originally intended by the author, that is not true. We must remember that we interpret the Bible like we interpret a letter from home. If my brother writes to me and tells me that he needs money to pay his school fees and that I should pray for another brother who is sick, we interpret all of that as being very straightforward truth. We do not look for hidden or secret meanings in normal communication.

Once again, there are exceptions to this rule. These exceptions are figures of speech and idioms and parables and allegories. All of these have slightly different meanings than the literal meaning of the words. However, there is still only one meaning. We will discuss those exceptions when we talk about the rule of figurative language.

Conclusion

The Bible is not a book of magic or a book that requires a secret code to be able to unlock it. It is a book written in normal language by people who were attempting to communicate in the most simple straightforward manner possible. Therefore, we should interpret the Bible in the most simple manner possible.

Study Questions

1. State in your own words the first part of the rule of simplicity.
2. Give an example of the rule that says that the most simple interpretation of a passage is usually the best interpretation.
3. Give an example of an obscure passage being made understandable by another clearer passage.
4. What did Jesus mean by this statement: Luke 14:26. "If anyone comes to me and does not hate his father and mother, his wife and children, his brothers and sisters—yes, even his own life—he cannot be my disciple?"
5. Explain why a passage can have only one meaning?
6. What is wrong with saying that a passage can have more than one meaning?

Chapter Thirteen

Rule 4
The Rule of Context

Context is everything in communication.

A student decides to come see me one day. He comes up to my office and is just preparing to knock on the door when he hears voices inside. He does not mean to be listening in on a private conversation but he suddenly hears me say in very clear voice: "I think I am just going to kill you right now." What would that student do? It is likely he would run down to the security personnel and report the matter. The security people would rush back to my office, force their way inside to see if they could rescue this person who was supposedly in great danger. When the security people get inside my office, they see me, sitting with another person, playing a game of chess. The student heard the correct words but he misunderstood the message because he did not understand the context. He knew the meaning of every one of the words, but those same words have different meanings in different contexts.

What is Context?

Context is the way God gave us the Bible, one book at a time. The first readers of Mark could not turn over to Revelation to help them understand Mark. Revelation had not been written yet. The first readers of Galatians did not have a copy of the letter Paul wrote to Rome to help them understand it. These first readers did share some common information. In this book, we call this shared information "background." The background information they shared includes some knowledge of the culture, earlier biblical history, and an excellent understanding of the Greek language. But, most importantly, they had the individual book of the Bible that was in front of them. Therefore we can be confident that the writers of the Bible included enough within each book of the Bible to help the readers understand that book. For that reason, context is the most important key to Bible interpretation.

Failure to Observe Context

Often popular ministers today quote various isolated verses they have memorized, even though this means that they usually leave 99% of the Bible's verses untouched. One seemingly well-educated person told a Bible teacher that she thought the purpose of having a Bible was to look up the verses the minister quoted in church! But the Bible is not a collection of people's favourite verses with a lot of blank space in between. The God of the Bible is not a God of isolated verses without their context.

As history testifies, by using verses out of context one could "prove" almost anything about God or justify almost any kind of behavior. Too often we take shortcuts to understanding the Bible by quoting random verses or assuming that others who taught us have understood them correctly. When we do so, we fail to be *diligent* in seeking God's wisdom and truth (Proverbs 2:2-5; 4:7; 8:17; 2 Timothy 2:15).

Reading in Context

After one begins reading the Bible a book at a time, one quickly recognizes that verses isolated from their context nearly always mean something different when read in context. The method of isolating verses from their context shows disrespect for the authority of Scripture. It leaves much of the Bible unread. Preaching and teaching the Bible the way it invites us to interpret it—in its original context—both explains the Bible accurately and provides our hearers a good example how they can learn the Bible better for themselves.

If we read any other book, we will not simply take an isolated statement in the middle of the book and ignore the surrounding statements that help us understand the reason for that statement. If we hand a storybook to a child learning how to read, the child will probably start reading at the beginning. That people so often read the Bible out of context is not because it comes naturally to us, but because we have been *taught* the wrong way by others' examples. Now we must accept the opportunity to begin teaching the next generation the right way to interpret the Bible. We must not get so wrapped up in the details of the text that we miss the larger picture of the context. Just as we would feel misrepresented if someone quoted us out of context, thus changing our meaning, we should avoid quoting the Bible out of context.

Ignoring Context

Many contradictions some readers claim to find in the Bible arise simply from ignoring the context of the passages they cite. They jump from one text to another without taking time to first understand each text on its own terms. For instance, when Paul says that a person is justified by faith without works (Romans 3:28), his context makes it clear that he defines faith as something more than passive assent to a viewpoint, He defines it as a conviction that Christ is our salvation, a conviction on which one actively stakes one's life (Romans 1:5). James declares that one cannot be justified by faith without works (James 2:14)—because he uses the word "faith" to mean mere assent that something is true (2:19). He demands that such assent be actively demonstrated by obedience to show that it is genuine (2:18). In other words,

James and Paul use the word "faith" differently, but do not contradict one another on the level of meaning. They differ linguistically but not theologically. If we ignore context and merely connect different verses on the basis of similar wording, we will come up with contradictions in the Bible that the original writers would never have imagined.

Types of Context

Most of us agree that we should read the Bible in context, but how far should we read in the context? Is it sufficient merely to read the verse before and the verse after? Or should we be familiar with the paragraphs before and after? Or should we be familiar with the entire book of the Bible in which the passage occurs?

As these questions imply, there are various levels of context for every text. First, most texts have an immediate context in the paragraph or paragraphs surrounding them. Second, we must look at the context of the entire book of the Bible in which every text appears. We can be sure that this is the "context" that the first readers had in front of them. Third, we sometimes need to look at the whole context of that writer's teaching. For instance, though the Corinthians could not consult Paul's letter to the Galatians, they were familiar with a broader backdrop of his teaching than what we find in 1 Corinthians alone, because Paul had taught them in person for eighteen months (Acts 18:11). Whatever we can learn about Paul's broader teaching may help us, provided we give *first* priority to what he tells his audience in the *particular* letter we are trying to understand.

Fourth, there is the context of shared information—the background that both the original writer and readers shared. Some of this background may be available for us in the Bible. For instance, Paul could expect many of his readers to know the Old Testament. But background may also require of us extra research though the first readers, who normally already knew it, could take it for granted. Finally, we can look at the context of God's entire revelation in the Bible. Too often we want to explain one verse in light of another before we have really understood either verse in light of the immediate context in which they occur.

We will now look at all of these levels of context in three broad areas. We will begin looking at the immediate context and then expand outward to include the broader areas of context.

The Immediate Context

There is a small river named Rigolette Bayou near where I was reared. Engineers have narrowed it down to flow through a very big culvert before it flows into a bigger river. I have looked at the water rushing into that culvert on one side and seen the water rushing out of the culvert on the other side. I have never been inside the culvert but what I see going in and coming out gives me some idea of what is happening inside the culvert.

The immediate context is what immediately precedes and follows after a passage. One must know something of the flow of thought that goes into a passage and away from a passage to be able to interpret it accurately. If one started reading in the middle of the Book of Job, he would not understand what was happening. One needs to read the whole book and understand the context of what is being said before he can know how to interpret the passage. There are two ways we can divide the immediate context.

Context Within Verses

Traditional English poetry balances sounds with rhymes, but ancient Hebrew poetry balanced ideas instead. Most modern translations place the poetry of Psalms and most of the biblical Prophets in verse form. There are different kinds of idea-balancing, or parallelism, in texts; we mention here only two of the most common. In one kind of parallelism, the second line repeats the basic idea of the first (sometimes adding or replacing some details)—for instance, *"Blessed is the man who does not walk in the counsel of the wicked or stand in the way of sinners or sit in the seat of mockers"* (Psalm 1:1). In another kind of parallelism, the second line is contrasted with the first; for instance, *"Ill-gotten treasures are of no value, but righteousness delivers from death"* (Proverbs 10:2). This kind of Hebrew parallelism affects the interpretation within verses.

Proverbs 29:18

We have perhaps often heard the expression, *"Where there is no vision, the people perish"* (Proverbs 29:18). But what does Proverbs mean by "vision"? Does it just mean having a good plan for the future? Does it mean that a driver who needs glasses might run over someone if he drives without his glasses? Because most of the Book of Proverbs is a collection of general principles rather than a sustained argument, the verses around Proverbs 29:18 do not help us interpret the verse very well.

The other half of the verse, however, does provide some context. *"Where there is no vision, the people perish; but happy is the person who obeys God's law"* (Proverbs 29:18). The second half of the verse parallels the basic idea of the first half. Visions and the law are both sources of God's revelation, sources of hearing from God. In other words, "vision" does not refer to mere natural sight; nor does it merely refer to having a plan for the future. It refers to hearing from God. The Hebrew term translated "vision" here in fact relates to dreams, revelations, or oracles, which confirms the point. God's people needed the Bible and genuine prophets who had heard from God to guide them in the right way. The NIV translation of this verse reflects that interpretation: *"Where there is no revelation, the people cast off restraint; but blessed is he who keeps the law."*

Proverbs 11:1

Proverbs 11:1 warns that God hates a *"false balance."* Unfortunately, some people today quote this verse to imply that God wants us to be "balanced" people, not too committed to a particular agenda. But the real point of the proverb is to avoid cheating our neighbors. The rest of the verse reads, *"but God delights in a correct weight."* In the markets of ancient Israel, people would weigh out grain or other items in return for a particular weight of money, but some people cheated their customers by changing the scales. This kind of parallelism is frequent in Israelite poetry. For instance, Mary means basically the same thing when she says that her soul "exalts" the Lord as when she declares that her spirit rejoices in God (Luke 1:46-47).

As helpful as it is to examine the context within a particular verse, in most cases we need a broader circle of context than simply within a verse.

Context within a Paragraph

A paragraph is a complete unit of thought. Therefore, it is reasonable to assume that any part of the paragraph will be best understood by knowing what the entire paragraph says. Paragraph context is usually what people mean when they talk about "reading in context." Therefore, when we read a particular very or phrase of a verse, we must identify the main theme of the paragraph. We should also identify the argument as it leads up to the verse or phrase we are looking at and also the arguments after that. It is only by seeing how every verse or phrase fits into the general argument of the paragraph that we will understand that passage.

The following are some illustrations of scriptures that are sometimes taken out of context:[1]

---

[1] Many more examples of "context problems" are found in the appendix.

The Thief in John 10:10

John 10:10 says, *"The thief comes only to steal and kill and destroy; I have come that they may have life, and have it to the full."* Many people assume that the thief in this passage is the devil. They assume this because they have heard this view many times, not because they examined the text in context. In John 9, Jesus heals a blind man and the religious officials expel the blind man from the religious community for following Him. Jesus stands up for the former blind man and calls the religious leaders spiritually blind (9:35-41). Because there were no chapter breaks in the original Bible, Jesus' words that continue into chapter 10 are still addressed to the religious leaders. He declares that he was the true Shepherd and the true sheep followed his voice, not the voice of strangers (10:1-5). Those who came before him were thieves and robbers, but Jesus was the sheep's true salvation (10:8-9). The thief comes only to destroy, but Jesus came to give life (10:10).

In other words, the thief represents the false religious leaders, like the Pharisees who kicked the healed man out of their synagogue. The devil certainly works behind such false teachers, and the devil certainly is a thief and a murderer. However, modern readers usually think immediately of the devil rather than of false religious leaders because they have not considered the text in its context. The background of the text clarifies this point further. In Jeremiah 23 and Ezekiel 34, God was the shepherd of his scattered people, his sheep; these Old Testament passages also speak of false religious leaders who abused their authority over the sheep like many of the religious leaders of Jesus' day and not a few religious leaders in our own day.

Jesus' Crucifixion in John 12:32

We often sing, *"Lift Jesus higher . . . He said, 'If I be lifted up from the earth, I will draw all men unto Me,'"* based on John 12:32. If we sing the song with the same meaning that the original text has, we would be singing, "Crucify Him! Crucify Him!" Of course God knows our hearts, but it is unfortunate that neither the song writer nor many of us who sing such songs have taken the time to look up the verse on which it is based.

Three times John refers to Jesus being *"lifted up."* In one case, he compares this event to the serpent being lifted up in the wilderness (John 3:14), to make eternal life available to everyone (3:15). In another, Jesus declares that his adversaries will lift him up (8:28). And in the final passage, where he says that he will draw all people to himself, John explicitly tells us what the lifting up means: *"He was declaring the kind of death He was going to die"* (12:33). In other words, John means by *"lifting up"* what Isaiah meant by it. Jesus would be crucified (Isaiah 52:13-53:12). John includes plays on words in his gospel, and may also indicate that we "exalt" Jesus by preaching the Cross; but leaves no doubt as to the primary sense of the term in this context: crucifixion. To read it any other way is to ignore his explicit, inspired explanation of the "lifting up."

The Day of Christ's Exaltation in Psalm 118:24

Many of us often sing, *"This is the day that the Lord has made."* When we sing this, most of us mean that God has made every day and what comes with it, and that we should therefore rejoice in what happens on that day. That is certainly a true principle, but we would do better to quote a different text to prove it (maybe Ephesians 5:20). In context, Psalm 118:24, from which this statement comes, refers not to every day, but to a particular day—the day when the Lord made the rejected stone the cornerstone (118:22-23), probably of the Temple (118:19-20, 27). It speaks of a special day of triumph, applicable in principle to many of God's great triumphs but often applied in the New Testament in a special way. If Psalm 118:22-23 was fulfilled in Jesus' ministry as He claimed (Mark 12:10-11), so also was Psalm 118:24—the great and momentous day the Lord had made. The day the Psalmist calls his hearers to celebrate is the prophetic day when God exalted Jesus, rejected by the chief priests, as the cornerstone of His new temple (cf. Eph. 2:20). The verse points to a truth far more significant than merely the common biblical truth that God is with us daily. It points to the greatest act of God on our behalf, when Jesus our Lord died and rose again for us.

Meeting our Needs; Philippians 4:19

Nearly every Christian has quoted Philippians 4:19 when he or she was in some kind of financial need. It says, *"And my God will meet all your needs according to his glorious riches in Christ Jesus."* We use this verse as an encouragement that God will meet our financial needs. However, we often fail to examine the context. Note these phrases which appear in the preceding context: "*it was good of you to **share** . . . not one church **shared with me** in the matter of **giving** and receiving, except you only . . . when I was in Thessalonica, **you sent me aid** again and again when I was in need . . . I have received **full payment** and even more; I am amply supplied, now that I have received from Epaphroditus **the gifts you sent** . . .*" It is in this context that Paul says that the Lord will supply all their needs. The Philippians had been very faithful in supplying Paul's needs. And now Paul promises that based upon their faithfulness in giving, God is going to supply their needs also. If we are not faithful in supplying the needs of others, we have no right to use this verse as a basis to request God to meet our needs.

In order to properly understand the immediate context, it may be necessary to go back two or three paragraphs to get the proper flow of the passage. Remember that the chapter and verse divisions are not inspired; they were placed there by a man riding horseback. One person has said, "The first step in interpretation is to ignore the modern chapters and verses." But in most cases context must go beyond the surrounding paragraph to surrounding chapters or even the entire book in which a passage occurs. Thus we turn in the next section to a discussion of a larger level of context.

The Context of the Book

While it is important to read each passage in the context that immediately surrounds it, it is also important to read it in the context of the entire book in which it appears—whether John or Judges or James or other books of the Bible. Often the particular passage fits into the argument of the entire biblical book, or sometimes it connects with themes that run through that book. In some cases, the story runs over several books in our Bible that were once connected as extended narratives. For instance, the Moses story in Exodus carries over from the Joseph story in Genesis and continues through Exodus, Leviticus and Numbers with Deuteronomy repeating some of the events.

To properly interpret a specific passage within a book, one must have a holistic understanding of the book. To do that we must do several things.

We must study the author of the writing.

Before we can understand the significance of any communication, we need to understand its author. For example, if I receive a note that says, "I would like to see you immediately," whether or not I take the note seriously depends upon who the author is. If the note is from a trader who is trying to sell me something that I do not want and do not need, I will not take the note too seriously. If the note comes from one of my students, I will probably try to find a convenient place to stop my work and then meet with the student, if I can. However, if the note comes from my Vice Chancellor, it does not matter what I have on my schedule, I will have to set it aside immediately in order to respond to the note. The point is that the authorship of any particular written document influences the way it is understood and responded to.

Personal Information

When one is studying the writings of a particular author in the Bible, it is always helpful to know some things about him. Where was he from? What were things he was interested in? Are there certain themes that he stresses? How did he relate to the ministry of Jesus?

To understand Paul's writings we need to understand all we can about Paul. He was a rabbi who was reared in a Gentile city. Even though his father was a Roman citizen, he grew up in a strict Jewish family. He studied in Jerusalem under the rabbi, Gamaliel. He was exposed both to non-Jewish people, practices, and literature, and to demanding Jewish life and culture.

It is helpful to know that Luke was a physician. When he gives a description of a disease, he is doing so from the viewpoint of a professional. This also helps to explain his particular interest in disease and healing.

Personal Style

In some cases, we have additional help in understanding a passage or statement in the Bible because we can look elsewhere at the particular author's style. Paul says that God inspired the Scriptures "through" people (Romans 1:2), which suggests that the author's point corresponds with God's point. It is therefore important to understand the author's point. Understanding inspiration recognizes that God inspired different writers in their own basic styles. Jeremiah and Isaiah and Ezekiel all heard God's message, but each has his own unique style of writing.

Personal Interests

Sometimes the author's personal interest is relevant to interpreting a word or phrase within a book. For example, some people today claim that *"abundant life"* in John 10:10 refers to material prosperity. However, we should note that this is not what John means by "life" anywhere else (1:4; 3:15-16, 36; 4:14, 35; 5:24, 26, 29, 39-40; 6:27) in his gospel. If this were not enough, however, one could also note references to "life" by the same author in 1 John (1:1-2; 2:25; 3:14-15; 5:11-13, 16, 20).

Personal Peculiarities

Matthew 4:23 says, "Jesus went throughout Galilee, teaching in their synagogues, preaching the good news of the kingdom, and healing every disease and sickness among the people." On the basis of this verse, some argue that Jesus healed everyone. But does "every disease" mean every individual in the whole region? Matthew also says that they brought him "all" the sick in the whole province of Syria (which included Galilee and Judea). If he meant that literally, no one would have needed healing after this point which is clearly contradicted by the testimony of Acts and even the rest of Matthew's Gospel. Jesus did not heal everyone who was sick near Him (13:58). The statement "every disease" or "all people" is a typical Hebrew way of saying that many came for healing. When we read Isaiah and the Psalms, "salvation" has a broader meaning than it usually bears in the New Testament. Therefore, we should respect the context of Isaiah's and the psalmists' usage and not read our own understanding of the word into these.

Example of "wrath" in Paul's Writings

Let us take an example from Paul's writings.[2] Some say that the Church will not go through the Great Tribulation at the end of the age because Paul declares that we will not experience God's *"wrath"* (1 Thessalonians 1:10; 5:9). This, however, is a questionable argument for that position. Occasionally Paul speaks of God's wrath in the present era (Romans 1:18), but usually when he uses the term he speaks of future wrath on the day of God's judgment (Romans 2:5, 8; 5:9; 9:22)—nowhere of the Great Tribulation before that day. Some interpreters want to appeal to the use of "wrath" in Revelation, but Revelation had not yet been written, so Paul could not expect the Thessalonians to simply turn over to Revelation to guess what he meant by wrath. (If one does appeal to Revelation, however, this particular Greek word for "wrath" always refers to judgment at the end of the tribulation. The word which sometimes—not always—refers to the tribulation as God's anger is not even the same word!)

Most of the letters of Paul are relatively short. By contrast, many of his congregations knew him and were familiar with some points he was making; it is therefore helpful for us to get to know him better by familiarizing ourselves with all his extant writings. This helps us whenever we approach any particular writing of Paul's.

We must study the occasion of the writing.

What is happening to the writer and the intended readers at the time of the writing? Why was this particular document written? Is it possible to discern the occasion for the writing of the specific book one is studying? Understanding the occasion will go a long way in helping one understand the meaning of specific passages.

Most interpreters agree that Psalm 51 was written after David had committed adultery with Bathsheba. Being able to tie this psalm with the actual historical situation goes a long way in helping us understand the

---

[2] In this example we are not advocating a particular doctrine. A doctrine often may be based on other texts. It is often helpful to pick examples that we misuse to make a point.

psalm. In fact, one of the most useful tools in helping to understand the psalms is to gain a good understanding about the historical context behind them.

The Epistle of Philippians is the "epistle of joy." It contains repeated exhortations to rejoice. These exhortations are even more meaningful when one understands that Paul was in prison when he wrote this epistle.

In Galatians, Paul refers to the *"Law"* several times. He frankly states that the Law has been annulled. What does he mean by "Law"? When we understand that the overall purpose of the book is to counter the teachings of the Judaizers who were demanding circumcision even on non-Jewish Christians, we can understand what Paul means by Law. He is not referring to national laws or laws of families or work places. He is specifically referring to the ritualistic laws of the Old Testament.

Some of these questions related to background can be answered with very diligent original research, but most of them will require some reading in the other Biblical study aids that have been discussed, particularly commentaries and Bible dictionaries.

We must study the purpose of the writing.

The interpreter needs to know something about the purpose the author was trying to accomplish in his book. The purpose of a book is to the author what goals and objectives are to a teacher. All teachers prepare their lesson plans with certain objectives in mind. When the teacher teaches that class, he or she is trying to accomplish those specific goals. Every Biblical writer had certain goals in mind as well. If we can discern those general goals, we will have taken a big step forward in interpreting the specific parts of the book.

How does one discover the purpose of a book? Some books specifically state the purpose. In 1 John, there are three specific purposes listed (1:4; 2:1; 5:13). If the purpose is not stated, we have to read and study until we understand something of the main reason that the book has been written. Ideally, we should first attempt to discover the basic purpose of each book ourselves. However, after that exercise, we should always consult other interpreters who have also spent time studying these books. None of us is so knowledgeable that we cannot learn from others. Remember:

interpretation of the details of a book is always influenced by the general purpose of the book.

A good way to understand the general context is to read rapidly through the book one is studying several times. By reading rapidly you will gain the most important ideas but will not flounder in the details.[3]

Whole Book Interpretation Principles

Before we look at some examples, we should summarize some whole book interpretation principles.

- We must not focus on the individual details so much that we miss the big picture. We must not "miss the forest for the trees"
- We must not focus so much on difficult details that we miss the main message of the book.
- We should look for the major themes that are found in any particular book in the Bible.
- We should try to see the flow of argument in any book of the Bible where that is relevant. How does the author develop the major themes?
- We must attempt to see how individual passages fit into the overall themes and the development of the argument in the book.

Examples

The following are some examples of material that one can only gain through having an understanding of the whole book:[4]

---

[3] A good exercise is to take three minutes to rapidly read over the Book of Habakkuk or Haggai or some other short book that you do not remember much about. In that brief period, you should be able to answer several questions: From whose viewpoint is the book written? What is the big problem in the passage? How is the problem solved?

David's Judgment in 2 Samuel 12:11

Sometimes we think that David's punishment for his adultery with Bathsheba and murder of Uriah ended with his son's death (2 Samuel 12:18). But because David was a leader in God's household, his behavior affected many others and required strict judgment (12:14); God takes sin very seriously, especially when it leads others to misunderstand His holiness. In 12:11, Nathan prophesies against David judgment from within his household, including the rape of some his wives (as he committed immorality with another man's wife) by a friend of his, in public. This prophecy provides almost an outline for the rest of 2 Samuel!

In chapter 13, David's son Amnon rapes his half-sister Tamar. Tamar's full brother Absalom avenges his sister's honour by killing Amnon—who also happens to be the brother immediately his elder, meaning that—if Chileab is uninvolved in politics (he is nowhere mentioned)—Absalom is also next in line for the throne by birthright (2 Samuel 3:2-3). Absalom returns from exile (ch. 14), and then leads a revolt that nearly destroyed David and his allies (chs. 15-18)—and broke his father's heart. Absalom slept with his father's concubines in the sight of Israel (16:21), despite the fact that this was against the law (Leviticus 20:11). Once this revolt was quelled and David returned to Jerusalem in peace (ch. 19), he had to deal with another revolt in the wake of the previous one, by a Benjamite usurper (ch. 20). By the opening of 1 Kings, the son immediately younger than Absalom is plotting to seize the throne (1 Kings 1).

Though forgiven by God and restored to his throne, David suffered the consequences of his pattern of sin for the rest of his life. This story provides a harsh warning for spiritual leaders today who forget their responsibility to live holy lives. It also illustrates how one story is part of an entire book.

Reproving Loveless Christians in 1 Corinthians 13

We often quote 1 Corinthians 13 as if it is an all-purpose description of love, for weddings, marriage counseling, friendships, and other occasions.

---

[4] A number of additional examples of whole-book context are found in the appendix.

The principles in this chapter are in fact universal enough to apply to those situations, but Paul originally wrote them to address a specific situation. Paul was addressing the appropriate use of spiritual gifts.

The Corinthian church was divided over a variety of issues. One issue, addressed in chapters 12-14, was the use of some spiritual gifts. Paul reminds the Christians in Corinth that the purpose of all publicly used gifts is to build up the body of Christ. In chapter 14, he emphasizes that prophecy is more important in public worship than tongues, because it builds up the church better. Between these two chapters is chapter 13, revealing love as the key virtue that moves us to use all our gifts to build up Christ's church.

Paul emphasizes that even if we have the greatest gifts, we are nothing without love (13:1-3). He points out that the gifts are temporary, due to pass away at Christ's return when we see him face to face (13:8-10). Love, however, is eternal (13:11-13). Between these two points he describes the characteristics of love—characteristics, which, in the context of the entire book, directly address what the Corinthian Christians lack (13:4-8). Love is not jealous or arrogant or boastful (13:4), but the Corinthian Christians certainly were jealous (3:3) and arrogant (4:6, 18-19; 5:2; 8:1) and boastful (see also 1:29; 3:21; 4:7; 5:6). In short, everything Paul says love is, he has already told the Corinthians they are not! Paul's praise of love is simultaneously a gentle rebuke![5]

But just as love is our first priority, love tells us which gifts to seek most for the building up of Christ's body. The verses immediately surrounding 1 Corinthians 13 remind us that we should seek from God for public worship especially the "greater" gifts, those like prophecy which build up others (12:31; 14:1).

Additional Observations on Whole Book Context

Sometimes today we start with specific doctrinal assumptions and read them into the Bible. The danger with this method is that it keeps us from ever learning anything new. If we read the Bible only as a textbook of

---

[5] An interesting project is to find examples things Paul condemned in 1 Corinthians 13 in the rest of 1 Corinthians.

what we already believe, we are likely to miss anything it has to teach and correct us. Thus it is important to learn the Bible's perspectives as they are written.

While we affirm that the Bible is correct and does not contradict itself, we recognize that some books of the Bible emphasize some themes more than other books do. Thus, for example, if we read the Book of Revelation, we are more likely to find an emphasis on Jesus' second coming than in the Gospel of John. In the Gospel of John, there is a heavier emphasis on eternal life available in the present. In the same way, when Paul writes to the Corinthians about speaking in tongues, he emphasizes its use as prayer. When Luke describes tongues in Acts, it functions as a demonstration that God transcends all linguistic barriers, fitting Luke's theme that the Spirit empowers God's people to cross cultural barriers. Different writers and books often have different emphases. These differences do not contradict one another, but we must study them respectfully on their own terms before we try to put them together.

When a specific passage seems obscure to us and we cannot tell which way the author meant it, it helps to look at the rest of the book to see what the author emphasizes. Thus, for example, the fact that the Gospel of John so often stresses that future hopes like *"eternal life"* are present realities (e.g., John 3:16, 36; 5:24-25; 11:24-26) may help shed light on how we approach John 14:2-3, as noted above. At the same time, we should never forget that each New Testament writing, however distinctive, is also part of a larger context of the teaching of apostolic Christianity, which had some common features. Thus, though the Gospel of John emphasizes the *presence* of the future, it in no way minimizes the fact that Jesus will return someday future as well (5:28-29; 6:39-40).

General Context

In any communication, some matters are stated but others can be left assumed. For instance, I am writing in English, on the assumption that I and my readers both know English. Since Paul wrote to the Corinthians in Greek, he assumed that they knew Greek. I assume that my readers know what a Bible is, and would be safe to assume that my readers know what a car is, what a radio is, and what pounded yam is (though Paul's readers knew none of these things, except what the Old Testament part of the

Bible was). Paul could likewise allude to specific customs his readers practiced without explaining them, because the Corinthians already knew exactly what he meant (e.g., "baptism for the dead," 1 Corinthians 15:29). But for us to understand Paul's meaning we must either know Greek or have a translation, and we must either know the culture the biblical writers shared with their audiences or have access to resources that help explain that culture. What the writer could *assume* as part of his meaning was as much a part of the meaning as what he had to state.

We have noted above the importance of whole-book context, because most books of the Bible stress particular themes addressing particular issues. Although people sometimes ignore such verses, many verses explicitly state particular audiences for these books—for instance, the Christians in Rome (Romans 1:7) or in Corinth (1 Corinthians 1:2). There are appropriate ways to apply these books to today, but first we must take seriously what these works explicitly claim to be: works addressed to specific audiences in specific times and places. In other words, before we can determine how to apply the ancient meaning for today, we must understand the ancient meaning. To skip this important step in Bible interpretation is to ignore what the Bible claims for itself.

When Paul wrote letters, the very genre in which he wrote reminds us that he addressed specific situations, as letters usually do. Thus, for example, in 1 Corinthians Paul addresses questions about food offered to idols, head coverings, and other issues that Christians today usually view as relevant only in some cultures. The letter also addresses division between followers of Paul and followers of Apollos. Though each interpersonal or inter-church conflict is different, solving differences between Christians was not unique to the Corinthians but is a very real problem today. If we read letters as letters, we remember to look for the specific situations they address.

We should consider the relevance even of narratives to the first audience they addressed. For instance, if Moses wrote Genesis to those who had just been released from slavery in Egypt, they could have identified readily with Joseph, who had also been a slave in Egypt before his exaltation. The repeated emphasis on the promise of the holy land in Genesis also would provide great encouragement for Israelites about ready to go in and conquer it. Considering such relevance of the Bible to its original hearers does not make the Bible any less relevant for us.

Rather, it teaches us how to discover its relevance properly. Everything in the Bible is for all time, but not everything in the Bible is for all circumstances.

Every written or oral statement is always given against a particular background and within a specific worldview. This includes the historical situation, the political climate, the geographical setting, the cultural condition and many other factors. Without having a general understanding of these issues, we may miss some of the fine nuances of the communication. The following are some specific details that we need to understand.

We must study the geography.

The events of the Bible occurred and were written in a certain geographical setting. One cannot understand the overall message of the Bible without understanding something about the geography of the Bible lands. This is more important sometimes than at other times. For example, when Jesus healed the leper (Matthew 8:2 following), he told him to go show himself to the priest. This incident occurred in Galilee. This meant that the man had to take a 150 kilometer overland journey to Jerusalem where he could show himself to the priest. He would likely have to wait at least thirty days for the priest to see him a second time before he would be allowed to return to his family. The leper would have to do all of this in order to fulfill the Law.

Without understanding Bible geography, one cannot appreciate what Jesus was doing in Samaria when he spoke to the woman at the well. Instead of taking the most direct route between Galilee and Judea, many Jews, because of their hatred and distrust of the Samaritans took a long circuitous route. For example, from Nazareth, they would walk east for one day, cross over the Jordan River and then walk south to Jericho. They would then cross over the Jordan River and make their way up to Jerusalem. They would walk at least two days out of their way to avoid going through Samaria. However, because Jesus did not have such prejudice, He and His disciples took the most direct route, which was right through Samaria. That is part of the context around Jesus ministering to the woman at the well.

We must study the customs.

The Bible was written in a cultural context. All the stories that Jesus told were told in a cultural context. If we do not understand the customs and culture of the ancient world, we are not going to be able to understand much of the Bible. One will not be able to understand the Parable of the Ten Virgins without understanding the marriage customs of that day.

We all recognize that some commands in the Bible were limited to the period that they address. Moses said that the Israelites were to build a "fence" around the roof lest they incur bloodguilt if anyone fell from it (Deuteronomy 22:8). Yet most of us today do not build fences around our roofs. Are we disobeying this passage? Back in Moses' day, people had flat roofs and would spend time on the roof, often with their neighbors. Yet if a neighbor's child fell off the roof, he or she could get hurt. So Moses commanded the Israelites to build a parapet or small fence around the roof to protect those who might be on the housetop. Today, if we do not build roofs so they can be walked on, so we do not take our neighbors on the roof. In that case, there would be no need to build a parapet. The point of application is that we must watch out for the safety of our family and neighbor. A modern application of the principles would be wearing a seat belt while riding in a vehicle. We may never have discovered this important principle if we had not understood the background.

Jesus told his disciples that they did not have to eat with washed hands (Matthew 15:2). Was Jesus unsanitary? No, this had to do with the ritualistic washing of the hands, not the proper washing of the hands to make them actually clean. Jesus and his disciples walked through someone's grain fields and plucked off grains of wheat to eat as they walked. Was this stealing? No, it was customary and acceptable to pick off grains of wheat to eat along the way, as long as one did not take any with him from the field.

Guidelines for Determining the General Context

1. Obtain the Correct Background.

In order to understand a passage, we must first take into account, as best as possible, the specific culture and situations in which the original writers lived and ministered. If we are going to practice or not practice wearing head coverings today, we should know what head coverings were like in Paul's day (hence what he meant by them) and why he supported their use.

From the Bible

Where do we get this background? Some of the background is often in the Bible itself. For instance, we can learn much about the times in which Isaiah prophesied by reading the accounts of the kings in whose reigns he prophesied (listed in Isaiah 1:1) in 2 Kings; likewise about the situations Jeremiah addressed roughly a century later. Acts 17:1-9 tells us about the founding of the church in Thessalonica, which in turn gives us some background for 1 and 2 Thessalonians. We can also reconstruct some of the specific situation addressed based on what the texts themselves emphasize. For instance, Paul seems to address Jewish-Gentile division in Rome and conflicts between the wealthier and less wealthy Christians in Corinth. Noticing the patterns in these letters can help us reconstruct the sorts of issues the writers had to contend with, shedding light on many details in the letters.

From Non-Biblical Sources

Not all the background is available in the Bible itself. When Paul wrote to the Corinthians, he did not provide a translation of his letter into Hausa, Igbo, Yoruba, English or Arabic. Later translators provide that for us. Paul wrote his letter in Greek, because that was the language most or all of the Corinthian Christians spoke. In the same way, he does not pause to explain customs or situations that he and the Corinthians both knew. They are *assumed* in his meaning, but modern readers need to do some research to find out what he meant. Paul would welcome later readers to learn from his letters, but he could not write a letter that would address all languages and cultures at once; he would expect us to learn his language and culture or use tools that provide it.

More specific knowledge of the culture requires more work, because not everyone possesses biblical background resources outside the Bible. On some issues (like holy kisses, Jewish burial customs or water pots in Cana) we recognize that the Bible's culture often differs from our own. But often even when we think we can take for granted that our own cultural background qualifies us to understand the Bible, we are mistaken. Many of us miss the shock that would have greeted the first hearers of Jesus' parable of the prodigal son. No respectable father would have divided his inheritance at a son's demand, run to greet his son, or welcomed him home safe without punishment. Jesus compares God to an overly lenient father—showing just how merciful he has been in view of our rebellion against him.

Often we miss the point of the passage because we are unfamiliar with the culture in which it was written. Some cultures, such as Middle Eastern and Mediterranean cultures or some traditional rural African culture, are closer to the cultures in the Old and New Testament than most western cultures are. But none of us dare assume that we will always interpret the Bible correctly without consulting the ancient culture. African cultures are closer to biblical cultures than western cultures are, but this makes it easy to miss the fact that sometimes African and biblical cultures differ. For example, in Corinth either husband or wife could divorce the other regardless of the other's protests (1 Corinthians 7:15).

From Jewish Writings

Various sources provide information on ancient Mediterranean cultures. Someone who wants to study the Gospels in detail, for instance, should read in addition to the Old Testament the Apocrypha (a section contained in Catholic Bibles), especially Wisdom of Solomon and Sirach; some of the Dead Sea Scrolls (especially the Manual of Discipline and War Scroll) and so-called Pseudepigrapha (especially 1 Enoch; Epistle of Aristeas; 4 Ezra and 2 Baruch); parts of Josephus (especially his *Life, Against Apion,* and parts of the *War*); and probably the tractate Aboth in the Mishnah.

From Bible Study Tools

Because most students do not have access to all these resources, one might use a Bible encyclopedia like the new *International Standard Bible Encyclopedia* to get answers for specific questions one has. But sometimes one does not even know which questions one should ask without knowing some of the background. For that reason, one of the simplest and most available beginning tools is the *IVP Bible Background Commentary*. The New Testament portion provides background on each passage or verse of the New Testament, and was written by Craig Keener, one of the co-authors of this book. Professor Keener spent many years researching ancient Mediterranean culture so he could provide it in one volume, passage-by-passage, to make the information widely available to all Bible readers. But though he tried his best to take into account all cultures, he could address most fully only those questions which he could anticipate, so there are still many questions unanswered. The *IVP Bible Background Commentary* provides a bibliography of sources useful for further research into ancient Mediterranean culture, for those who are able to pursue it further.

2. Determine How the Passage Relates to its Culture.

We should know the culture and situation well enough to understand why the biblical writers addressed issues the way they did. Once we understand the culture and situation, we need to understand what the writers say to the situation. In any passage you are studying, you need to determine whether the author agrees with the views of his culture. For instance, when Jesus tells his disciples to offer private reproof before public rebuke (Matthew 18:15-17), He is in agreement with the usual Jewish way of doing things in his day. In some other cases, biblical writers may adopt neutral aspects of the cultures they are addressing for the sake of being a relevant witness within those cultures, as Paul clearly explains that he does in 1 Corinthians 9:19-23. And at times, the writer is clearly in disagreement with the local culture. For instance, although the Israelites had some sacrifices the Canaanites had (like sin offerings), they did not have offerings to make it rain. Many pagans thought offerings to their gods could secure rain; but Israel's God promised to simply send rain if his people obeyed his covenant. Mesopotamian law required that any person who harbored an escaped slave should be executed. By contrast, God commanded Israelites to harbor escaped slaves (Deuteronomy 23:15).

Does the biblical writer modify a standard view of his culture, even while communicating his message in culturally intelligible forms? This is one of the most frequent ways biblical writers related to their cultures. For instance, from Aristotle onward Greeks and Romans often emphasized that the male head of the household must rule his wife, children and slaves. But Paul, while taking over the topic, modifies the instructions. He tells a husband not how to rule his wife, but how to love her (Ephesians 5:25). The wife must submit, but as a form of Christian submission that all Christians must learn to practice (Ephesians 5:21-22). If we read this passage as if Paul were saying exactly the same thing as Aristotle, we would miss his point.

Likewise, God instructs the Israelites to build the tabernacle with a holy of holies, sanctuary and outer court just as in Egyptian temples, but this makes the contrast all the more striking. Atop God's ark there is no image of the deity as in Egyptian temples. Sometimes biblical writers, for the sake of their witness, adopted aspects of their culture that were good or neutral; but this invites us to pay all the closer attention to where these writers departed from their culture.

3. Apply the Biblical Writers' Message

We cannot determine whether every culture or situation must address matters the same way the biblical writers did until we understand the biblical writers' reasons for making the particular arguments they do. But once we have a good idea about why the biblical writers addressed particular situations the way they did, we can begin to ask how they would have applied the same principles in very different situations.

Head Covering

For example, knowing why women wore head coverings in Paul's day helps us understand why he gives the instructions he does. Most women in the eastern Mediterranean world covered their hair in public as a sign of sexual modesty. Hair constituted the primary object of male lust in the ancient Mediterranean world, so married women were required to keep their hair covered. Thus the lower class women in the churches were concerned when some upper class women refused to wear them. Paul therefore addressed issues of ostentation, seductiveness, sexual modesty and class division in the church, all of which are trans-cultural issues.

But would Paul solve matters of sexual modesty or class division in the same way in every culture as he did in Corinth? Would the head covering provide a solution to such issues in every culture? Could head coverings in some cultures become signs of ostentation, showing off wealth? Could they in some cultures actually become tools of seduction the way jewels and costly array sometimes were in Paul's culture? What of a culture where only well-to-do people could afford to wear head coverings, thus introducing class division into the church? Is it possible that in churches in some parts of the world, *wearing* a head covering (as opposed to not wearing one) might draw attention to the wearer?

In such cases, do we follow Paul's specific example for his culture, or do we follow the transcultural principles Paul used to make a specific case for a specific culture? This is why it is so important for us to take into account cultural background and read Scripture consistently in light of it: If God inspired the writers to address their own culture in a particular way, how would they have addressed our culture today? Which are the principles and which are the specific examples that illustrated those principles in the situations the biblical writers addressed?

Example of Jesus

Jesus interpreted and applied Scripture this way. The Pharisees were interested in detailed regulations, but Jesus was more interested in the principles (Matthew 12:7). Jesus took into account the human *reasons* some Scriptures were given. For example, some things God permitted because of the hardness of their hearts (Mark 10:5), but their real goal should be to understand God's ideal purposes (Mark 10:6-9). Then Pharisees cited a law; Jesus cited a story. All Scripture is inspired and useful for teaching (2 Timothy 3:16), so the issue is not that one kind of writing is more useful than another. The issue is that they saw only details, whereas Jesus looked for the *reasons* for the details. Jesus claimed that what mattered most was justice, mercy and faith (Matthew 23:23)—the heart of God's word.

Paul in the same way disagreed with his contemporaries on what was fundamental, arguing that it is God's own power that saves us, not secondary issues like circumcision or food laws. This method of interpretation requires us to keep central what matters most (the gospel and obedience to God's will), rather than becoming legalistic on secondary matters that could distract us from the heart of the gospel.

Much of the New Testament consists simply of examples how to relate the basic message of the gospel to various concrete historical situations and challenges. We must likewise learn how to relate the central message of Christ to our various situations today, never losing sight of what is the central principle and what are simply the cultural expressions.

Misapplying Biblical Principles

Many early missionaries came to Africa with a gospel contextualized for their own culture, like the American or European versions of Christianity. Usually they remained largely faithful to the Bible, but they often failed to discern the difference between the Bible's actual teaching and the way they had applied it to the issues in their own cultures. Thus they sometimes encouraged African Christians to adopt western music styles, clothing styles, wedding ceremony styles, and similar things because they had assumed these customs to be Christian.

Today we know better, and today we must avoid making the same mistake. We should be able to distinguish between the Bible's universal principles and how it applied those principles in the cultures it addressed. Again, we affirm that all Scripture is God's message. But it was first God's message to the original cultures to which God sent it, so for us to hear it properly today we must take into account how God related it to those cultures. Likewise, we must distinguish between what the Bible teaches for all cultures and how we have applied it specifically to the situations we must address.

We must be aware that at times people will use culture to explain away things in the Bible. That is a danger we must strive hard to avoid. But people have been explaining away things in the Bible for centuries without using culture, so this danger should not make us afraid to use background in the appropriate manner. We simply need to use it conscientiously, diligent to find the truth. The only appropriate starting point for finding wisdom is the fear of the Lord (Proverbs 1:7). If we fear him we will be careful to truly understand his truth, wherever the evidence of the Bible genuinely leads us, rather than ways to explain that truth away.

Conclusion

Context is everything in communication. If we misunderstand the context, we misunderstand the communication.

Study Questions

1. What is meant by the "immediate context?"
2. Explain one of the ways that one can understand the context of the whole book.
3. Why is it important to know who the author and the readers of a document are?
4. Give an example of how knowing Biblical geography affects the interpretation of a passage.
5. What should be considered to be part of the general context?
6. What are some possible sources for background information?
7. Describe some of the dangers of failing to properly understand background information.
8. Explain how knowing the culture of the Biblical world helps in interpreting a specific passage.
9. Explain how the context helps to explain the statement in 1 Corinthians 10-23, *"all things are permissible."*
10. Give an example of how the context helps us understand a specific passage of Scripture?

Chapter Fourteen

Rule Five
The Rule of Words

Introduction

The most basic unit of communication is the word. It is possible to communicate using only one word. We frequently use such one-word communications: "Go," "Come," "Stop," "No." Since words are the lowest common denominator in communication, it is essential for interpreters of the Bible to have some understanding of how to interpret the words of the Bible. If one misunderstands a word, it can lead to a totally wrong interpretation of Scripture.

I once was teaching a course in New Testament Theology to a group of eight students. One day, a Chinese student, who did not speak English too well, raised his hand and asked a question. I thought he said, "I want to ask a question about the table?" I could not remember anything I had said about a table so I was confused. I said, "Excuse me, you want to know about the table?" He shook his head and said, "No, the Table." I still could not understand so I asked him, "What about the table?" Again, he shook his head vigorously and tried to explain, "The Table; the Table; the Table." His fellow students also tried to figure out what he was saying, but they were just as confused as I was. Finally, I said, "Just come up and right the word on the blackboard." He walked forward and carefully wrote, "D-E-V-I-L." I thought he was saying "table" but actually he was saying "devil." Not understanding that one word confused the entire communication. That is why studying Biblical words is essential.

All languages, both spoken and written, are made up of words. Since the Bible is written in normal language, it is written in words. Therefore, one of the basic aspects of Bible study is the study of the words of the Bible.

Most of the words in the Bible are very normal words, just like the words I am using to write this chapter. The Bible is filled with thousands of examples of "the," "and," "is" and other small words that are important to our communication.

In addition, the Bible is filled with other words that have major theological significance. Most of these words were borrowed from a non-theological part of society. However, having been used so much with theological language, we have often forgotten their original meaning and only think of them in theological terms. These include words like *righteousness, justification, grace, perfection, holiness, salvation,* and similar words.

Somewhere in between these two kinds of words lie other words that do not have as much theological significance but which are pregnant with meaning and insight and application. Into this category are words like *meekness, discipline,* and *restore.*

Some Problems with Biblical Words

Unfortunately, words do not come without problems.

1. The Bible was written in a different language.

Most Christians do not speak or read Hebrew or Greek, the languages in which the Bible was written. Therefore, we have to study the Bible in a translation. Words in one language rarely mean exactly the same when translated into another language. This is especially true with abstract concepts. It is the job of the interpreter to try to understand the concept behind the words as much as it is possible to do so.

There are blessings and dangers associated with the inter-linear Greek New Testament. (This is a Greek New Testament that has a literal word-for-word English translation written under the Greek words and a standard translation on the side of the Greek text.) This book can help the weak Greek student to understand the meanings of words and aid in his reading and translating. In addition, it can help one to see the variety of words used to translate English words. But the inter-linear Greek New Testament can be a problem also, because the translators selected one English word to reflect the meaning of the one Greek word. Many times it is not possible to accurately translate one word in a language with one word in another language. In addition, simply having a literal translation of the words of another language does not mean that one has understood the meaning of that particular document.

2. Certain Biblical words are used in a special sense.

Words like *justification* and *righteousness* have specialized meanings which are not found outside the Bible. Words like the Greek word for love, *agape*, developed new meanings in the Bible. Figurative words like *death* and *sleep* have different meanings in secular literature.

3. Words have more than one meaning.

In most languages, the same word can be used to mean many different things. For example, the English word "run" is an over-worked word. Water runs out of the tap. Vines run up on trees. An athlete runs in a race. An engine runs when the vehicle is moving. A person's nose runs when he is sick. A supervisor runs a program.

The Bible contains certain words which are used in different ways in the Bible: For example, death can refer to physical death. It can also refer to the fact that people were *"dead"* before they became Christians. It can mean the putting to death of the sinful deeds and attitudes. Sometimes it refers to the danger of death; Paul said, *"I die daily."* It also is the word used to describe eternal separation from God and which is sometimes called the *"second death."*

4. Different Greek and Hebrew words can be translated by the same English word.

All those who speak more than one language recognize that sometimes there is only one English word to describe several concepts from another language. For example, in Greek, there are two words for "new." *Neos* refers to new in existence, whereas *kainos* refers to something that has a new depth or fullness. There are two words translated "love" in the New Testament. *Agape* refers to unselfish giving regardless of the emotional attachment one has. *Philos* refers to the warm emotional love that one has for another person, the family type-love. *Eros,* another Greek word for a sensual type love, is not found in the New Testament.

There are two words for burden. *Baros* refers to a very heavy load, such as the cargo that would be found on a ship. This would be a load that would be impossible for a person to carry. *Phortion* refers to a pack, like a soldier would carry. It is heavy but bearable. Knowing this helps to clear up the apparent discrepancy between Galatians 6:2, *"Bear ye one another's burdens (baros),"* and 6:5 *"For every man shall bear his own burden (phortion)."*

There is also a difference between the words for anointing, *aleipho* (anointing for cosmetic and medicinal purposes) and *chrio* (anointing for religious purposes). This knowledge gives insight into the statement by James when he says, *"Is any one of you sick? He should call the elders of the church to pray over him, and anoint him with oil in the name of the Lord"* (5:14). The word "anoint" in this passage is *aleipho* which suggests anointing for medicinal purposes. Oil was a common medicine in those days. What James is apparently saying is that when one gets sick, he should ask the elders to pray for him in case God chooses to bring about supernatural healing. In addition, he should also use the normal medical treatment in case God chooses to use a natural means of bringing about healing.

5. The same original Greek or Hebrew word may be translated by several different English words.

Hebrew and Greek were very rich languages. It often takes many different English words to translate a Greek or Hebrew word—the meaning of which depends on the context. For example, the Hebrew word *yom* is used to refer to a twenty-four hour period, time, age, space and season, all in the first book of the Bible.

The Greek verb *katartizo* is translated in the following ways:

Rule of Words

1. Matthew 4:21; "**mending** their nets"
2. Luke 6:40; "Everyone, after he **has been fully trained**, will be like his teacher."
3. Romans 9:22; "Vessels of wrath **prepared** for destruction"
4. Galatians 6:1; "**Restore** such a one in a spirit of gentleness . . ."
5. 1 Peter 5:10; "will himself **perfect**, confirm, strengthen and establish you."

With all of these things being true, it is essential that the careful student of the Bible pay special attention to the words of the Bible.[1]

Doing Word Studies

There are many different ways that one can do word studies. However, we will concentrate on two of them. The first method demands that one has the right kind of theological tools and at least a working knowledge of the original Biblical languages. We refer to this as the "ideal method." The second requires only the use of a complete or exhaustive concordance.

The Ideal Method

The ideal method of doing a word study will require access to original language books and at least a working knowledge of the original language. We will use the Greek language in this model.

A. Determine which original Greek word you wish to study.

This has to be done either through consulting the Greek New Testament or through finding the Greek word in some other source. This implies that the student can read at least some Greek.

---

[1] Some of the above material was taken from J. Robertson McQuilkin, *Understanding and Applying the Bible* (Chicago, IL USA: Moody Press), pp. 83-89.

B. Look the word up in a Greek Concordance.

The most well-known is by William F. Mouton and Alfred S. Geden, *A Concordance to the Greek Testament,* (Edinburgh, Scotland: Clark). However, an easier tool to use is George Wigram, *The Englishman's Greek Concordance of the New Testament,* (Grand Rapids, MI USA: Zondervan Publishing House). This particular edition has all of the Greek words listed in alphabetical order in Greek, but the examples of the way the words are used are all found in English, which makes it easier for those who don't read Greek well. A parallel version in Hebrew is *The Englishman's Hebrew and Chaldee Concordance of the Old Testament* also by Zondervan.

C. Look up all the usages of that particular word, and study it in its context, noting the following things.

1. What is the basic meaning of this word in this passage? (That can usually be determined from the context.)
2. What are the words and concepts that surround this particular word? If it is found in a list of words, what are its closest neighbors?
3. Who are the people associated with this word? Are they godly people or ungodly?
4. What are the words that this word is linked with by "and" and similar conjunctions?
5. What are the words that this word is contrasted with by "but" and similar conjunctions?
6. Compile all the results of this study by demonstrating the different ways the word is used in the different contexts with appropriate illustrations.

D. For theological words make a special note of the way the word is used in non-theological settings.

Practically all theological abstract words, like righteousness or spirit or holiness, have their roots in some everyday concept. For example, the word "sin" is a very common theological word. The Greek word for sin, *hamartano* is used in the Septuagint version of Judges 20:16, "There were seven hundred chosen men who were left-handed, each of whom could sling a stone at a hair and not **miss**." Miss is translated from *hamartano.,* which is also the word for sin. From that we can assume that this particular word for sin, *hamartano,* means to "miss the mark."

E. Look up the word in a Greek or Hebrew Lexicon.

The following are the most well-known lexicons:

1. Francis Brown, S. R. Driver and Charles Briggs, *A Hebrew and English Lexicon of the Old Testament,* (Oxford, England: Claredon Press), (abbreviated *BDB*). 1979

2. William F. Arndt and F. W. Gingrich, *A Greek-English Lexicon of the New Testament and Other Early Christian Literature* (Chicago, IL USA: University of Chicago Press). 1957

3. Joseph H. Thayer, *A Greek-English Lexicon of the New Testament* (New York, NY USA: American Book Company). 1967

Note especially the meanings of the word in non-Biblical sources. If you are looking up a Greek word, frequently the lexicon will give references to the way the word is used in the *Septuagint,* the *Apocrypha* and *Classical Greek.* (There is a large body of extant classical Greek literature including Aristotle, Plato, Sophicles and many others.) If one has the skills and tools, it is good to look up the Classical references to see how the word was used in secular Greek. This type of study can yield tremendous benefits for illustrating and clarifying of the original word.

The Greek lexicon will frequently give illustrations of the way the word was used in papyri or other *koine* Greek sources. This is a large collection of literature that comes from around the first century AD, and it can yield a lot of insight into words. This would include ancient secular papyri texts and the church fathers such as the *Epistle of Barnabus* and other similar writings. The point is the more examples you can get from many different sources, the more confident you can be that you have accurately interpreted the original meaning of the word.

Another major function of the lexicon is to give some idea about the derivation of the word you are studying. Many lexicons will discuss the "root" word or concept. For example, when studying the word *"spirit"* we discover that the root meaning is wind or breath.

F. Check the conclusions of other word-study tools.

These are examples:

1. T. Robertson, *Word Pictures in the New Testament* (Nashville, TN, USA: Broadman Press).
2. M. R. Vincent, *Word Studies in the New Testament,* (McLean, VA USA: McDonald Publishing Company).
3. Robert Girdlestone, *Synonyms of the Old Testament,* (Grand Rapids, MI USA: Wm. B. Eerdmans Publishing Company).
4. Richard Trench, *Synonyms of the New Testament,* (Grand Rapids, MI USA: Wm. B. Eerdmans Publishing Company).
5. Stewart Custer, *A Treasury of New Testament Synonyms,* (Greenville, SC USA: Bob Jones University Press, Inc.).
6. William Barclay, *A New Testament Wordbook,* (London, UK: SCM).
7. William Barclay, *Flesh and Spirit,* (Nashville, TN USA: Abingdon Press).
8. William Barclay, *More New Testament Words,* (New York, NY USA: Harper and Row).
9. W. E. Vine, *Vine's Expository Dictionary of New Testament Words,* (McLean, VA USA: McDonald Publishing Company). This book would be one of the most useful for the non-Greek reader.

The following are some examples of more technical and exhaustive works:

1. Gerhard Kittel, Editor, *Theological Dictionary of the New Testament* (Grand Rapids, MI USA: Wm. B. Eerdmans Publishing Company). This is a massive ten-volume set of books that gives very exhaustive and comprehensive information about New Testament words.
2. Colin Brown, Editor, *Dictionary of New Testament Theology,* (Grand Rapids, MI USA: Zondervan Publishing House). A three-volume set that contains much of the same kinds of materials as Kittel.
3. R. Laird Harris, *Theological Wordbook of the Old Testament* (Chicago, IL USA: Moody Press). A similar work based upon Old Testament words.

You must now compare the results of your personal study with the results of the experts. Remember the experts used the same tools and methods that you used. Therefore do not automatically accept their conclusions instead of your own. However, remember also most of the experts have been doing this for many years. Therefore, disregard their interpretations very cautiously.

G. Write out the conclusions of your research.

Make sure that you write out all of the details, including your conclusions. Five years from now, you will not remember the details of this research. If you have not written them down, you will have to redo the work.

Word Study Using English Concordances

A. Look up the word in the concordance.

Notice that there is usually more than one Greek or Hebrew word translated into that particular English word. Find the transliterated Greek word (Greek word changed into English letters). Go to the back of the concordance and look up the original word with the transliterated spelling. Find all of the other ways the original word is translated into English.

B. Look up all of these references and answer the following questions about each passage.

1. What is the basic meaning of this word in this passage? That can usually be determined from your own reading of the context.
2. What are the words and concepts that surround this particular word? If it is found in a list of words, what words are closest to it?
3. Who are the people that are associated with this word? Are they godly people or ungodly people?
4. What are the words that this word is linked with by *"and"* and similar conjunctions?

5. What are the words that this word is contrasted with by *"but," "yet," "however,"* and similar conjunctions?

Compile the results of the study by showing the different ways the word is used in the different contexts with appropriate illustrations.

C. Compile all of your study, organize it and write it down.

1. Divide the word into the different ways it is used.
2. Use Biblical illustrations to show these different meanings.
3. Summarize the conclusions of the study in a brief paragraph.
4. File this information where it can be found.

D. Illustration of the Methodology using the Word "Meek"

We will now look up the word *"meek"* in *Young's Analytical Concordance*. It is found on page 652.[2] The word *meekness* is the noun form of the word *meek* (which is an adjective) so we decide to include it in our study. Under the word *meek* we observe that Greek words 3 and 4 are translated *meek*. They are *praos*, which is used one time, and *praus*, which is used three times.

We notice that the first three letters of the word are the same, *pra*. We can logically determine that these words come from the same Greek root word. They certainly will be related words; they may be different spellings of the same word. Under the word *meekness*, meanings 3 and 4 are *praotes* with 9 references and *prautes* with 3 references. Using the same reasoning that we used above, we decide to treat all of these words as one.

We now go to the back of the concordance to see what additional information is shed on these words. We look up *praos* and find it on page 87 of the index explaining the words. We see *praos* and *praotes* together. The concordance shows us the way these words are translated in the King

---

[2] The word study demonstration done here uses the King James Version since we are working with *Young's Analytical Concordance*. Page numbers may vary in different editions.

Rule of Words

James Version, which is *meek* and *meekness*. *Praus* is translated "meek" 3 times and *prautes* is translated "meekness" 3 times.

One important thing that we discover is that the words *praus* and its related words are always translated with the word *meek* or *meekness*. Therefore, we do not have to look up any additional words.

Now we must start examining the individual passages where the word is used and make some observations. We turn back to pages 653 in *Young's* and start looking up the individual passages asking the above questions about each reference.

Who had this quality?

1. Christ had the quality of meekness. Matthew 11:29 says, *"Take my yoke ... for I am meek and lowly in heart ..."* Matthew 21:5 adds, *"Behold, thy king cometh unto thee, meek, and sitting upon an 'ass. ."* In 2 Corinthians 10:1, Paul says, *"I beseech thee by the meekness and gentleness of Christ.."*
2. Paul also had the quality. In 1 Corinthians 4:21, Paul wrote, *"Shall I come unto you with a rod, or in love, and in the spirit of meekness?"*

Note these observations:

1. This word is not used in conjunction with unbelievers.
2. The word is not used in conjunction with God.
3. These observations may or may not be significant because we have such a small sample of references.

What are words associated with meekness?

There are five lists of virtues, similar to the fruit of the Spirit, that include *meekness*. These include Galatians 5:22-23, Ephesians 4:2, Colossians 3:12, 1 Timothy 6:11 and 2 Timothy 2:25. Note these additional words associated with meekness.

1. Lowliness: Matthew 11:29, *"I am **meek** and **lowly** ..."*
2. Love: 1 Corinthians 4:21, *"... come **in love** and in the spirit of **meekness**."*
3. Gentleness: 2 Corinthians 10:1, *"by the **meekness** and **gentleness** of Christ ..."*

4. Titus 3:2, "... to be **gentle**, showing all **meekness** unto all men."
5. Quiet Spirit: 1 Peter 3:4, "even the ornament of a **meek** and **quiet** spirit .."
6. Fear: 1 Peter 3:15, "reason for the hope that is within you with **meekness** and **fear**."

Note these observations:

1. The word is always found among positive character qualities.
2. From the words that surround it, we can discern that it is some kind of quality that is humble, gentle, quiet and even fearful in a positive sense.

What are the words it is contrasted with?

1. The rod: 1 Corinthians 4:21, "come with a **rod** . . . or in the spirit of **meekness**"
2. Gossip and brawling: Titus 3:2, "To **speak evil** of no man, to be **no brawlers**, but gentle showing all **meekness** unto all men . . ."
3. Filthiness: James 1:21,

   Wherefore lay apart all **filthiness** and **superfluity of naughtiness**, and receive with **meekness** the engrafted word, which is able to save your souls.

4. Ostentatious outward adorning: 1 Peter 3:3-4,

   Whose adorning let it not be that **outward adorning** of plaiting the hair, and of wearing of gold, of or putting on of apparel; But let it be the hidden man of the heart, in that which is not corruptible, even the ornament of a **meek** and quiet spirit, which is in the sight of God of great price.

Note these observations:

1. *Meekness* is contrasted with and assumed to be opposite of that which is harsh, loud, unclean and proud.
2. The *meek* person does not beat up people, does not criticize them, does not pollute himself with that which is unclean and does not dress in a proud and worldly manner.

Meekness is necessary for the following:

1. To inherit the earth: Matthew 5:5, "*Blessed are the **meek**: for they shall inherit the earth.*"
2. To restore a fallen brother: Galatians 6:1, "*Brethren, if a man be overtaken in a fault, ye which are spiritual, restore such a one in the spirit of **meekness**.*"
3. To teach: 2 Timothy 2:24-25, "*And the servant of the Lord . . . must be gentle unto all men, apt to teach, patient, in **meekness** instructing those that oppose themselves . . .*"
4. To be saved: James 1:21, "*Lay apart all filthiness and superfluity of naughtiness and receive with **meekness** the engrafted word which is able to save your souls.*"
5. To convince the doubters: 1 Peter 3:15, "*and be ready always to give an answer to every man that asked you a reason of the hope that is in you with **meekness** and fear.*"

Note these conclusions:

1. *Meekness is a very vital aspect of Christianity because it is even necessary for salvation.*
2. *Meekness is necessary to accomplish most of the ministries to which Christians are called.*

Meekness is exhorted for Christians in the following passages:

1. Ephesians 4:1-2: "*I . . . beseech you that ye walk worthy of the vocation wherewith ye are called, with all lowliness and **meekness** . . .*"
2. Colossians 3:12: "*Put on therefore, as the elect of God, holy and beloved, bowels of mercies, kindness, humbleness of mind, **meekness**, long-suffering .*"
3. 1 Timothy 6:11: "*But thou, O man of god, flee these things; and follow after righteousness, godliness, faith, love, patience, **meekness** . . .*"

When all of this is taken together, we get a good picture of meekness.

Additional Insights from Additional Study Aids

William Barclay discusses *meekness* in his commentary on Matthew 5:5. He shows the word is used three different ways in the ancient world.

1. Balance Between Two Extremes

Aristotle, the great Greek philosopher, attempted to define every virtue as the mean or the balance between two extremes. One extreme was excess; the other extreme was defect. For example, in eating, one extreme is gluttony; the other extreme is being too conscientious about what one eats. Aristotle maintained that *meekness* was the perfect balance between excessive anger (being a hothead) and excessive agelessness (never being angry at anything). This same concept is suggested in at least two of the verses on *meekness*. 1 Corinthians 4:21 *"shall I come . . . with a rod or in the spirit of meekness?"* and Titus 3:2 *" . . . to be no brawlers, but gentle, showing all meekness unto all men . . ."*

Moses was the *meekest* man on earth (Numbers 12:3). Yet he demonstrated anger and patience. Jesus Christ certainly is the epitome of *meekness*, yet He drove the money changers from the Temple.

2. Humility

The Greeks contrasted meekness with pride. *Meekness* was never considered a virtue to the Greeks. The Arndt/Gingrich definition of *praus* is *"gentle, humble, considerate, meek . . . unassuming."* Note that the words we observed earlier, which were associated with the word meekness, demonstrate the same thing.

3. Submission

The Greeks used this word to describe an animal who had been domesticated - trained to obey the commands of its master.

Some years ago, I had a dog named Sari. He was capable of doing many things. He would sit when I told him to sit, stay when I told him to stay, and come when I told him to come. I could tell him to go get his bowl for feeding and he would run to where his bowl was, pick it up and bring it to me. He was a domesticated animal who had learned to submit to authority.

This is the principle of authority and submission. When one submits to the authorities over him, he is demonstrating *meekness*.

Cautions about Word Studies

Preaching out of Lexicons or Concordances

Although word studies can yield very rich rewards, one must be careful not to overuse the technique. Occasionally someone with a little knowledge of Greek or Hebrew will develop a sermon based upon the multiple meanings of a Greek or Hebrew word in a lexicon. This becomes equivalent to preaching from a dictionary rather than from the Bible. Tracing all the uses of a particular word in the Bible with the help of a concordance is a useful exercise for finding out the different ways that word can be used. However, that approach should seldom be used to create a sermon outline.

Overusing Etymology

The etymology of a word relates to the history of the word. What are the distinct parts that made it up and how was it used in earlier times. One should be careful about determining the meaning of words purely based upon their etymologies. In other words, you cannot break a word down into its component parts and always come up with its meaning. You usually cannot determine the meaning a word has by looking at how it was used centuries earlier or how the word originated.

For a contemporary example, if one of my students called me a "nice professor," they might intend it as a compliment. But if I were committed to understanding words according to their origins, I could grow very angry. In English, "nice" is a friendly term; but its Latin source means "ignorant" or "foolish." So I might think the person was abusing me when he was actually trying to complement me. We know that English does not work that way, and we should not expect ancient languages to work that way, either.

For a Biblical example, some take the Greek word for "repent," *metanoieo*, and divide it into two parts, of which the second, *noieo*, is related to thinking. Therefore, they say, repent simply means a change of mind. The problem with this interpretation is that the meaning of words is determined by their usage, not by their origins! The New Testament generally uses "repent" not in the Greek sense of "changing one's mind" but in the Hebrew sense of "turning." The Old Testament prophets taught a repentance that was a radical turning of one's life from sin to God's righteousness.

Conclusion

Words are little pictures of information. The more we can understand them, the more we understand the truth that they represent. The serious Bible student must seriously study the words of Scripture if he or she is to rightly divide the word of truth.

Study Questions

1. Summarize five (5) common problems with interpreting Biblical words.
2. Give an example of an English word that comes from two Greek words.
3. Summarize the layman's way of doing a word study?
4. What are the questions one must ask when doing word studies?
5. List some of the blessings associated with word studies.
6. What are the dangers of doing word studies?

Chapter Fifteen

Rule Six
The Rule of Grammar

The smallest unit of communication is the word. However, whenever two words are joined together, that creates the need for grammar. Grammar is the glue that binds together words and phrases and gives them meaning. Just as certainly as God used words to communicate his will, he also used grammar, for without grammar the words would be meaningless.

Grammar is the dress of the truth; it is what adorns and illustrates and amplifies the truth. When you first saw your wife/husband, you probably noticed her/his clothing. The clothing was not the real person as you know, but it helped to communicate to you what the real person was like. Likewise, grammar is the adornment of truth. God himself is the one who chose to reduce His revelation into a written form. Therefore, we should never under-estimate the importance of studying grammar, so we can understand the Word of God. I will summarize the rules of grammar into two simple statements.

Never violate the basic rules of grammar.

Grammar does not deceive. The communicator selected the particular grammatical construction in each communication that best communicated the truth. We acknowledge that we are working with a translation of the original. However, we believe that translation is as accurate as conscientious men can make it. Therefore, we assume the grammar in our English translations accurately reflects the grammar of the original. We should always allow a passage to say what it naturally says based upon the grammar.

Use grammar as your tool to help discover the truth of the Bible.

Every rule of English grammar is designed to help us understand the communication better. Most of us have spent many years studying English grammar. Therefore what we have learned about grammar can be useful in helping us interpret the English Bible. Two techniques are included below that can be used to break apart sentences and see their individual components.

Diagramming

To diagram a sentence means to rearrange the sentence in a chart form that shows the relationship between the different words, phrases and clauses. The first thing you must do in diagramming a sentence is to find the subject and verb. Next you need to find the direct object, the modifiers and the subordinate clauses and phrases. The following is the basic pattern for diagramming:

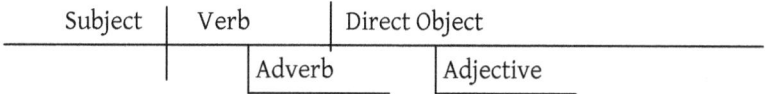

The following is a diagram of John 3:16.

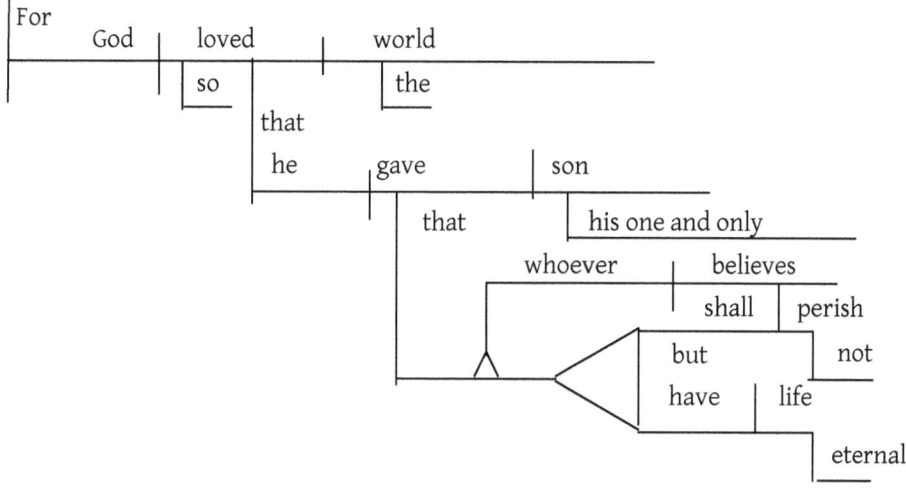

A Mechanical Layout[1]

A mechanical layout is a technique that helps one understand the relationship between the various words and phrases in a sentence. Unlike the diagramming technique, the words in a mechanical layout remain in the same order they occur in the text.

There are two advantages to the mechanical layout. First, the finished product will show at a glance the basic elements of the sentence and their relationship with one another. Second, the process of doing the work forces the person to think and analyze and understand the passage.

---

[1] J. Robertson McQuilkin, *Understanding and Applying the Bible* (Chicago, IL USA: Moody Press), pp. 116 following.

Before one can make any kind of diagram or outline, he or she must understand at least the grammatical make-up of the passage.

The following are the rules for doing a mechanical layout.

1. Place independent clauses on the extreme left margin. This same line should include subject, verb, and direct object.
2. Dependent clauses or modifying phrases are placed on the next line under (and sometimes over) the word they describe.
3. Connecting words (conjunctions) should be placed in front of the words or clauses they modify on the line between the two items being connected except when connecting independent clauses.

The following is a mechanical layout of John 15:1-3.

I am the true vine

and

my Father is the gardener.

He cuts off every branch

        that bears no fruit

    while every branch that does bear fruit

he prunes it

    so that it will be even more fruitful.

You are already clean

 because of the word I have spoken to you.

The following is an example of a mechanical layout of Matthew 6:1-4

Be careful not to do your acts of righteousness

      before men

     to be seen by them

   If you do

Rule of Grammar

you will have no reward

        from your Father

            in heaven.

    So when you give to the needy

do not announce it

    with trumpets

    as the hypocrites do

        in the synagogues

    and

        on the streets

        to be honored

           by men.

I tell you the truth

they have received their reward in full

But

    when you give to the needy,

do not let your left hand know what you right hand is doing

    so that your giving may be in secret.

Then your Father, who sees what is done in secret, will reward you.

Parts of Speech

When studying words, note what part of speech they are. For example, note whether a word is an adjective, adverb, or some other part of speech. Each part of speech has a different function. Knowing the part of speech a word is will help to give insight in interpreting that word.

In 1 Corinthians 11:27 (KJV), Paul uses the word *"unworthily"* to describe the way one should not celebrate the Lord's Supper. The word "unworthily" is an adverb. An adverb modifies the verb. In this case, it is telling the manner in which one was eating. The problem in the Corinthian church was that the church was filled with both the rich and the poor. When the church came together for a love feast—a meal that included the "Lord's Supper"—the rich people were going off in one corner and enjoying their expensive delicacies. The poor, on the other hand, were huddling over in the other corner with little or nothing to eat. The celebration that should have been bringing people together in humility and repentance was actually creating division. Therefore, when Paul tells them not to eat "unworthily" or in an "unworthy manner," he is warning them about the way they were celebrating the Lord's Supper. He did not mean that some were "worthy" of partaking of the Lord's Supper and some were not. In one sense of the word, none of us are worthy of partaking of the Lord's Supper. The point is the manner in which it was being celebrated.

This example should help you understand why it is helpful to go through a passage of scripture and identify the nouns, verbs, pronouns, adjectives, adverbs and other parts of speech. This practice will force you to think about a passage in a grammatical way. And often when we examine a passage this way, we will uncover truths that were hidden before.

Tenses

Tense describes the time of any action. One of the most simple, but rewarding, grammatical exercises is to identify the tenses of the verbs in Biblical sentences. Is the action of the verb something that happened in the past? Is it something that is ongoing right now? If it happened in the past, was it an ongoing activity in the past or was it some action that was completed in the past. All of these distinctions are fairly easy to determine by simply observing the tense of a sentence.

For example, the verbs for sin in 1 John 3:4-9 are all in the present tense, which could be translated *"sinning."* The emphasis on sin in this passage is not on a single isolated incident of sin. It is on the continuous practice of sin that is illustrated by the present tense verbs. In John 3:16, the verb "believes" (*believeth* KJV) is in the present tense, which indicates a continual practice of faith. The one who has eternal life is not the person who has believed sometime in the past, but the one who has believed and continues to believe. In fact, most of the verbs that deal with faith in the New Testament are in the present tense, suggesting a continual practice of faith, not a one-time incident.

There is a very difficult passage in Hebrews 6:4-6 (NIV). The question raised in the passage is whether a person who turns away from God can repent. On the surface, it would appear that it is impossible for such a person to return to God. However, when one examines 6:6 carefully the problem is solved. The verbs "crucifying" and "subjecting" in this passage are in the present tense. This suggests an ongoing habit of sin. What the passage is saying is that it is impossible to renew these people to repentance as long as they continue to crucify the Son of God and subject him to an open shame. However, the implication is that if they stop crucifying the Lord and stop subjecting him to public shame with their actions, there is hope of returning to God. Repentance is more than just saying that one is sorry. Repentance is stopping the sin.

One does not need to be a Greek scholar to be knowledgeable about the Bible. However, nearly all of the upper level Biblical scholars have some understanding of the original languages. Certainly one needs to have a basic understanding of Greek grammar to understand serious commentaries. Even without knowing how to read Greek, there is some basic information that one should know about Greek grammar to help in proper interpretation. This is especially true with Greek verbs.

There is one Greek tense that every serious student of the Bible needs to learn about. This is because there is nothing quite like it in English. It is the aorist tense. To understand the aorist, let us review briefly the other Greek verb tenses and the way they describe action.

Verb tenses that describe action as continuous or linear

1. Imperfect tense: "He was kicking the ball."
2. Present tense: "He is kicking the ball."
3. Future tense: "He will be kicking the ball."

Verb tenses that describe action as completed

The verb indicates a state or condition that has resulted from past action and remains in effect.

1. Perfect tense; "He has kicked the ball." This stresses the result of an action that remains in effect.
2. Pluperfect; "He had kicked the ball." This stresses a previous result of action

Verb tense used to describe an action as a totality, stressing wholeness of action

The aorist tense of the verb focuses attention upon wholeness of action. This is sometimes referred to as "point time" or "punctiliar" action. It looks at the action of the verb as it were completed at a point in time or in a single moment of time. And this is the significance of the aorist tense. The aorist would indicate the action described above as "He kicked the ball."

The significance of tenses are especially obvious when they change in the middle of a sentence. Romans 12:1-2 is a good example. The Romans are urged to present their bodies (aorist tense), which suggests a one-time event, but they are urged to *"be not conformed"* (present tense), which suggests continual nonconformity to the world. A very loose translation of this passage—stressing the significance of the tense of the verbs—would be this:

> *Therefore, I am urging you, brothers, in view of God's mercy to offer your bodies at a moment in time as living sacrifices, holy and pleasing to God—this is your spiritual act of worship. Stop being conformed to the pattern of this world, but be continually being transformed by the continual renewing of your mind . . .*

Promises

The Bible is filled with hundreds of promises. There are several questions one must ask when studying promises. Is the promise given to a specific person or is it a promise for all people? Was the promise restricted to a specific time period or is it a universal promise? From a grammatical point of view, one must ask whether the promise is a conditional promise or an unconditional promise. An example of a conditional promise is John

15:7, which says, *"If you remain in me and my words remain in you, ask whatever you wish, and it will be given you."* That sentence simply means that if the person meets the condition—remaining in Christ and having His words remain in him—he or she can make any request and it will be granted. An example of an unconditional promise is found in Matthew 16:18 where Jesus simply said, *"I will build my church and the gates of Hades will not overcome it."* What Jesus was saying in this passage is that regardless of what any other person does, He is going to make sure that the church is built.

It is important to remember that some promises may be conditional without using the "if" construction. Philippians 4:19 says, *"And my God will meet all your needs according to his glorious riches in Christ Jesus."* However, the preceding few verses suggest that the Philippian church had repeatedly given to the needs of others. There is an implied condition that God will supply our needs if we have been faithful to give to others. Parents do the same thing. We may tell our children that if they pass all of their examinations, we will buy suya for them. All during the preparation for the examination, we will talk about the suya, and we will not necessarily refer to the condition every time we talk about it. Even the verse in John 15:7 contains hidden conditions. The implication is that if one really remains close to Christ, he will only ask those requests that are consistent with the will of God. All the conditions are not stated but they are implied.

Conjunctions

Conjunctions show relationships by joining thoughts together. These may be words, dependent clauses or independent clauses. The following are some of the most important conjunctions:

1. Temporal or chronological: *now, then*
2. Reason or causal: Because, since, whereas
3. Purpose: in order that, so that, that
4. Contrast: Although, but, nevertheless, however, yet, otherwise, whereas
5. Result: so, then, therefore, thus

6. Comparison: also, as, just as ... so, likewise, so also, moreover, than
7. Emphatic: indeed, only
8. Continuative: *and*

Whenever a conjunction is used, one should attempt to understand why it is there. What is the relationship between the two parts of the sentence? What would be changed if a different conjunction were used?

A particular conjunction that is worthy of special note is the word "therefore." This is a word that nearly always introduces application. The word means something like this: "On the basis of what has just been said, here is the application." One person has said, *"If you ever see the word 'therefore,' you need to stop and see what it is there for."*

The first eleven chapters of Romans are fairly theological. Paul begins Romans 12 by saying, *"Therefore, I urge you, brothers, in view of God's mercy, to offer your bodies as living sacrifices ..."* In other words, Paul was saying something like this: "Up to now I have been providing some theological foundation. Now on the basis of what I have just said, this is what you are to do. 1 Corinthians 15 is a similar example. It is a long chapter that teaches the theology of the resurrection. The last verse in the chapter begins, *"Therefore, my dear brothers, stand firm."* Paul wanted the Corinthians to know that the resurrection was not just a theological possibility. It is the foundation of all Christian faith. And on the basis of that, we should be strong and steadfast.

Levels of Authority

Different grammatical constructions have different levels of authority. Therefore, it is always necessary to determine what the level of authority of a particular phrase or sentence has. Note these different levels of authority:

1. **Direct Command.** This is the highest level of authority. It is the most direct way that one can request someone else to do something. Ephesians 6:1 contains a command: *"Children, obey your parents...."*
2. **Exhortation.** An exhortation is a milder way of making a request. The speaker or writer is urging but not commanding the person to do a certain thing. Paul uses an exhortation in Romans 12:1: *"Therefore, I*

Rule of Grammar

> urge you, brothers, in view of God's mercy, to offer your bodies as living sacrifices, holy and pleasing to God—this is your spiritual act of worship."

3. **Wish or prayer.** A wish is not technically a request. However, it is used as the gentlest way of making a request. It does not contain the authority of a command but does express a desire for a certain thing to happen. Most of the prayers and benedictions in the Bible fall into this category. For example, the "grace" is such a grammatical construction. *"May the grace of the Lord Jesus Christ, and the love of God, and the fellowship of the Holy Spirit be with you all."*

4. **Examples.** An example shows one what to do or not to do without expressing an opinion about whether or not it should be done. All of the individuals in Hebrews 11 are examples of faith. The way the believers responded by praying when they heard Peter was in prison is an example of the way we should pray when we hear of some Christian brother who is facing trouble (Acts 12:12).

Paul and Silas' singing in the jail at midnight is an example of how one responds in a crisis (Acts 16:25).

Let me expand a bit more on the authority of an example. As a general rule, we can assume that the way the apostles did things is the way they should be done unless it is stated that they made a mistake. Paul says in 1 Corinthians 11:1 *"Follow my example, as I follow the example of Christ."* He stressed this two more times (Philippians 3:17 and 2 Thessalonians 3:7). It is true that the actions of the apostles are not necessarily inspired like their words are. However, they were apostles and they have a greater degree of authority than we do.

I have always been hesitant to criticize an apostle unless the Bible criticizes him (Galatians 2:11-14). Here is an example that is often debated. In Acts 21:11 Agabus predicted that Paul would be captured in Jerusalem. Some interpreters contend that this was God's warning to Paul not go to Jerusalem. The fact that he went and was captured is a proof that he was out of God's will. However, I seriously doubt if that is the correct interpretation. God was surely warning Paul, but he was doing so to prepare him for what he was about to face. The point is this: It is my conviction that without scriptural authorization, we do not have a right to criticize the apostles' behavior.

There is a grammatical way of looking at this same information. The Greek language has a grammatical construction known as the "mode" that is associated with verbs. The mode of a Greek verb has to do with the reality of the statement. There are four modes in the Greek language for expressing truth. These go from something being grammatically realistic to grammatically remote. The following is an example of these modes.

Indicative Mode. This is the mode of reality. It is the most common mode in Greek and simply describes what is. One might say "You are going to London." This may be an unrealistic statement but from a grammatical point of view, it is the clearest and most realistic way of describing something.

Imperative Mode. This is the mode of command. One might say, "Go to London." Though this is a command, there is some doubt about its fulfillment. Just because one commands something, there is no guarantee that that command will be fulfilled. Therefore, the imperative mode is a step less realistic than the imperative.

Subjunctive Mode. This is the mode of exhortation. One could say, "Let us be going to London," or "I encourage you to go to London." This is even further removed from reality. It is more likely that one would obey a command than obey an exhortation. There is more doubt about its fulfillment.

Optative Mode. This is the mode of a wish or prayer. One could say, "I wish you would go to London." This is the mode furthest removed from reality. It is expressed in a way that is not as definite as an exhortation and even less definite than a command. It is the least authoritative way one can make a request in the Greek language.

I could be sitting at my table eating my dinner. I notice that there is no water on the table. I desire that my daughter should get some water. There are several ways that I could express this.

- "You will bring me a cup of water." That is the indicative. It is a direct statement that is expressed in such a way that it is even more certain that a command.

- "Bring me a cup of water." This is the imperative. It is a direct command. To refuse to obey would constitute rebellion.

Rule of Grammar

- "I encourage you to get me a cup of water." This is the subjunctive. It is a much more gentle request. It is to make a suggestion but not to give a command. To refuse to get the cup of water would not constitute direct disobedience.

- "I wish I had a cup of water." This is the optative that is an expression of a wish. If my daughter really loves me, she will not wait for me to give a command but will go get the water.

Several years ago, I made an observation about the verses that describe the highest possible life of the believer. They are not commands. They are not even exhortations. They are optatives, which means they are found in prayers.

Christianity is a voluntary religion. No one can force anyone to become a Christian. In addition, no one can force any Christian to become a "better Christian." Certainly no one can force a believer to reach the highest levels of Christianity. Therefore, the apostles describe this "higher" level of Christianity in the wishes and prayers. Note these examples:

- 1 Thessalonians 3:12-13: *"May the Lord make your love increase and overflow for each other and for everyone else . . ."*

- 1 Thessalonians 5:23:

    May God himself, the God of peace, sanctify you through and through. May your whole spirit, soul and body, be kept blameless at the coming of our Lord Jesus Christ.

- Ephesians 3:16-19:

    I pray that . . . he may strengthen you with power through his Spirit in your inner being, so that Christ may dwell in your hearts through faith . . . you, being rooted and established in love, may have power, together with all the saints, to grasp how wide and long and high and deep is the love of Christ, and to know this love that surpasses knowledge—that you may be filled to the measure of all the fullness of God.

- 1 Peter 5:10-11:

    And the God of all grace, who called you to his eternal glory in Christ, after you have suffered a little while, will himself restore you and make you strong, firm and steadfast. To him be the power forever and ever. Amen.

These passages challenge all believers to draw close to God not because He commands it but because he wishes it.

Misusing Grammar

Danger of Manipulating Grammar

People can twist Greek the way they can twist English, Hausa, or any other language. When certain groups claim that John 1:1 calls Jesus "a God" because there is no definite article "the" in front of "God" there, they neglect several factors, of which I will briefly summarize two. First, "God" does not always have a definite article in John's Gospel. The God who sent John the Baptist does not have a definite article (John 1:6), but no one ever says he was simply "a god." Second, grammatically "God" is a predicate nominative in *"the Word was God,"* and predicate nominatives usually omit definite articles. Even without moving any further, we can see that the translation 'a God" is based on a lack of knowledge of Greek.

Some misinterpret Greek grammar, claiming that "faith of God" must mean "the God-kind-of-faith." It could mean that, but in context probably means "faith in God." Someone once claimed that Christians would all become Christ, because Jude 14 literally says He would come with "ten-thousands of himself." The person's error was simple—"ten-thousands of him" is the appropriate way to say in Greek, "ten-thousands belonging to him." More often than not, when someone comes up with an interpretation based on Greek or Hebrew that contradicts what one would have thought from reading the rest of the Bible, they may be reading into the Greek or the Hebrew something that is not there. It is helpful to learn Greek and Hebrew for yourself, but if you cannot, sticking with a couple good translations is usually safe.

Danger of Proof Texting

A very common abuse of grammar is widespread in churches of most denominations. We read into the text what we already expect to find there, because of our doctrine or because of how we have heard a story told! We commonly call this "proof texting." We read a text from the

Bible to prove something we already believe. How often have we read a Bible story only to realize that part of the story we always heard is not in that passage? How often have we read our doctrine (maybe even a correct doctrine, supported by other texts) into a text or texts that did not really address the issue?

When this kind of interpretation takes place, Christians from different groups can no longer use the Bible as a common basis for seeking truth. We are all "sure" of our own interpretations, which we sometimes cannot defend from the context! It is important to respect the Bible enough to let it speak for itself. If our doctrine is not in a passage, we do not need to read it in. Our doctrine is probably in some other passage. If not, respect for the Bible's authority may require us to change our doctrine.

In using this practice, we are open to fresh discoveries in the Bible each time we study it. At the same time, this does not mean that we throw away everything we have already learned and start with nothing each day. We build on what we have already learned, and go back and change particular interpretations only as we study the text as honestly as possible and find a need to change. In this way we can also dialogue with other honest Christians around the Scriptures.

Conclusion

Many people do not enjoy studying grammar. However, because it can become a tool for better interpreting the Bible, we must learn it and use it in our study.

Study Questions

1. What are the basic rules of grammar?
2. Give a simple definition of grammar.
3. What is one difference between a diagram and a mechanical layout?
4. Write out John 3:16 and identify which part of speech every word is.
5. Explain how knowing the tense of a verb can assist in interpreting a verse.
6. What is the significance of the aorist tense? Give an example from the Bible.
7. What is the difference between a conditional and unconditional promise?
8. What is the significance of the conjunction "therefore"?
9. To what extent should believers follow the examples of the apostles?
10. What is the optative mode and what does it mean?
11. What are two examples of misusing grammar?
12. Give an example of proof texting.
13. What are some of the advantages to recognizing the use of proof texting and being willing to change that practice?
14. Give a personal example of using grammar to help you better interpret a passage.

Chapter Sixteen

Rule Seven
The Rule of Figurative Language

Introduction

Languages tend to evolve from the simple to the complex. Complex ideas must at least in the early stages use simple language to express various ideas. Figures of speech, word pictures, metaphors and similes are all part of the way languages attempt to define and express complex ideas. Frequently, these figures of speech become so embedded in the language that they lose their figurative aspect and become idioms.[1]

Definitions

An idiom is an expression that does not mean what the literal words actually say. Most idioms are peculiar to one particular language[2] and involve some type of figurative language. However, the figure has become such a real part of the language that it ceases to be a figure and becomes an idiom, a frequently used saying. C. S. Lewis gives this illustration:

When a man says that he grasps an argument, he is using a verb (grasp), which literally means to take something in the hand, but he is certainly not thinking that his mind has hands or that an argument can be seized like a gun. To avoid the word *grasp,* he may change the form of expression and say, 'I see your point,' but he does not mean that a pointed object has

---

[1] Much of the material below comes from the chapter entitled, "Hebrew Idioms" in T. Norton Sterrett, *How to Understand Your Bible* (Downers-Grove, IL USA: InterVarsity Press), pp. 123-130.

[2] Sterrett, p. 123.

appeared in his visual field. He may try again and say, 'I follow you,' but he does not mean that he is walking behind you along a road.[3]

Examples of Idioms

Although English is not the first language in Sub-Saharan Africa, most people in countries where English is spoken, such as Nigeria and Ghana and Kenya, speak English very well. The thing that often surprises me as a non-African is how well Africans use English and American idioms, although sometimes they are used slightly differently than they would be used in the UK or the USA. For example, we often hear in Africa that someone has "kicked the bucket." People just learning English may really struggle with that statement. They know what the word "kick" means and they know what the word "bucket" means. They knew that the person who had "kicked the bucket" had been very seriously sick. They might be tempted to think, "How could this brother, who was so sick, get out of the bed and started kicking a bucket?" However, anyone who speaks English well will realize that the phrase "kick the bucket" is an idiom for death.

American Idioms

In America we have many idioms:

- "It is six of one and a half dozen of the other." That means there is not much different between two things.
- "I am between a rock and a hard place." That means that a person is in a difficult situation in which either decision he makes is bad.
- "Did the cat get your tongue?" That would be said when someone is expected to say something but is remaining silent.
- "Knock your socks off." This means that someone really did something very well.
- "He hit a homerun." This means that someone was very successful.

---

[3] C. S. Lewis, *Miracles* (New York, NY USA: Macmillan, 1947), pp. 88-89; quoted in Robertson McQuilken, *Understanding and Applying the Bible* (Chicago, IL USA: Moody Press, 1992), pp. 166-167.

I have learned quite a few idioms in Africa as well.

African Idioms

I frequently speak at places away from Jos and someone will come up to me and say, "Oga, I want to follow you to Jos." To follow means to come behind. I sometimes tease him and say, "Well, I will be going to Jos in one hour. You can follow me any time after that." However, in Nigerian English, "to follow" means "to go with." In addition, often when a person is leaving to go somewhere, he will turn around and say, "I am coming." In actual fact, he is going, but he says he is coming.

When I first came to Nigeria, I would often go to a church and preach a sermon. Someone would come up to me afterwards and say, "Oga, you really tried-o!" I would give a lecture, and my students would also tell me I had really tried. In American English, "to try," means to make an attempt, which may have not been successful. Usually when one of our students fails an examination, we will call him and tell him he failed the exam but we will conclude the discussion by saying, "But don't worry. You tried. Try harder next time." In other words, he made a good effort even though his effort was not successful. So when people kept telling me that I had tried, I was confused. I was wondering what I would have to do to really preach a good sermon. One day one of my students asked to give a testimony in one of my classes. I gave him permission. He was a businessman who owned a shop in the market. Unfortunately, the market had caught on fire the day before and burned. Though he was not present, the man who owned the shop next to his had broken down the door of his shop and packed all of his things out to safety. As he stood in front of the class and tried to find words to express his thanks to God, he finally said, "You know, God really tried." From that time onwards, I figured if God could try, it was all right for me to try.

Figures of Speech

Should we treat every passage literally? Do we interpret the Bible literally? The correct answer is that we should interpret literal passages literally, and figurative passages figuratively, and poetic passages poetically. It is not always easy to determine which passages should be taken figuratively and which should be taken literally. What did Jesus mean when he said, *"This is my body"*? About one third of the Christian world accepts this statement literally. Others take this statement and other events, such as the resurrection or the second coming of Christ, and say that they are just allegories—that these "events" should be interpreted as figures of speech. When John describes all of the strange figures in the Book of Revelation, was he actually describing real phenomena or were these simply a description of things that for political reasons were better described figuratively rather than literally?

An important guideline that bears repeating is this: One should always seek to find the single meaning of the passage intended by the author. That is the only correct interpretation. For example, when Jesus said, "I am the good shepherd," does this mean that Jesus, instead of taking up Joseph's trade of being a carpenter, had become a shepherd and took care of sheep in the hills? No, Jesus was not literally a shepherd. Jesus' statement obviously meant that he was "like a shepherd." He took care of His people like a shepherd takes care of his flocks. In this case, we do not take the literal interpretation of the passage because the actual meaning intended by Jesus was that he was like a shepherd. The single purpose of Biblical interpretation is to discover the meaning originally intended by the author. If the writer used a figure of speech, we have to look behind the figure of speech to the actual point that the writer was making.

The following are some of standard figures of speech used by practically all languages.[4]

Examples of Common Figures of Speech

A **simile** is a comparison using "like" or "as." Most languages are filled with similes. We say such things as, it is "cold as ice," or "heavy as lead." The psalmist declared (Psalm 103:13), *"As a father has compassion on his children, so the Lord has compassion on those who fear him."* One of the most well-known similes is Psalm 1:3: *"He is like a tree planted by streams of water . . ."* Peter says that the devil comes *"like a roaring lion"* (1 Peter 5:8).

A **metaphor** is a comparison without using like or as. It is an implied comparison. Genesis 49 is full of metaphors. To Judah, Jacob said, *"You are

---

[4] McQuilken, pp. 174-179.

a lion's cub" (49:9). *"Issachar is a rawboned donkey lying between two saddlebags"* (49:14). *"Dan will be a serpent by the roadside"* (49:17). *"Naphtali is a doe set free"* (49:21). *"Joseph is a fruitful vine"* (49:22). *"Benjamin is a ravenous wolf"* (49:27). In the New Testament, John the Baptist called the Pharisees and Sadducees a *"brood of vipers"* (Matthew 3:7). Jesus referred to Herod as a fox. In addition, all of the *"I am"* statements that Jesus gave are metaphors. There are literally hundreds of examples of metaphors and similes in the Bible. These are the two most common figures of speech.

Metonymy is an idea used to refer to an associated idea. It is a cause for an effect or *vice versa*. It is a substitution of one name for another. For example, the writer of the Book of Job uses a very strange construction in Job 34:6. The King James Version translates this *"My arrow is incurable."* Apparently he means that the sores on his body are like wounds from an arrow. Rather than making a comparative statement, he simply uses the word "arrow" as a substitute for his wounds. In the New Testament, Paul says in 2 Corinthians 3:15; *"Even to this day when Moses is read, a veil covers their hearts."* The author is used to refer to the books he has written. Moses is the cause; his writings are the effect. Thus, the effect is referred to by the name of the cause. Hosea 1:2 reads, *"the land is guilty of the vilest adultery . . ."* The land is not actually guilty. It is the people of the land who are guilty.

Hyperbole is a deliberate exaggeration or overstatement for effect. This is a figure of speech that is fairly common to all languages. I might say to my students, "I have told you a thousand times to bring a Bible with you to class." I know that I have not said that a thousand times. My students know that I have not said that a thousand times. We both know that I have deliberately exaggerated to make a point. Hyperbole is very common in the Bible. For example in Judges 7:12 we read, *"The Midianites, the Amalekites and all other eastern peoples had settled in the valley, thick as locusts. Their camels could no more be counted than the sand of the seashore."* It is doubtful if the people were actually as thick as locusts. And it is certain that there were not as many camels as there are grains of sand on the seashore. This is good hyperbole. The following are additional examples of hyperbole:

- 1 Samuel 11:11b: *"Those who survived were scattered, so that no two of them were left together."*

- Psalm 6:6 (KJV): "*All the night make I my bed to swim . . . with my tears.*" (NIV): "*All night long I flood my bed with weeping.*"

- Matthew 19:24: "*Again I tell you, it is easier for a camel to go through the eye of a needle than for a rich man to enter the kingdom of God.*"

- John 21:25: "*If every one of them [the acts of Jesus] were written down, I suppose that even the whole world would not have room for the books that would be written.*"

Personification is attributing human qualities to inanimate objects. Numbers 16:32 declares, "*The earth opened its mouth and swallowed*" Korah and friends. Jesus says in Matthew 6:34, "*Therefore do not worry about tomorrow, for tomorrow will worry about itself.*" The psalmists like personification. Psalm 114:3-4 says, "*The sea looked and fled.*" Psalm 24:7 says, "*Lift up your heads, O you gates; be lifted up, you ancient doors.*"

Synecdoche is using a part for a whole or a whole for a part. It is also the singular used for plural and *vice versa*. Luke 2:1 (KJV) says that "*all the world*" came to be taxed. It is unlikely that people from Africa or India came to be taxed. The people came from the part of the world that Luke was focusing on at that time. Matthew 12:40 says, "*For as Jonah was three days and three nights in the belly of a huge fish, so the Son of Man will be three days and three nights in the heart of the earth.*" The most common understanding of the chronology of Jesus death and resurrection has Jesus dying on Friday and being buried shortly before sundown and then rising from the dead before daylight on Sunday morning. That means that although he was in the grave parts of three days, he was actually there only a little over one day. However, synecdoche is attributing a part for a whole. It is almost certain that is what Jesus did in this statement. When Paul was on his way to Rome, Luke tells us in Acts 27:37 (KJV) that there were "*two hundred threescore and sixteen souls*" on board that ship. These people also had their bodies along with them. The term "soul" is frequently used to refer to the whole man. In Romans 12:1 Paul urges the Romans to present their "*bodies*" as a "*living sacrifice*" to God. I assume that Paul would have also expected the Romans to present their minds, their will, their emotions and every other part of their beings to Christ also. One of the most common examples of synecdoche is the phrase "*blood of Jesus.*" This phrase represents the death of Christ. Wherever the phrase is used, it always refers to Jesus' death.

Apostrophe is when a speaker or writer addresses directly persons or objects that are either absent or imaginary. This figure adds life and drama to the writing. Psalm 68:16 says, *"Why gaze in envy, O rugged mountains?"* Isaiah 54:1 declares, *"Sing, O barren woman, you who never bore a child; burst into song, shout for joy, you who were never in labor."* Ezekiel 37:4 gives this testimony: *"Then he said to me, 'Prophesy to these bones and say to them, "Dry bones, hear the word of the Lord!"'"*[5]

Interrogation (*Rhetorical Question*) is asking a question whose answer is obvious and which is not intended to be answered by the hearer or reader. There are literally hundreds of these in the Bible. Jeremiah 32:27 says, *"I am the Lord, the God of all mankind. Is anything too hard for me?"* Psalm 8:4 asks, *"What is man that you are mindful of him, the son of man that you care for him?"* Jeremiah 23:29 demands, *"'Is not my word like fire,' declares the Lord, 'and like a hammer that breaks a rock in pieces?'"*[6]

Irony is saying the opposite of what one means in order to better get the attention of the hearer or reader. In 2 Samuel 6:20, David's wife speaks after he had danced in the street: *"How the king of Israel has distinguished himself today, disrobing in the sight of the slave girls of his servants as any vulgar fellow would!"* David's wife spoke as if she were complimenting David, but she was really rebuking him with irony. In 1 Kings 22:15, Ahab inquires of the prophet Micaiah who gave the opposite advice from his other advisors; *"When he arrived, the king asked him, 'Micaiah, shall we go to war against Ramoth Gilead, or shall I refrain?' 'Attack and be victorious,' he answered, 'for the Lord will give it into the king's hand.'"* The king obviously detected the irony in his voice because he complained, *"How many times must I make you swear to tell me nothing but the truth in the name of the Lord?"*[7]

---

[5] See additional examples of apostrophe in 2 Samuel 18:33; 1 Kings 13:2; Isaiah 14:12; and Jeremiah 22:29, 47:6.

[6] See other examples of rhetorical questions in Job 21:22; Jeremiah 2:11, 13:23, 30:6; Amos 3:3-4; Obadiah 1:5; Matthew 7:16; and 1 Corinthians 10:22.

[7] See other examples of irony in Numbers 24:11; 1 Kings 18:27; Job 12:2, 38:21; Zechariah 11:13; 1 Corinthians 4:8; and 2 Corinthians 11:19.

Euphemism is substituting a more pleasant expression for a harsh or blunt statement. In Judges 19:22 (KJV), the homosexual crowd demanding that the Levite be brought outside that they may *"know him."* The word "know" is a euphemism for sexual activity. The phrase "fell asleep" is often used as a euphemism for death (Matthew 27:52 (KJV); John 11:11; Acts 7:60, 13:36; 1 Corinthians 11:30, 15:20, 51; 1 Thessalonians 4:13, 14, 15, 5:10).

Litotes is stressing a certain point by denying the opposite. This is commonly done today, especially in greetings. One asks, "How are you doing?" and the person replies, "There is no problem." Psalm 51:17 says *"The sacrifices of God are a broken spirit; a broken and contrite heart, O God, you will not despise."* The phrase *"you will not despise"* actually means that God will accept this kind of sacrifice. In 1 Samuel 26:8, Abishai wanted to kill Saul when he and David had slipped into their camp one night. He says to David, *"Now let me pin him to the ground with one thrust of my spear; I won't strike him twice."* The denial that he would strike him twice was an affirmation that he would only need to strike him once.

Pleonasm is the superfluous or unnecessary use of words. In 2 Samuel 7:22, David said to the Lord, *"we have heard with our own ears."* This is obvious; what other part of the body would one hear with? However, this is stated that way for emphasis. Genesis 37:24 describes the hole in which Joseph was placed: *"Now the cistern was empty; there was no water in it."* If it was empty, there would certainly be no water in it. However, this double statement is given for emphasis. In Deuteronomy 3:27, God instructs Moses shortly before he died, *"Look at the land with your own eyes, since you are not going to cross this Jordan."* It is obvious that Moses would not have been able to see the land with anyone else's eyes or with any other part of his body. That is a good example of pleonasm.

Anthropomorphism is attributing human characteristics to God. God is a spirit and does not have a physical body like human beings. However, the only way we human beings can understand God is to think of Him in the sphere we know—having a body like we have. Therefore, the psalmist says in Psalm 34:15, *"The eyes of the Lord are on the righteous."* Isaiah 52:10

declares, *"The Lord will lay bare his holy arm in the sight of all the nations."* The following is a list of human characteristics attributed to God:[8]

- A face: Exodus 33:23; Psalm 10:11; Jeremiah 21:10 (KJV)
- Eyes: 2 Chronicles 7:16; Psalm 11:4 (KJV); Jeremiah 16:17
- Ear: Psalm 10:17 (KJV); Isaiah 37:17; Daniel 9:18
- Nose: Exodus 15:8; Psalm 18:15; Isaiah 65:5
- Mouth: 1 Kings 8:24; Isaiah 34:16; Micah 4:4 (KJV)
- Voice: Job 40:9; Daniel 9:11, 14(KJV)
- Arm: Deuteronomy 11:2; Isaiah 62:8; Jeremiah 21:5 (KJV)
- Hand: Exodus 33:23; Isaiah 50:2; Jeremiah 1:9
- Back: Exodus 33:23; Isaiah 38:17; Jeremiah 18:17
- Soul and heart: Genesis 6:6; 2 Chronicles 7:16; Psalm 11:5
- Feet: Exodus 24:10; Psalm 77:19; Isaiah 60:13
- Form: Psalm 17:15

Other verses do not particularly mention bodily parts but do mention human actions like sitting and walking, remembering and repenting.

Examples of Hebrew Idioms

An Absolute for Relative

The western world is characterized by great precision in communication. Although people in the West do use hyperbole, as a general rule, they are very careful to speak precisely, and they usually mean exactly what they say. Exaggeration and embellishment tend to be frowned on in the

---

[8] In addition to anthropomorphism, there are examples of zoomorphism, which is attributing to God animal characteristics. Psalm 91:4 says, *"He will cover you with his feathers, and under his wings you will find refuge."*

society. However, the non-western world is much more open to hyperbole, overstatement, and similar kinds of dramatic and impressive speech. People in West Africa are known worldwide for the "West African hyperbole."[9]

Interestingly, the Semitic world, of which the Hebrews are a part, shares many of these same characteristics of communication with Africa. One of the most obvious illustrations is the use of an absolute statement for a relative statement. An absolute statement is independent from relationship to other statements. It is a statement that has no flexibility. It is an absolute declaration. On the other hand, a relative statement has relationship to other things. There is flexibility. For example, if I said, "the car is large," that would be an absolute statement. If I said, "this car is larger than that car," that would be a relative statement. The first statement is an independent statement, but the second contains a comparison of two things that shows their relationship. Hebrews and other Semitic people enjoyed making an absolute statement when they meant only a relative statement.

Example from Joseph

For example, in Genesis 45:8 Joseph said to his brothers, *"It was not you who sent me here, but God."* This is an absolute statement—but not absolutely true! The brothers did have something to do with sending Joseph to Egypt. However, Joseph realized that although his brothers were the immediate cause of his going to Egypt, it was really God who had arranged this whole thing. God's part in getting him to Egypt was far greater than their part. Therefore, he just made an absolute statement. "You did not bring me here. God did." This is a Hebrew way of emphasizing that God was involved in getting Joseph to Egypt. It is not an "untrue" statement but a perfectly legitimate Hebrew idiom.

---

[9] A European lady married to a Nigerian once told me, "When I heard my husband tell about something that had happened to us, I hardly recognized the story. However, his version was much more interesting than mine."

Example from Jeremiah

In Jeremiah 7:22-23, the Lord says,

> *For I did not speak to your fathers, or command them in the day that I brought them out of the land of Egypt, concerning burnt offerings and sacrifices. But this is what I commanded them saying, 'Obey My voice, and I will be your God, and you will be My people; and you will walk in all the way which I command you, that it may be well with you.'*

This statement makes western people uncomfortable, because it is obvious that God did speak to these people about burnt offerings. In fact, a large portion of the Pentateuch relates to burnt offerings. However, Jeremiah was stressing that what God was demanding, even more than the sacrifices, was obedience. A Hebrew way of emphasizing one truth is to negate or deny the opposite or a parallel truth. This is a linguistic issue not an ethical issue.

Example from Jesus

Jesus declared in Luke 14:26, "*If anyone comes to Me, and does not hate his father and mother, his wife and children, his brothers and sisters—yes, even his own life—he cannot be my disciple.*" This is an absolute statement. However, the literal interpretation of it contradicts other plain teachings of Scripture. It means that one should love God more than even the persons in his own family.

Other Biblical Examples

The following are some additional examples of this idiom:

- Exodus 16:8: Moses says to the people of Israel, "*You are not grumbling against us, but against the Lord.*" The Israelites were grumbling against Moses, but the point Moses wanted to stress was that they were grumbling against the Lord.

- Deuteronomy 5:2-3:

    > *The Lord our God made a covenant with us at Horeb. It was not with our fathers that the Lord made this covenant, but with us, with all of us who are alive here today.*

- Psalm 51:16: *"You do not delight in sacrifice, or I would bring it; you do not take pleasure in burnt offerings."*

- 1 Corinthians 1:17: *"For Christ did not send me to baptize, but to preach the gospel."* The Great Commission is pretty clear that baptism was part of the responsibility of those who preached the gospel. However, Paul was emphasizing that preaching the gospel is far more important than baptizing people.

- Philippians 2:4 (KJV): *"Look not every man on his own things, but every man also on the things of others."* The NIV puts this in terms more acceptable to Western English by saying, *"Each of you should look not only to your own interest, but also to the interests of others."* However, the Old KJV actually captures the Hebrew idiom better.

- 1 John 3:18: *"Dear children, let us not love with words or tongue but with actions and in truth."* Is it wrong to say "I love you" to those you love? Obviously not. What John was saying is that is better to express our love with deeds than with words.

Another Example from Jeremiah

Jeremiah is filled with this Semitic tendency to overstate. Jeremiah 44 talks about the Israelites who fled into Egypt to try to get away from the Babylonians. The Lord was not happy with this action and promised judgment on those who fled to Egypt. Note these two sections from the *New Living Translation* Jeremiah 44:7-12:

> *And now the Lord God Almighty, the God of Israel asks you: Why are you destroying yourselves? For not one of you will survive—not a man, woman, or child among you who has come here from Judah, not even the babies in your arms . . . (10) To this very hour you have shown no remorse or reverence. No one has chosen to follow my law and the decrees I gave to you and your ancestors before you. Therefore, the Lord Almighty, the God of Israel, says: I have made up my mind to destroy everyone of you! I will take this remnant of Judah that insisted on coming here to Egypt, and I will consume them. They will fall here in Egypt, killed by war and famine. All will die from the least to the greatest . . ."*

If one reads this passage literally, it is obvious that all of the Israelites will be annihilated in Egypt. Not a single person will be left. However, note what Jeremiah says a few verses later (44:28): *"Only a small number will escape death and return to Judah from Egypt."* This passage modifies the strong statements found earlier in the chapter. If we read this passage with Western eyes, we will be confused. We would think that Jeremiah was contradicting himself. However, in the earlier passage, his statement that everyone was going to be destroyed, was just a Semitic way of saying that there was going to be great destruction. It was not intended to be an absolute statement but a relative statement, even though it is expressed in absolute terms.

Example from Africa

This particular idiom is not unique to Semitic languages. We use it here in Africa. For example, when I lived in Port Harcourt, we lived across the street from a lady named Belinda. She was from Bonny, a village on the Atlantic Ocean. Most of these people are commercial fishermen and they know how to cook fish very well. Belinda was a very good friend of my wife. She knew I liked fish, so occasionally she would cook some fish and bring to us. One day, Belinda brought over a nice pot of "pepper soup" made from fresh fish. She said to me, "Oga, I prepared this just for you. I know you do not like too much pepper, so I did not put any pepper inside." However, when I ate the soup, the tears almost ran out of my eyes because it had so much pepper in it. What she said was "I did not put any pepper inside." However, what she meant was "I did not put as much pepper inside as I would for my own family." That was an absolute statement used to describe a relative fact.

If we do not understand this particular Hebrew idiom, there are going to be parts of the Bible that do not make sense to us. However, once we understand this truth, many things about the Bible will become clearer.

A Relative for an Absolute

This is the exact opposite of the previous idiom. The meaning is absolute but the form is comparative. This idiom is not used nearly as much as the earlier one. However, it is occasionally found. For example, in Luke 11:31-32, we read "... *and now one greater than Solomon is here.... one greater than Jonah is here.*" It is actually Christ who is being compared to these individuals. It is true that Jesus is greater than these other individuals, but He is so far greater, the comparison is weak. The point is that He is great which is an absolute statement.

Here are some other examples: 1 Samuel 15:22, *"Does the Lord delight in burnt offerings and sacrifices as much as in obeying the voice of the Lord?"* Ezra 9:13, *". . . our God, you have punished us less than our sins have deserved and have given us a remnant like this."*[10]

The "Son of" Expression

The expression "son of" (or "daughter of") and similar expressions do not always mean a child of a parent. The expression can mean many things in the Bible. The Hausa language has been influenced a lot by Arabic, which is also a Semitic language. Hausa also uses the "son of" construction in many non-literal ways. For example, the word *dan sanda* literally means "son of a stick." However, it is the word for "policeman." The word *dan kasuwa* literally means "son of the market," but means "trader" or "businessman."

The following is a partial list of the ways this expression is used in the Bible.

- It can refer to an actual son or daughter of someone. This is the normal way the word is used. It is used this way over one thousand times in the Bible.

- It can refer to a descendent, a grandson or later generation. Matthew 1:8 says that Jehoram was the father of Uzziah (Azariah). However, 1 Chronicles 3:11-12 explains that there were three generations between the two. See other examples in 1 Kings 15:3, 1 Chronicles 26:24.

- It can refer to one who has a certain quality. Barnabas is called a *"son of encouragement."* Ephesians 2:3 (KJV) says that we *"were by nature the children of wrath"* (NIV, *"objects of wrath "*).[11]

- It can be used affectionately, to refer to one who is like a son to another even though there is no blood relationship. In 1 Samuel 26:17

---

[10] See also Psalm 118:8-9, Proverbs 21:3, Hebrews 1:4, 3:3, 6:9.

[11] See also Job 41:34, Isaiah 14:12, Matthew 8:12, Luke 10:6, 1 Thessalonians 5:5.

Saul said to David, *"Is that your voice, David my son?"* Paul called Timothy his *"son in the faith."*

- The nation of Israel is called son of God. Jeremiah 31:9 says *"I am Israel's father, and Ephraim is my firstborn son."*

- Citizens are called sons of their respective nations. Lamentations 4:2 says, *"How the precious sons of Zion, once worth their weight in gold, are now considered as pots of clay, the work of a potter's hand!"*[12]

- Jesus is called the *"son of God."* In Luke 1:30-35, this expression may refer to Jesus' birth as a result of the conception of the Holy Spirit. The majority of the references to *"son of God"* refer to the eternal sonship that Jesus had with God the Father.

- Believers are also identified as sons of God. 1 John 3:2 says, "Dear friends, now we are children of God, and what we will be has not yet been made known."[13]

- *"Sons of God"* can refer to the creations of God, such as angels. In Job 1:6, we learned about the *"sons of God"* coming together. These *"sons of God"* even included Satan.

The Adverb "Forever"

The adverb "forever" literally means "unto the ages" and normally means something that continues without end. However, the word can have a more narrow meaning—to "continue without hindrance or interruption during the lifetime or existence of the subject referred to."[14] Exodus 21:6 (KJV) describes the servant who wishes to serve his master the rest of his life. *" . . . his master shall bore his ear through with an awl; and he shall serve him forever."* Actually in this case, he will only serve him the rest of his life.[15]

---

[12] See also Zechariah 9:13 and Lamentations 2:13.

[13] See also Revelation 22:3.

[14] Sterrett, p. 129.

[15] See also Psalm 72:17; 2 Kings 5:27; 2 Chronicles 7:16; Psalm 49:11; Isaiah 32:14-15; Jeremiah 31:35-36.

Observations about Interpreting Hebrew Idioms

The following are some guidelines for interpreting Hebrew idioms.

1. Identify the Idiom.

One should constantly be looking for idioms as he or she studies the Bible. One will not be able to interpret idioms until they have been identified.

2. Always attempt to interpret the passage under consideration literally.

If a statement in the Bible makes good sense and does not violate other teachings of Scripture, then it probably should be interpreted literally. If the literal interpretation of the passage violates other Biblical references or Christian doctrines or common reason, then one should try to see if it is a Hebrew idiom or some other figure of speech.

3. Convert the idiom to normal language.

If the idiom is "I see your point," in literal language it can be expressed, "I understand." The idiom, "I am the vine," can be expressed, "I am like a vine." Whenever one encounters an idiom, he should convert or translate it into normal straightforward language.

4. Be careful about overusing the "Hebrew idiom" phenomenon.

Whereas we must recognize the Hebrew tendency to concretize things that are not absolute, we must be careful about overusing this principle. One could use this explanation to undermine anything he does not like in the Bible. He would say, "Well, the Bible does not really mean that you should never commit adultery. It simply means that your life should mostly be characterized by faithfulness." That obviously is an abuse of the principle.

Example of Hosea

The Book of Hosea is a brilliant example of figurative language. It contains approximately 200 figures of speech in the 14 chapters. The book is rich in similes. The Lord says, *"The Israelites are stubborn, like a stubborn heifer. How then can the LORD pasture them like lambs in a meadow?"*[16] It also contains much metaphorical language. Hosea 2:6 is a typical example: *"Therefore I will block her path with thornbushes; I will wall her in so that she cannot find her way."* In fact, Hosea develops one metaphor as extensively as any in the Bible.

One of the major themes in the book is idolatry. Hosea describes idolatry in a figurative was as adultery. It is interesting that Hosea starts out referring only to adultery and gradually shifts until it is referring only to idolatry. In other words, in the early part of the book, idolatry is referred to in a figurative manner but the further Hosea developed the prophecy, the more he dropped the figure and addressed this issue directly. This is illustrated by the fact that in the first seven chapters of the book, there are 28 references to adultery and 8 references to idolatry. In the last seven chapters, there are only 3 references to adultery and 19 references to idolatry.[17]

Typology

Typology is a study that is almost unique to Christianity. It is at least unique to the religious world. The more I study the Bible, the more questions I have about what we commonly call "typology." I suspect that

---

[16] Other similes are found in 1:10; 2:3; 4:16; 5:12; 5:14; 6:3-5; 6:9; 7:4; 7:6-7; 7:11; 7:16; 8:9; 9:4; 9:10-11; 9:13; 10:4; 10:7; 11:10-11; 12:11; 13:3; 13:7-8; 13:13; 14:5-8.

[17] Many people do not like to write in their Bibles. I am sympathetic with that concern but do have one Bible in which I mark things. There are many ways to mark one's Bible, including color-coding (marking different themes in different colors), circling or underlining figures of speech and other literary techniques.. This provides a visual overview of the themes and literary techniques. For example, in Hosea I color-coded the book in three themes: Sin was marked in red; judgment was gray and God's mercy and blessing were blue. In addition, I circled all figures of speech and underlined key principles. I circled references to adultery and prostitution in red and references to idolatry in orange. In the first part of the book, there are exclusively red circles; in the middle of the book, there are an equal number of red and orange circles and at the end of the book there are only orange circles. This exercise helped me to see this literary technique even before I picked it up from reading.

what we consider to be typology is simply another form of figurative language.[18]

Most of the New Testament writers were so knowledgeable about the Old Testament that they not only wrote about its teachings but they used many of its persons, places and events as symbols or illustrations of truths they were attempting to communicate. Certainly there were specific prophesies about certain things that were to be fulfilled later in the New Testament. In addition, there is little question that God sovereignly created things like the sacrificial system and the law so that they would prepare people for the truths that were to be presented by Christ and his followers. However, whether or not there were specific persons, places and events that were divinely foreshadowed in the Old Testament is still unclear in my mind.

Definition

Because typology is very popular in some circles, there are many definitions of a type. The following are representative of these definitions:

1. Muenscher,

    In the science of theology it (typology) properly signifies the preordained representative relation which certain persons, events and institutions of the Old Testament bear to corresponding person, events and institutions in the New.[19]

---

[18] The original draft of this book had a separate chapter on "typology." However, the two contributors to this book have similar skepticism about the legitimacy of typology. Since it is such an important part of the Biblical study of many people, we did not want to ignore it altogether. However, by reducing this to one and a half pages in the Figurative Language chapter, we are hoping to reduce the emphasis of typology in Bible study.

[19] From Bernard Ramm, *Protestant Biblical Interpretation* (Grand Rapids, MI USA,1970), pp. 208-209.

2. T. Norton Sterrett, "A type can be defined as a divinely purposed, Old Testament foreshadowing of a New Testament spiritual reality."[20]

3. Woolcombe, A type is

> . . . the establishment of historical connections between certain events, persons, or things in the Old Testament, and similar events, persons or things in the New Testament.[21]

The general idea is that the Old Testament lays the foundation for the truths of the New Testament by teaching certain truths through events, persons or other things. The key characteristic of a type is that it was not like other illustrations but something that God purposefully created in an earlier era to prepare for a teaching or practice in a later era.

History of Typology

Typology has been stressed by certain persons or movements during different periods of church history. The Alexandrian school of interpreters from Egypt assigned three meanings to every passage of Scripture: 1) Its literal meaning; 2) Its typical (or allegorical) meaning; 3) Its theological or higher meaning. When it comes to typology, teachers and preachers can be extremely creative and unique. Typology may be good for illustrative purposes. However, we must develop our theology from the plain teachings of the Bible, not the obscure and figurative pictures.

Mark Twain, one of America's most well-known literary figures, said once, "It is not the parts of the Bible that I do not understand that bother me. It is the parts that I do understand." It must be the responsibility of preachers and teachers of the Bible to primarily concentrate on the parts "we do understand."

---

[20] *How to Understand Your Bible* (Downers Grove, IL USA: InterVarsity Press, 1974), p. 107.

[21] A. Berkeley Micklesen, *Interpreting the Bible* (Grand Rapids, IL USA: Eerdmans), pp. 237-238.

Conclusion

If we do not understand the figures of speech and idioms of the Bible, we will not understand the Bible.

Study Questions

1. Define the word "idiom." Give an example from the Bible and from your own language to illustrate an idiom.
2. Give contemporary examples of similes and metaphors.
3. Give an example of a Biblical hyperbole and an example of one from modern English.
4. Give a Biblical example and a modern example of personification.
5. Give a Biblical example and a modern example of euphemism.
6. What are some modern examples of anthropomorphism?
7. Explain the "absolute for a relative" idiom.
8. Give a modern example of an absolute for a relative construction.
9. Give five Biblical examples of the word "son of" not meaning the actual son of a person.
10. Identify as many figures of speech in Hosea as possible.

Chapter Seventeen

Rule Eight
The Rule of Progressive Revelation

Introduction

Many people fail to understand the true nature of the Bible. They view it as if it were all directly dictated by God to the various Bible writers. In addition, many people fail to understand that the Bible is a dynamic book. That means that for the 1500 years it was being written, it was a living document that was recording the events as they were happening and also documenting the beliefs of the Biblical characters as they were developing. The truth of the matter is that the Bible does not present a unified and organized set of doctrines like a systematic theology book would present. The Bible presents those events as they were progressively unfolding and the doctrines as they were progressively developing.

The doctrines in the Bible developed similarly to the way other beliefs develop. For example, it was over 250 years ago that many people in the world first began to speak publicly about the evils of slavery. The early opponents of slavery understood that all human beings were made in the image of God and, therefore, it was wrong for one person to own another person as if he or she were a piece of property. However, over the next two hundred and fifty years, the world's collective conscience continued to develop and understand what later became known as human rights. Not only is it wrong for a person to own another person, it is wrong to discriminate against any person based upon sex, race, color of skin, or national origin.

In this section, we will look at the principle of progressive revelation in the Bible.[1]

There are two important principles that I have observed in Scripture. They tell us about the way that God works in this world. As a general rule, God does not work as we do. His ways are different from our ways. Though there may be one or two exceptions in the Bible, these are certainly general principles.

Principle One: Whenever God works on earth, He always works through human beings.

Whenever God wanted to populate the world, he supernaturally created only one man and one woman. From that time onward, the population of the world was increased through the normal process of men and women bearing and rearing children who in turn would do the same until the earth was filled with people. When God wanted to punish the world but preserve it as well, he selected Noah to do all the work of building the ark and taking care of the animals. If I had been God, I could have punished the world and started over with a new world in five minutes by using purely supernatural means, but God works through human beings.

If you stop and think about it, every miracle performed in the Bible involved some kind of human effort, even though it may have only been a token amount. The greatest miracle in the Old Testament, the crossing of the Red Sea, did not take place until Moses stretched out his staff. The first miracle of Jesus was the turning of the water into wine. That miracle did not take place until the servants had filled the large stone jars with water and taken some of the "water" to the master of the banquet.

---

[1] I am indebted to Mr. James Hatch, one of my professors at Columbia International University, for helping me to observe the principles I present in this section. Although I already had a degree in Biblical education when I went to Columbia, it was Mr. Hatch who really helped to put the Bible together for me. His course in "Progressive Revelation" did more for my understanding of the Bible as a whole than any other single class. Though it has been over thirty years since I took the course, I still clearly remember the charts he wrote on the blackboard and many of the points he made orally.

Somewhere in that process, the miracle took place. Jesus could have instantly created a beautiful golden goblet of wine in front of each person at the wedding, but he did not. He worked through human beings. Jesus' most popular miracle was the feeding of the 5,000. Jesus could have created a beautiful lump of pounded yam and egusi soup instantly in front of each of the 5,000 people. However, that is not the way God worked. First, Jesus required his disciples to do research to see what resources were available. Then after he had blessed the available resources, he had the disciples distribute the food to the people who were present. Afterwards, he had them gather up the fragments. The miracle involved human effort at every level.

A miracle is simply the multiplication of human effort to a supernatural level. Even when God decided to redeem the world from sin, he involved a human being. Jesus himself became a man in order to save us, because that is the way God works.

This is the point: Whenever God works on this earth, he always works through human beings. If what I have said is correct, we can expect certain implications in the way we do things, but we will explore that later.

Principle Two: Whenever God works on the earth, He normally works the hard way, the slow way, the difficult way, the progressive way, the way that is opposite of the way man would do things.

One would think that since God is all powerful, he would do things in the fastest, most efficient manner possible. However, when we observe God's works in the Bible, we notice almost the opposite. It seems God takes delight in working the slow and difficult way. His projects often take a similar pattern. God starts with a very small project. It slowly and painfully grows. It has to overcome many difficulties until finally it accomplishes its goal.

Let us return to the illustrations mentioned earlier. If I were God and possessed all power, and I wanted to fill the world with people, I could have figured out a quicker way than God did. I would have just instantly created millions of people around the world at one time and the job would have been complete. If I wanted to destroy the world and preserve a remnant, I would have just picked up my remnant in my omnipotent hand, wiped the world clean, and set the remnant down. The job would have been finished in a few seconds. However, God's ways are not our ways, which means he does not do things the way we think he should.

On the basis of what I have said before, I suggest this major premise: **The Bible is a progressive unfolding of what God is doing and saying.**

Though we will review this in more detail at the end, note the preliminary implications of these premises:

- The earlier references to any given subject in the Bible will usually be found in a seed form.

- Later references will grow out of the early truths, and the doctrine will slowly develop.

The kingdom of God, which Jesus talks so much about in the Gospels, is obviously a typical project of God. The way God is building the kingdom is representative of the way he does other things.

Note these two parables:

> He told them another parable: "The kingdom of heaven is like a mustard seed, which a man took and planted in his field. Though it is the smallest of all your seeds, yet when it grows, it is the largest of garden plants and becomes a tree, so that the birds of the air come and perch in its branches," (Matthew 13:31-32)

Matthew 13:33 adds, "He told them still another parable: 'The kingdom of heaven is like yeast that a woman took and mixed into a large amount of flour until it worked all through the dough.'" These two parables illustrate the slow growth nature of the kingdom of God. In addition, they give another practical demonstration of the way God does all of his projects on this earth.

Illustration of God's Progressive Work

The Giving of the Seed

God spoke to Abram in Genesis 12:1 and told him to leave his homeland and go to a land he would show him. God then made this promise: (Genesis 12:2-3)

> *I will make you into a great nation and I will bless you; I will make your name great and you will be a blessing. I will bless those who bless you, and whoever curses you I will curse; and all peoples on the earth will be blessed through you.*

God made several specific promises to Abraham at this time. However, they can probably be summarized in two specific statements:

- God will make a great nation out of Abram.
- God will make Abram a blessing to all the peoples of the earth.

These promises that the Lord made are like a seed—a very tiny seed in which God outlines in a very simple way what he is going to do through Abraham. In fact, this statement contains in seed form everything else God is going to do in the Bible, because the Bible is a progressive unfolding of the expansion of these promises. It is like a seed growing into a mighty tree.

The Planting of the Seed

God promised to Abraham that he would make a great nation out of him. So that we will know when God has fulfilled that promise, we need to note the characteristics of a nation. In order to have a nation, there must be at least four components:

- People
- Law
- Land
- Leader

How did God go about building a nation? He selected the people who would accomplish this objective, Abraham and Sarah. In fact, he selected old people. Sarah was far beyond the age of bearing children. God started with a difficult situation. (Have your ever noticed how often God selected an old woman or a barren woman or a virgin to bear a special child?) When Abraham died, was there a nation? No, there was only one son by Sarah, and another son, who proved to be troublesome, from a slave woman. Sarah's son, Isaac, had two sons, but there was still no nation. Jacob had twelve sons but, though this did provide a framework for a nation, it was still a long way from being a nation. At the end of Genesis, there was still nothing like the nation that God had promised to build. There were only about seventy people who were living in a foreign land as virtual slaves to their Egyptian masters. However, seventy people are much better than nothing. We see a small amount of progress.

Exodus 1:6-7 says,

> Now Joseph and all his brothers and all that generation died, but the Israelites were fruitful and multiplied greatly and became exceedingly numerous, so that the land was filled with them.

It is estimated that two to three million eventually left Egypt to go back to Canaan. According to these verses, there is remarkable progress. There is now a large enough group of people to make up a nation. There are several nations of the world today with fewer people than three million. In the early part of Exodus, is there a nation yet? No, the promise to build the nation has not yet been fulfilled but there is progress.

Sinai

After the Israelites had been delivered from Egypt and were in the desert, God gives to Moses something else that is essential to a nation. Starting in Exodus 20:1-17, we read about the giving of the Law, which not only includes the Ten Commandments but a large portion of Leviticus and Deuteronomy. The Law is absolutely essential to forming a successful nation. However, having a law does not necessarily make a nation. At the end of the Pentateuch, though there has been a lot of progress, God's promise to make a great nation out of Abraham has still not been fulfilled.

Joshua

Joshua is able to lead the people successfully in to the land of Canaan. The Book of Joshua tells about the successful battles to drive the majority of the Canaanites from the land. A major step forward is taken at this time. Now the people of Israel are occupying their land. Could it now be said that God's promise to Abraham is fulfilled?

Judges

The answer to that question lies in the book of Judges. The book of Judges tells about a series of cycles.

- Step 1: Things are going well.
- Step 2: The people rebel against God.
- Step 3: God judges the people by raising up a foreign oppressor.
- Step 4: The people repent and call on God.
- Step 5: God raises up a "judge" or military leader who throws off the yoke of bondage of the foreign leader.
- Step 6: This returns things to normal once again.

Key to understanding the book of Judges is the fact that the judges were not really national leaders but regional leaders. The apostasy and repentance and deliverance did not really affect all twelve of the tribes at one time. The last section of the Book of Judges tells some of the most sordid and awful tales to be found in the history of Israel.

The first story tells about a Levite who became the personal priest of a family of pagans. Later the Danites came along, stole the gods, and persuaded this Levite to become their priest. The second story tells about a mad homosexual crowd who raped a man's concubine until she was dead. This made such a stir in the land that several of the tribes went together and almost destroyed the tribe of Benjamin.

Throughout this last section of the book, there is a reoccurring theme. It is found in one form or another four times in the last five chapters of the book (Judges 17:6; 18:1; 19:1) and, in fact, the book concludes with the refrain, *"In those days Israel had no king; everyone did as he saw fit"* (Judges 21:25). This reoccurring theme and the message of the whole book of Judges tells us that there was something missing in the nation of Israel. There was no national leader. The judges had been regional leaders. For about four hundred years, there has been twelve tribes acting independently of each other, or at least, only in conjunction with their closest neighbors.

Ruth

On the surface, one would wonder why this little book is included in the Scriptures. It is a very simple story. It simply tells about a man and woman who fall in love, get married and have a baby. What is so amazing about that? The last two verses give us a little hint (Ruth 4:21-22), *"Salmon the father of Boaz, Boaz the father of Obed, Obed the father of Jesse, and Jesse the father of David."* The Book of Judges shows us how important a good leader is, and the Book of Ruth shows God's sovereign preparation for that leader.

1 Samuel

There is more progress made in 1 Samuel. The early chapters of this book tell about the birth of a small boy. 1 Samuel 4:1a gives us a hint about the real significance of Samuel's life: *"And Samuel's word came to all Israel."* Samuel was the first national leader since Joshua. The judges had been only regional leaders, but Samuel was truly a national leader. He was not the king God was preparing for his people. But he was the person to bring the people together to prepare the way for the king God had selected for them.

Eventually Samuel anointed Saul to be the king over Israel. When that happened, Israel had finally achieved the status of an independent functioning nation. It had been almost a thousand years since God had promised Abram that he was going to make a great nation out of him. God kept his promise, but he did so in a very slow and painful and progressive manner.

2 Samuel, Kings, Chronicles

Eventually Saul fell away and David came to the throne. From the evidence in the Bible, it seems that David was the kind of king God had wanted the Israelites to have all along. He was a man after God's own heart. He was a man whom God could work through. David's son, Solomon, though he also had some personal problems, greatly expanded the kingdom of Israel. It is safe to say that the kingdom God had promised to Abraham, reached its peak of development under David and Solomon.

The Destruction of the Nation

Although God faithfully fulfilled his promise to Abraham to build a great nation out of him, the nation had serious problems because of its rebellion against God. The first problem came when the nation broke apart and became two nations. Though this was not part of the original seed statement to Abram, it was a part of the ongoing revelation. When the nations began to apostatize, God allowed them to slowly degenerate and eventually self-destruct. Ultimately both nations went into captivity because of their rebellion against God. A remnant of the Israelites came back to Israel. Though they enjoyed some good days after their return, they never really enjoyed the blessings and glory of the former days. Consequently, what we see in the latter kingdom period is "negative progress." If progress is an indication of God's blessing and work then "negative progress" is also a sign of God's work but a work of judgment and punishment rather than blessing.

By the time Jesus came along, the nation of Israel had basically been reduced to a people who were subservient to a powerful Roman government. They had lost their national independence and were maintaining their identity by clinging to memories. God is a God of progress. He always wants to move us forward. However, whenever we sin and rebel against God, God cannot allow progress and, in fact, we go backward.

Illustration of the Church

The Seed

God's promise to Abraham also stated that his seed would be a blessing to all the nations of the earth. That promise could never be fulfilled in the Old Testament period. Israel was basically an exclusivistic people who wanted little or nothing to do with Gentiles. However, the New Testament opens with the birth of another son of Abraham. He was given the name Jesus. He grew up to become a great blessing to the people of Palestine. However, he was not a typical Jew. We see several hints of his openness to non-Jews.

Instead of going over and walking on the east side of the Jordan River when traveling from Galilee to Jerusalem, Jesus took his disciples directly through Samaria, a small country that was hated by the Jews. We also see Jesus going to the Decapolis on the east side of the Sea of Galilee. We see him going up to the northern part of Palestine, to the Syro-Phoenician area. He was not afraid to be around Gentiles.

Throughout his ministry Jesus dropped hints that his kingdom would spread to all parts of the globe. For example, early in his ministry, after observing the faith of the Roman centurion, Jesus said, *"I say to you that many will come from the east and the west, and will take their places at the feast with Abraham, Isaac and Jacob in the kingdom of heaven"* (Matthew 8:11). The hint turns to a full-blown command as Jesus prepares to leave his disciples for the last time: *"Therefore go and make disciples of all nations, baptizing them in the name of the Father and of the Son and of the Holy Spirit,"* (Matthew 28:19). It was the blessings provided by Jesus that fulfilled God's promise to Abraham to make him a blessing to all people of the earth.

During the three years of Jesus' public ministry, he laid a very solid foundation for Abraham's seed to be a blessing to all the people of the earth. He healed the bodies of people, demonstrating that God's kingdom is a holistic kingdom. He taught people about peace and love, demonstrating that God's kingdom would be a diverse but a peaceful and compassionate kingdom. The most important thing that Jesus did was to become the sacrifice that would provide forgiveness to human beings and make it possible for them to be reconciled to God. The Lord also prepared his disciples to spread his new kingdom all over the earth.

The Church

In Matthew 16:18, we see another important seed statement made by Jesus: *"And I tell you that you are Peter, and on this rock I will build my church, and the gates of Hades will not overcome it."* In this simple statement, Jesus made a promise reminiscent of the promise that God had made to Abraham. In fact, this seed promise was a further outgrowth of the original promise to make Abraham a blessing to all the peoples of the earth.

The Book of Acts is a progressive unfolding of Jesus' promise to build his church. It is another illustration of the two important principles:

God works through men. Although the Holy Spirit did come upon the disciples in a very powerful way, nevertheless it was human beings who began spreading the word of God to the Jews, the Samaritans and the uttermost parts of the earth.

God also works the hard way, the slow way, the progressive way. We like to stress the fact that there were three thousand people who were converted on the Day of Pentecost. That was really wonderful. However, if you added three thousand people to the kingdom of God every day, you would never fill the world with the gospel of Christ. The early church actually grew slowly and progressively.

The Book of Acts shows many obstacles and problems that the young church had to overcome:

- The problem of prejudice against Gentiles
- The problem of interpersonal conflict
- The problem of persecution
- The problem of natural disasters
- The problem of doctrinal controversy

However, through very difficult means, the church slowly and gradually grew and expanded. Since the close of the Book of Acts, the church has continued to grow. It has expanded from the seed form and is filling the whole world like the yeast in the lump of dough.

What we have seen in this brief overview of Biblical history is that the Bible is a progressive unfolding of what God is doing on this earth. He started the redemption process with Abraham. And we have seen slow and steady progress ever since. However, the premise we stated at the beginning is that the "Bible is a progressive unfolding of what God is doing **and saying**." What we have seen so far is only the progressive unfolding of what God is doing. We will now see that just as certainly as God works progressively, he speaks progressively also. He reveals his will in slow and difficult and painful ways.

Illustration of God's Progressive Speaking

Just as certainly as God has been working in this world in a progressive manner, we believe that God is also speaking progressively. By that I mean that God reveals truth a little bit at a time. He gives us small nuggets of truth and then gradually expands our knowledge by releasing more and more knowledge to us. There are six major periods of revelation in the Bible.

Revelation to the Patriarchs

Although God revealed some basic facts to us prior to Genesis 12, God's real revelation of what he is doing on this earth began when God called Abraham and promised to make a great nation from him and make his seed a blessing to all the peoples of the earth. In addition to this first encounter with the Lord, the Lord spoke to Abraham at least six more times. In each of these meetings, the Lord expanded Abraham's understanding a little more about what God was going to do:

1. Genesis 12:1: The Lord speaks to Abram at the great tree of Moreh at Shechem and tells him that all of that land will belong to his descendants.
2. Genesis 13:14-17: The Lord speaks to Abram after Lot has left him and reconfirms that all the land he can see, including that which Lot has occupied will belong to his descendants.

Rule of Progressive Revelation

3. Genesis 15:1-21: The Lord promises Abram that his descendants will be from his own loins because he will have a son. In addition, God establishes a blood covenant with Abram in this section. The Lord further explained that the land he is giving Abram's descendants is from the land of Egypt to the Euphrates River.

4. Genesis 17:1-21: When Abram is 99 years old, the Lord appears to confirm his covenant. The Lord changes his name to Abraham. The Lord also tells Abraham that the sign of the covenant will be circumcision. He gives more information about the land that is being given to his descendants and promises a son through Sarah. It will be through this son of Sarah that the covenant will be fulfilled.

5. Genesis 18:1-33: The Lord appears to Abraham near the great trees of Mamre in the form of three men who come to visit Abraham at his tent. It is at this time that Sarah received the promise that she is to give birth to a son. The Lord also tells Abraham at this time about the destruction of Sodom.

6. Genesis 22:1-18: The Lord speaks to Abraham and requires him to offer his son at Moriah. This is the great test of Abraham's faith, a test he passes very well. After Abraham passes the test, the Lord reiterates his promise to bless his descendants and to make him a blessing to all the peoples of the earth.

It is very clear from the way the Lord spoke to Abraham that he reveals truth slowly—by giving a little bit at a time. The Lord also spoke to the other patriarchs in the same way.

1. Genesis 26:2-5: The Lord speaks to Isaac and tells him not to leave the land. Because Abraham has been faithful, the Lord is going to make the descendants of Isaac as numerous as the stars of the heavens.

2. Genesis 26:24: The Lord appears to Isaac in Beersheba and reconfirms he is going to increase his descendants.

3. Genesis 28:12-15: The Lord speaks to Jacob in a dream and reiterates the promise He has made to Abraham—that his children will be expanded and that they will be a blessing to all the peoples on the earth.

4. Genesis 31:3: The Lord speaks to Jacob while he is working for his father-in-law and tells him to go back the land of his fathers.

5. Genesis 31:10-11: The angel of the Lord speaks to Jacob in a dream and shows him how the Lord has controlled the mating of his livestock in such a way to increase his herds. He also tells him it is time to leave that land and go back to the land of his fathers.
6. Genesis 32:22-29: The Lord appears to Jacob and wrestles with him until he confesses his name.
7. Genesis 37:5-9: The Lord speaks to Joseph in a dream and gives him hints that he will be the brother who will rule over the others.
8. Genesis 46:2: The Lord speaks to Israel (Jacob) and encourages him to go down to Egypt where his son Joseph is.

God regularly spoke to the patriarchs. His main message was that God had given them a land and would make a great nation out of them and that this great nation would someday be a blessing to all of the peoples of the earth. This message was given in only seed form when Abraham first received it, but it had considerably expanded by the end of Genesis.

Revelation to Moses

God had given to the patriarchs a brief sketch of the nation that he was going to build. However, the information about that nation took a giant leap forward with the second major period of revelation in the Bible—the revelations that God gave to Moses, which eventually were encapsulated in the Law. This revelation that Moses received on Mount Sinai gave specific details about the structure of the nation God was going to make with the descendants of Abraham. It described laws related to worshipping God, laws related to getting along with one another, laws related to the land, laws related to foreigners—all of these instructions were given in the law. So by the time Moses died, the knowledge about these people and this nation God had promised to build was considerably expanded.

Revelation through David and Solomon

The third major period of revelation was after the nation had been established—when it was at its peak of health and development. During this pinnacle of success, there was something the people had learned that

God felt needed to be communicated to future generations. David and his colleagues had truly learned how to worship and praise God. Therefore, God chose a new method of speaking to his people. He inspired David and others to put into music and poetry important truths about worship, prayer, and praise. Though the psalms are in a different format than any of the earlier revelations, they expand our understanding of how God expects His people to worship and praise and pray to Him.

God had also revealed a lot of practical wisdom to Solomon and other wise men. He inspired them to reduce this wisdom into proverbs and other wisdom literature. This wisdom also gives us expanded insights into the ideal world that God expects the descendants of Abraham to develop.

Though this is a bit oversimplified the psalms are primarily vertical in their focus. They tell us how we can know God and interact with him. The proverbs and other wisdom literature are primarily horizontal in their focus. They tell us how we can interact successfully with our fellow human beings. The psalms and proverbs and other poetic literature from the time of David and Solomon continue to expand the truths that God wanted his people to know about his kingdom and about what he expects of us human beings.

Revelation through the Prophets

The kingdom reached its peak of development and expansion during the reigns of David and Solomon. From that time, the people and their leaders gradually began to rebel against God. As a result of their rebellion, the progress stalled. However, even in the midst of negative progress, the Lord continued to progressively expand his revelation through the prophets. The prophets contain two main messages:

- *A message of judgment.* Nearly all of the prophets warn of impending judgment upon Israel and Judah and their neighbors because of their sin of rebellion and neglect of God.
- *A message of hope.* Nearly all of the prophets have some kind of optimistic message in them as well. Although judgment was certain to come, the judgment would have a silver lining.

The prophets continue to expand our understanding of God by showing us his righteous side. He will not tolerate sin. The message of the prophets is nearly always wrapped up in the prophet. The prophet was usually a rather stern, uncompromising spokesman for God. This is what one would expect in a message of judgment.

Revelation through Jesus Christ

After 400 "silent years," God once again clearly spoke to the world. God had a very important message he wanted to communicate to the world through the teachings and ministry of Jesus Christ. We have already looked briefly at what God was doing through the ministry of Jesus. The next question is, "What was the message of Christ?" Does it continue to expand on what God has revealed in the Old Testament period?

The answer is an unqualified yes. Jesus taught many truths and they all expanded what the world knew about God and His expectations of the world. What was the message of Jesus?

It was a re-interpretation of the Law. Several times in the Sermon on the Mount, Jesus said, *"You have heard that it was said . . . but I tell you . . ."* It appears here that Jesus was not so much contradicting the teachings of the Law as giving their original meaning or the truth before it had become adulterated by the many interpretations of the rabbis.

It was an expanded understanding of the kingdom. The kingdom was not a kingdom with armies and boundaries. The kingdom was an internal kingdom not an external kingdom. The kingdom somehow included Israel but went beyond to include the Gentiles.

It was a message of personal spiritual salvation. Prior to Jesus, the concept of salvation was primarily one of delivering one from danger, and its primary application was national and not personal. Beginning with John the Baptist the importance of personal repentance and salvation began to be emphasized. Jesus picked up this same theme and explained that personal salvation involved being *"born again."*

It was a message of love and forgiveness. Jesus expanded our understanding about such things as anger and retaliation. He taught us to love our enemies and release them from the consequences of their wrong actions against us.

It was a message of faith. Even with Abraham, we see the importance of faith. However, when the Roman centurion demonstrated his great example, he received the highest compliment from Jesus. Jesus emphasized the need for faith even more than the earlier revelations.

It was a message of commitment, righteousness and personal holiness. Although righteousness was demanded in the Old Testament, Jesus raised the level of righteousness to a new level—it had to be internal righteousness. One had to be careful even of his thoughts. In the Old Testament, the stress on national salvation left the impression that to be blessed of God meant financial prosperity and material blessings. Jesus corrected that by warning about the evils of wealth and stressing the importance of self-denial and commitment.

It is interesting to note the method that God chose to communicate these truths. Jesus taught in a warm, friendly personal way, and he often taught them using stories.

Revelation from the Epistles

One of the greatest contributions of the early church was the writing of the Epistles that now make up a large portion of the New Testament. After Jesus ascended to heaven and the church had been planted, God saw that it was necessary for the young church to receive some additional information. Therefore, the Holy Spirit inspired the apostles and their close associates to write letters explaining the things that Christians needed to know.

The Epistles are the final revelation that God has given to us, apart from the Book of Revelation, which is basically a teaser about the future. The Epistles make the application of Jesus' teachings to the then contemporary church. The writers of the Epistles understood all of the revelations that had been given before and wrote as a commentary and final application of all these. Therefore, we must interpret everything in the Bible in the light of the truth that is shed on them by the Epistles.

One additional point: It is amazing how uniquely the method of the epistles fits the message. The epistles are warm and friendly and personal. They are letters that were written calmly and carefully—not quite like the bombastic declarations of the prophets or the thunderings of Sinai.

Summary

Remember, the Bible is a progressive unfolding of what God is doing and saying. There is a key verse that helps to see all that we have said in this section in a glance. Jesus said shortly before he ascended back to heaven (John 20:21b): *"As the Father has sent me, I am sending you."* The first part of the sentence is a summary of the Old Testament. The Old Testament tells about all the preparation that went into sending Jesus to this earth. The second part of the sentence tells about the New Testament and particularly Acts and the Epistles. Jesus is sending his disciples into the world to spread the good news about God's new kingdom on the earth. In fact, these verses tell us about Jesus sending us all into the world.

Implications of the Principle

Observations

1. *Early references to certain truths are likely to contain basic kernels of truth.* We have already illustrated this sufficiently. One danger to interpreters is the failure to recognize this, which means that we often give the same weight to these kernels of truth that we do to the fully mature fruit.

2. *Later references to these truths/doctrines will add to the truth already there.* This truth has also been illustrated. A key method of Bible study is to trace a certain doctrine as it progressively unfolds throughout the Scripture. Most doctrines can be studied this way, including topics like sin, the Holy Spirit, the family, life after death and so forth.

3. *The latest revelation (chronologically) is most likely to be the most complete and therefore the most authoritative.* The Epistles are the final word for Christians. The Gospels give us the life of Christ, but the Epistles interpret that life to us. If you want to know about a certain doctrine, go to the place where it is most fully discussed, which is usually in the Epistles.

A friend once said to me, "After hearing you preach, I take it that you like the Apostle Paul." I replied, "That is certainly true because Paul gives us the final revelation and basically interprets everything else that has gone on before him." Paul certainly understood God's original words to Abraham, as well as the Law, the Psalms and the Prophets. He knew the teachings of Jesus and, now, under the inspiration of the Holy Spirit, interpreted all of that for us in his Epistles.

If a passage is not discussed in the Epistles, then you can assume that God thought sufficient information had already been given elsewhere and that it did not need repetition there. For example, there is really not a lot of new information given about worship in the Epistles. God had already given ample teaching on that subject in the psalms.

Illustration of the Constitution and Supreme Court of the USA

When the Europeans had been in America for several generations, they eventually rebelled against England and established a new nation. One of the first things that they did was to write and approve a constitution. That constitution is a rather short document. It could be included on four or five typewritten pages. In that constitution were all the rights and privileges and laws for American citizens in seed form. However, it soon became obvious that the Constitution was not sufficient to meet the many needs of a diverse country like America. Therefore, other laws were added, which all grew out of the constitution. Eventually some of these laws were challenged as being in violation of the Constitution, so they were sent to the Supreme Court, which interpreted and explained the Constitution. After over two hundred years of history, there is an incredible amount of new information and interpretations that have been developed by the Supreme Court. Although the Constitution is still the foundation stone upon which all American laws are made, these laws have to conform to the latest interpretation of the Supreme Court.

For example, the Declaration of Independence, which became the foundational document to the United States Constitution, declared that "all men are created equal and are endowed by their Creator with certain inalienable rights and among these rights are life, liberty and the pursuit of happiness." However, in the 1850's a man named John Emerson died, leaving a slave named Dred Scott. Scott sued the widow for his freedom since he had at one time lived in the state of Missouri, which prohibited slavery. This lawsuit eventually came to the Supreme Court which ruled that Dred Scott had no right to bring a lawsuit since he was not a citizen of the USA. This was a great setback for slaves and former slaves.

Later, after slavery was abolished, the Supreme Court ruled in a case known as *Plessy vs. Ferguson* that a Louisiana law creating separate but equal laws for blacks and whites was constitutional. Technically, this was to ensure that everyone was treated equally, but in fact, it legally created a group of second-class citizens. However, in 1954, the Supreme Court reversed itself and ruled in a decision known as *Brown vs. Board of Education of Topeka* that legal segregation of public schools was unconstitutional. This forced all the states that had "separate but equal" laws to change them because of the latest interpretation of the constitution.

Genesis 3:15 and God's promises to Abraham serve as something of the Constitution of the kingdom of God. However, the Epistles of Paul are the final and authoritative supreme court rulings. They interpret the original constitution, the earlier rulings in the Scripture and the current situation and apply all of this directly to the Christian.

Key Questions

What about the Old Testament?

If what I have said is true, what should be the attitude of the Christian toward the Old Testament? If the revelation is progressive, how much of the Old Testament should we believe and obey? First, we should believe it all. All of its history is correct; its teachings are totally infallible for the nation of Israel, and the other people of that day. The Old Testament is the inspired word of God and is profitable to all believers (see 2 Timothy 3:16-17). Note the *"Scripture"* referred to in that passages is strictly the Old Testament. Some parts of the Old Testament no longer apply directly to the New Testament Christian because they were written exclusively for believers who were serving God in a theocracy. Galatians 3:15-29 tells us that the Law was in effect until the "seed" came. The seed is Christ so that means that we are no longer under the authority of the law as those people were. The law of Christ has superseded the law of Moses.

What about the "moral law of God"?

The "ceremonial," the "civil," and the "moral" laws of God are all distinctions that we Christians make. There was never any distinction made in these laws during the Old Testament period. When God said that the law was annulled, he meant exactly that; all of the law was annulled. However, God did not annul his basic moral principles that are embodied in the "moral" part of the Old Testament. Most of these were repeated in the New Testament. Even if they were not repeated in the New Testament, God's moral laws are for all of us for all time. It was just as wrong to lie or murder or commit adultery before the giving of the Law at Sinai as after Christ. These are all the basic laws of God that do no change.

A parallel situation is the relationship that Nigeria has with the colonial laws. I frequently ask my students, "How many of the laws of the colonial government are we presently under?" The answers vary. Some say we are under none of them and some say we are under many of them. Actually both statements are truth. Technically, we are under none of the colonial laws. All of those old colonial laws were annulled when Nigeria became an independent nation. However, there is much overlap between the laws of the colonial government and the current government of Nigeria. It was against the law to steal under the colonial government. It is against the law to steal today. In a similar way, though we are freed from any legal obligation to obey the Old Testament law, most of the law reflected in the Old Testament is upheld in the New Testament. However, we are grateful that many things like the sacrificial system have been rendered null and void by the sacrifice of Christ.

Are we freed from the Ten Commandments?

In a legal sense we are freed from all of the laws of the Mosaic Law, because we are not under that legal system. However, in a moral sense, we are not free from the Ten Commandments, because these commandments reflect the moral law of God.

In certain parts of the United States there are rules known as the "blue laws." They forbid certain things like drinking alcohol on Sunday. Let us say that I lived in Effingham County, Georgia and that county had a law forbidding drinking alcohol on Sunday. Tomorrow the law is changed to allow drinking alcohol on Sunday. Therefore next Sunday I could legally go buy a bottle of whisky in Effingham County. However, the changing of that law would not affect my lifestyle, because I live under a personal commitment to avoid drinking alcohol. My personal law related to alcohol is a higher law than the laws of Effingham County. In a similar way, the standard for the Christian is higher than the standard for the Old Testament believer. When Jesus came, he gave us more information and more knowledge means greater responsibility.

Is everything in the Psalms applicable to Christians today?

The psalms are hymns of worship for the Old Testament saint. In many ways the New Testament Christian worships like the Old Testament person. He prays; he gives thanks; and confesses sin. As a general rule, the worship of a particular people takes upon itself something of the culture of a given people and the matters of prayer and praise are distinctive to a particular society. There are definitely issues in the psalms that are not appropriate for the New Testament believer. In Psalm 149:6-9, the psalmist prays that the praise of God might be in our hearts and a double-edged sword in our hands to *"inflict vengeance on the nations."* We are no longer serving God in a theocracy, which has the responsibility of punishing evil. We pray for our political and governmental leaders to do justice, but that is not the direct responsibility of the Church. Although Christians have created their own pilgrim's board to visit Jerusalem and take advantage of the same benefits from the Nigerian Government that the Muslims receive in order to visit Mecca, there are no "holy places" for the New Testament believer as there were for the Old Testament believer. A misunderstanding of this led to the Crusades in the Middle Ages.

Psalm 147:12-13 says, *"Extol the Lord, O Jerusalem; praise your God, O Zion, for he strengthens the bars of your gates and blesses your people within you."* A similar psalm, Psalm 137, is almost exclusively about Jerusalem. This would be an appropriate psalm for a Jew to sing but not really for a Christian. At least we cannot apply it like it was written to be applied. In fact, this psalm also rejoices when the enemies of Babylon dash their infants against stones. Sometimes Christians spiritualize this type of psalms by interpreting "Zion" to refer to heaven. However, this is a misinterpretation of the real meaning of these psalms.

The point is this: The psalms are inspired in the sense that they are an accurate reflection of the methods and messages of worship under the nation of Israel. They are very valuable because they show us how the Old Testament person worshipped. And, to the point that the means and words of our worship overlap with theirs, they are to be used by us in our worship. However, not all of them apply as directly to the New Testament Christian, as they did to the Old Testament saint.

Conclusion

It is my conviction that unless we understand something about the progressive unfolding of the word of God, we will not understand the Bible. Remember, the Bible is a progressive unfolding of all that God is doing and saying. That unfolding includes the record of what God said to a nation and it also includes the unfolding of what God said to the church. There are things that apply to both the nation and the church, but there are also things that apply exclusively to one. The careful Bible student must be able to separate the two.

Study Questions

1. Explain the two foundational principles related to understanding the way God works on this earth.
2. Give some scriptures that illustrate the slow progressive way that God operates on this earth.
3. What were the two main things that God promised to do for Abraham?
4. What are the four essential ingredients to making a nation and when did the Lord complete each one of them in building the nation of Israel?
5. How does the story of Ruth contribute to the progressive unfolding message in the Old Testament?
6. What does the downfall of Israel teach about progress?
7. What is the seed that relates to the planting of the church?
8. Give the six major periods of revelation in the Bible and show how each period builds on and is related to the others.
9. What are the implications of the doctrine of progressive revelation?
10. What is the correct attitude of the New Testament Christian toward the Old Testament?

Chapter Eighteen

Symbolism in the Bible

Introduction

I was born and reared in the small rural village of Rigolette in the American state of Louisiana. The earliest words that I heard spoken were English with a deep-south American accent. The first words that I spoke were English. As I grew up, whenever someone wanted to communicate with me, he or she spoke to me in English. If someone wanted me to come he would say, "Come 'ere." If my mother wanted me to get some water she would say, "Go get some water." In my village, as in all villages, the primary means of communicating was by the use of words.

However, words were not the only means of communicating in my village. Whenever my mother did not want me to do something, all she had to do was to shake her head from side to side. Without any words being spoken, she had communicated. Whenever I was talking too much or too loud, she would simply raise her forefinger to her lips. In my culture that meant that I should be quiet. Whenever someone passed by our house in his vehicle and the noise from the engine was so loud that we could not hear the greetings, we would simply lift our hands and wave and everyone would interpret that as a greeting even though no words had been spoken.

There were still other ways of communicating in my village. When someone bought or sold a piece of property, a certain person would come out and measure the property with a big tape measure. He would then take an iron stake and drive it deep in the ground. Everyone who later saw the iron stake knew that this was the corner of the property. There were no signs that said that. It was simply understood.

I suspect in African cultures there are other unwritten and unspoken means of communication. For example, when a person plants his farm, he may put a certain combination of leaves and old rags near it. Everyone recognizes this as a symbol representing a curse upon anyone who would disturb that property. There are neither words nor even any physical actions of the body but still there is communication through symbols.

A more modern illustration can be seen at a traffic signal. When the light is green, all the vehicles facing the light proceed through the intersection. However, when the light turns red, everyone stops. Even an illiterate driver knows that while driving, the color green means to go and the red means to stop. This also is communication through symbols.

God's Primary Means of Communication—Words

Of all the ways God could have chosen to communicate with humanity, most of the time he chose to speak to us in words. The very first communication God made with Adam and Eve was in words. He said, *"Be fruitful and increase in number; fill the earth and subdue it"* (Genesis 1:28). God later spoke to them and said, *"You are free to eat from any tree in the garden; but you must not eat from the tree of the knowledge of good and evil, for when you eat of it you will surely die"* (Genesis 2:16-17). After Adam and Eve had sinned, God said, *"Where are you? . . . Have you eaten from the tree that I commanded you not to eat from?"* (Genesis 3:9, 11).

From this time onward in human history, God communicated to the human race primarily in direct words. God spoke to Abraham and said that he was going to make a great nation out of him (Genesis 12:2). God spoke directly to Moses and gave him the Law that was written down for later generations to be able to read and understand. Sometimes God spoke indirectly to individuals. God rebuked David for his sin with Bathsheba through words given to the prophet Nathan. Many of the latter kings of Israel and Judah received messages indirectly through the prophets.

When John the Baptist came, he announced the coming of the Messiah through words, *"Repent, for the kingdom of heaven is near. This is he who was spoken of through the prophet Isaiah . . ."* (Matthew 3:2-3). Nearly all of Jesus' communications to humanity were in simple straight forward words. On the Day of Pentecost when Peter wanted to explain the miracle of the outpouring of the Holy Spirit, he explained it very clearly in plain simple words. When God wanted to communicate to the first Christians in the early church, God inspired the apostles to write letters to these new Christians and these letters were all written in simple straight forward words.

Symbolism in the Bible

God's Secondary Means of Communication—Symbols

However, in addition to using words, God also used symbols to communicate. Sometimes symbols communicate better than words. There are thousands of different languages in the world. Certain symbols cut across these language barriers when words cannot do it. At times I have met people who did not speak a single word that I could understand. However, we shook hands with one another and smiled at one another and, thus, communicated with one another through symbolic acts.

One of the first possible symbols in the Bible was the fruit that God told Adam and Eve they were not to eat. Was there anything particularly poisonous or odorous about the fruit? Probably not. However, the fruit was a symbol. It was a symbol of something that was forbidden to the human race. It would become a part of the test of humanity to determine whether they would obey or disobey. In this instance, though God did not explain the symbol, He did give in plain words what was also taught elsewhere in symbolic words.

Perhaps another early symbol was what God did after the first couple had sinned. Prior to that time Adam and Eve were naked and felt no shame. However, by partaking of the fruit, their eyes were opened and they felt ashamed. To cover their nakedness, God killed an animal and used the skins to cover their nakedness. Theologians throughout all ages have seen this as involving more than just a means of making garments. It was a symbolic act showing Adam and Eve the seriousness of their sin. Because of their sin, an innocent animal had to die. The Bible was to later say in plain words, *"The wages of sin is death,"* but Adam saw this same truth illustrated in a symbolic way when God killed the animal to make clothes for them.

Old Testament Symbols

With the giving of the Law, the creation of the sacrificial system and the institution of the priesthood, God used many more symbols. The priests were to dress a certain way. The tabernacle was to be continually lit by a lamp stand with places for seven small lamps to burn at one time. There was to be bread placed on an altar daily and incense was to be continually burning. At certain times, animals were to be sacrificed and their blood was to be sprinkled on various objects. Buildings and furniture were all built in a certain way because these things had symbolic meaning. Sometimes the meanings were explained. More often they were not. Because their particular culture had developed symbolic meaning for these objects, it was not always necessary to explain the symbolism.

The nature of a symbol is that it is always illustrating or pointing toward something else. The real meaning of the green light on the traffic light is to "go." There is no particular significance to the shape of the light or the fact that the light is green as opposed to being blue. It is simply universally understood among those who drive vehicles that the meaning of green is go. The symbols of oil and incense and lamps and sacrifices and garments in the Old Testament were all symbols of things which later became reality in the New Testament period. Once Jesus came and died and rose again and poured out the Holy Spirit upon the human race, the symbols were no longer important. They were superseded by a better communication. This would be like a policeman standing at an intersection where there is a traffic light. A policeman standing at an intersection supersedes the symbolic communication of a traffic light.

This is much like what we do when we prepare for a big convention. A committee meets and decides upon a theme and an advertising strategy. Advertisements are printed and posted all over the city. Announcements are prepared and played on the radio and TV. Special letters of invitation are prepared and sent to the pastors in the city. All of this is part of the preparation which goes into the upcoming convention. However, once the convention has arrived and certainly after it is over, there is no need to play the announcements on the radio again. Those advertisements which have been placed on various walls and utility poles are soon forgotten. No one talks about the advertisements for the convention. They talk about the convention itself. The pictures and posters, which symbolized the upcoming crusade, have now been replaced by the memory of the event itself.

New Testament Symbols

With the coming of the New Testament, the need for symbols in religion was drastically reduced. In fact, God only ordained two ongoing symbols. The first is the Christian rite of baptism and the second is the celebration

Symbolism in the Bible 255

of the Lord's Supper. The first is a once-for-all act which is done when a person becomes a believer. Paul himself explains the significance of the symbol in Romans 6:3-4. The second Christian symbol is the celebration of the Lord's Supper. This is an ongoing symbolic act, one that is to be repeated over and over again. Jesus himself gave the meaning of the Lord's Supper when he originally instituted it (Matthew 26:26-30). Paul also later reemphasized what Jesus had taught (1 Corinthians 11:23-26). The bread represented the broken body of Jesus and the wine represented his blood. Together these two elements symbolized the death of Christ, which is the very heart of Christianity. Jesus instituted a symbolic ceremony, which would be celebrated regularly so that even illiterate people would be reminded regularly of the heart of the gospel.

Cultural Symbols in the Bible

Baptism and the Lord's Supper are the only two truly Christian symbols in the New Testament. However, the Bible also recognizes other cultural symbols. For example, long and short hair were recognized as having symbolic meaning in the ancient Greek culture. Paul mentioned this in 1 Corinthians 11 where he talked about the appropriate authority structure. Long hair on women was considered a sign of submission to her husband, and short hair was considered a sign of rebellion and often associated with prostitutes. Because these were important cultural symbols in those days, Paul encouraged men to have short hair and women to have long hair because of their symbolic meaning. Once again, the real significance of the passage was not the symbol. The real significance of the passage is the fact that the man should not embarrass his master, who is Jesus, and the woman should not embarrass her husband by wearing her hair in a culturally offensive way.

Five times in the New Testament, the Bible writers declare, *"Greet one another with a holy kiss"* (Romans 16:16, 1 Corinthians 16:20, 2 Corinthians 13:12, 1 Thessalonians 5:26, 1 Peter 5:14). This is a direct command in the Bible, and yet seldom, if ever, has anyone come up to me and greeted me with a holy kiss. We here in Africa rightly recognize that a kiss was a symbolic greeting much like shaking hands is a greeting in African culture. Once again, the symbol is not what is important. What Paul and Peter were really saying is that we should greet one another appropriately. In the Semitic culture, the appropriate way to greet was to kiss one another. In South America, the culturally appropriate greeting is a big hug. Here in Africa we certainly know how to greet one another, but we use different symbolic acts than the Semitic people did. It would be culturally offensive to kiss another person in public.

Misuse of Symbolism

The second of the Ten Commandments says, *"You shall not make for yourself an idol in the form of anything in heaven above or on the earth beneath or in the waters below"* (Exodus 20:4). What is an idol? Webster's Seventh New Collegiate Dictionary says an idol is "a representation or symbol of a deity used as an object of worship." Basically an idol is a physical object, which symbolizes or reminds the worshipper of the real god he is worshipping. After God had warned that the Israelites were to have no other gods before them, he warned about the abuse of religious symbolism. He did not want his followers to try to reduce God to any kind of symbol. He wanted his followers to focus their attention upon him alone.

When Moses came down from the mountain and found that Aaron had built a golden calf, it was the second commandment that was being violated. Aaron was not saying that some other god represented by this golden calf had delivered Israel from Egypt. He was saying that Jehovah, the God who delivered them out of Egypt was represented by this golden calf. His argument to Moses was that he had created this golden calf because the people were demanding some symbol of worship. This they had learned in Egypt. It would be better to give them a symbolic representation of the true and living God than for them to turn and worship the gods around them. This made Moses very angry because he saw it as a violation of the second commandment and a means of the enemy to deviate the people from the true worship of Jehovah.

The danger is no less today. Because the old religions had symbols, or because some of the other religions have physical symbols, many modern Christians and some Christian leaders are crying for symbols as well. As certainly as this was sinful and wrong in the days of Moses, it is likely sinful and wrong today. Putting forward symbols instead of the truth is a perversion of the truth and becomes "truth idolatry."

Observations about Symbols in the Bible

1. Symbols are tools of communicating truth just like words are. However, they are less precise and of less value than words.
2. The real significance of the symbol is the truth it is communicating.
3. A symbol has no more value than the truth it is communicating. If one does not understand the truth behind the symbol, the symbol is worthless or even dangerous.
4. Certain Old Testament symbols have little significance today because the truth they were illustrating has been made much more clear through direct revelation.
5. The Christian symbolic acts of baptism and the Lord's Supper have ongoing value and must be continued.
6. Certain cultural symbols in the Bible days may have limited application today because of a different understanding of that cultural symbol.
7. The importance of all symbols is on the truth they are communicating and not upon the physical acts or substance of the symbols.
8. The misuse of symbols is a very serious sin in the eyes of God Almighty and must be rejected. It is basically the sin of idolatry.

Conclusion

Words can be used to bless and to curse. Words can be used to communicate health and healing, and words can also be used to deceive, manipulate and steal. Therefore, there is a right and wrong use of words. The same can be said of symbols. God used many symbols in the Bible. The proper use of symbols can help people understand certain concepts even better, or in a different way, than words. However, the abuse of symbolism was a serious offense to God. To focus on the symbol rather than the reality represented by the symbol is the sin of idolatry.

Study Questions

1. List some of the ways that we communicate through symbols.
2. What were some of the ways that God communicated to Adam and Eve through symbols?
3. What was the primary purpose of symbols in the Old Testament?
4. What are the New Testament symbols? What do they represent?
5. What is the danger in misusing symbols?
6. Summarize in five sentences the correct use of symbols for Christians.

Chapter Nineteen

Biblical Genres

Although we have surveyed and illustrated many of the most important *general* rules for interpretation, we must now note that some interpretation skills depend on the kinds of writing in the Bible one is studying. For example, Revelation is prophetic and apocalyptic literature, which means it is full of symbols. If interpreters today debate how literal some of Revelation's images are, no one doubts that much of Revelation such as the prostitute and the bride, are each symbols representing something other than what they would mean literally (Babylon and New Jerusalem versus two literal women).

The Psalms are poetry, and also often employ graphic images. Poetry involved a certain amount of poetic license. For example, when Job claims that his steps were *"bathed in butter"* (Job 29:6), he means that he was prosperous, not that his hallways were packed with butter up to his ankles. One could provide hundreds of similar example. Those who deny the use of symbolism in some parts of the Bible, especially poetic portions, have simply not read the Bible very thoroughly.

On the other hand, narratives are not full of symbols. One should not read the story of David and Goliath and think, "What does Goliath stand for? What do the smooth stones stand for?" These accounts were written as literal historical stories. We seek to learn morals from these accounts the same way we would seek to learn them from the testimonies of others today. The difference between biblical experiences and modern experiences is that the biblical ones more often come with clues to the proper interpretation from God's perfect perspective. We may apply what we learn from Goliath to other challenges that we face, but Goliath does not "symbolize" those challenges. He is simply one example of a challenge.

Even our most important rule, context, functions differently for different kinds of writings. Most proverbs, for instance, are not recorded in any noteworthy sequence providing a flow of thought. They are isolated, general sayings, and were simply collected (Proverbs 25:1). This is not to suppose, however, that we lack a larger context in which to read specific proverbs. By reading these proverbs in light of the entire collection of proverbs, and especially in light of other proverbs addressing the same topic, we have a general context available for most individual proverbs.

Scholars use the term "genre" for the different kinds of literature found in the Bible. Poetry, prophecy, history and wisdom sayings are some of the genres represented in the Bible. Genre is not a word that is unique to hermeneutics. Examples of different kinds of genres exist in our written documents today. And we approach each of those genres differently. For example, one would interpret fiction differently than he would a newspaper. One would take a written note telling about a bomb threat much more seriously that he would a child's poem about butterflies.

We will now survey some of the most common "genres" in the Bible and some important interpretation principles for each.

Study Questions

1. Give an example of a Biblical statement that we do not take literally.
2. Take a Biblical story and draw legitimate principles from it.
3. Write out a definition of "genre."
4. List all the forms of genre found in the Bible that you can think of.

Chapter Twenty

Interpreting Narrative

Narrative is the most common genre in the Bible. Narrative simply means a "story." This may be a true story like history or biography, which would include most of the Bible's narratives, or a story meant to communicate truth by fictional analogy, like a parable. All stories are placed in the Bible for a purpose. Most of them are designed to provide the necessary historical framework to understand God's revelation to humankind. Some stories were added to the Bible to teach some kind of lesson. All stories were added to the Bible for a purpose. All stories, like all other parts of Scripture, are inspired by God and profitable to us (2 Timothy 3:16-17).

Guidelines for Understanding Narrative

The following are some guidelines for interpreting stories.

Avoid Allegory.

The first principle related to understanding the narratives in the Bible is actually a warning: Do **not** allegorize the story. That is, do not turn Biblical stories into a series of symbols as if the events in the story did not happen. If we turn a narrative into symbols, we are tempted to interpret the narrative to say whatever we want. When we read a text in this way, we read into it what we already think—which means that different people could read the same narrative and come up with opposite interpretations!

Examples of Allegory

For example, when David prepared to fight Goliath, he gathered five smooth stones. One allegorist might claim that David's five stones represent love, joy, peace, longsuffering, gentleness, and goodness. Another might claim that he picked five stones to represent five particular spiritual gifts; or perhaps five pieces of spiritual armor listed by Paul in the New Testament.

Such interpretations are unhelpful. First, they are unhelpful because there is no objective way for everyone to find the same point in the text. Second, they are unhelpful because it is really the allegorist and his views, rather than the text itself, which supplies the meaning. Third, it is unhelpful because it obscures the real point of the text. Why did David pick smooth stones? They were easier to aim. Why did he pick five instead of one? He selected five in case he missed the first time. The lesson we learn from this example is that faith is not presumption: David knew God would use him to kill Goliath, but he did not know if he would kill him with the first stone.

History of Allegory

Where did allegory come from? Some Greek philosophers grew embarrassed about the myths of their gods committing adultery, robbery, and murder, so they turned the myths into a series of symbols rather than taking them as true teachings about their gods.

Some Jewish philosophers, trying to defend the Bible against accusations by Greeks, explained away uncomfortable portions of the Bible by taking them as mere symbols. Thus, instead of allowing that biblical heroes like Noah had weaknesses, a Jewish philosopher might claim that he did not actually get drunk with wine, but rather was spiritually drunk on the wonderful knowledge of God.

Christian scholars from Alexandria, whose schools were controlled by Greek philosophical thought, often practiced allegory, though some other church leaders like John Chrysostom preferred the literal meaning. Gnostics like Valentinus mixed some Christian ideas with pagan philosophy. They often used the allegorical method to justify blurring the distinction between Christianity and other thought systems. Many later Christian thinkers borrowed the allegorical method, which became quite common in Europe in the Middle Ages.[1]

---

[1] On Gnostic use of allegory, see e.g., Stephen M. Miller, "Malcontents for Christ," *Christian History* 51 (1996): 32-34, p. 32; Carl A. Volz, "The Genius of Chrysostom's Preaching," *Christian History* 44 (1994): 24-26, p. 24. For the Alexandrian school (perhaps a little too favorably), see Robert M. Grant with David Tracy, *A Short*

Motivation for Allegory

Many people practice allegory because they want to discover some hidden meaning in every word or phrase of Scripture. The problem with this approach is that it defies the way Scripture was actually given to us, hence disrespects rather than respects Scripture. The level of meaning is often the story as a whole, and individual words and phrases normally contribute to that larger contextual meaning. To read into the story meaning that is not there is in essence to attempt to *add* to Scripture, as if it were inadequate by itself.

Allegory in Numbers

Allegorical attempts to find a deeper meaning behind the actual words of Scripture takes on many forms. In recent years some have looked for numerical patterns in the words of Scripture, but these ignore the hundreds of "textual variants," mostly spelling differences, among different ancient copies of the Bible. The numbers three (Trinity), seven (days of creation) twelve (tribes of Israel; disciples; foundations of New Jerusalem) and multiples of twelve like 144 are often viewed as having special significance. The problem is that there is no place in the Bible where the significance of these numbers is given. The attempts at seeing significance in numbers is harmless speculation at best and counterproductive misinterpretation at worse because they focus attention away from the main point of the text.

Read the Story as a Whole.

Sometimes we cannot draw a correct moral from a story because we have picked too narrow a text.

Story of David and Abishag

I had a friend once who doubted the usefulness of the passage where Abishag lies in bed with David to keep him warm. What moral would we

---

History of the Interpretation of the Bible, 2d ed. (Philadelphia: Fortress, 1984), 52-62; on the Antiochenes like Chrysostom, see *ibid.,* pp. 63-72.

draw from such a story? We would be wrong if we supposed that the moral was that young people should lie with older people to keep them warm. True as it might be that we should look out for the health of our leaders, that is also not the moral. Nor is the moral that live humans work better than blankets. Some might wish to extract a lesson that contradicts other moral teachings in the Bible. But all these interpretations miss the point, because the writer did not intend us to read one paragraph of the story and then stop. We should read the entire story, and in the flow of the entire story, this paragraph identifies that David is dying and prepares us for why Solomon must later execute his treacherous brother Adonijah. It helps us understand the rest of the story, and the point comes from the larger story, not always all of its individual parts.

Whole Book Reading

How much do we need to read to get the whole picture? As a general rule, the more context you read, the better. We need not spend much time here, because this is the principle of whole book context we illustrated at length above. We should pause merely to point out that the literary unit is sometimes longer than what appears as a book in our Bibles. Because it was difficult to get a very long document on a single scroll, longer works were often divided into smaller "books." Thus 1 Samuel through 2 Kings represents one continuous story (with smaller parts); 1 and 2 Chronicles represents another story. Although our Bibles place John between them, Luke and Acts together comprise a single, united work and should be read together.

Stories within Stories

There is also a sense in which larger stories may contain smaller ones. For example, many of the stories in Mark can be read on their own as self-contained units with their own morals. Some scholars have argued that the early church used those stories as units for preaching the way they used many Old Testament readings. But while this observation is true, modern scholars recognize that we should also recognize these smaller stories in their larger context to get the most out of them.

One can follow the development of and suspense in Mark's "plot" and trace the themes of the Gospel from start to finish. This prevents us from drawing the wrong applications. For instance, we might read Mark 1:45

and assume that if we are sent from God and fulfill God's mission like Jesus did, we will be popular with the masses. But if we read the whole Gospel, we see that the crowds later clamor for Jesus' execution (Mark 15:11-15). The moral is not that obedience to God always leads to popularity. The moral is that we cannot trust popularity to last, for the crowds are often easily swayed. Jesus thus focused on making disciples more than drawing crowds (Mark 4:9-20).

Narratives and History

Following the influence of the Western Enlightenment, many western scholars grew skeptical of miracles and thus skeptical of biblical accounts as history. Discovery after discovery from the ancient world has challenged this skepticism, new trends have begun to challenge old Enlightenment views, and today most scholars, whether Christian or not, focus more on the *meaning* of the text than its relation to history.

But the early church did expect Christian leaders to be able to respond to objections raised against the faith (2 Timothy 2:25-26; Titus 1:9), so we will briefly introduce some of these issues here. Because some of my scholarly work published so far is in Gospels, I can best illustrate the methods with respect to the Gospels (whose historical reliability I affirm).

If an honest skeptic had no evidence for or against the reliability of the Gospels, should that skeptic accept or doubt the Gospels? A growing consensus of scholars is arguing that the Gospels are ancient biographies. This means that at the very least they are historically reliable. They fit all the characteristics of ancient biographies and not the characteristics of other genres; thus even a skeptic should regard them as at least generally reliable.

Some nineteenth-century scholars asking historical questions noted that some parts of the Bible overlapped, such as Kings and Chronicles or Mark and Matthew. Thus they developed a method called "source history," trying to reconstruct what sources biblical writers of history used. Clearly, if they depended on earlier sources, they did not simply make things up from their imaginations. Many passages in the Bible mention their sources (Numbers 21:14; Joshua 10:13; 2 Samuel 1:18; 1 Kings 14:19; 1 Chronicle 29:29; 2 Chronicles 27:7); 1 and 2 Chronicles cite a "Book of Kings" ten times (nine of them from 2 Chronicles 16 on). Although the

Gospel writers write closer to the time of the events they describe, when many sources probably reported similar events, hence they do not need to name their sources, they do make it clear that many were available (Luke 1:1). Although there remains some debate, most scholars recognize that the synoptic writers borrowed from one another and from other sources.

Beyond such a basic consensus, however, source history provided few widely accepted views. Early twentieth-century "scissors-and-paste" approaches (where skeptics chopped up Scripture to their liking) are now almost universally rejected, weakening the value of those commentaries that followed it. We also know that ancient Mediterranean storytellers drew on a wide variety of sources, including oral traditions, so we cannot always identify which report derives from which source.

Some other scholars advanced a method called "form history"; Jesus' teaching and works were reported in several different literary forms. Some of these distinct forms (such as parables) are clear, but traditional form-historians speculated too much about which forms were used by the church in particular ways, and most of their early speculations have been refuted by later scholars.

Scholars then moved to redaction history (editorial history). If Matthew used Mark as a source (or vice versa), why does Matthew edit or adapt Mark the ways that he does? Ancient biographers had complete freedom to rearrange sources and put them in their own words. A simple comparison of Matthew, Mark and Luke will indicate that they do not always follow the same sequence or use the same wording to describe events. When we find consistent patterns in Matthew's editing, we may learn about Matthew's emphases and hence what he wanted to communicate to his first audience. Some early redaction historians were too confident of their abilities to understand why some changes were made. Later scholars have recognized that some changes were purely stylistic or for space constraints!

While there is some value in each of the above approaches, modern scholars have turned especially in two directions. The first is various forms of literary criticism, a basic component of which is usually reading each book as a whole unit to understand its meaning. The second is the social history approach, which focuses on what we have called "background." Nearly all biblical scholars today, across the entire range

Interpreting Narrative

from "conservative" to "liberal," accept the validity of both these approaches.

Study Questions

1. Give a one sentences description of narrative.
2. Explain the danger of allegorizing the Bible.
3. Summarize an example of an allegorical sermon you have heard.
4. Define and illustrate "source history."
5. Define and illustrate "form history."
6. Define and illustration "redaction history."

Chapter Twenty-One

Interpreting Law

Biblical laws have much to teach us about justice, even if we need to take into account the culture and era of history they addressed. Thus God informs Israel that no other nation has such righteous laws as they do (Deuteronomy 4:8) and the psalmist celebrates and meditates continually on God's law (Psalm 119:97).

Transcultural Laws

Some laws, like the Ten Commandments, are stated largely as transcultural principles. It is also difficult to find genuine parallels to them in other ancient Near Eastern legal collections. Most laws, however, addressed ancient Israel as civil laws for how Israel's society should work. These were addressed specifically within an ancient Near Eastern framework, and we need to think carefully when we look for appropriate analogies in how to apply them today.

Ancient Near Eastern law set the tone for which issues had to be addressed. Actually, Israel's laws addressed many of the same issues as Mesopotamian law. The Code of Hammurabi and other legal collections addressed: ear-boring (Exodus 21:6); debt-slavery (21:7); the treatment of enslaved captives (21:9); causing a miscarriage (21:22); eye for an eye and tooth for a tooth (21:23-25); negligence regarding an ox (21:28-36); bride price (22:16-17); local responsibility for bloodguilt there (Deuteronomy 21:9-10); and similar issues.

Variations in Legal Systems

At the same time, there were significant differences between the Near Eastern legal tradition and Israel's laws. In other societies, one received a harsher penalty if one belonged to a lower social class. Israel's law distinctively eliminates that injustice. Whereas in Babylonian law the punishment for a man who caused the death of another's daughter would have been his own daughter executed, in Israelite law the man who did the killing would die. We do not know of other societies that protected ancestral lands the way Israel's laws did (Leviticus 25:24). This law prevented a monopolistic accumulation of capital that would make some people wealthy at others' expense. Some offenses have more lenient penalties in Israelite law (thieves who break in during the day are executed under Babylonian law) and some have harsher penalties (Israelite law was harsher toward disobedient children). Babylonian law mandated the death penalty for those who harbored escaped slaves. God's law commanded Israel to harbor escaped slaves (Deuteronomy 23:15).

Israelite Laws not the "Ideal" Form of Justice

The laws in the Old Testament, while improving the standards of their culture, do not always provide us with God's *ideal* of justice. In any culture, civil laws provide a minimum standard to enable people to work together efficiently, but do not address all moral issues. For instance, a law may say, *"Do not kill"* but only God can enforce the fullest implications of that law for moral standards (i.e., *"You shall not want to kill."* Matthew 5:21-26).

We may take for example the law concerning a slave who is beaten and dies in Exodus 21:20-21, where the slaveholder is not executed if the slave survives a day or two. To some extent, this follows the law for anyone who does not die immediately from injuries (21:18-19), but in this case the law specifically states that this is because the slave is the slaveholder's "property." Given what we read about slavery in Philemon and Ephesians, slavery hardly seems God's ideal purpose! Likewise, although the law condemns the sexual use of another's slave, it is condemned less harshly than adultery because she is a slave (Leviticus 19:20; cf. Deuteronomy 22:23).

The Law and Slavery

Two centuries ago some people tried to argue from such texts that God supports slavery, but no text specifically endorses slavery. Rather, the texts address a system that already practiced slavery and made it more humane. Fellow-Israelites could not be enslaved permanently. They would serve for a time, then be set free and given capital by which they could provide for themselves (Deuteronomy 15:12-15). Israel usually did not even meet this divine standard, according to Jeremiah 34:11-22. Christians who opposed slavery cited broader biblical principles such as loving one's neighbor as oneself (Leviticus 19:18) or all people being the same before God (Acts 10:28). It is this latter group of interpreters who correctly articulated the ideal of Scripture.

Concessions to the Ideal Standard

When some scholars cited Deuteronomy 24 as permission for a man to divorce his wife, Jesus said that law was a "concession" to human sinfulness (Mark 10:5). That means that God did not raise the standard to its ultimate ideal because he was working within their culture. To provide workable laws in a sinful society, God limited sin rather than prohibiting it altogether. But the morality God really demands from the human heart goes beyond such concessions. God never approved of a man divorcing his wife, except for very limited reasons (Mark 10:9; Matthew 19:9). Other concessions in the Old Testament may include polygamy, indentured servanthood, and perhaps holy war. God worked through or in spite of these practices, but his ideal in the New Testament is better. Ritual and civil laws may contain some moral absolutes, but they also contain concessions to the time and culture they addressed, just as Jesus recognized.

The Death Penalty

Some offenses in the Old Testament always carried the death penalty, suggesting that God took these quite seriously for all cultures. These included murder, sorcery, idolatry, adultery, premarital sex, homosexual intercourse, extreme rebellion against parents, and some other offenses. This does not mean that we should enforce the death penalty against all these sins today, but we should take all these offenses seriously.

In interpreting Old Testament laws, we must take into account the difference in era as well as the difference in culture. Just as people in Moses' day could not ignore God's revelation to Moses by citing the earlier revelation to Abraham, so today some things are different because of the coming of Jesus. Human nature is largely the same; God's ways of working have much in common with his ways of working in the Old Testament, but now he sometimes works in very different ways. In Moses' day, God drowned the Egyptians in the Red Sea. In Jesus' day, God unleashed a spiritual revolution that within three centuries converted much of the Roman and Axumite (East African) empires. The old covenant was good but worked by death. The new covenant works by life (2 Corinthians 3:6).

Applying the Law

The law remains good and useful for ethical teaching, provided we use it properly (Romans 3:27-31; 7:12; 1 Timothy 1:8-11). But mere obedience to the law without faith has never brought salvation; God always saved people by grace through faith (Romans 4:3-12), and since the coming of Jesus he has saved people through faith in Jesus Christ. When we consider how to apply particular details of the law today, we should also take into account other factors. Some biblical patterns, like God's command to us to rest, were given prior to the law (Genesis 2:2-3; Exodus 20:11), and God also gives us commands in the New Testament (John 13:34; Acts 2:38; 1 John 2:7-11). Also, although the Spirit was quite active in the Old Testament era (1 Samuel 19:20-24; 1 Chronicles 25:1-2), but has become active in a new way in Christ (John 7:39; Acts 1:7-8; 2:17-18).

Study Questions

1. What are transcultural laws or principles? Give a specific example.
2. Gives some of the Israelite laws that overlapped with ancient neighbors and some that were opposite.
3. What was the Israelite law not the "ideal" form of law?
4. Explain whether or not one can justify slavery based upon the laws of the Old Testament.
5. What is the application of the death penalty laws to us today?
6. What would be an example of a principle that transcended Old Testament legislation?

Chapter Twenty-Two

Interpreting Poetic Literature

Introduction

Even from a secular point of view, the Bible is one of the greatest collections of literature in the world today. One of the things that makes it so rich is the great variety of styles of literature that it possess. And one of the great types of literature that is found in the Bible is Hebrew poetry.

Types of Hebrew Poetry

There are three important types of Hebrew poetry found in the Old Testament.

Lyric Poetry

Lyric poetry is primarily poetry that was written to be accompanied by a lyre or other musical instrument. We would call them songs today. Most of the psalms fall into this category. Some psalms even specify the particular kind of musical instrument or the tune to be used when this psalm is sung. The stress on this type of poetry is on the beauty of expression. Words are arranged in such a way as to appeal to the aesthetic part of man's nature. This type of poetic expression is beautiful and we feel good when we hear it.

Didactic Poetry

Didactic poetry is primarily poetry whose object is to teach some truth. It is usually arranged in a way so as to enhance memory and prolong the lessons learned. Most proverbs can be placed in this category. They teach some kind of wisdom. The primary stress in this type of poetry is on teaching the listener an important truth in such a way that he or she will remember it. The appeal is not so much to the aesthetic or emotional part of man's being as to the intellectual part.

Dramatic Poetry

This poetry is designed in such a way that various speakers/actors physically interact with one another to convey a certain message. In most Hebrew drama, the action is largely limited to conversations between the major players. Job and the Song of Solomon fall into this category. The purpose of drama is to act out a play in such a way as to communicate a message. It must be remembered that whereas truth is being communicated in all the parts, the major stress of a drama comes from the overall message. Therefore, more stress should be given to the overall message of the drama than to the individual parts. To state it another way, the individual parts of the drama must be interpreted in light of the overall message.

Characteristics of Hebrew Poetry

Parallelism

When many people think of poetry, they think of rhythm and parallel sounds. For example, I learned the following little poem as a child:

> Mary had a little lamb, his fleece was white as snow;
> And everywhere that Mary went, the lamb was sure to go.

It is easy to hear the rhythm, or the bounce of the words, as one recites the poem orally. It is also obvious that "snow" rhymes with "go." It is true that not all poetry rhymes, but there is usually rhythm or meter involved.

Hebrew poetry does not rhyme. Instead of having parallel sounds, it has parallel thoughts. In fact, the key word in Hebrew poetry is *parallelism*. Hebrew poetry, like nearly all poetry, is made up of different lines. The minimum number of lines to make a verse is two (known as *distich*). However, *tristichs* (three lines) are also common as well as *tetrastichs* (four lines) and even *pentastichs* (five lines). There is normally some kind of parallel thought in the second and subsequent lines that can be expressed in many ways.

Normal Types of Parallelism

Synonymous Parallelism

The second line essentially repeats the first line except it uses different words. Note these examples:

Job 8:3. Does God pervert justice?
 Doest the Almighty pervert what is right?

Psalm 70:1. Hasten, O God, to save me;
 O Lord, come quickly to help me.

Psalm 37:1. Do not fret because of evil men
 or be envious of those who do wrong.
 for like the grass they will soon wither,
 like green plants they will soon die away.

Proverbs 20:1 .Wine is a mocker
 and beer a brawler.

Ecclesiastes 2:10. I denied myself nothing my eyes desired;
 I refused my heart no pleasure.

Song/Songs 5:1b. Eat, O friends and drink;
 drink your fill, O lovers.

Isaiah 53:6. We all, like sheep, have gone astray,
 each of us has turned to his own way.

One should recognize synonymous parallelism and not try to make too much out of the distinction of words. One of the dangers of interpretation is over-interpretation—that is, seeing more in the passage than was intended by the author. If we fail to recognize the principle of synonymous parallelism, we could fall into the trap of over-interpreting.

For example, Job 38:7 says, *"while the morning stars sang together and all the angels shouted for joy."* This is obviously an example of synonymous parallelism. The *"morning stars"* and the *"angels"* obviously mean the same thing. One should not try to create another category of spiritual beings known as *"morning stars."*

Antithetic Parallelism

The second line makes a contrast with the first line. In this kind of parallelism, the second line nearly always will begin with "but" or similar contrasting conjunction. Note these examples:

Psalm 1:6   For the Lord watches over the way of the righteous,
*   but the way of the wicked will perish.*

Psalm 30:5   For his anger lasts only a moment,
*   but his favor lasts a lifetime;*
*   Weeping may remain for a night,*
*   but rejoicing comes in the morning.*

Proverbs 10:1[1] A wise son brings joy to his father,
*   but a foolish son grief to his mother.*

Proverbs 14:34 Righteousness exalts a nation,
*   but sin is a disgrace to any people.*

Synthetic Parallelism

The second line adds to or completes the thought of the first line.

Note these examples:

Psalm 1:3 He is like a tree planted by streams of water,
*   which yields its fruit in season*
*   and whose leaf does not wither.*
*   Whatever he does prospers.*

---

[1] Nearly all of the proverbs in Proverbs 10-15 are antithetic proverbs.

Interpreting Poetic Literature

Psalm 2:6 I have installed my King on Zion,
my holy hill.

Proverbs 16:3 Commit to the Lord whatever you do,
and your plans will succeed.

Ecclesiastes 12:1 Remember your Creator in the days of your youth,
before the days of trouble come . . .

Song/Songs 2:3 Like an apple tree among the trees of the forest
is my lover among the young men.

Jeremiah 47:2a See how the waters are rising in the north;
they will become an overwhelming torrent.

Climactic Parallelism

The first line is incomplete; it needs something from the second line to complete and emphasize the thought. Note this example.

Psalm 29:1   Ascribe to the Lord, O mighty ones,
Ascribe to the Lord glory and strength.

Emblematic Parallelism

One of the lines gives an illustration to explain the other line but does so without any words of contrast. So one of the lines serves as an emblem or illustration of the other. Note these examples:

> *Proverbs 11:22* **A gold ring in a swine's snout—**
> *a fair woman and without understanding.*

> *Proverbs 25:25* **Cold water to a thirsty soul,**
> *And good news from a far country.*

Multiple Types of Parallelism

Double Parallelism

One parallel couplet is set against another parallel verse. Psalm 32:1-2 is a good example:

> *Blessed is he whose transgressions are forgiven*
> *whose sins are covered.*

> *Blessed is the man whose sin the Lord does not count against him*
> *and in whose spirit is no deceit.*

Note the pattern: A - B - A - B; the two couplets are parallel with each other. The following is an even more sophisticated example:

Psalm 24:7-10
> *Lift up your heads, O you gates;*
> *be lifted up, you ancient doors,*
>
> *that the King of glory may come in.*
> *Who is this king of glory?*
>
> *The Lord strong and mighty,*
> *the Lord mighty in battle.*
>
> *Lift up your heads O you gates;*
> *lift them up, you ancient doors,*
>
> *that the King of glory may come in.*
> *Who is he, this King of glory?*
>
> *The Lord Almighty—*
> *he is the King of glory.*

Notice the pattern in the first six lines: A - A - B - C - D - D. This exact same pattern with the same subjects is found in the second part, verses 9-10.

Chiastic Parallelism

The Greek letter "chi" looks like an X which has four points. In this kind of parallelism the first line is parallel with the fourth line and the second

Interpreting Poetic Literature

and third lines are parallel with one another. It follows a pattern of A - B - B - A. Note this example:

> Psalm 51:1 Have mercy on me, O God,
> according to your unfailing love;
> according to your great compassion
> blot out my transgressions.

Lines 1 and 4 are parallel and lines 2 and 3 are also parallel.

Figurative Language

Nearly all poetic literature contains highly figurative language. Sometimes we refer to the language as being "flowery" because it contains such rich descriptions of its subjects. Hebrew poetry has this same feature. It is filled with many rich figures of speech and other word pictures.

Often nature is used to describe things. Psalm 91:4 says, "He will cover you with his feathers, and under his wings you will find refuge." Psalm 92:12 declares, *"The righteous will flourish like a palm tree, they will grow like a cedar of Lebanon."*

Here are some examples of other very rich language being used:

1. Psalm 11:2: *"For look, the wicked bend their bows; they set their arrows against the strings to shoot from the shadows at the upright in heart."*

2. Psalm 7:14: *"He who is pregnant with evil and conceives trouble gives birth to disillusionment."*

3. Psalm 90:3-6:

    > You turn me back to dust, saying, 'Return to dust, O sons of men,' For a thousand years in your sight are like a day that has just gone by, or like a watch in the night. You sweep men away in the sleep of death; they are like the new grass of the morning—though in the morning it springs up new, by evening it is dry and withered.

Psalm 23 is the classic psalm of descriptive language. It uses various parts of nature including the green grass, the quiet streams as well as other pastoral terminology.

Rhythm and Meter

There is no general agreement about the question of rhythm or meter in Hebrew poetry. There are some scholars who think that they observe some rhythm in certain passages but this is not conclusive. Even if there were rhythm in the Hebrew poetry it would be difficult, if not impossible, for us to appreciate for at least two reasons. First, most of us do not read Hebrew, and second, all sense of rhythm is lost in translation. Therefore, there is very little use in a general biblical scholar trying to study the rhythm of Hebrew poetry.

Other Literary and Stylistic Devices

Acrostics

An acrostic is a literary device in which every line begins with a new letter. Three of the five chapters in Lamentation are alphabetical acrostics meaning that each of the verses in the chapter begins with a word that starts with the next Hebrew letter in the alphabet. Chapter three is a triple acrostic containing 66 verses. Since the Hebrew language has 22 letters in its alphabet, that means three verses begin with each of the letters of the Hebrew alphabet. This type of construction cannot be completely appreciated or illustrated in a translation. An even more sophisticated variation of this is Psalm 119. In this psalm, there are 22 sections each containing eight verses. Each of the eight verses begins with the particular letter of the Hebrew alphabet being featured in that section and all twenty-two of the letters are featured in the poem.

Alliteration

This is using words or phrases that begin with similar sounds such as *"Peter Piper picked a peck of pickled peppers."* This is occasionally used in Hebrew poetry but is also lost in translation.

Onomatopoeia

This is using words that sound like what they are describing. The Greek word for murmuring is *goggurmos*. It sounds like murmuring and grumbling. Unfortunately, all such interesting sounds are lost in any English translation.

Paronomasia

This is the use of puns in which a word is used which sounds much like or even identical to another word. For example, in Amos 8:1 (KJV) God asked Amos, *"Who do you see?"* Amos replied, *"A basket of summer fruit."* Interestingly the word for *"summer fruit"* sounds almost identical to the word *"end"* in God's next statement, *"The end has come upon my people Israel."* Unfortunately, like onomatopoeia, the richness of puns cannot be appreciated in translations.

Rules for Interpreting Hebrew Poetry

Recognize It.

If we do not know what kind of literature we are studying, it is unlikely that we will be able to interpret it properly. The failure to recognize poetic parallelism, for example, may encourage a person to think that a passage is saying more than it is.

Analyze It.

This can be done several ways:

1. Identify the Types of Parallelism.

Whether it is synonymous parallelism or antithetic parallelism or another form will not drastically affect the interpretation. However, it will affect our understanding of the thinking of the writer and help us to appreciate the writings more. The more we focus on the passage, and the more we learn about the passage, even if it is technical grammatical and literary things. The more we concentrate by analyzing these things, the more we will learn.

2. Identify the Literary Devices.

As stated earlier, the Biblical writers used many of the standard literary devices we use today. Thinking through these, and identifying which ones are used in a given passage, will improve concentration and produce more riches from one's study.

3. Identify the Types of Figures of Speech.

It is not absolutely necessary to know that a comparison without using like or as is called a metaphor. It is nice to know these things, and a serious student of the Bible should know them. However, it is important that we know and recognize various phrases in the Bible as figures of speech. Otherwise, we will be forced into thinking that the Pharisees were snakes and that Herod was actually a fox. Identifying and understanding the figures of speech in the Bible will avoid the trap of being overly literal in our interpretation.

4. Identify the Central Truth.

After we have identified the form, it is essential to understand the main thought in the passage. Remember that the poet is often concentrating on the form of his writing. The message is often very simple but the poet is expressing it in a variety of ways for aesthetic reasons. For doctrinal purposes, the message of the poetry is more important than the form. Therefore, it is important to be able to identify the central theme in the verse or the section.

5. Identify any Unique Characteristics.

Poetry is obviously different from straightforward prose. We have identified many of the unique characteristics of poetry. However, there may be additional things that are not part of the general characteristics outlined above. To state it once again: the more elements that one can observe about a passage of scripture, whether they are grammatical, literary, linguistic, theological, or other observations, the more one is going to improve one's concentration and the more one will get from the passage.

Summarize or Paraphrase It.

One of the good ways to determine whether or not one understands a passage is to summarize or paraphrase it in one's own words. Remove the poetic features and express the main message in words that your friends would understand. For those who speak a second language, it is good to translate the passage into another language. The process of translating will force you to think through the passage in a way no other method will do.

Conclusion

Some of the richest portions of the Scriptures are found in Hebrew poetry. The Book of Psalms has always been the hymnbook of the church. The greatest collection of wisdom anywhere in the world is in the Book of Proverbs. Therefore, we should make every effort to learn all we can about Hebrew poetry so we can mine out the riches that are found inside it.

Study Questions

1. Give a Biblical example of five different literary techniques used in the Bible.
2. List three different kinds of Hebrew poetry and give examples of each.
3. What is the primary characteristic of Hebrew poetry? Give an example.
4. List three different kinds of Hebrew parallelism and give examples of each.
5. Give an example of multiple parallelism.
6. Give an example of beautiful or colorful language found in Hebrew poetry.
7. What is acrostic? Give an example of an acrostic found in the Bible.
8. Summarize the best way to identify Hebrew poetry.

Chapter Twenty-Three

Interpreting Psalms

The Book of Psalms was originally the hymnbook of ancient Israel. The ancient Hebrew title was *Tehillim,* which means "praise," or "songs of praises." The word *psalm* comes from the Greek. The verb form of the word means "I sing" but the noun form means "songs set to music." The word *psalter* comes from a word that referred to a stringed musical instrument which was used to play and sing the psalms. The word eventually came to refer to the collection of psalms.

The psalms are the poetic expressions of the Old Testament saints. They are internal thoughts, meditations, questions and prayers of God's people. As poetry they tend to be more pleasing to the aesthetic and emotional nature of humanity than prose. They are written for the heart not the mind. All legal proceedings are carried out in straightforward prose. It is doubtful whether a judge would allow a lawyer to cross-examine a witness in poetry.

W. T. Purkiser says this about the psalms:

> The psalms, sacred songs of the Hebrews, are a mirror into which one can peer and see himself and his emotions reflected. This is why the psalms are so important, for in them we find not only a profound revelation of the inner spiritual life of the Hebrews, but also a striking picture of the inmost religious life of all sincere followers of God. Here, as Martin Luther so aptly put it in his Second Preface to the Psalter, 'we can look into the hearts of all the saints.'"[1]

An Old Testament psalm provides a window into the soul of the Old Testament saint. The psalms give us a diary of meditation—the innermost thoughts, feelings, frustrations, questions, and blessings of the Old Testament child of God.

---

[1] W. T. Purkiser, *Exploring the Old Testament* (Kansas City, MO USA: Beacon Hill Publishers), p. 215.

The psalms are generally attributed to David. However, David probably wrote only about half of them.[2] The first psalm was probably written by Moses and the last one was written during or after the Babylonian Captivity. However, the majority of the psalms were written during the days of David and Solomon, during the time when the Israelite kingdom had reached its peak of geographic expansion and military might.

Types of Psalms

There are at least eight different types of psalms. These are not necessarily mutually exclusive categories. In other words, some psalms might fit into two or more categories.

1. **National Psalms.** The Hebrews had a holistic view of life, much like Islam. There was not much distinction between their religion, business, family and politics. They were almost inseparable. The Hebrews recognized that God was directly involved in the nation of Israel as He was no other nation. Therefore, their poetry tends to reflect that relationship. National Psalms are those that are particularly written for and about the nation of Israel. They are patriotic in nature. Many of them reflect God's divine care and protection upon Israel and are written to express praise and thanksgiving. Such is Psalm 46 which begins, *"God is our refuge and strength, an ever present help in trouble."* The national psalms do not just concentrate on the blessings and good things about the nation. Sometimes they lament about the deplorable conditions of God's people. Psalm 137 was apparently written in Babylon during or shortly after the Babylonian Captivity. It reads in part, *"By the rivers of Babylon we sat down and wept when we remembered Zion"* (137:1). Psalms 44, 66 and 79 are additional illustrations of national psalms.

---

[2] The following is an estimate of the number of psalms written by various individuals and groups: David, 73; Moses, 1 (Psalm 90); Solomon, 2 (Psalms 72, 127); Jehoshaphat, 2 (possibly Psalms 75, 76); Jeremiah (could have possibly written Psalms 31, 35, 38, 43, 55, 69, 71); Asaph, 12 (Psalms 50, 73-83); Sons of Korah, 11 (Psalms 42-49, 84, 85, 87); Heman, 1 (Psalm 88); Ethan, 1 (Psalm 89); Psalms without an inscription, Psalm 49.

2. **Royal or Messianic Psalms.** These are psalms that are written about the glorious king of Israel's future. Some of these psalms are prophetic in nature. They are actually looking forward to the coming Messiah. Others are describing a contemporary king, but a king that in some way foreshadows the Great King that is coming. Psalm 110 is perhaps the best example. It begins this way: *"The LORD says to my Lord: 'Sit at my right hand until I make your enemies a footstool for your feet. . . . you will rule in the midst of your enemies.'"* Psalm 45 describes the anointing by the Holy Spirit:

    Your throne, O God, will last forever and ever; a scepter of justice will be the scepter of your kingdom. You love righteousness and hate wickedness; therefore God, your God, has set you above your companions by anointing you with the oil of joy (45:6-7).

3. Other Royal Psalms or portions of psalms are Psalms 2, 16, 18, 20, 21, 22, 40, 45, 73, 89, 110, and 132.

4. **Nature Psalms.** Nature Psalms are not necessarily written about nature but use nature extensively to illustrate the main point of the psalm. Nature is usually used to offer praise and worship to the Creator of nature, God Himself. These psalms constantly attribute the beauty and power of nature to a sovereign God. Psalm 8 is perhaps the best example of a nature psalm. It begins *"O Lord, our Lord, how majestic is your name in all the earth!"* He then describes how nature illustrates the power and perfection of God. Psalm 19 is another nature psalm. It begins *"The heavens declare the glory of God; the skies proclaim the work of his hands."*

5. **Penitential Psalms.** These are psalms of repentance. The psalmist confesses either personal or national sins. The most well-known of the penitential psalms is Psalm 51. In this psalm David confesses his sin. This was, no doubt, David's confession of the sin of adultery with Bathsheba, though the specific sin is not mentioned. The sin of murder is suggested in the passage in verse 14 where David prays, *"Save me from bloodguilt, O God."* The psalmist prays in Psalm 6:3-4, *"My soul is in anguish. How long, O Lord, how long? Turn, O Lord, and deliver me; save me because of your unfailing love."* He prays in Psalm 38:18, *"I confess my iniquity; I am troubled by my sin."* Other penitential psalms include Psalms 32, 102, 130 and 143.

6. **Didactic Psalms.** These are psalms whose basic purpose is to teach a lesson. Nearly all psalms have some type of didactic goal but some are more specifically designed for teaching than others. Psalm 1 falls into this category. It is teaching about the characteristics of the blessed man, especially as they are contrasted with the wicked man. Other examples of didactic psalms include Psalm 14, 34, 94, 112, 119, 127 and 128.

7. **Historical Psalms.** These may also be considered didactic, because they are teaching about history. Their basic purpose is to remind the Israelites of their history, which was sovereignly guided and controlled by God Himself. These historical psalms are basically found in Psalms 105-107.

8. **Psalms of Praise and Thanksgiving.** These are psalms whose main purpose is to praise God. Nearly all psalms have some element of praise in them. A group of these is found in Psalms 113-118. Also Psalms 144-150 fall into this category. In fact, they contain some of the riches praises found in the whole Bible.

9. **Imprecatory Psalms (or Psalms about Enemies).** An imprecatory psalm prays for or wishes judgment to fall upon one's enemies. Psalm 35: 4-5, *"May those who seek my life be disgraced and put to shame; may those who plot my ruin be turned back in dismay. May they be like chaff before the wind, with the angel of the Lord driving them away."* The language of imprecatory psalms can be very graphic. For example, Psalm 58:6-8 says,

    Break the teeth in their mouths, O God; tear out, O Lord, the fangs of the lions! Let them vanish like water that flows away; when they draw the bow, let their arrows be blunted. Like a slug melting away as it moves along, like a stillborn child, may they not see the sun.

    Perhaps the majority of the psalms in the first section of the psalter contains some element of imprecation or at least some thoughts about enemies. Enemies is one of the major themes of the psalms. In fact the word enemy appears 92 times in the NIV translation of the psalms.

Titles of Superscriptions

In all but 34 of the psalms, there is editorial information placed at the beginning of the psalm. This information was not a part of the original psalm. However, these are very old additions. They were apparently handed down orally for generations until they were included in the text. These titles are normally considered the first verse in the Hebrew Bibles. Therefore the verse designations may not be exactly the same when referring to technical commentaries that contain a lot of the original language. The following types of information are given in the titles:

- Technical names, which identified the type of psalm
- Musical terms
- Hymn tunes
- Liturgical information
- Historical information

Interpreting Psalms

The following are some guidelines for interpreting the psalms.

1. **Observe any useful information given in the title.** It may provide you historical or other information that will make interpretation easier.
2. **Note the kind of parallelism found in the psalm.** For example, if the psalm is using synonymous parallelism, you compare the two lines to see the common teaching in the section. If it is using antithetic parallelism, the second line will help in interpreting the first by pointing to the opposite teaching.
3. **Translate any figures of speech or idioms into the non-figurative meanings they were intended to communicate.** To really interpret figurative language, it is best to take it out of the figurative format and put it in a form that you could easily explain to others. For example the statement *"the tongue of the righteous is choice silver"* (Proverbs 10:20a) simply means that the speech of a righteous man is very valuable.

4. **Determine which of the major categories the psalm fits into.** This is one of the most helpful things you can do when studying psalms. If a psalm is a royal psalm, it will be interpreted differently than if it is a penitential psalm. Certainly, imprecatory psalms must be applied differently today than they were applied when they were written.

5. **Remember that the psalm was written as a song of a Hebrew saint who was living in a nation that considered itself a theocracy.** The psalmist made no distinction between his government and his "religion." A patriotic song was as holy as a song about God. The psalmist had a very holistic view of life. This affects interpretation and application as well.

Conclusion

A psalm like all other forms of music was an outstanding communication device in the ancient world. The more we understand this part of the Bible, the more we will understand the mind of God.

Study Questions

1. What is a psalm?
2. List and give an illustration of the eight types of psalms.
3. What are some of the kinds of information given in the titles of the psalms? To what extent is this material helpful in interpretation?
4. What is the main rule for interpreting psalms?
5. Find an imprecatory psalm. Explain it and then make an appropriate contemporary application.
6. Explain how understanding Hebrew poetic parallelism will help one interpret the psalms.

Chapter Twenty-Four

Interpreting Proverbs

Wisdom teachers, or sages, often taught in easily memorizable sayings called proverbs. Most cultures have some familiarity with this genre.

A proverb is a short wise statement that teaches a general principle in a memorable manner. From the very beginning of time, humankind has been passing along bits of advice and wisdom in the form of short pithy sayings. In fact, much of ancient education used to involve the memorization and utilization of the proverbs. No one really knows who was the first person to use a proverb. Most of the early proverbs were created primarily for oral transmission rather than written transmission. This is an important thing to remember. Proverbs were not designed to be written and analyzed grammatically and linguistically. They were designed to make a point orally.

International Proverbs

Here are some examples of English proverbs:

- A stitch in time saves nine.
- A bird in the hand is worth two in the bush.
- Don't cry over spilt milk.
- An ounce of prevention is worth a pound of cure.
- Many hands make light work.
- Better late than never.
- Curiosity killed the cat.
- Many cooks spoil the broth.
- A word to the wise is sufficient.

- Spare the rod and spoil the child.
- Two heads are better than one.
- You cannot get blood out of a turnip.
- Easy come; easy go.

The following are examples of German proverbs:

- The last person is bitten by the dogs.
- The cruse goes to the well until it breaks.
- A bad workman blames his tools.
- New brooms sweep well.
- As one makes his bed, so one lies.
- At night all cows are black.

African Proverbs

The following are examples of African proverbs:

- A toad does not jump in the daytime without a cause.
- An old man never runs in vain.
- One who defecates along the road will meet the flies when he returns.
- Little drops of water make a mighty ocean.
- You look for a black goat when it is not yet night.
- The proverbs are the oil with which words are eaten.
- You don't need a long stick to kill a snake.
- If you want to eat with Satan, eat with a long spoon.
- You don't live by the seashore and sharpen your knife with spit.
- If you eat a frog, eat one with a big head.

- A young boy plans to kill a snake while the snake plans where the boy's body will be.
- He who is bitten by a snake will run at the sight of a worm (or rope).
- Reserve wet clothes for the dry season.
- A man bitten by a bee runs at the sound of a fly.
- A boy is no longer a child when he kills a big meat.
- A Reverend Father is not a small boy in the church.
- A rat with only one hole dies quickly.
- If you look at how the moon gives light, you will not shut your door.
- The first animal drinks clean water.
- A father slaps his child with one hand but draws him with the other.
- One who has a monkey as his friend never gets his stick stuck in the tree.

What are the marks of a successful proverb? R. C. Trench gives the following:

- *Brevity:* Bulky sayings will not lodge well in the memory and proverbs must be memorable.
- *Intelligibility:* The meaning of a proverb must be grasped easily.
- *Flavor:* Only the pungent proverb will stick in people's minds.
- *Popularity:* Even a good saying will die if not repeated frequently and passed along through the generations.[1]

---

[1] LaSor, (Grand Rapids, MI USA: William B. Eerdmans Publishing Company, 1929) p. 538.

Biblical Proverbs

The book of Proverbs begins by attributing the proverbs to Solomon. However, Solomon is actually the author of only some of them. It is more likely that he is the collector of many of the proverbs. In addition, there were several other authors mentioned who contributed to the Biblical collection of proverbs, including Agur son of Jakeh (chapter 30) and King Lemuel (31:1-9). The proverbs found in the Bible provide us with a brief snapshot of the way people thought during that particular time in history. They tell us the ideal way to interact with our friends and neighbors, how to take care of your family and certainly how to please God. They do not represent just the wisdom of Solomon. They represent the consensus of practical wisdom in the ancient Hebrew world. Though the proverbs represent all periods of the Old Testament, most of them probably come from the Solomonic era.

We should also note the "rhetorical function" of proverbs. Ancient sages offered proverbs in short, succinct statements as general principles. Proverbs were poetry (often with the second line contrasting with the first line), and they were short summaries that would not list all possible exceptions to the principles they articulated. They might use humor, hyperbole (rhetorical overstatement), irony, and other means to communicate graphically; proverbs were intended to be memorable and practical, not detailed statements of philosophy and certainly not legal guarantees. We must read them according to the character in which they were written.

Guidelines for Interpreting Proverbs

1. **Check the context.** Many of the proverbs are simple short one-verse proverbs, which are unrelated to the context. They are found in long lists. Therefore, the context is often of little value. However, at times the context is valuable because sometimes proverbs are grouped together. Sometimes the proverbs are expanded in length. For example, Proverbs 7 is a description of the ways of a harlot. In order to study any portion of that chapter, one would need to have a general understanding of the whole chapter.

Interpreting Proverbs

2. **Group proverbs.** One who preaches or teaches from Proverbs may wish to gather different proverbs on the same topic and preach them together. This is important because most of the Book of Proverbs consists of sayings in random order, so normal rules of context do not apply. But the broader context of genre does apply, and pulling together other wisdom-sayings on the same topic can be very helpful.

3. **Observe the different literary styles found in the proverb.** All kinds of figures of speech are found in the proverbs. Therefore one needs to analyze every proverb by asking is it a simile or a metaphor or some other figure of speech? What type of parallelism is it made of? Determine the type of proverb this is: Is it a command? Is it a statement of fact? Is it an exhortation? Does it appear to be a general principle?

4. **Remember proverbs contain general truths not absolute facts.** It is essential to remember that a proverb does not contain the same degree of absolute truth as historical narrative or prose. I frequently make this point when teaching about proverbs. "A Biblical proverb is still a proverb." The point is that a Biblical proverb, like all other proverbs, usually teaches a general truth, not an absolute truth. There may be exceptions to most of the general principles found in most proverbs. For example, the proverb that says "Better late than never" is generally true. However, there could be some meetings where it would be just as bad to be late as to not attend at all. The proverb, "many hands make light work" is generally true. However, there are some jobs that would be better done by one good person rather than ten people. Many people would just confuse things. And so there is a proverb that says the opposite, "Too many cooks spoil the soup."

The following are some examples of Biblical proverbs that teach general truths but may have exceptions. Proverbs 13:11 *"Dishonest money dwindles away, but he who gathers money little by little makes it grow."* There have probably been examples in the history of the world of people who have gotten wealth through some inappropriate means and have died wealthy men. On the other hand, there have been people who have worked hard all their lives and still have not increased much. The point of the proverb is not to make an absolute statement of fact but to state that which is generally true—that those who gain things dishonestly will eventually fail while those who gain honestly will prosper. The fact that there might be exceptions to this statement does not negate the truth of it. It is a proverb not a statement of fact.

Each of the following illustrations falls into the same general category.

- 15:1 *"A gentle answer turns away wrath, but a harsh word stirs up anger."* Does this mean that every time a person gives a gentle answer, all harsh words will be quieted? Obviously not.

- 16:7 *"When a man's ways are pleasing to the Lord, he makes even his enemies live at peace with him."* Does every godly man always have peace with all people? If a man has an enemy, does that mean his ways are not pleasing to God? Did Stephen and James and other Biblical martyrs please God? Was Jesus displeasing to God because people were angry with Him?

- 18:22 *"He who finds a wife finds what is good and receives favor from the Lord."* Has there ever been a time when a man found a wife but she turned out to be not such a good thing?

- 19:4 *"Wealth brings many friends, but a poor man's friend deserts him."* Has every poor man lost all of his friends?

- 21:17 *"He who loves pleasure will become poor; whoever loves wine and oil will never be rich."* Does this mean that everyone who loves pleasure will eventually become poor? No, it simply means that if you focus too much on pleasure it will rob you of time, energy, and money.

- 23:13 *"Do not withhold discipline from a child; if you punish him with the rod, he will not die."* I have read examples of parents who beat their children to death. However, this does not negate the general truth that is being taught.

- 28:27 *"He who gives to the poor will lack nothing, but he who closes his eyes to them receives many curses."*

The point is that proverbs are general principles not absolute promises. When we elevate a proverb to the status of a promise or a doctrine, we are elevating it beyond what it was intended to be. We must always remember that the Bible is using literary devices in the same way as the society as a whole. For example, a hyperbole is a deliberate exaggeration given to make a strong point. No one accuses a person using hyperbole of lying. The hyperbole was given under the inspiration of the Holy Spirit. However, it was given to be interpreted in light of the rules of hyperbole. The same principle applies to the proverbs. They are inspired by the Holy Spirit, but, they are inspired to be interpreted as proverbs.

In light of this truth, one should always interpret proverbs in light of the more clear teachings of the Bible. The prophets and the words of Jesus and the Epistles all contain information that is designed to teach. Therefore, if a proverb appears to be teaching some unusual belief or practice, evaluate it by other parts of the Bible that are not poetic in nature and whose primary purpose is to make the truth as plain as possible.

Study Questions

1. Give a definition of a proverb. Give an example of an African proverb.
2. What are the characteristics of good proverbs?
3. How does understanding Hebrew poetic parallelism help one to under-stand a specific proverb?
4. What is the most important rule for interpreting proverbs?

Chapter Twenty-Five

Interpreting Prophecy

Introduction

God made human beings in such a way that they are constantly striving to learn more and more. The human appetite for knowledge and truth is never quenched. Proverbs 25:2 says, *"It is the glory of God to conceal a matter; to search out a matter is the glory of kings."* This verse tells us that you can do something that God cannot do. You can learn. One of the greatest things in all the world is learning. Even if a man is a king (he has reached the ultimate pinnacle of success), he can do nothing more exciting and fulfilling than to "search out a matter" which is another way of describing learning.

On the other hand, God has never had the privilege of learning. Because God is omniscient—he knows all things, he has never learned anything. So God receives glory in concealing things, and then watching the creature that He has made search out and discover truth. God told us many things about our past in order to particularly satisfy the craving for knowledge that he placed within human beings. However, he left many things unsaid so that man could and would continue to dig and search and learn.

We humans have an innate desire to know the future. God has revealed a few facts about the future in plain terms but most of the future is veiled in mystery. Some details are suggested in figurative language. A diligent student can discover a few more things about the future than the casual student will.

One of the basic principles of Biblical interpretation is the principle of emphasis. What does the Bible emphasize? One can partially answer that question by simply counting the verses or measuring the amount of space that is given to a certain subject. If this principle is true, then prophecy is a very important study because it occupies a major portion of the Bible.

Definitions[1]

A prophet is a spokesman for God. He is a person to whom and through whom God speaks. A prophet speaks about things in the past, present and future. A New Testament description of the work of the prophet is given in 1 Corinthians 14:3, *"But everyone who prophesies speaks to men for their strengthening, encouragement and comfort."*

Prophecy is simply the writings or utterances of the prophets. However, the word "prophecy" has evolved in modern English language to the extent that it is now most often associated with the predictions of future events. However, we must not always assume that in studying Bible prophecy.

Types of Prophecy in the Bible

Short-Term Predictions

These are the predictions that were fulfilled in a short period of time. In Exodus 14:4, God promises to harden Pharaoh's heart. God fulfilled that promise within a few days or even a few hours. Jesus predicted his own death and resurrection (Mark 9:31). This occurred within a relatively short time.

Old Testament Predictions Fulfilled in the Old Testament

The Babylonian captivity is predicted as early as Deuteronomy 28:32. The restoration from the captivity was predicted by Isaiah well over 150 years before it occurred with such accuracy that Isaiah even gave the name Cyrus as the person who would deliver them from their captivity (Isaiah 44:28f.)

---

[1] Much of the material in this chapter is taken from T. Norton Sterett, *How to Understand your Bible* (Downers Grove, IL USA: InterVarsity Press), pp. 139-147.

Old Testament Predictions Fulfilled in the New Testament

There are many prophecies in the Old Testament of a coming Messiah. Isaiah 53 contains many prophecies that particularly focus on the sufferings of Jesus. These are some of the most precise prophecies in the Bible. In addition, Joel 2:28-29 gives a very precise prediction of the events that occurred on the Day of Pentecost in Acts 2.

New Testament Predictions Fulfilled in the New Testament

Most of these prophecies were short term predictions because the events of the New Testament cover a period of a little over 90 years. Jesus' prophecy of the betrayal of Judas and the denial of Peter fit into this category. Though it is not mentioned, Jesus' prophecy of the destruction of the Temple was fulfilled in AD 70, still within the period the New Testament era.

Biblical Prophecies Yet to be Fulfilled

There are many prophecies that are yet to be fulfilled. Many relate to the second coming of Christ.

Characteristics of Prophecy

Prophecy is not a kind of writing that we use every day. It has some unique characteristics. We need to familiarize ourselves with them.

Prophetic Perspective

To correctly interpret prophecy, we must place ourselves back into the prophets situation. When we do that, the prophecy might look differently than it would in if we looked at it purely from a contemporary point of view. Theologians frequently refer to the "mountain range perspective" when discussing prophecy. If a person is many miles away from a mountain range, the mountains all appear to be grouped together. One mountain peak sticks up and then another sticks up behind it. From a long distance, it appears all of the mountains are grouped together. As one gets closer, however, one can see that the mountains in the rear may be many miles away from the first mountain.

From the prophet's perspective, certain of the events they prophesied about looked as if they were all bunched up together. However, as the events began to occur it became obvious that they were actually many centuries separated. For example, in one verse, Isaiah predicts that it will be the responsibility of the Lord to *"proclaim the favorable year of the Lord, and the day of vengeance of our God"* (Isaiah 61:2). However, these two events are separated by millennia. The first and second comings of Christ are often viewed as one from the prophet's long range view.

Figurative Language

Prophecy by its very nature contains much figurative language. God does not usually state exactly what is going to happen in the future. He gives hints through figurative language. For prophecy to be understood, one must use all the rules for interpreting figures of speech. When we examine the New Testament to see which verses were fulfilled, we see some were literal fulfilled while some were figurative in nature. I will say more about this later.

Special Grammar

Verbs used in the past tense may refer to future events. The great prophecy of the sufferings of Christ in Isaiah 53 is in that category. Verbs in the present tense may refer to the future. The prophecy of the triumphant entry of Jesus into Jerusalem in Zechariah 9:9 is an illustration: *"See, your king comes to you, righteous and having salvation, gentle and riding on a donkey."*

Conditional and Unconditional Predictions

God makes both conditional and unconditional promises in the Bible. These are found in both the Old and New Testaments. However, frequently God makes what appears to be an unconditional promise or prophecy. However, in reality the fulfillment of that prophecy depends upon the response of the people. Therefore, it has a hidden condition.

God promised to David that there would always be one of his descendants sitting upon the throne. However there was a period of time during the Babylonian Captivity when there was no such thing as a throne much less a descendant of David sitting upon it. This was a conditional promise. It was conditional upon the response of David's descendants.

Guidelines for Interpreting Prophecy

1. Find out who and what the prophecy originally addressed.

To learn the circumstances prophecies addressed, the place to begin is to look at the beginning of the book, which usually (though not always) lists the reigns of the rulers during which the prophet prophesied. Then you can turn to 1 and 2 Kings and 1 and 2 Chronicles to learn what was happening in Israel in that period of time.

2. Use the law, historical books and earlier prophets as background.

The prophets saw themselves as calling Israel back to the covenant. Many judgments they announced simply fulfilled the warnings of curses in Deuteronomy 27-28. Their language regularly echoes and recycles the language of earlier prophets. Many of the prophets repeat the same basic message over and over, except in creatively new, poetic ways. Some surrounding cultures claimed prophets, but none of them had a succession of prophets with the same basic message generation after generation.[2]

---

[2] The city of Mari had prophets whose most "moral" reproof to a king might be that he was in danger of losing a battle because he was not paying enough money to the temple. Egypt had prophetic writers who denounced injustices of past rulers, which is a little closer but still not with the courage and passion of the Biblical prophets.

Ask this question: How would the original interpreters have understood this prophecy? The original hearers or readers did not always understand the prophecies given to them. However, looking for the things that would have influenced their perspective on any prophecy is always valuable.

In each prophecy, first try to understand the prophecy in its most literal sense. This is one of the fundamental rules of interpreting the Bible. Always accept any particular Biblical statement literally if it will allow you to do so.

3. Interpret poetic prophecy in light of poetic rules.

That prophets often prophesied in poetry invites us to interpret them in a particular manner. First, most ancient poetry was rich in symbolism, worded so as to capture attention. Most people knew that not all the details were literal. Rather, the reader should strive to catch the basic point. Some details were even deliberately obscure until their fulfillment, though clear enough in retrospect that one would recognize both God's wisdom and humanity's foolishness in not understanding it.

Second, Israelite prophecy involved parallelism, as in the psalms and proverbs. Some modern poetry and songs balance sound, for instance, by rhyme and rhythm; but the Israelites balanced especially ideas. Thus the second line might repeat the thought of the first line (either in the same words or in similar ones that might slightly develop the thought). Or the second line might give the opposite point.[3] For example, if the first line says the memory of the righteous will be blessed, the second might note that the name of the wicked will rot. In such cases, we should not read into parallel lines different thoughts. Some preachers have even taken separate points of their sermon from parallel lines, but in the original poetry, these separate lines were not separate ideas; they were simply varied ways of stating the same idea.

As stated above, one should always attempt to interpret every passage including prophecy literally. If it does not make sense literally, then attempt to see if a figure of speech or some other poetic device is being used and what type of meaning is intended. Prophetic scriptures are filled

---

[3] For a fuller explanation of Hebrew poetry, see Chapter 22.

with figurative language. We will not understand prophetic scriptures without understanding something about the use of figurative language.

4. Try to determine whether the prophecy was fulfilled.

Observing the way prophecies were fulfilled in the Bible will give one a good understanding of how unfulfilled prophecies might be fulfilled. Here you should check historical parts of Bible and other historical information to see if a prophecy was fulfilled. Often prophecies are poetic ways to give the general sense, while the particular application remains ambiguous (Isaiah 37:29, 33-37). God does not give prophecy to satisfy our curiosity, but to tell us just what we need. In light of that, we should not expect literal fulfillment of every detail as if prophecies were prose rather than poetry, although God sometimes did fulfill details literally.

All scholars agree that Jeremiah prophesied before Jerusalem's fall, announcing in advance judgment on his own people. This was unusual in the ancient Near East, where prophets were often expected to be patriotic and encourage their people to victories. But Jeremiah (and Deuteronomy) prophesied the restoration of Israel to the land. When the Assyrians had carried people into captivity, no one ever returned, and no one expected matters to be different with the Babylonians. But a generation after Jeremiah's death the Judean exiles returned to their land. This was a remarkable, large-scale fulfillment, not naturally expected and not able to be viewed as coincidence, which validates Jeremiah's prophecy even if some details were intended poetically. Jeremiah's very writing style lets us know that many of his details are merely poetic, graphic ways of communicating his broader point (Jeremiah 4:7-9, 20-31).

A few prophecies were never fulfilled and never will be (Jeremiah 46:13; Ezekiel 29:19; 30:10), because they were conditional prophecies. Either the people responded to the threats or took for granted the promises, so the future was altered, either for the better or worse. Just as many of God's promises were conditional, many prophecies were also (Jeremiah 18:7-10).

5. Try to determine if a prophecy was partially fulfilled.

Prophecies are not always fulfilled at one time. One reason for this is there are consistent patterns in God's dealing with humanity. Both God and human nature have remained the same. Thus, for example, the temple was repeatedly judged in *"abominations of desolation,"* by the Babylonians (587 BC), by Antiochus Epiphanes (second century BC), by Pompey (first century BC), by Titus (first century AD) and by Hadrian (second century AD). Referring in advance to Titus' destruction of the temple, Jesus could speak of an abomination of desolation within one generation (Matthew 23:36-38; 24:1-3, 15, 34) that was fulfilled forty years after Jesus predicted it. Because there are many evil emperors in history, the *"mystery of lawlessness is already at work"* (2 Thessalonians 2:7). Because deceivers remain, there are already many antichrists (1 John 2:18). It is important to note that these are "partial fulfillments" and not "double fulfillments."

When a prophecy was not fulfilled, one must try to determine whether the promise was an unconditional promise and what parts still remain unfulfilled. For example, the Israelites' return from Babylon was a clear miracle. But Isaiah's exalted prophecies of the deserts blossoming with lilies were not fulfilled at that time. Israel remained a very small kingdom. Some aspects of Isaiah's prophecy were fulfilled in Jesus' ministry, both physically and spiritually (e.g., Isaiah 35:5-6; 61:1-2; Matthew 11:5; Luke 4:18-19). But history also suggests that God is preserving Israel for a purpose. Israel was scattered again a generation after Jesus' crucifixion, as He warned would happen in judgment (Luke 21:20-24). Yet the Jewish people never disappeared, in contrast to the Hittites, Edomites, Philistines and other nations that were assimilated into other peoples.

Jesus' coming may appear at first sight a less dramatic deliverance than the first exodus or the return from Babylon, but within a few centuries Judea's oppressors were converted to belief in Israel's God—something more dramatic than happened with Pharaoh or Cyrus. Today perhaps half the world's population acknowledges that there is one God; much of this faith may be inadequate in many respects, but from the standpoint of Jeremiah's or Jesus' day it would appear an amazing miracle. All this leads us to expect the fulfillment of future promises of restoration, though we cannot get past the prophets' symbolic language to fathom all the details.

Interpreting Prophecy

Those who have been grafted into the biblical heritage and hope by faith (Romans 2:26-29; 11:17-24) share in those future promises.

6. Beware of "double fulfillments."

We must be careful, however, in speaking of "double fulfillments." Many of the "secondary fulfillments" of Scripture we see in the New Testament are actually applications or analogies with the Old Testament, not claims to primary fulfillment. Thus, for example, when Hosea said, *"Out of Egypt have I called my son,"* the context makes clear that he speaks of Israel in the exodus (Hosea 11:1). When Matthew applies this to Jesus, it is because he recognizes an analogy between Israel and Jesus, who repeats Israel's history but overcomes. For example, Jesus was tested forty days in the wilderness (as Israel was for forty years), but passed the very temptations Israel failed (note the context of the verses he quotes from Deuteronomy.

The Fulfillment Passages in the Gospels

The gospel writers frequently say that a certain thing happened that the scripture might be fulfilled. The word most often used in those references is the Greek word *pleroo*.[4] This word literally means "to fulfill." Matthew and the other biographers of Jesus often used this word in a proverb-like manner. In other words, rather than using the word to refer to a literal prophecy and fulfillment, they often used it to refer to an event in their day like they would use a proverb. For example, when Herod murdered the children in Bethlehem, Matthew says,

> Then what was said through the prophet Jeremiah was **fulfilled**: 'A voice is heard in Ramah, weeping and great mourning, Rachel weeping for her children and refusing to be comforted, because they are no more' (Matthew 2:17).

Was the killing of the infants in Bethlehem actually a prophecy and fulfillment? It may not have been. That even may have been simply another application of a Biblical text that related to the same topic. It was a fulfillment like a proverb is fulfilled. In this case, Jeremiah's comment about the children of Ramah weeping over the loss of her children

---

[4] Matthew uses *pleroo* many times. See 1:22; 2:15, 17; 4:13-16; 8:17; 12:17; 13:35; 21:4; 26:54, 56; 27:9; 27:35 (textual problem).

(Jeremiah 31:15) was an appropriate Biblical statement that would apply to the weeping that went on when the children of Bethlehem were killed.

Does this mean that Matthew misunderstood the Jeremiah passage or misused the word "fulfill." No, the word "fulfill" is capable of that kind of fulfillment. In addition, it was common for people who knew the Old Testament so much to frequently quote the scripture when making a certain point. In quoting the scripture, they were not implying that this was the original meaning of the passage. Rather this passage served as an appropriate commentary on a contemporary event and, thus was used like a proverb.

Interestingly, we use the Bible this way today. Someone is caught doing something that he should not do and we say, "You see, the Bible is fulfilled, *'Be sure your sins will find you out'*" (Numbers 32:23). We are not implying that the person's actions were prophesied in the Bible and this was a specific fulfillment of that passage. However, it is a fulfillment in the sense that the conditions are the similar enough to be another form of fulfillment.[5]

Richness of Scripture

The whole Old Testament bears witness to Christ because it reveals God's character, his way of saving by grace, his ways of using deliverers, his principles for atonement, covenant and promise, his purposes for his people and so many other things. This means that understanding it properly leads us to recognize in Christ the promised deliverer, and God had all this in mind when he inspired the Old Testament Scripture.

It does not mean, however, that we are free to come up with new "fulfillments" of Scripture randomly. The writers of the New Testament were guided by special inspiration, but we cannot make the same claim. That is not to deny that we should be led by the Spirit in understanding Scripture. It is rather to claim that if we say, "The Bible says," we dare say only what it specifically says. If we read into the Bible what is not there, we should be honest and say, "This is my view, not the Bible's," or "I felt

---

[5] See Danny McCain "The Proverbial Use of Pleroo in Matthew's Fulfillment Passages," *Jos Bulletin of Religion*, Volume III, No 1, 1997 for a more complete description of this phenomenon.

as if God were leading me this way." The safest way to read Scripture is to look for its one meaning. With so much of the Bible yet to understand correctly, we have no reason to go looking for "hidden" meanings!

7. Beware of sensational or divisive interpretations of prophecy.

Through most of church history and especially in the past two centuries, many interpreters have reinterpreted biblical prophecies to apply to their own generation. Every decade or two, as news events change, "prophecy experts" have to revise their interpretation of Scripture. In such cases teachers are not reading Scripture on its own authority, but interpreting it in light of current events. This is problematic because they do it on two assumptions: first that all prophecy applies to the final generation which is not true; and second, that we must be the final generation. But most generations in history believed they were the final generation! God says that for all we know we might be—or we might not (Mark 13:32); we must always be ready (Mark 13:33-37). In the New Testament, the *"last days"* included the entire period between the first and second coming, including the first century (Acts 2:17; 1 Timothy 4:1; 2 Timothy 3:1; Hebrew 1:2; James 5:3; 2 Peter 3:3).

In light of the many things that can affect interpretation of prophecy, we must not be dogmatic about our conclusions. We will not likely know the absolute truth until the future unfolds before us. Only a few doctrines about the future are vitally important. We must not allow issues relating to prophecy to divide and separate us.

Conclusion

Prophecy is a very rewarding Biblical field of study. There are many prophecies in the Bible. No one has all the answers, so there is plenty of room for everyone to make a contribution.

Study Questions

1. Give at least one reason why God conceals truth?
2. What is a prophet?
3. List and briefly describe the types of prophecy found in the Bible.
4. What is meant by the "mountain peak perspective" in prophecy?
5. Explain the pros and cons of the "near and far fulfillment" principle.
6. Find 5 examples of figurative language in prophetic portions of the Bible.
7. What is "double fulfillment? Give a specific example.
8. Give an example of a "sensational" prophecy teaching.

Chapter Twenty-Six

Interpreting Jesus

Jesus' Teachings

Jesus' teachings are not a broad genre like poetry or narrative. In fact, they mix together elements of several different kinds of genres. Jesus was, among other things, a Jewish sage, so he often uses the teaching style used by Jewish teachers in his day, including rhetorical overstatements, wisdom proverbs, and parables. At the same time, Jesus was a prophet, and sometimes gave oracles like prophets did (*"Woe to you, Capernaum . . . !"*) Of course, as the Messiah, Jesus was more than a prophet or a sage, and he often spoke with greater authority than either prophets or sages did. But he also used many teaching techniques that were familiar to the people in his day.

Many people assume that what Jesus said on a particular occasion covers every situation, sometimes Jesus himself provided different perspectives for different kinds of situations. Thus we recognize that while Jesus wants us to love him more than our parents, we "hate" them only by comparison with our love for him (Luke 14:26). In another place he instructs us to provide for them in their old age (Mark 7:10-13). Therefore, either teaching taken in isolation creates a misunderstanding of Jesus' teachings.[1]

---

[1] A demonstration of the variety of Jesus' styles and emphases within different contexts related to divorce is found in the appendix.

Gospels

The Gospels are a specific kind of narrative,[2] but rather than treating them only as narrative we make some special points here. The Gospels fit the format of ancient biographies. Some early twentieth century scholars disputed this premise, but more recent scholarship has increasingly returned to the historic view that the Gospels are ancient biographies.

Techniques of Ancient Biographers

Ancient biographers followed some fairly standard procedures in their writing, but some of these differed from the ways we write biographies today. For example, ancient biographies sometimes started with their subject's adulthood as in Mark or John. Sometimes they arranged their story in topical more than chronological order similar to the way Matthew arranges Jesus' teaching. This is why events are not always in the same order from one Gospel to another. Nevertheless, biographers were not free to make up new stories about their heroes. They could choose which stories to report and put them in their own words, but other writers criticized those who made stories up. Further, one need not quote people verbatim, though one did have to get correct the sense of what they meant. This was especially true when one was writing about events in one language that occurred in another language, as was the case with Jesus. He spoke in Aramaic but the Gospel writers wrote in Greek. Knowing such details about various kinds of ancient narratives helps us be even more precise when we learn principles for interpreting narratives.

Trustworthiness of the Gospel Writers

Here we offer just a few comments on the historical trustworthiness of the Gospels as ancient biographies, using Luke 1:1-4 as a simple outline. We know from Luke 1:1 that by the time that Luke wrote, many written

---

[2] We can also identify other kinds of narratives in the Bible more specifically than we have. For example, the Book of Acts is a special kind of history book that was common in the first century.

sources (other Gospels) were already in circulation.³ Luke himself writes in the lifetime of some of the apostles, and already many others have written before him! People were writing Gospels when others still remembered Jesus' teachings very accurately.

Further, there were many oral stories about Jesus being passed on that went back to the eyewitnesses (Luke 1:2). Many African societies have members of the tribe (in some places called a griot) who can recall centuries of information that matches well with written records of European travelers. Ancient Mediterranean people were excellent with memory. Schoolchildren learned by rote memorization, focusing on sayings of famous teachers. Orators regularly memorized speeches that were hours in length. Teachers expected their students and disciples to memorize and propagate their teachings—that was the main duty of disciples. Students regularly took notes, and often ancient teachers attest that students reported their teachings exactly as the teachers gave them.⁴ It is actually historically naive to doubt that Jesus' disciples accurately passed on his teachings.

Further, we can trust the testimony of these eyewitnesses. The apostles remained in positions of leadership in the early church. Both Acts and Paul mention Jesus' brother and the leading apostles in Jerusalem. No one had any reason to invent such people, and the spread of Christianity started somewhere. In addition, diverse sources attest these people. So virtually no one today denies their existence. Because of their leadership, no one could make up stories about Jesus that contradicted their true reports about Jesus. Further, no one can accuse them of lying about Jesus. They were so convinced that they spoke truth about him that they were prepared to die for their claims. Moreover, they were not simply dying for what they believed. They were dying for what they saw and heard when they were with Jesus.

---

³ Most of those Gospels no longer exist. Apart from the Gospels in the New Testament, all first-century Gospels have been lost. The so-called "Lost Gospels" some people speak about today are forgeries, novels, or sayings-collections from later eras.

⁴ For documentation, see the introduction in Craig Keener, *Matthew* [InterVarsity, 1996], or the more detailed volume he wrote for Eerdmans.

Third, Luke had the opportunity to investigate their claims (Luke 1:3, according to the Greek and most translations). Luke verified his sources by interviewing witnesses, wherever possible. Some sections of Acts say "we" because Luke was traveling with Paul at those points, and those sections include their journey to Jerusalem and Palestine, where they remained two years (Acts 21:15-17; 24:27; 27:1). That gave him the opportunity to interview Jesus' younger brother James, among others (Acts 21:18).

Finally, Luke himself would not be able to make these stories up. He is confirming accounts for Theophilus, not introducing new ones (Luke 1:4). That is, while some eyewitnesses are still alive, the stories Luke records were already known by Theophilus. This further confirms to us that, even on purely historical grounds, the Gospels are trustworthy.

Parables

No one can study the life of Jesus without being impressed by how often he used parables in his teaching. A story is one of the most common ways of communicating. However, the lack of understanding the nature of parables has led to some remarkable misunderstandings of Jesus' teachings.

Definition

A parable is a short real-to-life story which is designed to illustrate and support a certain truth. The word comes from two Greek words. *Para* means "alongside of" and *ballot* means "to cast or to throw." When we combine these two words, we get the idea of "to throw alongside of." The idea is that when a person is attempting to communicate a certain truth, he states the truth and then "throws in beside" that truth a story that will help illustrate that truth.

Parables are not unique to the Bible. People have been telling stories, which have figurative meaning, throughout the history of humankind. People are often able to identify more closely with stories than with abstract concepts. Therefore, a story often makes a point better than a straightforward statement. Jesus understood this very well and used many stories in His teaching.

An Ancient Teaching Tool

Parables are a specific kind of narrative that differs somewhat from other kinds of narrative. Ancient Israelite sages in the Old Testament and in the time of Jesus used various graphic teaching forms to communicate their wisdom. These forms were designed to make their hearers think carefully about what they were saying. One such kind of teaching was the proverb. A larger category of teaching (covered by the Hebrew word *mashal*) includes proverbs, short comparisons, and sometimes more extended comparisons, including some actually intended to be allegorized (unlike most kinds of narrative in the Bible)!

By Jesus' day, Jewish teachers often communicated by telling stories in which one or two or sometimes more characters might stand for something in the real world. Often they told stories about a king who loved his son, in which the king was an analogy for God and the son for Israel. When Jesus told parables, therefore, his hearers would already be familiar with them and know how to understand them.

But even though Jesus' parables sometimes were extended analogies with truths in the real world like the four different kinds of soil in the parable of the Sower (Mark 4:3-20), they often included some details simply necessary for the story to make good sense, or to make it a well-told story. For instance, when the Pharisee and the tax-gatherer pray in the temple (Luke 18:10), the temple does not "represent" something. That was simply the favorite place for Jerusalemites to pray. When the owner of the vineyard built a wall around his vineyard (Mark 12:1), we should not struggle to determine what the wall represents. It was simply a standard feature of vineyards, and forces the attentive reader to recognize that Jesus is alluding to the Old Testament parable in Isaiah 5:5. The readers then would know that the vineyard represents Israel.

In the Parable of the Prodigal Son, the father represented how compassionate God is; the younger brother was an analogy for sinners and the older brother is a possible reference to the scribes and Pharisees. But the pigs do not "represent" something in particular. They merely illustrate the severity of the prodigal son's suffering and uncleanness. The prostitutes (Luke 15:30) do not represent false teaching or idolatry or anything else. They simply illustrate how immorally the son squandered his father's earnings.

Parable of the Good Samaritan

Let us look at the parable of the Good Samaritan in Luke 10:30-35. In this parable, a man goes "down" from Jerusalem toward Jericho, when he is overtaken by robbers who beat him and leave him nearly dead. A priest and Levite pass by him, but finally a Samaritan rescues him and takes him to an inn. Augustine, a profound thinker and church father from the coast of North Africa, decided that this was the gospel story: Adam went "down" because he fell into sin, was abused by the devil, was not helped by the law but was finally saved by Christ as a good Samaritan. One could preach this interpretation and actually expect conversions, because one would be preaching the gospel. But one could preach the gospel without attaching it to this particular parable, and in fact this is not what the parable means in its context in Luke.

In Luke 10:29, a lawyer asks Jesus who is his "neighbor" that the Bible commands him to love (see also 10:25-28). Jesus responds that his neighbor might even turn out to be a Samaritan—that real love must cross racial, tribal, even religious lines. This was probably not the answer the lawyer wanted to hear. The answer remains offensive enough even to many people today to suggest why they would not want the parable to mean this! But why would the man go "down" from Jerusalem to Jericho? Simply because Jericho is lower in elevation than Jerusalem! Further, the road to Jericho (like many roads) hosted many robbers. A man who traveled alone would make an easy target, especially at night. The priest and Levite who passed by on the other side of the road (10:31-32) probably did so to avoid contracting ritual impurity. Many Jewish teachers felt that one would become unclean for a week if even one's shadow touched a corpse. And one could not tell, unless one got close, if someone "half-dead" (10:30) were really dead or alive.

The point of the story is that some very religious people did not act very neighborly, but that a person from whom one would not expect it did so. Perhaps if we told the story today we would talk about a Sunday School teacher or minister who passed by on the other side, but someone from a hostile tribe rescued the person. Our hearers might react with hostility to such a comparison—but that is exactly the way Jesus' hearers would have reacted to his. The lawyer's "neighbor" might be a Samaritan. Ours might be someone we are tempted to dislike no less intensely, but Jesus commands us to love everyone.

Rules for Interpreting Parables

1. **Study the Context.** Every parable was given in a specific context and cannot really be understood apart from that context. The context includes the immediate context—that which immediately preceded and followed the parable. It also includes who was in the setting in which the story was given, as well as, who was in the audience, the atmosphere of the event and other details.

2. **Observe the clear teachings near the parable.** Most of the parables are given against a backdrop of teachings. For example, all of the parables in Matthew 13 are given in the context of Jesus' teachings about the kingdom of God. They must be interpreted in light of the overall teachings Jesus was giving about the kingdom.

3. **See if Jesus has given the interpretation of the parable.** In many of the parables, Jesus gave the interpretation. For example, after one of the longest parables in the gospels, the Parable of the Ten Virgins, Jesus gives a very simple interpretation (Matthew 25:13), *"Therefore keep watch, because you do not know the day or the hour."*

4. **Remember that a parable is usually making one central point.** The most common mistake that interpreters make in interpreting parables is to turn them into allegories. An allegory is a story that has meaning and application in several of the parts of the story. The Parable of the Sower is an example of an allegory. The different places that the seed fell illustrate the different ways that the truth is received, so there are multiple points of application in the story. On the other hand, as a general rule, a parable makes one point. It illustrates one truth. We must remember that the details of a parable are given to make the story interesting, not to create additional points of application.

5. **Remember that a parable was originally spoken and not read.** All of the parables from the life of Jesus were given through Jesus' oral teachings and later written down by the apostles. The impact and application the parable had was immediate and not derived from some kind of academic analytical analysis later. One must remember that semi-literate people who heard Jesus speak one time, understood Jesus' communication and got the full impact of the parables.

Conclusion

The teachings and example of Jesus are the heart of Christianity. These teachings are found in several different kinds of genres. Without a proper understanding of these genres, we will not have a proper understanding of Christianity.

Study Questions

1. Give some ways that ancient biographers were similar and some ways they were different from modern biographers.
2. Write a paragraph explaining what the Gospels are trustworthy.
3. Define and explain the word "parable."
4. How were Jesus' parables similar to other stories that were told in his day?
5. What is the difference between a parable and an allegory?
6. What is the most common mistake made in interpreting parables?
7. Demonstrate how Jesus often gave the interpretation to his parables.
8. How does the fact that a parable was first heard and not read influence its interpretation?

Chapter Twenty-Seven

Interpreting the Apostles

Jesus spent three years preparing his disciples to implement what he had come to this world to do. They had heard all of his teachings. They had observed his lifestyle. They had participated in his activities. They had asked him questions and responded to his questions. They had experienced the "ups and downs" of his ministry. When he was crucified, they were deeply disappointed. However, when he was resurrected, they were overjoyed. When they stood on the Mount of Olives and watched Jesus ascend to heaven, something descended upon them. It was their responsibility to carry on everything Jesus had taught and demonstrated.

The apostles used several means to promote the message of Jesus. They preached. They healed. They cast out demons. They witnessed privately. They responded to questions. They went to court. And they wrote. It is two genres of their writing that we are interested in examining in this section.

Epistles

The most common literary device in the New Testament is the epistle.

Definition

An epistle is simply a letter. However, we normally think of an epistle as more than just a friendly letter that would convey greetings or personal information. It is a literary device that is designed to communicate substantive information. It is a didactic tool, the primary purpose of which is to teach. Another way of saying this is that a Biblical epistle is hortatory in nature. That means that it gives instructions, exhortations and clarifies doctrines. However, it does so in a warm and friendly manner. The fact that the Biblical epistles are actual letters, tells us that they are giving instruction to real people who had real questions and real problems. The epistle is not just a collection of theoretical religious thoughts. It is God's chosen tool to communicate His truth to His people.

Although the epistle is not unique to the Bible, the Biblical writers of the New Testament used it as a tool more than most other ancient writers. The use of the epistle was a very natural development in the early church period. The epistles proved to be the best means of passing along accurate information to the young Christian movement.

For example, shortly after Paul completed his first missionary journey, he was informed that some Christians from Jerusalem had visited those same areas. These Jewish Christians were insisting that the new Gentile converts become circumcised. Paul needed to communicate the truth to them. He basically had three options. He could have returned to this area himself and clarified the problem. He could have sent someone to correct the problem. He could write a letter and send it to these converts. He chose the latter. Paul used the other two options at times as well, but whenever he chose to use the epistle option, he put his thoughts into writing. These writings are preserved for us and give us insight into his thinking and that of the early church.

Rules for Interpreting Epistles

1. **Get as much background of every epistle as you can.** You need to know the author, the readers, the date, the circumstances, the problems faced by the recipients, the condition of the author and the purpose of the writing.

2. **Make sure you understand the whole message before trying to understand the individual parts.** The Epistles were given to real people in a real historical and cultural context. Galatians was written against the backdrop of certain Jewish teachers demanding that Gentiles be circumcised. The Thessalonians Epistles were written to answer questions about the second coming of Christ, particularly how that related to believers who died before Jesus returned. The Corinthian Epistles were written to solve several different kinds of internal problems in the church. If we fail to understand the purpose for the writing of the individual Epistles and the circumstances that prompted them, we will misunderstand the various parts of the epistle.

3. Remember that most of the recipients of the Epistles had less knowledge about Christianity than the average Christian today. Christianity was a very young movement when the Epistles were being written. Most of the Gentile converts were coming straight out of paganism and had little understanding of the God of the Old Testament. There was no "New Testament" at that time and the "Old Testament" was only in Jewish synagogues. Very few people had access to read and study sacred scriptures. There were few if any trained Christian leaders. Approximately half of the early Christians were slaves. Many early Christians were illiterate. When most of the Epistles were written, the recipients had been Christians less than ten or at most twenty years. Few if any of the early churches had access to the knowledge being conveyed in the other Epistles that were being written

4. Remember that although the Epistles were written, many of them were designed to be read orally to the members of the various churches. Even with the great limitations outlined above, we must assume that the average Christian who heard these Epistles read orally, understood the main communication intended by the author.

5. Although the Epistles address specific problems within a specific culture, they have application to all people in all cultures. Paul addressed many kinds of problems in 1 Corinthians including divisions in the church over leadership, fellow Christians going to court against each other, immorality in the church, misunderstandings about marriage, about eating meat offered to idols, about the proper means of worshipping, about the way to celebrate the Lord's Supper, about the resurrection and other issues. Many of those are the exact same problems we face today. However, the principles in the Epistles may apply to one culture in a slightly different way than they do another culture. For example, there are general principles about marriage in 1 Corinthians 7. However, various cultures also dictate customs related to marriage, which are not addressed by Paul. The principle of disrespecting authority found in 1 Corinthians 11:1-16 may have a different application in a culture that does not have the cultural practices of the ancient Greeks. Interpreting the Epistles should focus on extracting the general principles and making them applicable in the new culture as closely as one can.

Revelation

The Book of Revelation is a unique kind of literature. It begins and ends like an epistle but the majority of it reads like prophecy. It contains a very large section of apocalyptic imagery, similar to parts of Daniel, Isaiah, Ezekiel, and Zechariah.

Genre and Symbolism

Although scholars debate the specific type of literature into which Revelation falls, most agree that it fits at least in part what modern scholars call "apocalypses." These are Jewish texts that focus on revelations relevant to the end-time. Almost everything in Revelation can be paralleled at least somewhere in the Old Testament prophets, suggesting that Revelation fits into more than one category.

Just as Jewish teachers used riddles, so Jewish prophetic writers used mysterious predictions or riddles, often to provoke thought. Revelation's riddles are primarily to provoke thought, not to conceal most of its meaning. As noted above, on any view, Revelation employs much symbolism. Although one should read most narratives in the Bible literally, prophetic and apocalyptic texts are quite different, as anyone who has spent much time reading them will recognize. They contain considerable symbolism, and often were fulfilled in unexpected ways. Revelation's symbols may appear obscure to us, but they would have made good sense to the believers in the seven churches, at least after some reflection. Most of these symbols were more widely used by their contemporaries.

Revelation is also full of implicit allusions to the Old Testament. Indeed, it contains more biblical allusions than any other early New Testament writing, though it includes no extended quotations of the Old Testament. Many of the allusions recall also the context of their biblical source. Many, however, blend various biblical allusions, and Revelation regularly recycles its images to apply them in a fresh way. For instance, one expects the lion from the tribe of Judah (Revelation 5:5) to be a conquering Messiah (Genesis 49:10), as interpreted in Jewish tradition. Instead, this lion is a slain lamb, conquering by martyrdom (Revelation 5:6). Revelation frequently reapplies standard Old Testament and Jewish end-time symbols in fresh ways.

Approaches to Revelation

History has produced various approaches to the Book of Revelation. Many of these have some elements that commend them, provided we do not press too far their denials of elements in other positions.

1. **The Idealist Approach.** The idealist approach finds timeless principles in the Book of Revelation, but in its extreme form, denies any specific historical or future meaning for Revelation. That Revelation contains timeless principles is hard to dispute, but does that explain the source of its images? Was Revelation teaching merely timeless general principles, with no concern for pressing issues at hand in the churches to which John wrote?

2. **The Historicist Approach.** Some have argued, from at least the time of the fourteenth-century writer Nicolas of Lyra, that Revelation provides a detailed map of history from its own day until Jesus' future return. This historicist view of Revelation as church history dominated views about the book through the seventeenth and eighteenth centuries. It is rarely advanced today. Though there are interesting parallels, if the symbolism is interpreted in the right way, the links between Revelation's contents and history's events are always forced.

3. **The Preterist Approach.** Preterists read the Book of Revelation the way they believe John's original audience in the seven churches would have. In other words, they seek to apply to Revelation the same interpretive method we apply to every other book of the Bible, namely, that we should read it in its historical context. Because more radical preterists insist, however, that the events of Revelation were entirely fulfilled in the first century, they read it in a manner that John's original audience probably would not have. Whatever else may already have been fulfilled, most early Christians would not have recognized in any first century events the fulfillment of the great white throne judgment (20:11-15) or the arrival of the holy city (21:1-22:5). Thus more moderate preterists do not insist that every event of Revelation was fulfilled in the first

century. Most commentators today accept at least the preterist belief that the Book of Revelation must have made sense to its first readers.

4. **The Futurist Approach.** Futurists are certainly right to claim that some events in the book await fulfillment, such as God's unchallenged eternal city supplanting the kingdoms of this world (21:1-22:5). But the futurist position, like the other positions, can be pressed too far. In its radical form, it implies that the book has little truth to communicate to the fifty or more generations between the first and second coming of Jesus. Further, some pivotal clues in the book (see 12:5-6) may suggest that the time frame much of the book reports is not merely future.

5. **An Eclectic Approach.** Many Christian scholars prefer some mixture of historical or preterist approaches with a futurist approach. Late sixteenth-century Spanish Jesuit Ribeira suggested that Revelation portrays events about to occur in John's day as well as immediately preceding Jesus' return, with not much in between. Alcasar, another Spanish Jesuit (d. 1614), suggested that Revelation 4-19 were fulfilled in the conflicts of John's era but Revelation 20-22 represent the church's triumph after Constantine.

Today most commentators who seek to apply Revelation opt for other eclectic approaches, usually combining some futurist, preterist, and idealist elements. Some elements in the book are clearly future; some are past; some probably typify characteristic judgments in the present age. A basic problem is distinguishing which elements belong to which categories. Many believe that much of Revelation provides principles for the end-time church living in the present era between the first and second comings, and argue that chapters 19-22 are future. On any interpretation, all elements warn us to contemplate God's ways and to live accordingly.

Once we understand what God was saying to the churches of Asia through John, we can begin to draw analogies for how the same message would be relevant to our churches today. Thinking concretely how to bridge the gap between Scripture's words in the past and our culture today is important. Sometimes we and our historical predecessors have simply passed on others' ideas without researching them, adding a few new ones along the way for future generations. Many leaders through church history, however, have sought to recontextualize the biblical message for their generation and culture just as the biblical writers contextualized their revelations for their generations and cultures. We must do the same, but before we can do so, we must make sure we understand the Bible properly.

Guidelines for Interpretation

J. Scott Duvall and J. Daniel Hays, in their book, *Grasping God's Word*, outline seven steps in interpreting the Book of Revelation.[1]

1. **Read Revelation with humility.** Because there is so much room for interpretation, there is no room for arrogance or exclusive types of interpretations. One should beware of anyone who has all the answer or provides the correct interpretation for every symbol.

2. **Try to discover the message to the original readers.** John was doing his best to explain truths to the people of his day in a way that would communicate most clearly to them. Any interpretation that ignores the way the original readers would have received this message is doomed to failure.

3. **Do not try to discover a strict chronological map of future events.** Apocalyptic literature is designed to make an impact on people not teach a time line of future events. For example, the sixth seal seems to take the reader to the end of the age (6:12-17) but there is a seventh zeal with additional judgments.

4. **Take Revelation seriously but do not always take it literally.** The use of symbolic or figurative language in no way changes the truth or seriousness of what is being taught.

5. **Pay attention when John identifies an image.** For example, the golden lamp stands in 1:20 are identified as the church; the Lion in 5:5-6 is identified as the Lamb; the dragon in 12:9 is identified with Satan. Since John has given the interpretation of these, when these

---

[1] J. Scott Duvall and J. Daniel Hays, *Grasping God's Word*, Zondervan, Grand Rapids, MI USA, 2001; pp. 278-283.

symbols are found elsewhere in the book, unless otherwise indicated, it can be assumed that these symbols mean the same thing.[2]

6. **Look to the Old Testament and historical context when interpreting images and symbols.** The only two tools the ancient readers had to assist with the interpretation of this book were their own social and cultural background and the Old Testament scriptures. Therefore, the book must be read and interpreted with those two contexts in mind.

7. **Above all, focus on the main idea and do not press all the details.** In apocalyptic literature, it is the big picture that is in focus. The details are there to make the images interesting. We err when we seek meaning in the details.[3]

A general principle for interpreting any text is to take into account the kind of writing a work is. Thus, for example, we read Mark as an ancient biography, Acts as a work of ancient history, Isaiah as a book of prophecies (mostly poetic in form), Psalms as a collection of prayer and praise songs, and Revelation as prophecy or apocalypse (including many symbols). Each kind of literature has some special characteristics.

Conclusion

The New Testament contains various kinds of literary devices which teach the eternal truth that God wants us to know. All of these devices are designed to communicate truth. It is our responsibility to understand

---

[2] Duvall and Hays add a qualification to this point. Sometimes John will use one symbol to refer to more than one thing. "For example, the seven stars are the angels of the seven churches (1:16, 20; 2:1; 3:1). But John also uses the image of a star (not the seven stars) to refer to other things, such as God's agents of judgment (8:10-12) or even Jesus himself (22:16). In the same way, the image of a woman can be used for a false prophetess (2:20), the messianic community (ch. 12), the harlot city or empire (ch. 17), and the bride of Christ (19:7; 21:9)." p. 281.

[3] Duvall and Hayes make this interesting observation: "With most literary genres in the Bible, we begin with the details and build our way toward an understanding of the whole. With Revelation, however, we should start with the big picture and work toward an understanding of the details." p. 282.

these tools as best we can, so that we can understand the truth God is trying to communicate to us.

Study Questions

1. Define and explain the word "epistle."
2. Why is an epistle especially good at communicating truth?
3. Explain this statement. "The average Christian in the first century had less knowledge about Christianity than the average Christian today."
4. How can an epistle addressed to a specific problem 2000 years ago have any bearing on our lives today?
5. Give an example of a symbol in Revelation that comes from the Old Testament.
6. Give an example of a part of the Book of Revelation that is historical and a part that is futuristic.
7. Give an example of how one of the seven principles for interpreting Revelation has been violated.
8. Why should one not stress the details in the Book of Revelation

Chapter Twenty-Eight

Application in the Bible

Introduction

"How do we interpret the statement Paul made to Timothy, 'be not drunk with wine?'" That is a common question that I occasionally ask my students. Most of the time, the student will reply, "That means that we should not drink wine or beer or *burukutu* and get drunk." When I get that answer, I frequently say, "No, that is not the correct answer." That usually creates something of a surprised atmosphere in the class so I continue, "What you have given me is the application of the passage. You have not yet given me the interpretation." The correct interpretation is the meaning that the writer had in his mind when he wrote it. Whenever I ask my students interpretive questions from the Bible, I am sure that over ninety-five percent of the time, they go directly to the application before establishing the correct interpretation. Perhaps one of the reasons for this is because interpretation is usually easier and less controversial than application. Interpretation was for "them" and does not affect our lives. Application is for "us" and should have a direct impact on our lives.

Whether we like to admit it or not, all of us make a distinction between the clear interpretation of the Bible and the application of the Bible. There are some parts of the Bible that are very clear and which were practiced in the past but that we no longer do. For example, all of the sacrifices in the Old Testament, the celebration of the various Old Testament feasts, the treatment of women during their menstrual cycles, the observance of the Sabbath day (though many have attempted to transfer the observance of this to Sunday), even the practice of circumcision and other practices are very clearly understood but not necessarily practiced and certainly not required. There is no problem with interpretation in these passages. The problem is with application.

We usually interpret most of these practices in light of the theological progress that has been made in the New Testament. The death of Christ rendered the additional sacrifices and certain Old Testament practices null and void. This was clearly illustrated in the issue of circumcision. However, we have also abandoned and modified some commands given in the New Testament. We do not share all things in common as the early church did (Acts 2:44). We now worship the Lord on Sunday instead of Saturday, and there is no clear teaching to demand such a thing. We have done so based upon cultural and historical practices. In some parts of Christianity there has been a serious re-interpretation of Jesus' pacifist teachings on *"turning the other cheek."* Some Christian leaders have developed a radicalism that tolerates and even encourages violence toward Muslims that goes beyond legitimate self-defense. Most of these practices reveal that there is a difference between our interpretation of the text and our application of the principles.

In fact, all Scripture is universally applicable (2 Timothy 3:16). This does not mean, however, that it is not articulated in culture-specific and language-specific ways. Rather, it means that we have to take the situation into account when we interpret Scripture, reading it like case studies applying to specific situations to find its principles that we can then apply in other situations.

Inspiration does not change a writing's *genre,* or type of literature. Proverbs are still proverbs, narrative is still narrative, and epistles are still epistles. Pastoral letters, like sermons addressed to local congregations, can contain universal and culture-specific exhortations side-by-side. This is true in inspired, biblical letters just as it is true in other letters.

Illustration of a Modern Letter of Exhortation

For example, I sometimes write letters of exhortation to my children containing mainly universal principles relevant to their lives. Yet in those same letters I may include some exhortations relevant only to our family and their specific situation. Unless I consciously write expecting other, future readers outside the situation, I may never stop to distinguish my universal and situation-specific exhortations. Because I intend all my exhortations to be relevant to my children I do not write these two kinds of exhortations in different ways or express them in different literary forms.

A later reader might therefore distinguish which I thought was which only by reconstructing the situation and comparing my other writings addressing specific situations. To carry this principle over to Paul's writing we can see that murmuring is always wrong (1 Corinthians 10:10; Philippians 2:14); eating idol-food is sometimes wrong (1 Corinthians 8-10); women's authority as ministers of the word was sometimes limited but sometimes commended (see also Romans 16:1-12; Philippians 4:3); drinking wine was sometimes commended (1 Timothy 5:23) and sometimes cautioned against (1 Timothy 3:8).

New Testament Commands Impossible to Obey

Paul provides many direct commands that we do not observe today, and some that we cannot observe today. How many Christians put money into savings the first day of every week for a collection for the saints in Jerusalem (1 Corinthians 16:1-3)? Paul commands his readers to receive Epaphroditus (Phil 2:29), but since this man is now dead, we cannot fulfill this command literally. Paul exhorts his readers to pray for the ministry of himself and his companions (2 Thessalonians 3:1-2), but it is too late to pray for their ministry today. Instead we learn more general principles about hospitably receiving and praying for God's servants.

Must a transcultural application be absurd before we will limit it? Or do these "absurd" examples point out to us the way we ought to read Paul's letters consistently? To claim that only the *obviously* culturally limited passages are in fact culturally limited is simply to beg the question of interpretation methods. If these examples remind us of the *genre* in which Paul writes, they remind us that Paul could freely mix directly transcultural statements with those that addressed merely specific situations. It should not surprise us that Paul relates to his readers where they are at; he specifically states that this is his missionary strategy (1 Corinthians 9:19-23; 10:31-33), and most of us today similarly try to be relevant to those to whom we speak.

"Impossible" Commands Have Application

But none of this means that these passages have nothing to teach us. Paul specifically writes to Timothy, Titus, or to particular churches, but we can learn from his inspired wisdom for their situations as long as we pause to think how it might translate differently into our somewhat different situations. Human nature and God's nature have not changed, and we can take into account the changes in culture as long as we know something about the original cultures of the Bible. For example, Paul specifically left Timothy in Ephesus to warn against those teaching false doctrines (1 Timothy 1:3), and exhorts Timothy to do so according to the prophecies given him (1:18; 4:14; cf. 2 Timothy 1:6); he also addresses specific false teachers (1:20), who are now dead. Although Paul did not leave us in Ephesus nor did we receive Timothy's prophecies, there are plenty of transcultural principles here, such as fighting dangerous doctrines, or heeding words of wisdom or properly tested prophecy. But again, noting that specific exhortations can have more general relevance does not allow us to simply assume that we *know* that transcultural relevance before we have studied the situation carefully.

When Paul tells Timothy to drink a little wine for his stomach's sake (1 Timothy 5:23), we learn that it is sometimes necessary to take medicine. God often heals instantly in answer to prayer, but at many other times he has provided us natural means by which to improve our health. (By "natural" we mean what he has created in nature, not occult practices which involve evil spirits.) Yet recognizing that this is the only way we can apply some Scriptures must summon us to consistency. Perhaps this is the way all Scripture is to be read to be profitable for teaching (2 Timothy 3:16).

Transferring Interpretation into Application

This is how Paul often read the Old Testament: those events were written down as examples for us, both positive and negative (1 Corinthians 10:6, 11). In the same way, we should read the stories in the Bible as case studies—as examples how God dealt with people in particular kinds of situations. Then we can take warning or encouragement when we recognize analogous situations today! But we must make sure the situations are really analogous. That is, God destroyed the disobedient in the wilderness (1 Corinthians 10:6-10); that does not mean that *obedient* people should fear destruction! We do not simply apply *directly to ourselves* every passage we read without taking into account the difference in situation.

The same is true for Paul's letters. Paul addressed specific situations in a specific culture. We cannot simply apply his words to all cultures directly, as if we can ignore differences. When Paul says to *"Greet one another with a holy kiss"* (Romans 16:16; 1 Corinthians 16:20; 2 Corinthians 13:12; 1 Thessalonians 5:26), he uses the standard form of intimate greeting in his culture. Familial kisses were often light kisses on the lips. Today Christians should still greet one another affectionately, but in most of our cultures few of us actually use kisses to do it, especially the kinds of kisses used back then. Although Christian interpreters today differ as to where to draw the line, *no* one tries to fulfill literally every command of the Bible with no account for the difference in situation. No one tries to get Paul's cloak at Troas and bring it to him.

In light of this, we must attempt to understand better the link between interpretation and application.

General Observations about Interpretation and Application

Although these often get confused, there is a significant difference between interpretation and application.

- Interpretation focuses on the past. Application focuses on the present.
- Interpretation focuses on what a passage says. Application focuses on what a passage means.
- Interpretation deals with theory. Application deals with practice.
- Interpretation deals primarily with the mind. Application deals primarily with the will.
- Interpretation is relatively simple. Application is often very difficult.
- Interpretation is often agreed upon quickly. People of diverse backgrounds will often agree upon what a passage says. However, because application actually affects the lives of people, it becomes more controversial.

- Interpretation focusing on the original meaning. Application focuses on how the original meaning fits into our particular culture.

- Interpretation focuses on what the original writer was thinking and how the original reader understood the communication. Application focuses on how that communication should be viewed and responded to by the contemporary believer.

- Interpretation is the job of the theologian. Application is the job of the preacher.

- Interpretation is always first. Application is always second.

- Interpretation is necessary. Application is just as necessary.

Biblical Example of Application

The early church had one very serious issue to deal with. All through the history of Israel, from the time of Abraham, onwards, the Jewish people practiced circumcision. Every Jewish male—every male who wanted to be identified with God—would be circumcised. All of the first Christians were Jews. Since circumcision had been required of them by God, they assumed that the issue of circumcision would continue to be applied to all followers of Jesus exactly like it had been applied to all worshippers of the true God. However, as Christianity spread outside of Judaism and Gentiles became believers, the Christian leaders had to take another look at the issue of circumcision. The issue was not interpretation. The Old Testament scriptures had not changed. What had changed were the circumstances. The original scriptures on circumcision were given in a specific context to a specific group of people. Now that there was a different context and a different group of people, was there a possibility that there would be a different application or even no application to this particular issue? The early church eventually concluded that the issue of circumcision did not apply to Gentile Christians.

Principles Used in Settling Cultural Issues

What were the principles the early church used to settle cultural issues? The following points summarize how the church dealt with this issue.

1. Church leaders came together (Acts 15:4).

The early church did not solve this problem on an individual basis. This is an important principle to note. There is always safety in consulting with others (Proverbs 11:14; 24:6). The final authority for an interpretation may lie with a person, but in the New Testament the issue was resolved by consensus of church leaders. There may be times when an individual church leader has to make a decision for his people. However, as a general rule, there should be consultation and consensus on controversial issues.

2. Various positions were presented (Acts 15:5-18).

The Jews requiring circumcision for the Gentiles, spoke first. Peter, Paul and Barnabas spoke against the practice of circumcision being required of Gentiles. James, the leader of the church at Jerusalem, spoke last.

3. A consensus was reached (Acts 15:19-21).

After all of the discussion, a consensus was reached. It was not a unanimous verdict but there was a clear consensus. The amazing thing is that we are not told how the consensus was reached. Was there a democratic type vote? Perhaps the Holy Spirit left the specific way this was resolved a bit ambiguous so that different cultures could use their cultural ways of coming to a consensus.

For example, in America, we usually reach a consensus by a straight up and down vote. After the issue has been thoroughly discussed, the chairman will ask members to vote. However, I have discovered that in Africa, seldom do we use a straight up and down vote. Usually someone will offer a suggestion. If the chairman thinks it is a good idea and there is no alternate suggestion and, if in the opinion of the chair, most people seem to agree, the chairman will say, "Well, then it is decided . . ." Which way is better? Neither way is better. They both work well. The African method tends to fit into the African sensitivity to the person better than the western method that places less stress on persons and more on ideas.

4. Results were published (Acts 15:22-29).

Although the church did not require circumcision, they did require that the new Gentile converts be sensitive to the convictions of their Jewish Christian fathers by observing some of the Jewish dietary regulations. They put these guidelines in writing. All of this is consistent with the principles found in Romans 14 about not offending a weaker brother.

5. Results were distributed to those affected (Acts 15:30-32).

After the issue was decided and reduced to writing, the decision was sent to the Gentile churches where the people were invited together and the decision was read to them.

What was the result of this approach to application? As far as we know, the issue of circumcision was resolved. Circumcision was not required of non-Jews. There continued to be some grumblers and Paul referred to those who promote circumcision a time or two, but it appears the church had taken an issue that had been considered a moral issue and resolved in successfully.

Follow-Up to the Issue

There is an interesting follow-up to this issue. The church that Paul planted in Corinth was filled almost entirely with people with pagan roots. There were so many pagans in Corinth that all of the meat sold in the public meat markets had been sacrificed to idols earlier that day. The Corinthians sought Paul's opinion about what they should do. If they could not eat meat offered to idols, that would mean that they would eat almost no meat.

Interestingly, Paul had a very clear statement from the Jerusalem Council on this issue. The published document that came out of the Jerusalem Council stated very clearly that the Gentiles were not supposed to eat any meat offered to idols. However, once again, the Corinthians were a different people in a different context and so this demanded a different application. Paul responded to their question by stating that an idol is really nothing (1 Corinthians 8:4), especially for the believer who knows that there is only one God (8:6). Therefore the believer has freedom in this matter (8:9). However, Paul urged the believers to be very careful

Application in the Bible

with this liberty because it might make a fellow believer stumble if he saw one eating meat offered to idols (8:10-12). Paul reiterates that it is legitimate to eat anything sold in the market place including meat offered to idols (10:25). In addition, Christian believers were allowed to go to the homes of pagans and eat any food set before them, even though it may have been offered to idols. However, if the host specifically stated that the food had been offered to idols, it was only then that the believer should refuse to eat (10:28). The summary of the issue is that the believer is free to eat anything, including meat that had been offered to idols. However, each believer has an overriding responsibility to make sure that he does not offend a brother by exercising this liberty.

This is another example of an application that becomes different from the original instruction. The context had changed. The people involved had changed. The issues were different. Therefore, the application of eating meat offered to idols was different in Corinth than it had been in Palestine.

Why did the Church in Palestine and the Church in Corinth come to two different applications? The answer lies in looking at the issues that were involved in the two different cases. There were actually two issues involved in the Jerusalem Council. First, *the Mother Church should not require cultural practices from the Daughter Church.* This was true even when the cultural practices had religious overtones. Second, *the Daughter Church should not needlessly offend the Mother Church with practices considered repugnant.* In other words, we should be sensitive to the cultural feelings of other believers. This is illustrated by the dietary requirements of the Jewish leaders.

The latter principle was the same principle that we see in 1 Corinthians 8 and 10. The Christian did not have to worry about Jewish believers who were far away. However, they did have to worry about the consciences of the local people, including the pagans whom they were attempting to reach with the gospel. Romans 14 discusses the same principle. It teaches us how to resolve "cultural" type problems—that is issues that are viewed in different ways primarily because of differences in cultural backgrounds.

To understand Romans 14, it is essential for one to understand the meaning of the "weak" and "strong" in this passage. The "weak" are not necessarily new believers or carnal believers or those inferior to the other believers in any way. In addition, the "strong" believers were not necessarily the mature, more committed believers. The "weak" represent those who have "weak consciences." That means that they have sensitive consciences. Their consciences cannot stand up to a lot of weight. They feel badly about small things. The "strong" on the other hand are those who have a conscience that is not easily bothered. They can do things that others cannot do and their consciences never bother them at all.

The first illustration given in this context is that of eating. One person who has a very sensitive conscience will not eat meat because an animal has to die. That person's conscience is so weak that he or she cannot even bear to think about that animal dying. On the other hand, another person has no conscience at all about eating meat. He or she can even kill the animal personally and still enjoy the meat because his or her conscience is very strong. The rest of the chapter is reasonably self-explanatory if one will simply read it with this understanding of the weak and strong.

Questions about Interpreting and Applying

What are the different levels of authority found in the Bible?

- **Commands.** A command carries the highest level of authority. Most Christians try to obey the commands of the Bible.

- **Exhortations.** Exhortations encourage us to do something. It is milder than a command. If one fails to fulfill the exhortation, there has been no rebellion.

- **Prayers.** This is the mildest form of attempting to get someone to do a certain thing. A wish or a prayer presupposes that the person to whom the wish is directed has a strong relationship with the person making the wish and a desire to please that person. A wish or prayer is also based upon a strong recognition of the free will of the person involved.

- **Examples.** The question is to what extent do we follow the example of Christ or the example of the apostles. Baptism is a good illustration of an example that needs some clarification. The unanimous example of the early church was that a person was baptized immediately after conversion. Do we baptize our converts here in Africa immediately after conversion? Note also that in Acts, the example is that they were baptized in the name of Jesus. However, the clear instructions are that we are to baptize in the name of the Father, the Son and the Holy Spirit. Do we go by the example or do we go by the instructions?

What are the criteria for following an example in the Bible?

- *Is the example possible to follow?* Jesus prayed all night on one occasion (Luke 6:12). That is something that we can do. However, Jesus did other things that are impossible for an ordinary person to do, such as, Jesus walked on the water (Matthew 14:25). One does not have to walk on the water to be a follower of Jesus.

- *Is the practice permissible?* The way that some of the Old Testament characters responded to violence is no longer permissible in the New Testament according to the teachings of Jesus.

- *Will the practice be understood the same way today as it was originally understood?* Though this is not stated very clearly, it is assumed that one of the reasons that the Jewish church leaders were willing to forego circumcision for Gentile believers was because it would not mean the same thing to them as it meant to the Jews. Therefore, the ceremony would be irrelevant. It is very unlikely that greeting one another with a holy kiss would be viewed in Africa today like it was viewed in the first century world.

- *Is there any teaching from the Bible to support the practice?* Jesus washed his disciples' feet. Later Jesus said, *"you also should wash one another's feet"* (John 13:14). The question is whether this was meant as a literal washing of feet or simply encouragement toward humility.

Why do we accept the Bible as authority?

This is not a book on apologetics. However, the following are at least some of the reasons why we accept the Bible as authoritative in our lives:

- Parts of it were given directly by God.

- Parts of it were written by the apostles who were closest to Jesus.
- It contains amazing prophecies that imply supernatural knowledge.
- It claims to have been inspired by the Holy Spirit.
- It has been respected as authoritative by the church.
- It has a unique way of speaking to us.
- It makes sense that an intelligent God would want to communicate with us. Communicating through writing is a good strategy.

What are some rules for application?

1. Summarize the interpretation of every passage.

Before you can make application to a passage, you must interpret that passage. A good way to do that is to simply summarize what the passage says in your own words. Usually the general interpretation of a passage is easier than one might think.

2. Extract the key principle(s) from the passage.

Once a person has a good understanding of what a passage says, he or she should ask the following questions to try to determine the principles underlying the passage:

- What is the core truth being taught in the passage?
- Is the core truth being taught appreciated in the local culture?
- Is that core truth expressed in a different way in the local culture?
- Is the application of the core truth consistent with other scriptures?
- Are there examples of the practice being "violated" in other parts of the Bible? For example, the prohibition on women leaders is not entirely consistent. On the other hand, the principle of respect for authority was practiced by David, even when it was to his personal detriment to do so.

- Is the practice repeated in different contexts, particularly in Jewish and Gentile contexts?

- Are there examples of exceptions to this practice in the Bible?

- Are there examples of cultures that have no understanding of this practice?

- Are there examples of different cultures expressing the principle in a different way? This can be illustrated by the way different cultures express respect for elders. An example of African and American cultures viewing things differently is the issue of bodily functions. Bodily functions are considered very normal in Africa. For one to relieve himself in public is not uncommon. However, bodily functions are considered very private in America. For one to relieve himself in public would be considered very rude and is illegal in most places. Greetings are considered very important in Africa. Before one can address problems, there must be appropriate greetings. Time is considered important in America. Therefore, greetings are not very important. When you visit someone, you get immediately to the point. This kind of impersonal approach to things is considered rude and improper by Africans.

- Does a local practice abuse anyone? Does the strict application of the Biblical practice abuse anyone in a different culture? If so, perhaps we have misunderstood the practice or the culture?

3. Attempt to determine whether the application has cultural or cross-cultural consensus.

There are many principles that extend across practically all cultures. For example, no culture believes that it is right to sexually abuse small children. So when making an application of a Scriptural principle, one should ask the following questions:

- Do most cultures of the world have consensus on this issue?

- Do honorable and noble people practice such things?

- Is there near unanimous consensus among religious leaders, including other religions, on the issue?

4. Look at your culture or area of influence and observe ways the principle is being violated.

If the truth being investigated has a cultural application, there will be some manifestation of this principle, either positively or negatively. A good exercise is to name practically any principle in the Bible (respect for authority; importance of truth; value of personal relationships). How is that principle being violated in your culture? Once you have observed how several Biblical principles are being violated, it should be easier to determine whether or not the application you are considering has eternal or only cultural ramifications.

5. Determine how one can observe the principle in a culture.

When one extracts a truth from the Bible and attempts to make an application to a local culture, he or she should first see if the application of the principle in this culture could be done as it was in the Biblical culture. However, if it appears to be clumsy or inappropriate to fulfill the principle exactly as it was fulfilled in the first century, is there some alternative way it can be fulfilled?

6. Attempt to find other scriptures to support that application.

When studying principles in the Bible, it is ideal to look at how this principle was manifested in more than one context. The more different ways that we can see how a principle was applied in the Bible, the better this will help us to apply that principle in our own context.

Examples and Projects for Consideration

The following questions and projects will help you to sharpen your ability to make appropriate application from Biblical principles:

1. What are some Old Testament laws that are no longer practiced or which are controversial in our modern Christian world?

Although Christians love and revere the Old Testament, we often do not know what to do with it. Do we interpret it literally? Do we observe all of its guidelines? Are there commands or guidelines in the Old Testament that are no longer applicable today? What about the following:

- Sprinkling the blood on the doorpost
- Wearing of men's clothing
- Keeping the Sabbath day
- Restitution
- Dietary Regulations

2. What are some potential "cultural" practices in the New Testament that need to be studied?

We often think of the Corinthian church as being the most troublesome for Paul. That may or may not have been true. If it were true, it was because the Corinthians had a lot of cultural issues to deal with. The contemporary Christian world struggles with some of the same issues that were practiced in the first century. Many of the issues came from Corinthians. Note the following issues which were applied quite clearly during the first century but which are often applied differently today.

- Going to law against a brother
- Confusion in the church service

- Eating meat offered to idols
- Head covering in 1 Corinthians 11
- Drinking alcohol
- Participation of women in church activities
- Submission of women to authority
- Instruction of slaves to obey their masters
- Speaking in tongues and prophesying
- Praying for the dead
- Toleration for slavery
- Turning the other cheek
- Taking a little wine for the stomach's sake

3. What are some cultural examples of things that may be applied differently in contemporary cultures?

The following are some examples of things in our contemporary world that may be applied a bit differently than they were in the first century.

- **Respect for Elders.** Africans are very extremely respectful to elders. However, some demonstrate that respect in more obvious ways than others?

- **Worship Styles.** Some church services are very quiet and personal. Others are very loud and participatory. The noise level in a worship service and the extent to which one participates in the worship appears to be a cultural issue and not an eternal principle.

- **Family Life.** Western families feel much more need to be together most of the time. However, African families are often split up. In Western families the nuclear family is important. In African families the extended family is what is important.

- **Market Chatter.** Americans feel compelled to always speak true words. Africans frequently say things in a market bargaining situation that are not true. Is this a cultural issue or a moral issue?
- **Mercy and Justice.** Western people tend to focus more on justice while Africans tend to focus more on mercy. Americans always want to see justice done when they have been offended. Africans tend to be more forgiving when they have been offended.

4. What are some examples of cultural customs that were practiced in Biblical days that are not practiced now?

The following customs may have been practiced a bit differently in the first century than they are today:

- Greeting one another with a Holy Kiss
- Eating meat offered to idols
- Wearing of a head covering
- Submission of the wife
- Wearing that which pertains to the opposite sex. This custom has to be culturally determined, because it is culture that determines what belongs to another sex.

Project

A helpful exercise is to select a contemporary problem in your church—a problem where there is fairly strong differences of opinion (the head tie issue; women in leadership and ministry; styles of worship; use of African instruments in church). Take the following steps in trying to understand and apply the Biblical principles to the issue:

- Identify the problem.
- Identify the key scriptures that relate to the problem.
- Make sure that you understand the way all sides support their positions from the Bible.

- Work your way through the application process as described above.
- Using the principles of creating appropriate application, formulate an application scheme for that issue for your church.
- Summarize the process and results of your research.

Exercise

A good activity for a group is to go through 1 Corinthians 11:1-16 and do an "application study" of the issues in that section of scripture.

Conclusion

Christianity is a practical religion. We study the Bible not to be philosophers and theologians but to find practical guidance for our lives. In order for the Bible to be a meaningful guide to our lives, we must understand both interpretation and application.

Study Questions

1. List five differences between interpretation and application.
2. How does the issue of circumcision illustrate the difference between interpretation and application?
3. Give an example of a contemporary practice that applies scripture differently than in the Biblical days.
4. What were the principles used in settling the issue of circumcision in the early church?
5. What are the different levels of authority found in the Bible? What are some scriptures more authoritative than others?
6. What are the guidelines for determining whether we should follow or imitate a Biblical practice?
7. What are the general rules for application?
8. What are some Old Testament practices that we no longer practice?
9. What are some New Testament practices that we no longer practice?
10. List some practices in your culture that are not practiced in other cultures.

Chapter Twenty-Nine

Application in the Narratives

Introduction

Many believe that Muslims take more seriously what Mohammed *did* in established Islamic doctrine than Christians do in building doctrine out of what Jesus *did*. Are Christians bound to follow the examples of Christ and the other godly characters in the Bible? After referring to a story in the Old Testament, twice Paul declares, *"These things occurred as examples"* (1 Corinthians 10:6, 11). If they are examples, how do we convert them into useful beliefs and practices for Christians? How do we identify what particular historical practices and events are useful to us in creating doctrine?

Modern Practices

Most cultures in the world teach lessons through stories. Most theologians who question the use of narrative are westerners or those trained by them, children of Enlightenment thought. In fact, not even all westerners find Bible stories inaccessible. Even in the United States, African American churches have for generations specialized in narrative preaching. In most churches children grow up loving Bible stories until they become adults and "learn" that they must now think abstractly rather than learning from concrete illustrations. Just because our traditional method of extracting doctrine from Scripture does not work well on narrative does not mean that Bible stories are unimportant. Instead our fear of narrative suggests the inadequacy of our traditional method of applying God's Word.

Traditional Practices

When Jesus' followers were writing the New Testament, everyone in their culture already understood that narrative conveyed moral principles.

Biographers and historians expected readers to draw lessons from their examples, whether these lessons were positive or negative. Students recited such stories in elementary school exercises, and in more advanced levels of education learned how to apply these examples to drive home moral points.

If this was a legitimate form of teaching doctrine in the Bible days, how should we go about doing it today?

Identifying Lessons from Stories

The first step in application is interpretation. The first step in applying narrative to contemporary life is to understand very clearly exactly what happened in the Bible story. It is only as we understand what happened, that we can make appropriate application. We must resist the temptation to read Bible stories in light of our modern context. We must make the effort to place ourselves back in the ancient world and see the events from their perspective.

After, establishing the fact of the story, we must start looking for lessons or principles that transcend the time and culture barriers. A good place to begin is to look at the characters in the stories. They have things to teach us.

Positive and Negative Qualities

Most narratives involve characters. One can try to determine whether the examples of the characters were good or bad ones in any given case by several methods:

When the writer and readers shared the same culture and it assumed an act was bad or good, we can assume that the readers knew which was which, unless we disagree with the views of the culture.

- If we read through the entire book, we may notice patterns of behavior. An evaluation of the behavior in one case would apply to similar cases of the behavior in that book.
- By deliberately highlighting the differences among characters, we can usually see which were good and which were bad examples.

Contrasting Characters

Sometimes we learn from a story by looking at positive and negative characters in the story and contrasting them. We can do this in 1 Samuel 1-2. We learn that humble Hannah, who was looked down on by many of the people who knew her, was godly, whereas Eli the high priest, whom everyone respected, had compromised his calling. Hannah offered to give up her son for God. Eli, refusing to give up his sons for God, ultimately lost them and everything else as well. After this, the story compares the boy Samuel, who hears God and delivers his message, with Eli's ungodly sons, who abuse their ministry by making themselves rich and having sexual relations with many women. God ultimately exalts Samuel but kills the hypocritical sons. Later 1 Samuel contrasts David and Saul; by examining the differences between them, we can learn principles for fulfilling God's call and also dangers to avoid.

Positive and Negative Qualities in the Same Person

One warning we need to keep in mind is that not all human actions recorded in Scripture are intended as positive examples, even when performed by generally positive characters. Scripture is realistic about human nature and openly reveals our frailties so that we can be realistic about our weaknesses and our need to depend always on God.

Most characters in the Bible, just like most characters in Greek histories and biography, included a mixture of positive and negative traits. The Bible tells us about real people, and we learn from that record not to idolize as perfect good people or demonize as wholly evil people today.

Jonah is such a person. He illustrates many negative qualities such as stubbornness, disobedience, lack of compassion and selfishness. On the other hand, he illustrates repentance, perseverance and humility (by later writing down a story that portrayed him in a very embarrassing light).

In the New Testament, John the Baptist was the greatest prophet before Jesus (Matthew 11:11-14). However, he was unsure whether Jesus was fulfilling his prophecy (Matthew 11:2-3) because Jesus was healing sick people but not pouring out fiery judgment (Matthew 3:11-12). John was a man of God, but he did not understand that the kingdom would come in two stages because its king would come twice.

Note these good Biblical characters who had weaknesses in their lives:

- Abraham and Sarah each laughed when they heard God's promise (Genesis 17:17; 18:12-15).
- David almost snapped under the pressure of Saul's pursuit and Samuel's death, and thus would have slaughtered Nabal and his workers had Abigail not stopped him (1 Samuel 25:32-34)
- Elijah actually asked to die, when faced with Jezebel's evil control over Israel (1 Kings 19:4).
- Jeremiah cursed the day of his birth because he was so discouraged that no one was listening to his message (Jeremiah 20:14-18).
- Peter denied Jesus three times (Mark 14:72).

As Paul said, we have this treasure in earthen vessels, so people may recognize that the power comes from God (2 Corinthians 4:7). Jesus alone exhibits no moral weaknesses, and even He identified with our being tempted (Mark 1:12-13; 14:34-42). Scripture shows the weaknesses of men and women of God so we will recognize that there are no spiritual superhumans among us—just, at best, men and women who depend on the power of God's perfect Spirit to give us victory.

Distinguishing positive from negative examples takes much work, but is rewarding. It requires us to immerse ourselves in the entire story over and over until we can see the patterns in the story that give us the inspired author's perspectives.

Listing Characteristics

A very helpful technique that lays a good foundation for application is to make a list of characteristics or character qualities associated with a certain Bible character, especially if the text specifically calls him or her righteous.

Example of Joseph

Matthew 1:18-25 specifically states that Joseph, the husband of Mary was "*righteous.*" Before listing lessons, we must provide some background.

Given the average age of marriage among first-century Jews, Joseph was possibly less than twenty and Mary was perhaps in her mid-teens. Joseph probably did not know Mary well. Sources suggest that parents did not allow Galilean couples to spend much time together before their marriage day. Also, Jewish betrothal was as binding legally as a marriage, hence could be ended only by divorce or the death of one partner. If the woman were charged with unfaithfulness in a court, her father would have to return to the groom the bride price he had paid. Also the groom would keep any dowry the bride had brought or was bringing into the marriage. By divorcing her privately the groom would probably forfeit such financial remuneration.

The following are some lessons we can learn from Joseph:

1. The narrative implies something about **commitment.** Joseph was righteous even though he planned to divorce Mary, because he thought she had been unfaithful, and unfaithfulness is a very serious offense.

2. The text also teaches us about **compassion.** Even though Joseph believed (wrongly) that Mary had been unfaithful to him, he planned to divorce her privately to minimize her shame, thereby forgoing any monetary repayment for her misdeed and any revenge. Here Joseph's "righteousness" (1:19) includes compassion.

3. The passage further emphasizes **consecration.** Joseph was willing to bear shame to obey God. Mary's pregnancy would bring her shame, perhaps for the rest of her life. If Joseph married her, people would assume either he impregnated her or, less likely, that he was a moral weakling who refused to punish her properly. In either case, Joseph was embracing Mary's long-term shame in obedience to God's will.

4. Finally, we learn about **self-control.** In their culture, everyone assumed that a man and woman alone together could not control themselves sexually. But in their obedience to God, Joseph and Mary remained celibate even once they were married until Jesus was born, to fulfill the Scripture that promised not only a virgin conception but a virgin *birth* (1:23, 25).

Identifying qualities like these in the life of Joseph leads to very easy and natural application.

Some passages do not yield as many specific principles as this passage. The story of the lepers' discovery of the abandoned Aramean tents (2 Kings 7:3-10) functions as part of larger story about God's provision for Israel, judgment on those who doubted his prophet, and how God could replace His judgment on the nation with extraordinary mercy according to His prophetic message. At the same time, this smaller unit probably does provide some insights that also fit into the larger pattern of Scripture as a whole. God chooses not the mighty (see 7:2) but lepers excluded from the city (7:3) to make the discovery—desperate people who had nothing more to lose (7:4). The Bible indicates that these are often the kind of people God chooses.

Can We Learn Doctrine from Narratives?

Some modern theologians have been skeptical about learning doctrine from narratives. However, 2 Timothy 3:16 explicitly declares that all Scripture is profitable for teaching, so to rule out a teaching function for narratives altogether, these theologians would have to deny that narratives are part of Scripture! But narrative makes up more of the Bible than any other genre does, and Jesus and Paul both teach from Old Testament narratives (e.g., Mark 2:25-26; 10:6-9; 1 Corinthians 10:1-11).[1]

If narratives did not teach, there would be no reason for different Gospels. Because Jesus did and taught so much, no single Gospel writer could have told us everything that he said or did as John 21:25 explicitly points out. Rather, each Gospel writer emphasized certain points about Jesus, the way we do when we read or preach from a text in the Bible.

Yet despite considerable historical precedent for using biblical historical precedent, many theologians suggest that one should feel free to find in narrative *only* what is plainly taught in "clearer," "didactic" portions of Scripture. Although some of these scholars are among the ablest exegetes of other portions of Scripture, I must protest that their approach to Bible stories violates the most basic rules for biblical interpretation and in

---

[1] Some of what follows below is borrowed from the appendix of Craig Keener's book, *3 Crucial Questions about the Holy Spirit* (Grand Rapids, MI, USA: Baker Book House, 1996).

practice jeopardizes the doctrine of biblical inspiration. Did not Paul say that *all* Scripture was inspired and therefore useful for "doctrine," or teaching (2 Timothy 3:16)? Certainly the teaching passages interpret and explain the things that have happened beforehand but to ignore history as a means of teaching Biblical history is a serious omission.

Getting the Author's Perspective

When we read Bible stories, we not only learn the historical facts, we listen to the inspired writer's *perspective* on what happened. When the writer "preaches" to us from the stories he tells us, he often gives clues for recognizing the lessons. For example, he often selects stories with a basic theme(s) that repeatedly emphasize particular lessons.

One of the most basic principles of Bible interpretation is that we should ask what the writer wanted to convey to his contemporary audience. This principle applies to narratives like the Gospels as much as to epistles like Romans. If one could simply write a "neutral" Gospel that addressed all situations universally, the Bible would undoubtedly have included it. Instead, the Bible offers us four Gospels, each selecting some different elements of Jesus' life and teachings to preach Jesus to the needs of their readers in relevant ways. The way God chose to give us the Bible is more important than the way we *wish* He would have given it to us.

Reading Books as Units

More importantly, we must be able to read each book first of all as a self-contained unit, because that was how God originally inspired these books. God inspired books of the Bible like Mark or Ephesians one at a time, inspiring the authors to address specific situations. The first readers of Mark could not cross-reference to Ephesians or John to figure out an obscure point in Mark. They would have to read and reread Mark as a whole until they grasped the meaning of any given passage in Mark. When we read a passage in such books of the Bible, we need to read the passage in light of the total message and argument of the book as well as reading the book in light of the passages that make it up.

This is not saying that we should *not* compare the results from our study of Ephesians with the results from our study of Mark. On the other hand, it is to say that we discount the complete character of Mark when we resort to Ephesians before we have finished our examination of Mark. For instance, the opposition Jesus faces for healing a paralytic does provide a lesson for the hostility we can expect from the world for doing God's will. The opposition to Jesus, which builds in early chapters of Mark and climaxes in the cross, parallels the suffering believers themselves are called to expect (Mark 8:31-38; 10:33-45; 13:9-13; 14:21-51). Mark summons Christians to endure. That Mark provides negative examples of this principle (e.g., 14:31-51) reinforces his point.

Case Study of the Lord's Supper

The Lord's Supper is a helpful example of how we combine historical teachings with didactic teachings. Matthew, Mark and Luke provide us with the original creation of the ceremony. However, because there was a controversy over this, Paul wrote to clarify the issue (1 Corinthians 11:17-34). Obviously, Paul's interpretation is an inspired commentary on the practice. However, we do not get our theology of Holy Communion just from Paul's writings. The way it was celebrated the first time as well as hints of the way it was celebrated in another history section (Acts 2:42; 46; 20:7) all work together to create the Christian doctrine of the Lord's Supper.

Conclusion

I suspect that many scholars—including myself in earlier years—have felt uncomfortable with finding theology in narrative largely because of our western academic training. In the world of the theological academy, one can feel satisfied addressing important issues like Christology while ignoring other necessary issues like domestic abuse and how to witness on a secular job. But pastors, people who do much personal witnessing and other ministers cannot ignore issues that exceed the bounds of traditional doctrinal categories. I believe that the more we are forced to grapple with the same kinds of situations with which the writers of Scripture grappled, the more sensitively we will interpret the texts they wrote. When that happens, we will need to re-appropriate all of Scripture for the life and faith of the Church.

Study Questions

1. In your opinion do Christians or Muslims take most seriously the example of their founders? Explain your answer.
2. Give an example of a Bible doctrine in which we build that doctrine with historical as well as teaching passages.
3. Select a Bible story with a positive and negative character. Give a list of five characteristics of the positive character and five characteristics of the negative character.
4. Select a Bible character and list six positive characteristics about him/her.
5. Select a Bible character and list six negative characteristics about him/her.
6. Select a Bible character and list three negative and three positive characteristics about him/her.
7. Explain why or why not we should use narrative to build doctrine.
8. What does a "writer's perspective" teach us about application?

Chapter Thirty

Application in the Epistles

The epistles are the final written portions of the sacred scriptures. They comment on, interpret and apply all of the other written scriptures to the early Christian era. In light of this unique perspective, it is essential for us to focus specifically on interpreting New Testament epistles.

Interpretation - the Bases of Application

As we read the epistles in the Bible, we must read them first of all as letters addressed to real people in the writer's own day, for this is what they explicitly claim to be (Romans 1:7). Only after we have understood the letters in their own historical context can we consider how to rightly apply them to our situations today. In contrast to those who assume that letters require less interpretation than other parts of Scripture, they are actually among the parts of Scripture *most* closely tied to their historical situation.

For example, how does one apply the teachings of 1 Corinthians in a very different cultural setting? The promise of future resurrection (1 Corinthians 15) seems easy enough. A topic that is more controversial in many cultures and in many churches is the practice of women wearing head coverings (1 Corinthians 11:2-16). Is it necessary for modern Christian women to wear head coverings, even if the practice is no longer part of the broader culture? But what about food offered to idols (1 Corinthians 8-10)? In cultures where people no longer sacrifice food to idols, like much of the western world, are they free to simply skip over those chapters? Or are there transcultural principles that Paul uses there which would also be relevant to other cultures?

Cultural Background

As we noted in more detail above, cultural background in Bible study is not optional; we must take the original situation into account to fully understand the Bible. This is at least as true of letters as it is of every other part of the Bible, and maybe more so, because letters explicitly address specific congregations or people facing specific situations. Some passages are difficult to understand because the original audience already knew what was being addressed, and we are not always able to reconstruct it (2 Thessalonians 2:5). In such cases we must learn humility! After all, if Paul was with the Corinthians for eighteen months (Acts 18:11), one might expect him to talk about some issues with them that we know little about (1 Corinthians 1:16; 3:4-6; 15:29). But even in such cases we can often catch the general point of the passage as a whole, and that is what we need most. Further research into the background usually reveals more details, but there will always be some things we do not know until Jesus returns (1 Corinthians 13:12).

Common Communication Means of the Ancient World

Writers of biblical letters often followed standards of "rhetoric," which were the proper speaking and writing principles of their day. Knowing some of those customs can help us understand the letters better.[1] At the same time, those writers were not simply showing off their writing abilities. They were making points, correcting problems and encouraging Christians in particular situations. Once we understand the situation, we can usually understand how the writer is addressing that situation. These writers applied eternal principles to concrete situations in their own day. To allow for an equivalent impact, we must reapply those principles to the concrete situations of our day, taking into account the differences in culture.

When we apply the teachings of the epistles, we must make sure that we find the appropriate analogies between the situations Paul addresses and our situations today. For example, some interpreters believe that Paul prohibits the women in one congregation from teaching because they were generally uneducated, hence could prove easily misled (1 Timothy 2:11-12). In that culture, his command that they should *"learn"* (2:11) actually liberated women, who normally did not receive direct

---

[1] For example, Paul often opens all of his epistles with "grace and peace be with you, from God and Christ." Understanding why he did this will help in interpreting the book.

instruction except by sitting in services. It makes a difference whether or not this is the issue. If not, the appropriate application today may be that women should never teach the Bible though this would leave in question what to do with other texts, like Romans 16:1-2, 7; Philippians 4:2-3; Judges 4:4; and 1 Corinthians 11:4-5. If so, the analogy today may be that unlearned people, whether male or female, should not teach the Bible.

Two Principles for Interpretation

Gordon Fee suggests two main general principles for interpreting letters. First, "a text cannot mean what it never could have meant to its author or his or her readers."[2] He notes for instance that one cannot argue that the *"perfect"* in 1 Corinthians 13:10 refers to the completion of the New Testament—since Paul's readers had no way of knowing that there would be a New Testament. Second,

> Whenever we share comparable particulars (i.e., similar specific life situations) with the first-century setting, God's Word to us is the same as his Word to them.[3]

Murmuring, complaining, sexual immorality and greed will always be wrong, no matter how much or little any culture practices them.

Contemporary Application

What do we do with texts that address situations very much unlike our situations today? Jewish and Gentile Christians divided over food laws and holy days. Paul warned them in Romans 14 not to divide over such secondary matters. If we live in a social circle where we do not know any Christians who keep Old Testament festivals and who abstain from pork, do we simply skip over this chapter? Yet Paul's advice in this chapter works from a broader principle in addressing the specific situation. The principle is that we should not divide from one another over secondary issues, issues that are not at the heart of the gospel and Christian

---

[2] Gordon Fee and Doug Stuart, *How to Read the Bible for All Its Worth* (Grand Rapids, MI USA Zondervan, 1993), p. 64.

[3] Fee and Stuart, p. 65.

morality. The particular issue Paul was addressing was eating various kinds of meat. The real principle was offending a Christian brother.

Paul wrote to specific, real-life congregations. Because he was not expecting Christians many centuries later in different cultures and situations to keep reading his letters (cf. Mark 13:32), he did not stop to distinguish for us his transcultural principles on which he based his advice from the concrete advice he gave to these congregations in their situations.

Determining Transcultural Principles

Gordon Fee lists several principles for distinguishing transcultural principles, the most important of which we have adapted here.

1. Look for the "core" principle in any passage.

We should look for the "core," or the transcultural principle in every text. This is important so we keep the emphasis on Christ's gospel and do not become legalists on details like some of Jesus' enemies were. The Bible itself presents some matters as transcultural moral norms, such as Paul's vice lists (Romans 1:28-31; 1 Corinthians 6:9-10). But in different cultures the Bible described different customs related to women's work outside the home (Proverbs 31:16, 24; 1 Timothy 5:14) or various forms of ministry (Judges 4:4; Philippians 4:3; 1 Timothy 2:12). If different passages allow different practices, we see these practices as providing guidelines in a specific culture. However, those guidelines may not be transcultural principles that apply to all cultures without exceptions.

2. Identify the cultural options available to the writer.

To really make contemporary application, we must understand the cultural options available to the original writers. For example, biblical writers wrote in an era where no one was trying to abolish slavery. That the Bible's writers do not explicitly address an issue that no one had raised does not suggest that they would have sided with slavery's supporters had the question been raised! On the other hand, Greeks in Paul's day held various views regarding premarital sex, homosexual intercourse, and other issues. However, the Bible is unanimous in condemning such practices, even though its opposition was contrary to commonly accepted beliefs in that culture.

3. We must take into considerations differences between the original readers and those to whom we are making contemporary application.

There are some major differences between the average Christian in the first century and the average Christian today. For example, in the first century, men were far more apt to be educated, than women. In fact, boys were taught to recite God's law but girls almost never received this education. In light of that, would Paul have written exactly the same applications for today, when women and men are more likely to share equal opportunities for education?

Case Study of Women Keeping Silent in the Church

We may provide one stark example of how we need to take Paul's situation into account. In two texts, Paul requires women to keep "silence" in church (1 Corinthians 14:34-35; 1 Timothy 2:12). If we press this to mean all that it could mean, women should not even sing in church! Few churches today press these verses this far, but are they ignoring the passages' meaning? Not necessarily. In other texts, Paul commends women for their labors for the kingdom (Philippians 4:2-3), and in Romans 16 commends more women for their services. Moreover, he at least occasionally uses his most common terms for his male fellow workers to some women, including: "fellow worker" (Prisca, Romans 16:3); *diakonos* ("servant," Phoebe, Romans 16:1); and once even "apostle" (Junia, according to the best translations; Romans 16:7)! Even more importantly, he accepts women praying and prophesying with their heads covered (1 Corinthians 11:4-5). How can they pray and prophesy if later in the same letter he requires them to be completely silent in church (1 Corinthians 14:34-35)? Does the Bible contradict itself here? Did Paul contradict himself in the very same letter?

The two texts about silence probably do not address all kinds of silence, but deal with special kinds of situations. The only kind of speech specifically addressed in 1 Corinthians 14:34-35 is asking questions (14:35). It was common for people to interrupt teachers and lecturers with questions in Jewish and Greek cultures alike. But it was rude for unlearned people to do so, and they might have considered it especially rude for unlearned women.

As to 1 Timothy 2:11-12, scholars still debate how Paul uses the Old Testament background (he applies Old Testament examples in different ways in different passages, even the example of Eve: 2 Corinthians 11:3). But one point, at least, is interesting: Paul's letters to Timothy are the only letters in the entire Bible where we know that false teachers were specifically targeting women with their false teachings (2 Timothy 3:6). In fact, they may have targeted widows (1 Timothy 5:9) who owned homes so they could use their houses for churches (one of the Greek terms in 1 Timothy 5:13 nearly always meant spreading "nonsense" or false ideas). Those who knew less about God and his truth were naturally most susceptible to false teachings. So the principle is those who do not know the Bible should not be allowed to teach it. Whatever other conclusions one may draw from this, it seems unlikely that Paul would have refused to let women sing in church!

Limitation of the Principle

We must be careful not to extend the application too far beyond the point in the text. If the law is summed up in love (Romans 13:8-10), we apply the text rightly to love our neighbor as ourselves, a principle which has a potentially infinite number of applications. But some people have taught as if this principle empties all the moral content of the law, so that adultery or bank robbery are acceptable as long as one is motivated by love. That such an application twists the meaning of the text is obvious, but we practice other such distortions all the time.

For instance, we sometimes quote 1 Corinthians 3:16, *"you are a temple of God,"* and use this against smoking, because smoking is bad for your body. The text in context, however, means that we as a church are God's temple and dwelling-place (3:9-15), and anyone who defiles that temple by causing division incurs God's judgment (3:17). This text applies even to nonsmoking Christians to the extent that we are unloving toward other Christians! A better verse would be 1 Corinthians 6:19, *"your body is the temple of the Holy Spirit."* This verse refers to our individual bodies, which should be used for the Lord only (6:20).

Paul's own primary point, however, is that our bodies should not be joined to prostitutes (6:15-17). This is a text to be used against sexual immorality! If we try to apply the principle also to smoking, because that is not glorifying God with our bodies, then we should also apply it to gluttony, lack of exercise, poor nutrition, and other problems damaging to our bodies. Our extension of Paul's principle in this verse may be legitimate, but it is certainly secondary to Paul's own focus, and Paul's own focus should be primary to us: if we are joined to Christ, we must avoid sexual immorality.

Different letters were written in different ways, but for the most part we need to read letters carefully in sequence and the entire way through. Romans develops an argument through the entire book. 1 Corinthians takes on several related issues, but most of those issues take up many paragraphs through several chapters (1 Corinthians 1-4, the church divided especially over the most skilled speakers; 1 Corinthians 5-7, mainly sexual issues; 1 Corinthians 8-11, mainly food issues; 1 Corinthians 12-14, spiritual gifts). A good project would be to illustrate Paul's argument by thinking up titles for each paragraph and show how these paragraphs relate to one another, developing a continuous argument.

Guidelines for Making Application from Epistles

We provide here a summary of our guidelines for understanding and applying the Bible's letters:

1. **Read the epistles first as letters addressed to real people**
2. **Learn the situation. How does writer address situation?**
   a. What is the culture and (as best as we can tell) the specific situation he addresses?
   b. Are there cultural reasons for why he constructs his argument in a particular format?

c. Determine how he addresses the situation (agreeing, disagreeing, a mixture of both elements, etc.)
3. **Is the writer's application transcultural, or is what is transcultural merely the principle behind this application?**
   a. In different cultures or situations, does the Bible present alternative teachings?
   b. Does the writer agree or disagree with majority views in his culture?
   c. If he agrees on some points, he *may* be embracing morally neutral elements of his culture for the sake of relating to it positively.
   d. If he disagrees on some points (or if he takes a firm position and his culture holds diverse views), he is likely articulating a transcultural norm.
4. **For equivalent impact, we must apply principles to equivalent situations today.**
   a. What situations today are almost exact analogies to those of the first audience?
   b. What situations today (in our lives, others' lives, and society) are similar to the original situation in various respects?
   c. What other situations might the principle address (provided we have correctly ascertained the principle behind the application)?
   d. Make sure your application fits the kind the original writer would have given. If he had lived in our day, what would he have said to this situation?

Study Questions

1. Explain what is the foundation of all application.
2. Find a cultural practice that Paul addresses in one of his epistles and explain how it relates to our contemporary culture.
3. Summarize in your own words Gordon Fee's two principles for interpreting epistles.
4. Explain and illustrate the difference between a specific situation in the Bible and a universal principle.
5. Study 1 Corinthians 11:1-16 and state what you think is the "core principle" in that passage.
6. What would be one difference between the Corinthians to whom Paul wrote and your own culture?
7. What was the main reason suggested in the Bible for women keeping silent in the churches?
8. Give an example of how application being separated from interpretation can be abused.

Appendix 1

Paragraph Context Examples

1. Is God's announcement that he owns *"the cattle on a thousand hills"* (Psalm 50:10) an assurance that he can supply all our needs?

Some people insist that God can supply all our needs because, after all, He *"owns the cattle on a thousand hills"* (Ps. 50:10). Some go beyond God supplying all our needs to suggest that he will supply anything we want. Again, it is true that God can supply all our needs, but there are many more appropriate texts to demonstrate that point. Psalm 50:10 does not address the issue of God supplying our needs (and certainly not all our wants); rather, it declares that God does not need our sacrifices.

The figurative setting of Psalm 50 is a courtroom, where God has summoned his people to respond to his charges. He summons heaven and earth as his witnesses (50:1-6). As witnesses of the covenant (Deut. 32:1; see also Ps. 50:5), they would be witnesses concerning Israel's violation of that covenant. Israel has some reason to be nervous. God is not only the offended party in the case, but the Judge (Ps. 50:4, 6). Testifying against them, God declares, *"I am your God"* (50:7)—reminding them of the covenant he had made with them. They had not broken faith against him by failing to offer sacrifices (50:8). In fact, God does not care about that.

> *I don't need your animal sacrifices, for all the animals belong to Me, including the cattle on a thousand hills. I don't eat animal flesh, but if I did, would I tell you if I were hungry? Since I own these creatures, wouldn't I just take them if I wanted them? (50:9-13).*

The sacrifice which he really requires is thanksgiving and obedience (50:14-15; cf. 50:23).

Most peoples in the ancient Near East believed that their gods depended on them for sacrifices, and if their gods were overpowered, their nation would be overpowered as well. The God of Israel reminds them that he is not like the pagan gods around them. Unlike Baal of the Canaanites (whose temples included a bed), Zeus of the Greeks (whom Hera put to sleep so her Greeks could win a battle), and other deities, the God of Israel neither slumbered nor slept (Ps. 121:3-4). God does not mention the cattle on a thousand hills to promise us anything we want. He mentions the cattle to remind us that he is not dependent on us, and we are not doing him a favor by serving him.

2. What does the *"baptism of fire"* refer to in Matthew 3:11?

One modern denomination in America is the "Fire-Baptized Holiness Church." Many Christians happily claim to be "baptized in the Holy Ghost and fire." We know and appreciate, of course, what they mean. They mean they have been baptized with holiness. But is that what John the Baptist means by "fire baptism" in this passage? Fire is sometimes used as a symbol of God's consuming holiness or of purifying trials in the Bible; but when fire is conjoined with the image of baptism in the New Testament, it has to do not with mere purification of the individual, but with purifying the whole world by judgment. Rather than cross-referencing to other passages that use the image of fire in different ways, we ought to examine what the *"baptized in fire"* text means in its own context. We ought to use the passage itself before jumping to a concordance.

The context is a call to repentance, and much of the audience promised this fire baptism was unwilling to repent. John the Baptist was immersing people in water as a sign of their repentance and preparation for the coming Kingdom of God (Matt. 3:2, 6). (Jewish people used baptism when non-Jews would convert to Judaism, but John demanded that even religious Jewish people come to God on the same terms on which Gentiles should; see also 3:9.) John warned the Pharisees about God's coming wrath (3:7), and that unless they bore fruit (3:8) God's ax of judgment would cast them into the fire (3:10; see also 12:33). Fruitless trees were worthless except for fuel. But chaff was barely even useful as fuel (it burned quickly), yet the chaff of which John spoke would be burned with "unquenchable"—eternal—"fire" (3:12).

In this context, "fire" is hellfire (3:10, 12). When John the Baptist speaks of a baptism in fire, he uses an image of judgment that follows through the whole paragraph. Remember John's hearers are not repentant people (3:7). The Messiah is coming to give his audience a twofold baptism, and different members of his audience would experience different parts of it.

Some may repent and receive the Spirit. The unrepentant would receive the fire!

3. By calling us to *"imitate"* God (Ephesians 5:1), does Paul want us to speak planets into existence? Or to be everywhere at once?

This passage summons us to imitate God the way children imitate a father. The text is also specific, however, in the ways that we should imitate God: we should forgive as God in Christ forgave us (4:32) and love one another, just as Christ sacrificially loved us (5:2). Happily, the text does not require us to imitate God by being all-powerful or everywhere at once!

4. What does it mean to *"resist the devil"* in James 4:7? In 1 Peter 5:8? In Ephesians 4:27? Some people use these verses to support rebuking the devil whenever something goes wrong. Is that the point?

James contrasts the peaceful wisdom which is from God (3:13, 17-18; *"from above"* was a typical Jewish way of saying, "from God") with the contentious wisdom which is from the devil (3:14-15). Then he warns his audience not to try to hold both perspectives as if they were compatible. Those who try to follow both God's and the world's wisdom at the same time are spiritual adulteresses (4:4). Submitting to God and resisting the devil (4:7), then, is rejecting the world's evil way of treating one another and preferring the gentle approach that comes from God. To adopt this new way of treating others requires repentance (4:8-10).

First Peter refers to a situation in which Christians are being persecuted (1 Pet 4:12-16). In 1 Peter 5:8-9, the devil apparently seeks to crush believers by seeking to turn them from the faith. Resisting him therefore means withstanding the persecution. In the context of Ephesians 4:27, one resists the devil by refusing to deceive or stay angry with one's fellow-believers (4:25-26); in the whole context of Ephesians, this is part of "spiritual warfare" (6:11-14, 18).

5. Some people quote Joel 2:11 to say that we are God's mighty army (in a spiritual sense). Other texts may say that, but is that the point of this text?

Joel 2:11 says,

> The Lord thunders at the head of his army; his forces are beyond number, and mighty are those who obey his command. The day of the LORD is great; it is dreadful. Who can endure it?

Although the third chapter of Joel seems to describe a future war, chapters one and two identifies the invading army as a devastating locust plague (Joel 1:4; 2:25). This text does not depict the church as a spiritual army of evangelists. It depicts locusts as an agricultural judgment against the sins of God's people.

6. Some people quote Joel 3:10 (*"let the weakling say 'I am strong'"*) to say that we should claim God's strength when we are weak. While that is a biblical principle (2 Corinthians 12:10), is it the point here?

This passage is not an invitation to the weary righteous to strengthen themselves. God is speaking in judgment to the nations gathered against his people for the final war (Joel 3:9). God commands them to make their weapons and make themselves strong, when in fact they are hopelessly weak before them. He is actually mocking the enemies of his people as He invites them to judgment (3:12-14).

7. Read Isaiah 14:12-14 in view of the whole of Isaiah 14. To whom does this text refer?

This passage begins, *"How you have fallen from heaven, O morning star, son of the dawn! You have been cast down to the earth, you who once laid low the nations!"* The full context of this passage would let us know that Isaiah is denouncing a ruler, even if he did not tell us so explicitly. Like many other ancient Israelite prophets, Isaiah includes oracles against various nations: Babylon (Isaiah 13-14), Moab (Isaiah 15-16), Damascus (Isaiah 17), the Nubian and Egyptian empires (Isaiah 18-20), Babylon again (21:1-10), Edom (21:11-12), Arabia (21:13-17), Jerusalem (22), and Tyre (23). Isaiah

14:3-4 explicitly tell us that the following oracle is directed against the ruler of Babylon—an oppressor (14:4), a ruler (14:5), who conquered other nations (14:6). As he is defeated, the nations rejoice (14:7); figuratively speaking, even the trees of Lebanon rejoice, for he will no longer be cutting them down for his building projects (14:8). How has the Lord brought this king low, breaking his rod and scepter (14:5)? The text clearly indicates that he is **dead.** He goes to Sheol, the realm of the dead (14:9), and other rulers there rejoice that the ruler who defeated them has died just like them (14:9-10). His pomp and dignity ruined, his court harpists silenced, he now rots with maggots and worms consuming his flesh (14:11). That means he is a corpse.

Like Israel whose glory was cast from heaven to earth (Lam. 2:1), this ruler has been cast from heaven to earth. At this point some readers want to ignore the context and insist that the text refers to a literal fall from heaven, in which case, they say, it must be applied to a fallen angel like the devil. But the jubilant outcries of Lebanon's cedars in 14:8 was hardly literal; neither was the image of dead rulers rising from their thrones in the realm of the dead in 14:9 (would they still be enthroned?). Hebrew poetry painted pictures with words, just as poetry normally does today. In contrast to non-poetic parts of Isaiah, the poetic portions are consistently full of figurative speech. Other texts also speak of figurative falls from heaven (Amos 9:2; Matthew 11:23; Luke 10:15).

Kings of Babylon, like some other ancient near Eastern kings, actually claimed to be gods (compare, for example, Dan. 3:5; 6:7). Claiming to be a deity like the morning star or offspring of the sun god or deity of dawn would not be unnatural for an ancient near Eastern ruler, but Isaiah grants the title only in contemptuous mockery: *"Poor king of Babylon! You reached for heaven, but have been cast down to earth! You tried to raise yourself above God, but now you have died like a man!"* (compare the similar taunt in Ps. 82:6-8). Verses 12-14 refer to the king of Babylon just like the preceding verses do. He once conquered nations (14:12), wanted to be enthroned on the sacred mountain (perhaps referring to Babylon's future conquest of Mount Zion in Jerusalem) (14:13), and he was brought down to Sheol, the realm of the dead (14:15).

The following context drives home the point still more thoroughly. This is *"the man"* who struck fear into the hearts of nations (14:16), *"the man"* whose conquests made lands deserted, destroying cities, carrying peoples off into captivity (14:17). Unlike the other nations' kings who at least were buried in dignity in royal tombs (a final honor very important to ancient people's sense of honor), this king's corpse was thrown out in the open to rot, trampled underfoot in punishment for the violent destruction he had brought upon his own people (14:18-20). His descendants and those of his people, Babylon, would be cut off (14:21-22). The text could not be any plainer in context. This explicit oracle against the king of Babylon (14:3-23) would be fulfilled in its time, and God's oppressed people vindicated.

Despite the clarity of this text, some people remain so committed to their earlier understanding of the text that they are determined to get around the context. "Well, maybe it does refer to the king of Babylon, but it must refer to the devil, too," they protest. But why *must* it refer to the devil? Is the text not clear enough as it stands? Do any of the oracles against other nations (chs. 13-23) contain hidden prophecies against the devil? Was the devil a mere earthly conqueror, brought to the realm of the dead after he was thrust from heaven (14:12, 15)? "But we all know that Lucifer refers to the devil, and that the devil said he would ascend to heaven," one student protested to me. "How do we know it?" I replied. I pointed out that the view that "Lucifer" refers to the devil and that the devil promised to ascend to heaven is based on an interpretation of the King James translation of this text. If "Lucifer" appeared here, it would be the only place in the Bible it occurred, but it does not in fact occur here, either. The Hebrew does not speak of "Lucifer" here; that is a Latin title for the "morning star" which the King James Version used in its translation here. "Therefore," I responded sadly, "you have told me nothing but that some people interpret this text as referring to the devil—an opinion of which I was already aware." Unable to make their case in Isaiah 14, some students have then declared that Isaiah 14 must refer to the devil because Ezekiel 28 does.

There are two fallacies in this argument. First of all, Ezekiel 28 and other passages could refer to the fall of the devil without Isaiah 14 having to do with that subject. Nowhere in my exposition have I denied that the devil fell. I only denied that this was the point of Isaiah 14. The second fallacy of the argument is that Ezekiel 28 does not clearly refer to the fall of the devil, either.

8. Many people apply Ezekiel 28:12-14 to the devil, just as they apply Isaiah 14 to him. In context, is that really the point of this passage?

This is the passage that begins, *"You were the model of perfection, full of wisdom and perfect in beauty. You were in Eden, the garden of God . . ."* Ezekiel also has oracles against the nations: Ammon (25:1-7), Moab (25:8-11), Edom (25:12-14), Philistia (25:15-17), Tyre (26:1-28:19), Sidon (28:20-26), and Egypt (29:1-32:32). The passage sometimes applied to the devil, 28:12b-19, is in the heart of an oracle against the ruler of Tyre. In fact, verse 12 begins, *"Son of man, take up this lament against the ruler of Tyre."* No one disputes that the context refers to the ruler of Tyre, but those who apply the text to the devil declare that it also applies to him, because (they claim) some features of the text cannot apply to anyone but the devil.

This argument, as we shall see, is not actually accurate. The lament calls this ruler arrogant about his wisdom and perfection of beauty (28:12, 17)—just as Tyre claimed to be perfect in beauty (27:3-4, 11) and full of wisdom that brought wealth (28:3-4), self-proclaimed wisdom that made the ruler think he was a god (28:6) though he was but a human being (28:8-10). This ruler was in Eden, the garden of God (28:13), which advocates of the devil-interpretation think must be taken literally. Only the devil was in Eden, they say. But this claim is not true; Adam and Eve, who did seek equality with God (Genesis 3:5), also lived in Eden, and Ezekiel could compare the Tyrian ruler's boasting with that of the first people.

Yet another explanation is better than either the devil-interpretation or the Adam-interpretation: Ezekiel explicitly compares the ruler of Babylon to a cherub (28:14-15). Genesis calls neither Adam nor the serpent a cherub, but does refer explicitly to cherubim in the garden: God's angels stationed there to keep Adam and Eve out after their fall (Genesis 3:24; see also Ezekiel 28:14-15 NIV: "guardian cherub"). In other words, this is an image representing great prestige in God's garden. (The *"holy mountain of God"*—28:14—might allude to Mount Zion, as often in Scripture, in which case the image of cherubim probably also recalls the cherubim on which God was enthroned on the ark in the Temple. The blamelessness until found wicked—28:15—may also be part of the cherub image.)

Some have objected that the king cannot simply be *compared* to a glorious cherub in Eden. The text calls him a cherub, and must be interpreted literally. Those who insist that all details of such prophecies should be taken literally, however, simply demonstrate that they are unfamiliar with the prophets' writings in general. Ezekiel himself is full of graphic, poetic images and metaphors, one of which is a statement that Pharaoh was a tree in Eden, God's garden (Ezekiel 31:1-18; he is also a sea monster, 29:3-5). Drawing on various images from the account of Adam and Eve's fall, Ezekiel's prophecies speak both of the stately cherubim and the greatest trees in Eden (perhaps the tree of life or the tree of the knowledge of good and evil?) Perhaps advocates of the devil-interpretation press their case that being in Eden refers to the devil in Ezekiel 28 but not in Ezekiel 31 because they can only fit Ezekiel 28 into their view in some other respects.

The adornment of precious stones (28:13) alludes to Tyre's great wealth, elsewhere described in terms of gorgeous array (27:4-7, 24) and trade in diverse merchandise including precious stones (27:16, 22). The wickedness of 28:15 is the wickedness of Tyre's merchant interests (28:16), her *"dishonest trade"* (28:18 NIV) elsewhere referred to in the context (27:2-36; 28:4-5; see also 26:17). The king's pride on account of his beauty (28:17) recalls the pride of the ruler of Tyre who claims to be a god yet is merely a man (28:2), proud because of the wealth Tyre had amassed through trading (28:5). That fire would come forth from the ruler of Tyre (28:18), just as ancient cities were normally destroyed by burning in their midst (see also, for example, Amos 1:4, 7, 12; 2:2, 5—especially Amos 1:10, against Tyre).

Ezekiel refers to an arrogant human ruler. The ruler in this passage exalts himself in pride and is cast down; the casting down is more explicit in the oracle earlier in the chapter (28:2-10). He claimed to be a god, enthroned in the heart of the seas (28:2; Tyre was off the seacoast of Phoenicia). God has Ezekiel mock this ruler: You think that you are as wise as a god (28:6), but God would bring judgment on this ruler by other nations (28:7). Then would he still pretend to be a god in front of those who would kill him (28:9)? He was a *"man,"* not a god, and he would die a horrible and violent death (28:8-10). This is hardly a description of the devil, an immortal spirit. This is an earthly ruler who claimed to be a god, who would learn his mortality at the time of God's judgment on Tyre.

Yet even if these two passages referred to the devil as well as to earthly rulers—though in context they do not—why do defenders of this view often apply these passages to the devil yet never apply them also to earthly rulers judged by God for their arrogance? Would not examples of human arrogance make even more useful passages for preaching or teaching matters relevant to our hearers? I suspect that many believers simply assume these passages refer to the devil because that is the way we have always heard them interpreted, but many of us never closely examined them in context. Whatever their views, I do not believe any reader can miss our point. This passage has a broad context in the surrounding chapters, and our short-cuts to learning the Bible have failed to study the books of the Bible the way God inspired them to be written.

9. When Paul says, *"I can do all things through Christ who strengthens me"* (Philippians 4:13), does he have anything in particular in mind?

I heard of a football player who approached a Bible professor, greatly troubled. His coach had encouraged the team that they could *"do all things through Christ who strengthens"* them, citing Philippians 4:13. Yet the team had lost a few games. The student was unable to understand why his team was not always winning. The problem, of course, is not with the text, but with the view that the player and apparently his coach had read into the verse; Thanking the Philippians for sending him a love-gift (4:10, 14), Paul noted that he had learned contentment with both little and with much (4:12). He could do all things through Christ (4:13). In this context, he is saying that by Christ's strength he could rejoice whether he had much or little. Today we should learn to rejoice in whatever our situation, knowing that Christ strengthens us to endure (whether persecution, ridicule, or even losing a football game).

10. What is the *"word of God"* (or, "word of Christ" in most translations) in Romans 10:17? Does it specifically refer to the Bible in this case or to something else?

Some people quote Romans 10:17 to support repeating Bible verses to ourselves aloud: *"Faith comes by hearing, and hearing by the word of God."* Of course, repeating the Bible to ourselves is important (if we understand it in context). But those who quote this particular *verse* to support this practice have neglected the context of Romans 10:17. Paul argues that no one could be saved unless they heard this word, this message of Christ (10:14-15), the "report" of the witnesses (10:16), the "word" in their mouths and hearts (10:8-10). Faith could only come from hearing this word, the gospel of Christ (10:17). In contrast to Hebrews 11:1, where "faith" in context means persevering faith, this passage refers to saving faith. One cannot get saved till one hears the truth about Jesus. This verse does not directly address reciting Bible verses.

11. According to 1 Corinthians 13:8-10, when will the gifts of the Spirit pass away? What is the immediate context? (cf. 12:31; 14:1) What is the function of 13:4-6 in the context of the letter to the Corinthians?

Paul says that spiritual gifts like prophecy, tongues and knowledge will pass away when we no longer need them (1 Corinthians. 13:8-10). Some Christians read this passage as if it said, "Spiritual gifts like prophecy, tongues, and knowledge passed away when the last book of the New Testament was written." This interpretation of 1 Corinthians 13 ignores the entire context of 1 Corinthians, however. It is a letter to the Corinthians in the middle of the first century, and they had never yet heard of a New Testament in the middle of the first century. Had Paul meant the completion of the New Testament, he would have had to have made this point much more clearly—starting by explaining what a New Testament addition to their Bible was.

In the context we find instead that Paul means that spiritual gifts will pass away when we know God as he knows us, when we see him face to face (13:12; when we no longer see as through a mirror as we do in the present—see also 2 Corinthians 3:18, the only other place where Paul uses the term). In other words, spiritual gifts must continue until our Lord Jesus returns at the end of the age. They should remain a normal part of our Christian experience today.

A broader examination of the context reveals even more of Paul's meaning in this passage. In chapters 12-14, Paul addresses those who are abusing particular spiritual gifts, and argues that God has gifted all members of Christ's body with gifts for building up God's people. Those

Paragraph Context Examples

who were using God's gifts in ways that hurt others were abusing the gifts God had given to help others. That is why Paul spends three paragraphs in the midst of his discussion of spiritual gifts on the subject of love: gifts without love are useless (13:1-3); love seeks to edify (13:4-7); the gifts are temporary (for this age only), but love is eternal (13:8-13). We should seek the best gifts (1 Corinthians. 12:31; 14:1), and love gives us the insight to see which gifts are the best in any given situation—those which build others up.

The context of Paul's whole letter drives this point home further. Paul's description of what love is in 1 Corinthians 13:4-7 contrasts starkly with Paul's prior descriptions of the Corinthians in his letter: selfish, boastful, and so on (1 Corinthians 3:3; 4:6-7, 18; 5:2). The Corinthian Christians, like the later church in Laodicea (Revelation 3:14-22), had a lot in their favor, but lacked what mattered most of all: the humility of love.

12. Revelation 3:20. When Jesus knocks at the door, is he trying to get someone converted? To whom is the verse addressed?

Here Jesus knocks not at the door of the individual sinner, but rather at the door of a church that was acting like one! Whereas Jesus had set before another church an open door, inviting them into His presence despite the false accusations of their persecutors (Revelation 3:8), He was here locked out of another church. Ancient hospitality required sharing food with a guest, but the Laodicean church had locked Jesus out by their arrogant self-sufficiency (3:17-18). He wanted these Christians to repent and express again their need for Him (3:19).

13. One could say that when God "gave" his Son (John 3:16), this refers to giving Jesus at his birth or giving him to the world when God raised him from the dead. What does "giving" him mean in context?

The context is clear that God gave his Son (3:16) when Jesus was lifted up (3:14-15). In the context of the rest of the Gospel of John, this must mean that he was *"lifted up"* on the cross (see 8:28; 12:32-33). God gave his Son when Jesus died for our sins.

14. When we seek first the kingdom, *what* things are added to us (Matthew 6:33)?

Jewish people sometimes used Gentiles—non-Jews, who were usually what they would have regarded as "pagans"—as examples of what upright Jews should avoid. "Pagans" seek food, drink, and clothing, Jesus said, but you should not seek these things (6:31-32). Instead, Jesus' followers should seek his kingdom, and these other things—the basic necessities of life— would be taken care of (6:33). It may be no coincidence that Jesus had just taught his disciples to pray first for the agendas of God's kingdom (6:9-10) and only after that for their own basic needs (6:11-13).

15. Who are Christ's ambassadors in 2 Corinthians 5:20? Whom are they entreating to be reconciled to God?

In every, or almost every instance of "we" in the preceding chapters (and probably even in 5:21 which follows, though that is debated), Paul refers to himself and his ministry colleagues. Probably in 5:20, then, Paul also refers not to all Christians as ambassadors, but only to those who are bringing God's message of reconciliation. After all, those he is entreating to be reconciled to God are the Christians in Corinth, who are not ambassadors but those who need ambassadors to them (6:1-2)! Perhaps ideally all Christians *should* be bringing God's message of reconciliation, but in practice most Christians in Corinth were not. The Corinthian Christians were acting like non-Christians, so Paul and his colleagues act as representatives for Christ's righteousness to them, just as Christ represented our sin for us on the cross (5:21).

16. Some people say that the *"witnesses"* in Hebrews 12:1 are the dead watching us from heaven. But in the context of Hebrews chapter 11, does "witnesses" refer to those who watch us?

In this case not all translations make equally clear the terms in the context related to the term for "witnesses" in 12:1. The concept, however, is evident in at least some of them. In the preceding context, God frequently *"testified as a witness"* or provided "testimony as a witness" that his servants had proved faithful (11:2, 4-5, 39). It is therefore possible that he speaks of the righteous listed in Hebrews 11 as those who also testified what they knew about God. These may be not "witnesses" like those who watch a sports match in a stadium, but rather those who "witness" for or "testify" about the truth they have discovered about God.

17. Some people claim the promise that no weapon formed against them would prosper (Isaiah 54:17). Is this a guarantee for every individual Christian?

The context indicates that the passage focuses on God's people. Israel had sinned, been judged, but now would be restored, and those who had tried to oppose Israel would be crushed. There is a principle here that God vindicates his people, but it is not an ironclad guarantee for every circumstance in the short run for each individual. It does encourage us, however, that God will ultimately vindicate his servants and his plans for history. So whatever we must face in the short run, in the long run we can be sure of God's faithfulness and vindication if we remain faithful to Him.

18. Does Proverbs 23:7 mean that whatever we think about ourselves will come true? Or does it mean something else? (Read 23:6-8.)

This passage says *"As a person thinks in their heart, so they are."* In the ancient Mediterranean world, sharing food obligated people to loyalty to one another. But Proverbs warns that you cannot trust your host if he is selfish. He may encourage you to eat as much as you like, but you will be sorry if you trust him. What matters is not what he says to you, but what he really thinks in his heart (23:6-8).

19. Who is the rose of Sharon, the lily of the valley, in Song of Solomon 2:1-2?

Many Christian songs depict Jesus as the *"lily of the valley,"* the *"rose of Sharon,"* and the *"fairest of ten thousand."* The songs are beautiful, and their point is that Jesus is the greatest beauty and desire of our souls. We should not read the meaning of those beautiful songs back onto the meaning of the Song of Solomon, however. The *"rose of Sharon"* in this book does not refer to Jesus, directly or indirectly. This book is an ancient love song, which provides wonderful insights into romance, the language of marital desire and appreciation, dealing with conflicts in marriage (the brief conflict is 5:2-6), the power of jealousy (8:6), and similar things. To the extent that it reflects the beauty of marital love, it may also supply us with words in our passionate pursuit of Christ, but this is not the subject of the book. The book is a practical example of romantic, married love. For instance, the *"banquet house"* and *"banner"* in 2:4 may refer to ancient wedding customs: while guests were banqueting at the wedding feast, bride and groom consummated their marriage and reportedly hung out a banner when they had sealed their union sexually. It is doubtful that this is a symbol of Christ. It reads much better as a picture of married sexual love in ancient Israel.

But even if Song of Solomon were but a symbol of Christ and his Church, as some have supposed, *"rose of Sharon"* and *"lily of the valley"* could not refer to Christ. As in the NIV, it is the bride who declares, *"I am a rose of Sharon, a lily of the valley"*—i.e., as beautiful as the most beautiful of flowers; her groom had made her feel loved, despite her own insecurities (1:6). The groom also compares her to a lily (2:2; 7:2). She compares his approach to one who moves among the lilies (2:16; 6:2-3; he also applies this image to her in 4:5). Even if Song of Solomon were an allegory of Christ and the Church (which is very unlikely), *"rose of Sharon"* would not refer to Christ, but to his Church. More likely, it is an example of the beautiful romantic language that an inspired author could apply to his bride, as an inspired guide emphasizing the importance of romantic affection in our marriages today.

20. In Matthew 18:18, what does Jesus mean by *"binding and loosing"*? Does he refer to how to treat demons here, or does he refer to something else?

I used to follow a popular misinterpretation of this verse. As a young Christian, I used to use Matthew 18:18 to "bind" and "loose" demons when I would pray. Fortunately, God is more concerned with our faith than with our formulas, and graciously answered my prayers whether or not I threw any "binding" in. But one day I read Matthew 18:18 in context, and I realized that I had been misinterpreting the passage. Because my prayers had "worked," I decided to keep "binding" and "loosing"—but now that I knew better, it did not work anymore, because my heart could no longer be right while doing it! Happily, I found that God still answered my prayers prayed in Jesus' name without "binding." What do "binding" and "loosing" mean in this context?

In the context, Jesus indicates that if one's fellow-Christian is living a sinful lifestyle, one must confront that Christian. If he or she refuses to listen, one should bring others so one will have two or three witnesses if one must bring the matter before the church. If despite repeated loving confrontations that person refuses to repent, the church must put that person out of the church to teach the person repentance (Matt. 18:15-17). In this context, Jesus declares that whatever they "bind" or "loose" on earth will have already been "bound" or "loosed" in heaven. In other words, under these circumstances, they clearly act on God's authority (18:18). Because the terms "binding" and "loosing" literally have to do with imprisoning or releasing people, and Jewish teachers used these terms to describe their legal authority, the terms make good sense in this context. The church must discipline its erring members, removing them from participation in the church if they continue in unapologetic sin.

The *"two or three"* who pray in this context (18:19) refer to the two or three witnesses (18:16). I used to read this passage and worry that my prayers would be less efficacious if I could not find someone to join me in prayer; I did wonder, however, why my own faith would be insufficient. But this verse does not imply that prayer is efficacious only for a minimum of two persons. It promises that even if only two witnesses are available, and even if the prayers or actions on earth involve something as serious as withdrawing a person from the church, God will back up his servants whom he has authorized. Perhaps the specific prayer in mind is a prayer that God will bring the dis-fellowshipped person to repentance and restoration. If so, Jesus deliberately contrasts the attitude required of his followers with the two or three witnesses in the Old Testament law, who were to be the first to stone those against whom they testified (Deuteronomy 17:7). Probably alluding to a Jewish saying circulating in the early centuries of this era—"Wherever two or three gather to study God's law, His presence is among them"—Jesus assures his followers (specifically the witnesses) of his presence even in the difficult situation of church discipline (Matthew 18:20).

Although we cannot take space here to comment further on the matter, this particular passage offers no support for the common practice of "binding" demons as it is done today. Whereas "binding demons" in the way it is generally practiced today has no warrant in this text. However, it does appear in some ancient magical texts, which makes this practice even more suspect.

21. What is the "coming" to which Jesus refers in John 14:1-3? Does he refer here to his second coming or to something else?

Jesus tells his disciples, *"In my Father's house are many 'dwelling-places'"* (14:2; "mansions" comes from the Latin translation—it is not in the original Greek text). Jesus said (John 14:2b-3), *"I am going there to prepare a place for you. And if I go and prepare a place for you, I will come back and take you to be with me that you also may be where I am."*

Usually readers today assume that Jesus here refers to his future coming to take us to heaven or the new earth. If we had these verses by themselves, that view would make as much sense as any other. After all, Jesus often spoke of his second coming. But the context indicates that Jesus is speaking of an *earlier* coming here.

Peter wants to follow Jesus wherever he goes, but Jesus tells him that if he wants to follow Jesus where he is going, he must follow him to the death (John 13:31-38). Nevertheless, Peter and the other disciples should not be afraid. They should trust in Jesus the same way they trusted in the Father (14:1). He would prepare a dwelling-place for them in his Father's house, and would come back afterwards to receive them to himself (14:2-3). *"You know where I'm going and how I will get there,"* He told them (14:4). Perhaps like us, the disciples were confused, and Thomas spoke for all of them: *"Lord, we don't even know where You're going; how can we know the way you're getting there?"* (14:5) So Jesus clarifies his point: where he is going is to the Father (14:6). He is going there by dying on the Cross but would return afterward to give them the Spirit (14:18-19; 16:18-22). How would they get to the Father? By coming through Jesus, who is the way (14:6).

We often cite John 14:2-3 as a proof-text for Jesus' future coming. Conversely, we cite John 14:6 as a proof-text for salvation. But if we follow the flow of conversation, we have to be wrong about one of them. John 14:2-3 declares that Jesus will bring them where he is going, but 14:6 tells us where he's going and how we his followers will get there: he is going to the Father, and we come to the Father when we get saved through Jesus

(14:6). The entire context makes this point clear. We enter the Father's house when we become followers of Jesus Christ!

In the context of John's entire Gospel, there is no reason to assume that the *"Father's house"* refers to heaven, though it might be an allusion to the Temple (John 2:16) or to the Father's household (John 8:35). More helpfully, Jesus goes on to explain the *"dwelling-places"* (NIV: *"rooms"*) in the following context. The Greek word for *"dwelling-place"* used in 14:2 occurs in only one other verse in the New Testament—in 14:23, part of Jesus' continuing explanation of 14:2-4. *"The one who loves Me will obey Me, and My Father will love that one and we will come make our 'dwelling-place' with that person"* (14:23). The related verb appears throughout John 15:1-10: "Dwell [abide]" in Christ, and let Christ "dwell" in you. We all know that Jesus will return someday in the future, but if we read the rest of John we learn that Jesus also returned to them from the Father after his resurrection, when he gave the disciples the Spirit, peace and joy (20:19-23). This is in fact the only coming the context addresses (14:18 in the context of 14:15-27; 16:12-24).

What is the real point of John 14:2-3? It is not that Jesus will return and we will be with him someday—true as that teaching is from other texts. It is that Jesus returned after his resurrection so Christians could have life with him (14:18-19), that he has already brought us into his presence and that we can experience the reality of his presence this very moment and at all times.

Appendix 2

Whole Book Context Examples

1. Jewish-Gentile Reconciliation in Romans

Many Christians urge non-Christians to be converted by believing in Jesus' resurrection with their heart and confessing with their mouth that Jesus is Lord. This summary of how to respond to the gospel is based on Romans 10:9-10. Romans 10 does in fact describe salvation in these terms. But have we ever stopped to examine why Paul specifically mentions the mouth and heart here rather than in some other passages which describe salvation? Would Paul deny that deaf mutes could be saved simply because they could not confess with their mouths? Or does Paul choose his particular words "heart" and "mouth" for more specific reasons?

We look first at the immediate context, as we did in passages above. Paul believes that we are saved by God's grace, not by our works. Contrary to the means of justification proposed by Paul's opponents (Romans 10:1-5), Paul demonstrates from the law of Moses itself that the message of faith is the saving word (10:6-7). As Moses said, *"the word is near you, in your mouth and in your heart"* (10:8). Moses was referring to the law (Deuteronomy 30:10-11, 14), but the principle was also applicable to the gospel, which was also God's word. In Moses' day one could not ascend to heaven to bring the law down from above. God in his mercy already gave it to Israel on Mount Sinai (30:12). Nor was it necessary to descend again into the sea (30:13). God had already redeemed his people and brought them through the sea. They could not save themselves. They had to depend on God's mighty grace (see also Exodus 20:2). In the same way, Paul says, we do not bring Christ up from the dead, or send him down from the Father. Like the law and Israel's redemption, Christ's salvation is God's gift to us (Romans 10:6-7). Moses declared that this message was *"in your mouth and in your heart"* (Deuteronomy 30:14), In other words, it had already given to Israel by God's grace. Paul explains that likewise God's message was in your mouth when you confessed Christ with your mouth and in your heart when you believed in him in your heart (Rom 10:9-10). Faith could come only from hearing this word, the gospel of Christ (10:17), as we noted above.

The immediate context explains why Paul mentions the "mouth" and the "heart" in this specific passage, but it also raises a new question. Why did Paul have to make an argument from the Old Testament that salvation was by grace through faith? Was there anyone who doubted this? Reading Romans as an entire book explains the reason for each passage within that book. Paul is addressing a controversy between Jewish and Gentile Christians.

Paul begins Romans by emphasizing that the Gentiles are lost (1:18-32). Just as the Jewish Christian readers are applauding, Paul points out that religious people are also lost (Romans 2), and summarizes that everyone is lost (Romans 3). Paul establishes that all humanity is equally lost to remind us that all of us have to come to God on the same terms. None of us can boast against others.

But most Jewish people believed that they were chosen for salvation in Abraham. Therefore Paul reminds his fellow Jewish Christians that it is spiritual rather than ethnic descent from Abraham that matters for salvation (Romans 4). Lest any of his Jewish readers continue to stress their genetic descent, he reminds them that all people—including themselves—descend from sinful Adam (5:12-21). Jewish people believed that most Jews kept all 613 commandments in the law (at least most of the time), whereas most Gentiles did not even keep the seven commandments many Jews believed God gave to Noah. So Paul argues that while the law is good, it never saved its practitioners, including Paul (Romans 7); only Jesus Christ could do that! And lest the Jewish Christians continue to insist on their chosenness in Abraham, Paul reminds them that not all Abraham's physical descendants were chosen, even in the first two generations (9:6-13). God was so sovereign, he was not bound to choosing people on the basis of their ethnicity (9:18-24); he could choose people on the basis of their faith in Christ.

But lest the Gentile Christians look down on the Jewish Christians, Paul also reminds them that the heritage into which they had been grafted was, after all, Israel's (Romans 11). God had a Jewish remnant, and would one day turn the majority of Jewish people to faith in Christ (11:25-26). And at this point Paul gets very practical. Christians must serve one another (Romans 12). The heart of God's law is actually loving one another (13:8-10). Ancient literature shows that Roman Gentiles made fun of Roman Jews especially for their food laws and holy days. Paul argues that we should not look down on one another because of such minor differences of practice (Romans 14). He then provides examples of ethnic reconciliation. Jesus, through Jewish Christians, ministered to the Gentiles (15:7-12) and Paul was bringing an offering from Gentile churches for the Jewish Christians in Jerusalem (15:25-31). In the midst of his closing greetings, he offers one final exhortation: beware of those who cause division (16:17).

Getting the whole picture of Romans provides us a clearer understanding of the function of each particular passage in the work as a whole. It also suggests the sort of situation which the letter addresses. What we know of the "background" sheds more light on this situation: Rome earlier expelled the Jewish Christians (Acts 18:1-3), but now they have returned (Romans 16:3). This means that the Roman house churches, which had consisted completely of Gentiles for many years, now face conflict with Jewish Christians who had different cultural ways of doing things. Paul's letter to the Romans summons Christians to ethnic, cultural, tribal reconciliation with one another by reminding us that all of us came to God on the same terms, through Jesus Christ alone.

2. Justice for the Poor in James

Some people, reading the letter of James, have thought that the letter collects miscellaneous exhortations that do not fit together very well. But their view is unlikely. When one examines James carefully, most of the book actually fits together quite well.

In the "immediate context" section above, we asked how James expected us to resist the devil (4:7), and argued that he referred to resisting the world's values. This is a valid general principle, but were there any specific values that James was especially concerned about among his readers? Most certainly, there were.

In the introduction to James' letter he introduces several themes which recur through the rest of the letter. By tracing these themes, we get a simple outline of the basic issues the letter addresses. (When I preach on James, I often like to preach from the introduction of the letter, which allows me to actually preach most of the letter using just one or two paragraphs as my outline.)

First of all, we see the problem James confronts: his readers were encountering various trials (1:2). As one reads through the letter, one gathers that many of his readers are poor people who are being oppressed by the rich (1:9-11; 2:2-6; 5:1-6). Some of James' readers appear tempted to deal with their problem of various trials in the wrong way—with a violent (whether verbally or physically) response (1:19-20; 2:11; 3:9; 4:2).

So James offers a solution demanding from them three virtues: endurance (1:3-4), wisdom (1:5), and faith (1:6-8). They need God's wisdom to properly endure, and they need faith when they pray to God for this wisdom. James returns to each of these virtues later in his letter, explaining them in further detail. Thus he deals with endurance more fully near the end of his letter, using Job and the prophets as biblical examples of such endurance (5:7-11). He also demands sincere rather than merely passing faith (2:14-26). What he says about faith here is instructive. Some of the poor were tempted to lash out and kill their oppressors, and might think God would still be on their side so long as they had not committed sins like adultery. But James reminds them that murder is sin even if they do not commit adultery (2:11). The basic confession of Jewish faith was the oneness of God, but James reminds his friends that even the devil had "faith" that God was one, but this knowledge did not save the devil (2:19). Genuine faith means faith that is demonstrated by obedience (2:14-18). Thus if we pray "in faith" for wisdom, we must pray in the genuine faith that is willing to obey whatever wisdom God gives us! We must not be *"double-minded"* (1:8), which means trying to embrace both the world's perspective and God's at the same time (4:8).

James especially treats in more detail the matter of wisdom. He is concerned about inflammatory rhetoric—the sort of speech that stirs people to anger against others (1:19-20; 3:1-12). This does not mean that he remains silent toward rich oppressors; in fact, he prophesies God's judgment against them (5:1-6)! But he does not approve of stirring people to violence against them. James notes that there are two kinds of wisdom. One kind involves strife and selfishness and is worldly and demonic (3:14). This is the sort of view and attitude that tempts his readers. James instead advocates God's way of wisdom, which is gentle (3:13); it is pure—unmixed with other kinds of wisdom—and peaceable, gentle, easily entreated, full of mercy and the fruit of righteousness which is sown in peace (3:17-18). His readers were tempted to use violence (4:2) and desire the world's way of doing things (4:4). But rather than taking matters into their own hands, they should submit to God (4:7).

James is calling us to keep peace with one another. And if he calls the oppressed not to seek to kill their oppressors, how much more does he summon all of us to love and remain gentle toward those closest to us, even those who are unkind to us? *"Resisting the devil"* may involve more work than some people think!

3. The *"least of these"* in Matthew 25:40

Many people today emphasize the importance of caring for the poor by reminding us that Jesus warned us we would be judged by how we treat *"the least of these"* Jesus' brothers (25:40, 45). While it is true that God will judge us according to how we treat the poor, is the "poor" what Jesus means here by his "brothers"? Will the nations be judged (25:32) only for this? The immediate context does not settle the issue, but the broader context of the Gospel tradition may help more. What does Jesus mean elsewhere by "brothers" and by the "least"?

Because ancient readers would unwind a scroll from the beginning, the first readers would have already read the preceding chapters before coming to Matthew 25. Thus they would know that Jesus' brothers and sisters included all those who did his will (Matt 12:48-50), that all Jesus' disciples are brothers and sisters (23:8), and, before they finished the Gospel, would know that Jesus' disciples remained his brothers after his resurrection (28:10). (Because of the way the Greek language works, "brothers" often can include "sisters" as well, but in 28:10 the women disciples are addressing specifically the men disciples.) When Jesus speaks of the "least" in the kingdom, he sometimes also refers to some disciples (11:11).

Who then are the least of these disciples of Jesus that the nations accepted or rejected? It is at least possible that these are messengers of the gospel, missionaries, who bring the gospel to all unreached people groups before the day of judgment. Certainly the message about the kingdom would be spread among all those people groups before the kingdom would come (24:14). These messengers might be hungry and thirsty because of the comforts they sacrificed to bring others the gospel. They might be imprisoned because of persecution. They might even be worn down to sickness by their efforts (like Epaphroditus in Phil 2:27-30).

But those who received such messengers would receive Jesus who sent them, even if all they had to give them was a cup of cold water to drink—as Jesus had taught earlier (10:11-14, 40-42). It is possible, then, in light of the entire Gospel of Matthew, that these *"least brothers and sisters"* are the lowliest of the missionaries sent to the nations. The nations will be judged according to how they respond to Jesus' representatives.

4. What it means to "believe" in John 3:16

John 3:16 does refer to salvation from sin through faith in Jesus, as we usually expect. But we do not catch the full meaning of this verse unless we read the Gospel of John the whole way through. The rest of the Gospel sheds light on what this verse means about the "world" (for instance, it includes Samaritans—see 4:42 in context), on how God expressed his love (by describing the cross), and other issues. We focus here on what John 3:16 means by saving faith. Someone may say he believes in Jesus, yet this person may attend church once a year and continue to live in unrepentant sin (let us say this person commits adultery every other weekend). Is this person really a Christian? What does it really mean to "believe" in Jesus?

The rest of the Gospel of John clarifies what Jesus means here by saving faith. Just before the conversation in which Jesus speaks 3:16, John tells us about some inadequate believers. Many people were impressed with Jesus' miracles and "believed" in him, but Jesus refused to put his faith in them because he knew what was really inside them (2:23-25). They had some sort of faith, but it was not saving faith.

What would happen if someone professed faith in Christ, then later renounced Christ and became a member of another religion or worshiped at the shrine of some traditional god? Would their earlier profession of faith be enough to save them in the end? The question is not hard to answer in light of the rest of John's Gospel, though some of us may not like the answer. Later in the Gospel of John, some of Jesus' hearers "believed" in him, but he warned them that they must continue in his word, so proving to be his disciples and learning the truth which would free them (8:30-32). By the end of the chapter, however, these hearers have already proved unfaithful. They actually want to kill Jesus (8:59). Jesus later warns that those who fail to continue in him will be cast away

(15:4, 6). In John's Gospel, genuine saving faith is the kind of faith that perseveres to the end.

The purpose of John's Gospel was to record some of his signs for Christian readers who had never seen Jesus in person, that they might come to a deeper level of faith, the kind of faith that would be strong enough to persevere in following Jesus to the end (20:30-31). John makes this comment right after narrating the climactic confession of faith in this Gospel. Jesus summons Thomas to "believe," and Thomas expresses his faith by calling Jesus, *"My Lord and my God"* (20:27-28). Jesus' deity is an emphasis in John's Gospel (1:1, 18; 8:58), so of all the other confessions about Jesus' identity in this Gospel (1:29, 36, 49; 6:69), this is the climactic one: he is God. The content of Thomas's faith is correct, but John wants more from his own readers. Correct information about Jesus is necessary, but by itself correct information is not necessarily strong faith. Thomas believed because he saw, but Jesus says that he wants greater faith that can believe even before it sees (20:29). John's readers believe because he narrates his eyewitness testimony to them (20:30-31), confirmed by the power of the Holy Spirit (15:26-16:15).

In John 3:16, saving faith is not just praying a single prayer, then going on our way and forgetting about Jesus for the rest of our lives. Saving faith is embracing Jesus with such radical dependence on His work for us that we stake our lives on the truth of His claims.

5. Under the Law in Romans 7

Earlier we noted the importance of the entire structure of Romans, which teaches us about ethnic reconciliation. In this context, the specific function of Romans 7 is significant: Paul notes that believers are no longer *"under the law"* (7:1-6). But he also notes that the problem is not with the law itself (7:7, 12, 14), but with humans as creatures of "flesh." Many people take this chapter as also depicting Paul's present enslavement to sin, and some even use it to justify living sinfully, saying, "If Paul could not keep from living in sin, how can we?" Is that really Paul's point?

In 7:14, Paul declares that he is *"fleshly, sold into slavery to sin."* In surrounding chapters, however, he declares that all believers in Jesus have been freed from sin and made slaves to God and righteousness (6:18-22). In 7:18, Paul complains that *"nothing good dwells"* in him, but in 8:9 he explains that the Spirit of Christ dwells in all true believers. In 7:25 he confesses that he serves with his body the *"law of sin;"* but in 8:2 he declares that Jesus has freed believers from *"the law of sin and death."*

Why this apparent confusion? Probably only because we have missed the primary issue. Although Paul speaks graphically about life under the law in Romans 7, he is not implying that this is his typical daily Christian life. He says that when believers "were" in the flesh (probably meaning, ruled by their own desires), their sinful passions stirred by the law were producing death in them. By contrast, Paul says, "But now" believers have been *"freed from the law,"* serving instead by the Spirit (7:5-6). That is, most of Romans 7 depicts the frustration of trying to achieve righteousness by the works of the law, that is, by human effort (Romans 7 speaks of "I," "me," "my" and "mine" over forty times). When we accept the righteousness of God as a free gift in Jesus Christ, however, we become able to walk in newness of life, and the rest of the Christian life is daring to trust the finished work of Christ enough to live like it is so (6:11). To the extent that our lives resemble Romans 7 at all, it is because we are trying to make ourselves good enough for God instead of accepting His gracious love for us.

6. The Spirit-baptized life in Mark 1:8-13

The Gospel of Mark explicitly mentions God's Spirit only six times, but half of them appear in his introduction (1:8-13), where he introduces several of his central themes for his audience. His other uses emphasize the Spirit's work in empowering Jesus for exorcism (Mk 3:29-30), Old Testament prophets to speak God's message (12:26) or Jesus' witnesses to speak His message (13:11).

In the introduction, John the Baptist announces the mighty one who will baptize others in the Holy Spirit (1:8). This Spirit-baptizer is Jesus of Nazareth. Immediately after this announcement, we see Jesus baptized and the Spirit coming on him (1:9-10). The Spirit-baptizer thus gives us a model of what the Spirit-baptized life will look like, for he himself receives the Spirit first. That is why what the Spirit does next appears all the more stunning: the Spirit thrusts Jesus into the wilderness for conflict with the devil (1:12-13). The Spirit-filled life is not a life of ease and comfort, but of conflict with the devil's forces!

The rest of the Gospel of Mark continues this pattern. Shortly after Jesus emerges from the wilderness, He must confront an evil spirit in a religious gathering (1:21-27). Throughout the rest of the Gospel, Jesus continues to defeat the devil by healing the sick and driving out demons (see also 3:27), while the devil continues to strike at Jesus through the devil's religious and political agents. In the end, the devil manages to get Jesus killed—but Jesus triumphs by rising from the dead.

In the same way, Jesus expects his disciples to heal the sick and drive out demons (3:14-15; 4:40; 6:13; 9:19, 28-29; 11:22-24), and also to join him in suffering (8:34-38; 10:29-31, 38-40; 13:9-13). His disciples seemed more happy to share His triumphs than his sufferings, but the Gospel of Mark emphasizes that we cannot share his glory without also sharing his suffering. That lesson remains as relevant for modern disciples as for ancient ones!

7. How to Make Disciples in Matthew 28:18-20

The immediate context of 28:18-20 provides us examples for how to testify about Christ (28:1-10) and how *not* to testify about Christ (28:11-15). But the context of the whole Gospel of Matthew further informs how we should read this passage, especially because it is the conclusion of the Gospel and readers would have finished the rest of this Gospel before reading this.

The command to "make disciples" of all nations (KJV has "teach" them) is surrounded by three clauses in Greek that describe how we make disciples of the nations: by "going," "baptizing," and "teaching." Jesus had spoken of "going" when he had sent his disciples out even within Galilee (10:7), but here disciples must go to other cultures and peoples because they will make disciples of the "nations."

Making disciples of the "nations" fits an emphasis developed throughout this Gospel. The four women specifically mentioned in Jesus' ancestry (1:2-17) appear to be Gentiles: Tamar the Canaanite, Rahab the Jerichoite, Ruth the Moabitess, and the "widow of Uriah" the Hittite (1:3, 5-6). Ancient Jewish genealogies normally emphasized the purity of one's Israelite lineage, but this genealogy deliberately underlines the mixed-race heritage of the Messiah who will save Gentiles as well as Jews.

When many of his own people ignored or persecuted him, pagan astrologers from the East came to worship him (2:1-12). God and his Son could raise up Abraham's children even from stones (3:9), work in *"Galilee*

Whole Book Context Examples

of the Gentiles" (4:15), bless the faith of a Roman military officer (8:5-13), deliver demoniacs in Gentile territory (8:28-34), compare Israelite cities unfavorably with Sodom (10:15; 11:23-24), reward the persistent faith of a Canaanite woman (15:21-28), allow the first apostolic confession of Jesus' Messiahship in pagan territory (16:13), promise that all nations would hear the gospel (24:14), and allow the first confession of Jesus as God's Son after the cross to come from a Roman execution squad (27:54). Matthew probably wrote to encourage his fellow Jewish Christians to evangelize the Gentiles, so the Gospel fittingly closes on this command.

"Baptizing" recalls the mission of John the Baptist, who baptized people for repentance (3:1-2, 6, 11). Baptism in Jewish culture represented an act of conversion, so as "going" may represent cross-cultural ministry, we may describe Jesus' command to "baptize" as evangelism. But evangelism is not sufficient to make full disciples; we also need Christian education. "Teaching" them all that Jesus commanded is made easier by the fact that Matthew has provided us Jesus' teachings conveniently in five major discourse sections: Jesus' teachings about the ethics of the kingdom (chs. 5-7); proclaiming the kingdom (ch. 10); parables about the present state of the kingdom (ch. 13); relationships in the kingdom (ch. 18); and the future of the kingdom and judgment on the religious establishment (chs. 23-25).

But in Matthew's Gospel, we do not make disciples the way most Jewish teachers in his day made disciples. We make disciples not for ourselves but for our Lord Jesus Christ (23:8). This final paragraph of Matthew's Gospel fittingly concludes various themes about Jesus' identity in this Gospel as well. John (3:2), Jesus (4:17), and his followers (10:7) announced God's kingdom, His reign; now Jesus reigns with all authority in all creation (28:18). Further, we baptize not only in the name of God and His Spirit, but in the name of Jesus (28:19), thereby ranking Jesus as deity alongside the Father and the Spirit. And finally, Jesus' promise to be with us always as we preach the kingdom until the end of the age (28:20) recalls earlier promises in the Gospel. Jesus himself is *"Immanuel," "God with us"* (1:23), and wherever two or three gather in his name he will be among them (18:20). To any ancient Jewish reader, these statements would imply that Jesus was God.

Does the promise that Jesus will be with us *"till the end of the age"* (28:20) imply that once the age ends he will no longer be with us? Such an idea would miss entirely the point of the text. Jesus is promising to be with us in carrying out His commission (28:19); that must be accomplished before the age ends (24:14), so the nations can be judged according to how they have responded to this message (25:31-32). Taking this passage in the context of the entire Gospel provides us plenty of preaching material without even stepping outside Matthew!

8. Loyalty to the Death in John 13:34-35

When Jesus commands us to love one another as he has loved us, why does he call this a "new" commandment (13:34)? Did not God command all believers to love one another even in the Old Testament (Leviticus 19:18). What makes this commandment a new commandment is the new example set by the Lord Jesus.

The immediate context makes this example clearer. Jesus takes the role of a humble servant by washing his disciples' feet (13:1-11); He also calls on his disciples to imitate his servanthood (13:12-17). In the same context, we understand the degree to which he became a servant for us by noting what he would suffer. Jesus and the narrator keep talking about Jesus' impending betrayal (13:11, 18-30). Jesus explains that he is being "glorified" (13:31-32), i.e., killed (12:23-24); he is about to leave the disciples (13:33), and Peter is not yet spiritually prepared to follow Jesus in martyrdom (13:36-38). This is the context of loving one another "as" Jesus loved us. We are called to sacrifice even our lives for one another!

The rest of the Gospel of John illustrates more fully Jesus' example of love and servanthood that culminates in the cross.

9. Judah's Punishment in Genesis 38

In his attacks on Christianity, South African writer Ahmed Deedat complains that the Bible is full of pornography and that Genesis 38, the story of Judah and Tamar, is a "filthy, dirty story." Did the Bible include this story simply to satisfy base interests of ungodly readers? Or have Deedat and others missed the entire point of the story?

The story can be summarized briefly, after which we will quickly see a moral lesson in it. Judah has three sons, Er (38:3), Onan (38:4), and Shelah (38:5). When God killed Er for sinful behavior (38:7), his younger brother Onan automatically inherited Er's responsibility to raise up offspring for his brother's name. Some cultures where women cannot earn money practice widow inheritance, where another brother takes over the deceased brother's wife. In the cultures around this family, however, normally a brother would simply get the widow pregnant, so that she could have a son who would receive her first husband's share of the inheritance. This son would in turn support her in her old age.

But Onan spills his seed on the ground, and God angrily strikes him dead (38:9-10), as he had struck his brother before him. Why did Onan *"spill his seed"*? And what was so sinful about him doing so? The firstborn (in this case Er) normally received twice as much inheritance as any other brother. If Onan raised up a son for his brother, that son would be counted as his brother's son and would receive half the inheritance, leaving only a quarter for Onan and a quarter for Shelah. But if Tamar could not become pregnant, Onan would receive two-thirds of the inheritance and Shelah one-third. Onan was greedy, and cared more about the extra inheritance than about honoring his brother and providing for Tamar. God defended Tamar's honor, because he cared about Tamar. The text teaches us about justice.

But the story goes on. Judah, fearing that allowing his sons to sleep with Tamar is leading to their deaths, refuses to give his final son to Tamar. In some of the surrounding cultures (though never in later Israelite law), if a brother were unavailable, a father was considered acceptable so Tamar takes matters into her own hands. She disguises herself as a prostitute, knowing what kind of person Judah is. Then she allows him to impregnate her, but keeps his signet ring so she can later prove that he is the father (38:18).

When Judah learns that Tamar is pregnant, he orders her to be executed. This reflects a double standard practiced in many cultures: the idea that a man can have sex with anyone (as Judah slept with what he thought was a prostitute) but a woman cannot. But God has no double standard. Sin is as wrong for a man as it is for a woman. Tamar sent him the signet ring, forcing Judah to release her and admit, *"She is more righteous than I"* (38:26). That was the moral of the story: Judah was immoral and raised two immoral sons, and now is caught in his guilt. By challenging the double standard of his culture, the writer argues against sin. This is not a "dirty story" at all!

But whole-book context shows us more. The chapter directly before chapter 38 is chapter 37, where Judah takes the lead in selling his brother

Joseph into slavery. In chapter 38, Judah's lifestyle of sin finally catches up with him, and he suffers for it! He sold his father's son into slavery. Now he loses two of his own sons to death. The chapter after 38 is chapter 39, where Joseph resists the sexual advances of Potipher's wife, despite the penalty he faces for doing so. Joseph does not practice a double standard. He lives holy no matter what the cost. And a few chapters later, God rewards Joseph for his obedience. He becomes Pharaoh's special assistant, and the agent through whom God can actually rescue the very brothers who sold him into slavery. And when Joseph is exalted, Pharaoh gives Joseph his signet-ring (41:42)—inviting us to remember Judah who lent his to what he thought was a prostitute (38:11). The larger story has a moral: those who live sinful lifestyles may prosper in the short run, but eventually they suffer. By contrast, those who remain faithful to God may suffer at first, but in the end they will be blessed.

This, however, is not the end of the story. Although Judah took the lead in selling his half-brother Joseph into slavery, Judah learned from his mistakes. Later he takes responsibility for Joseph's full brother Benjamin before their father Jacob (43:8-9), and for his father's sake takes responsibility for Benjamin before Joseph (44:16-34). Judah is ready to become a slave himself to keep Benjamin from becoming one—and this is what convinces Joseph that his brothers finally have changed. The final moral of the story, then, is one of forgiveness and reconciliation, and the faithfulness of God who arranged events to bring it all about. Ahmed Deedat did not read far enough to understand the story!

10. Rivers of Living Water in John 7:37-38

Jesus' promise of rivers of living water in John 7:37-38, referring to the coming of the Holy Spirit (7:39), is exciting in any case. But it is especially exciting if one traces through the rest of the Gospel the contrast between the true water of the Spirit and merely ritual uses of water by Jesus' contemporaries.

John's baptism in water was good, but Jesus' baptism in the Spirit was better (1:26, 33). Strict Jewish ritual required the water pots in Cana to be used only for ritual waters to purify, but when Jesus turned the water into wine he showed that he valued his friend's honor more than ritual and tradition (2:6). A Samaritan woman abandons her water pot used to draw water from the sacred ancestral well when she realizes that Jesus offers new water that brings eternal life (4:13-14). A sick man unable to be healed by water that supposedly brought healing (5:7) finds healing instead in Jesus (5:8-9). A blind man is healed by water in some sense but only because Jesus "sends" him there (9:7).

The function of this water is suggested more fully in John 3:5. Here Jesus explains that Nicodemus cannot understand God's kingdom without being born *"from above"* (3:3, literally)—that is from God. Some Jewish teachers spoke of Gentiles being "reborn" in a sense when they converted to Judaism, but Nicodemus cannot conceive of himself as a Gentile, a pagan, so he assumes Jesus speaks instead of reentering his mother's womb (3:4). So Jesus clarifies his statement. Jewish people believed that Gentiles converted to Judaism through circumcision and baptism, so Jesus explains to Nicodemus that he must be reborn *"from water."* In other words, Nicodemus must come to God on the same terms that Gentiles do!

But if Jesus means by "water" here what he means in 7:37-38, he may mean water as a symbol for the Spirit, in which case he is saying, *"You must be born of water, i.e., the Spirit"* (a legitimate way to read the Greek). If so, Jesus may be using Jewish conversion baptism merely to symbolize the greater baptism in the Spirit that he brings to those who trust in him. The water may also symbolize Jesus' sacrificial servanthood for his disciples (13:5).

So what does Jesus mean by the rivers of living water in John 7:37-38? First, in most current translations, at least a footnote points out an alternate way to punctuate 7:37-38 (the earliest Greek texts lacked punctuation, and the early church fathers divided over which interpretation to take). In this other way to read the verses, it is not clear that the water flows from the believer. It may flow instead from Christ. Since believers "receive" rather than give the water (7:39), and since they elsewhere have a "well" rather than a "river" (4:14), Christ may well be the source of water in these verses. (This is not to deny the possibility that believers may experience deeper empowerments of the Spirit after their conversion.)

Jewish tradition suggests that on the last day of the Feast of Tabernacles, priests read to the people from Zechariah 14 and Ezekiel 47, which talk of rivers of living water flowing forth from the Temple in the end time. Jesus is now speaking on the last day of that feast (7:2, 37), probably alluding to the very Scriptures from which they had read (*"as the Scripture said,"* 7:38).

Jewish people thought of the Temple as the "navel" or "belly" of the earth. So Jesus may be declaring, *"I am the foundation stone of the new temple of God. From me flows the water of the river of life; let the one who wills come and drink freely!"*

Normally one should not read symbolism into biblical narratives, but the end of John's Gospel may be an exception, a symbol God provided those who watched the crucifixion. (John uses symbolism a little more than narratives normally do.) When a soldier pierced Jesus' side, water as well as blood flowed forth (19:34). Literally, a spear thrust near the heart could release a watery fluid around the heart as well as blood. But John is the only writer among the four Gospel writers to emphasize the water, and he probably mentions it to make a point. Once Jesus was lifted up on the cross and glorified (7:39), the new life of the Spirit became available to His people. Let us come and drink freely.

11. Rebecca's Deceit (Genesis 27:5-10)

Some readers have accused both Isaac and Rebecca of equal fault in favoring their sons (Esau and Jacob respectively; Genesis 27:1-10). But in context of the entire book of Genesis, the motives of the two parents are quite different. Isaac favors the elder son (25:25; 27:4), but the whole patriarchal line suggests that God does not always choose the elder son (21:12; 49:3-4), and paternal favoritism produces problems (37:4). Jacob himself finally learns and practices this in his old age (48:14-20). What are Rebecca's motives? The clearest clue the text itself provides is in 25:22-23. She had sought God, and God had told her that the younger would prevail. In contrast to Isaac, Rebecca acts on the basis of a word from God. Further, Esau had married pagan wives and sold his birthright, with apparently no sense of responsibility for the call on this family to be God's blessing to the earth (25:31-34; 26:34-35). In a culture where the husband's will was law and Isaac was blind to God's choice, Rebecca took the only route she knew to secure God's promise.

Genesis is full of accounts that underline for Israel the miracle of their blessing and existence—three barren matriarchs (18:11; 25:21; 30:22), royal abduction or threatening of matriarchs (12:13; 20:2; Isaac repeated his father's example—26:7), and so on. Elsewhere in Genesis someone other than the patriarch makes a choice, nevertheless leaving the right land to the patriarch (13:9-13; 36:6-8). In the context of the themes the

Whole Book Context Examples

entire book emphasizes, it is consistent to believe that God worked through Rebekah's deception, as he worked through a variety of other means, to protect his chosen line.

This is not to say that the deception was God's preferred means to accomplish this, though he sometimes blessed deception when it would save human life from unjust oppressors (Exodus 1:18-21; Joshua 2:5-6; 1 Samuel 16:1-3; 2 Samuel 17:19-20; 2 Kings 8:10; Jeremiah 38:24-27). When Isaac asked Jacob his name, he lied to get the blessing (Genesis 27:18-19), hence incurring his brother's murderous anger (27:41). His mother promised to send for him when it proved safe to return (27:45), but apparently she died in the meantime hence could not send for him, so when he is returning he expects that Esau still desires to kill him (32:11). Thus he struggles all night with the Lord or his agent, and he is confronted with his past. This time, before he can receive the blessing from God, he is asked his name and must tell the truth (32:26-27; and then gets a new name—32:28), in contrast to the time he sought his father's blessing (27:18-19). But God was with Jacob even in spite of himself. He met angels both going from (28:12) and returning to (32:2) the land. In this story, though Isaac outlives Rebekah, she was the one with the greater perception of God's purposes for their descendants.

12. Casting Lots in Acts 1:26

Some interpreters today suggest that the apostles made a mistake in casting lots for a twelfth apostle, even though it was before the day of Pentecost. The immediate context, however, suggests something positive; the believers were in prayerful unity (1:12-14; 2:1), and now Peter has exhorted them to replace the lost apostle (1:15-26). Would Luke spend so much space to describe a practice he disagreed with, and then fail to offer any word of correction?

Whole-book context in Acts actually invites us to read Luke and Acts together, for they were two volumes of one work (Acts 1:1-2; cf. Luke 1:1-4). When we read them together we see that Luke's Gospel also opens with a casting of lots, in this case, one used to select which priest would serve in the temple (Luke 1:9). In that case, God certainly controlled the lot, for by it Zechariah was chosen to serve in the temple, and subsequently received a divine promise specifically designed for himself and Elizabeth, the promise of a son, John the Baptist (1:13). If God controlled the lot in the opening story of volume one, why not in the opening story (after repeating the ascension) in volume 2? The background would help us further. If God controlled the lot throughout the Old Testament, including for selection of levitical ministries, why should we doubt that he used this method on this occasion in Acts, before the Spirit's special guidance inaugurated with Pentecost (2:17).

Appendix 3

Background Context Examples

Here we provide only a few limited samples concerning the use of background; fuller details are available in my book the *IVP Bible Background Commentary: New Testament*. Some background is available in the Bible itself. This is especially true when biblical writers depend on what other biblical writers proclaimed before them; the prophets often depend on the law of Moses (though usually without quoting it) and the New Testament regularly depends on the Old.

1. God's Message in the Tabernacle

Egyptians built temples differently than Mesopotamians; because the Israelites had been slaves in Egypt used in building projects, they undoubtedly knew what Egyptian temples looked like. They would have known about portable tent-shrines used in Egypt and Midian, as well as about the structure of Egyptian temples (and palaces), with an outer court, inner court, and the innermost shrine, the holiest place. God chose a design with which the Israelites were familiar so they could understand that the tabernacle they carried through the wilderness was a temple.

Some aspects of the tabernacle parallel other temples, and the parallels communicate true theology about God. In the tabernacle, the most expensive materials were used nearest the ark of the covenant: gold was more expensive than copper, and blue dye than red dye. These details reflect an ancient Near Eastern practice: people used the most expensive materials nearest the innermost sanctuary to signify that their god should be approached with awe and reverence. The tabernacle uses standard ancient Near Eastern symbols to communicate its point about God's holiness.

Some aspects of the tabernacle include both parallels and contrasts, which also communicate theology about God. For instance, some of the furniture of the Tabernacle resembles the furniture of other ancient temples: a table of offerings, an altar, and so forth. But Canaanite,

Egyptian and Hittite temples included other features like a chest of drawers and bed. Priests would wake their idols in the morning, give them their morning toilet, entertain them with dancing girls, feed them, and eventually put them back to bed at night. There was none of this in the Lord's temple, for he was not merely an idol dependent on his priests to assist him.

Some features of the tabernacle contrast starkly with their culture. The climax of other ancient Near Eastern and northern African temples was the image of the deity, enthroned on its sacred pedestal in the holiest innermost sanctuary; but there is no image in God's temple, because he would allow no graven images of himself (Ex. 20:4). Further, many massive Egyptian temples included shrines for tutelary deities flanking the inner sanctuary; but there are no other deities associated with the Lord's tabernacle, for he would tolerate the worship of no other gods in his sight (Ex. 20:3). God communicated his theology to Israel even in the architecture of the tabernacle, and he did so in cultural terms they could understand.

2. Why Sarah used Hagar's womb and later expelled her.

As an Egyptian, Hagar may have been one of the servants Pharaoh gave to Abraham and Sarah several years earlier (Gen. 12:16). In passing, we should note what the presence of Egyptian servants of Abraham implies for the matter of some African elements in Israel's ancestry. Abraham later passed his entire estate on to Isaac (25:5); when Jacob went down to Egypt with "seventy" people in his immediate family (46:27), this number does not include all the servants who also went with him, who were presumably retained as slaves when the Israelites were later enslaved (Ex. 1:11). This means that the later Israelites included much Egyptian blood, in addition to the two half-tribes of Joseph (Gen. 41:50).

But returning to the matter of Hagar: in some ancient Near Eastern cultures, if a woman could not bear her husband a son some other way, she might have her servant do it for her. So Sarah, following some assumptions of her culture, had Abraham get Hagar pregnant (16:2-3). In such cases, however, it was understood that the child would be legally the child of Sarah; but Hagar began to boast against Sarah as if she were better than Sarah (16:4).

After Isaac is born, Sarah finds Ishmael mocking him (21:9), and she realizes that Ishmael's presence threatens the birthright of the son God had promised, Isaac. According to some ancient Near Eastern customs, if Abraham had regarded Ishmael as his son, Ishmael would be treated as his firstborn. The way to prevent this was to free Hagar before Abraham's death, and send her and Ishmael away without the inheritance (21:10).

It was Sarah's initial suggestion that got Hagar in trouble, Hagar's arrogance that perpetuated it, but in the end, Sarah did act to preserve God's promise that she had endangered by her previous suggestion to Abraham. With the exception of Jesus, all biblical characters, including Abraham, Sarah and Hagar, were flawed in some ways; but understanding the customs of their day helps us better understand the decisions Sarah made.

3. Matthew 2:1-16

Ancient narrators often taught moral lessons by contrasting various characters, some good, some bad, and some mixed. In the Matthew 2:1-6 narrative, there are three characters or sets of characters that warrant special attention. They are the Magi ("wise men"), Herod the Great, and the scribes.

Magi were a caste of Persian astrologers—that is, those who practiced a profession explicitly forbidden in the Old Testament (Deut. 18:10; Isa. 47:13). The term is actually used in Greek translations of the Old Testament to describe Daniel's enemies who wanted to kill him! One of their jobs as Magi was to promote the honor of the king of Persia, whose official title was "king of kings and lord of lords." But these Magi come to honor the true king of kings born in Judea. Matthew thus shocks his Jewish-Christian readers by telling them of pagans who came to worship Jesus, implying that we cannot predict beforehand who will respond to our message.

Herod the Great was a ruthless ruler who was paranoid about anyone threatening his kingship. Not being Jewish by birth (he was a descendant of the ancient Edomites) he was insecure about his title, "King of the Judeans," and did not want to share it with anyone else. He had two of his sons executed because he was told they were plotting against him (the rumor turned out to be false), and another son executed for plotting against him—while Herod himself was dying. ("Better to be Herod's pig than his son," the emperor was reported to have complained.) A young high priest who was getting too popular and might have provided competition for Herod had a drowning accident—in a very shallow pool. Herod was the sort of person that this narrative describes! But killing the male children of Bethlehem (perhaps twenty boys) recalls how Pharaoh treated Israelite boys in Exodus. The pagan Magi worshiped the true king of the Jews; Herod the king of God's people, however, acted like a pagan king.

Most troubling of all, however, are the leading priests and scribes (2:4). These were the Bible professors and leading ministers of their day. They know where the Messiah will be born (2:5-6), but do not join the Magi on their quest. The people who knew the Bible the best took it for granted—a sin that only people who know the Bible can commit. And a generation later, when Jesus could no longer be taken for granted, their successors wanted him dead (Matt. 26:3-4). The line between taking Jesus for granted and wanting him out of our way may remain rather thin today as well. Especially when background helps us learn more about the characters in this narrative, it warns us in stark terms not to prejudge who will respond to the gospel—and not to think of ourselves more highly than we ought.

4. Keeping God's Word in Matthew 5:18-19

In 5:18, Jesus says that not the smallest letter or mark will pass from God's law. He probably refers at least partly to the *yod*, the smallest letter in the Hebrew alphabet. Later rabbis told the story that when God changed Sarai's name to Sarah, the *yod* that was removed complained to God for generations till he reinserted it, this time in Joshua's name. Some teachers also said that Solomon tried to uproot a *yod* from the Bible, whereon God announced that a thousand Solomons would be uprooted, but not a single *yod*. Jewish teachers used illustrations like this to make the point that the law was sacred and one could not regard any part as too small to be worthy of keeping.

When Jesus goes on to say that breaking the least command makes one least in the kingdom whereas keeping it makes one great in the kingdom, a modern reader might ask, "What happens if you break one and keep another?" But such a question misses the point of this typically Jewish language. Later rabbis decided that the greatest commandment was honoring one's father and mother, and the least, respecting a mother bird; they reasoned that both merited the same reward, eternal life (based on "life" in Ex. 20:12; Deut. 22:7). Thus if one broke the least commandment, one would be damned; if one kept it, one would be saved. Yet these same sages recognized that everyone sinned, including themselves. They were not saying that some people never broke any commandments; rather, they were saying that people could not pick and choose among the commandments. One could not say, "I am righteous because I do not kill, even though I have sex with someone I am not married to." Nor could one say, "I am godly because I do not steal, even though I cheat." All of God's commandments are his word, and to cast off any is to deny his right to rule over us, hence to reject him. Thus Jesus was saying in a similarly graphic way, "You cannot disregard even the smallest commandment, or God will hold you accountable."

5. The Kingdom Prayer in Matthew 6:9-13

Many pagans added up as many names of their deities as possible, reminding the deities of all their sacrifices and how the deities were therefore obligated in some sense to answer them. Jesus, however, says that we should base our prayers instead on the relationship our heavenly Father has given us with himself: we can cry out to him because he is our Father (Matt. 6:7-9).

Jesus used some things in his culture, which was already full of biblical knowledge. Jesus here adapts a common synagogue prayer, that went something like this: "Our Father in heaven, exalted and hallowed be your great and glorious name, and may your kingdom come speedily and soon . . ." Jewish people expected a time when God's name would be "hallowed," or shown to be holy, among all peoples. For Jewish people, there was a sense in which God reigns in the present, but when they prayed for the coming of God's kingdom they were praying for him to rule unchallenged over all the earth and his will to be done on earth just as it is in heaven. Jesus therefore taught his disciples to pray for God's reign to come soon, when God's name would be universally honored.

To ask God for "daily bread" recalls how God provided bread each day for Israel in the wilderness; God is still our provider. To ask God to forgive our "debts" would stir a familiar image for many of Jesus' hearers. Poor peasants had to borrow much money to sow their crops, and Jesus' contemporaries understood that our sins were debts before God. To ask

God not to "lead us into temptation" probably recalls a Jewish synagogue prayer of the day which asked God to preserve people from sinning. If so, the prayer might mean not, "Let us not be tested," but rather, "Do not let us fail the test" (compare 26:41, 45).

6. Enemy Soldiers Torture and Mock Jesus in Matthew 27:27-34.

Over six hundred Roman soldiers were staying at the Fortress Antonia and at Pilate's palace (which once belonged to Herod the Great). Not recognizing that the true king of Israel and humanity stood before them, they mocked him as a pretend king. Roman soldiers were known for abusing and taunting prisoners; one ancient form of mockery was to dress someone as a king. Since soldiers wore red robes, they probably used a faded soldier's cloak to imitate the purple robe of earlier Greek rulers. People venerating such rulers would kneel before them, as here. Military floggings often used bamboo canes, so the soldiers may have had one available they could use as a mock sceptre. "Hail!" was the standard salute people gave to the Roman Emperor.

Spitting on a person was one of the most grievous insults a person could offer, and Jewish people considered the spittle of non-Jews particularly unclean. Romans stripped their captives naked—especially shameful for Palestinian Jews; then they hanged the convict publicly.

Normally the condemned person was to carry the horizontal beam (Latin *patibulum*) of the cross himself, out to the site where the upright stake (Latin *palus*) awaited him; but Jesus' back had been too severely scourged beforehand for him to do this (27:26). Such scourging often left the flesh of the person's back hanging down in bloody strips, sometimes even leaving his bones showing. Scourging sometimes led to the person's death from shock and blood loss. Thus the soldiers had to draft Simon of Cyrene to carry the crossbeam. Cyrene, a large city in what is now Libya in North Africa, had a large Jewish community (perhaps one quarter of the city) which no doubt included local converts. Like multitudes of foreign Jews and converts, Simon had come to Jerusalem for the feast. Roman soldiers could "impress" any person into service to carry things for them. Despite Jesus' teaching in Matthew 16:24, the soldiers had to draft a bystander to do what Jesus' disciples proved unwilling to do.

Crucifixion was the most shameful and painful form of execution known in the Roman world. Unable to privately excrete his wastes the dying person would excrete them publicly. Sometimes soldiers tied the condemned person to the cross; at other times they nailed them, as with Jesus. The dying man thus could not swat away insects attracted to his bloodied back or other wounds. Crucifixion victims sometimes took three days to finish dying.

The women of Jerusalem prepared a pain-killing potion of drugged wine for condemned men to drink; Jesus refused it (see 26:29). The myrrh-mixed wine of Mark 15:23, a delicacy and possibly an external pain reliever, becomes wine mixed with gall in Matthew. Even without myrrh, wine itself was a painkiller (Proverbs 31:6-7). But Jesus refused it. Though we forsook him and fled when he needed us most, he came to bear our pain, and chose to bear it in full measure. Such is God's love for us all.

7. Adultery and Murder in Mark 6:17-29

Herod Antipas's affair with his sister-in-law Herodias, whom he had by this time married, was widely known. Indeed, the affair had led him to plan to divorce his first wife, whose father, a king, later went to war with Herod because of this insult and defeated him. John's denunciation of the affair as unlawful (Lev. 20:21) challenged Herod's sexual immorality, but Herod Antipas could have perceived it as a political threat, given the political ramifications that later led to a major military defeat. (The ancient Jewish historian Josephus claims that many viewed Herod's humiliation in the war as divine judgment for him executing John the Baptist.)

Celebrating birthdays was at this time a Greek and Roman but not a Jewish custom, but Jewish aristocrats had absorbed a large amount of Greek culture by this period. Other sources confirm that the Herodian court indulged in the sort of immoral behavior described here. After taking his brother's wife (Lev. 20:21), Antipas lusts after his wife's daughter Salome (see Lev. 20:14). He then utters the sort of oath one might give while drunk, but which especially recalls that of the Persian king stirred by Queen Esther's beauty (Esther 5:3, 6, 7:2). But as a Roman vassal Herod had no actual authority to give any of his kingdom away anyway.

Salome had to go "out" to ask her mother Herodias because women and men normally dined separately at banquets. Excavations at Antipas's fortress Machaerus suggest two dining halls, one for women and one for men; Herodias thus was probably not present to watch Herod's reaction to the dance. Josephus characterizes Herodias the same way Mark does: a jealous, ambitious schemer.

Although Romans and their agents usually executed lower class persons and slaves by crucifixion or other means, the preferred form of execution for respectable people was beheading. By asking for John's head on a platter, however, Salome wanted it served up as part of the dinner menu—a ghastly touch of ridicule. Although Antipas's oath was not legally binding and Jewish sages could release him from it, it would have proved embarrassing to break an oath before dinner guests. Most people were revolted by leaders who had heads brought to them, but many accounts confirm that powerful tyrants like Antipas had such things done.

If a man had sons, normally the eldest son was responsible for his father's burial. Here, John's disciples must fulfill this role for him. Since he had been executed, the disciples performed a dangerous task unless they had Herod's permission to take the body. Their courage underlines by contrast the abandonment of Jesus' male disciples during his burial!

8. A New King's Birthday in Luke 2:1-14

Censuses were used especially to evaluate taxation requirements. A tax census instigated by the revered emperor Augustus here begins the narrative's contrast between Caesar's earthly pomp and Christ's heavenly glory. Although Egyptian census records show that people had to return to their homes for a tax census, the "home" to which they returned was where they owned property, not simply where they were born (censuses registered persons according to property). Joseph thus must have still held property in Bethlehem. Betrothal provided most of the legal rights of marriage, but intercourse was forbidden; Joseph was courageous to take his pregnant betrothed with him, even if (as is quite possible) she was also a Bethlehemite who had to return to that town. Although tax laws in most of the Empire only required the head of a household to appear, the province of Syria (then including Judea) also taxed women. But Joseph may have simply wished to avoid leaving her alone this late in her pregnancy, especially if the circumstances of her pregnancy had deprived her of other friends.

The "swaddling clothes" were long cloth strips used to keep babies' limbs straight so they could grow properly. Midwives normally assisted at birth; especially since this was Mary's first child, it is likely (though not clear from the text) that a midwife would have been found to assist her. Jewish law permitted midwives to travel a long distance even on the Sabbath to assist in delivery.

By the early second century even pagans were widely aware of the tradition that Jesus was born in a cave used as a livestock shelter behind someone's home. The manger was a feeding trough for animals; sometimes these may have been built into the floor. The traditional "inn" could as easily be translated "home" or "guest room," and probably means that, since many of Joseph's scattered family members had returned to the home at the same time, it was easier for Mary to bear in the vacant cave outside.

Many religious people and especially the social elite in this period generally despised shepherds as a low-class occupation; but God sees differently than people do. Pasturing of flocks at night indicates that this was a warmer season, not winter (when they would graze more in the day); December 25 was later adopted as Christmas only to supersede a pagan Roman festival scheduled at that time.

Pagans spoke of the "good news" of the emperor's birthday, celebrated throughout the empire; they hailed the emperor as "Savior" and "Lord." They used choirs in imperial temples to worship the emperor. They praised the current emperor, Augustus, for having inaugurated a worldwide "peace." But the lowly manger distinguishes the true king from the Roman emperor; Jesus is the true Savior, Lord, bringer of universal peace. God is not impressed with human power or honor; he came as the lowliest of all among the lowliest of all, revealing God's special heart toward those who most depend on him for their help.

9. Demands of Discipleship in Luke 9:58-62

Warning a prospective disciple that the Son of Man has less of a home than foxes and birds indicates that those who follow him may lack the same securities. Disciples usually sought out their own teachers (in contrast to Jesus, who called some of his own). Some radical philosophers who eschewed possessions sought to repulse prospective disciples with enormous demands, for the purpose of testing them and acquiring only the most worthy disciples. Many Palestinian Jews were poor, but few were homeless; Jesus had given up even home to travel and was completely dependent on the hospitality and support of others.

The man who wants to bury his father is not asking for a short delay: his father has not died that day or the day before. Family members carried the body to the tomb shortly after its death and then remained at home for seven days to mourn. The man could be saying, as in some similar Middle Eastern cultures, "Let me wait until my father dies someday and I fulfill my obligation to bury him." The other possibility is that he refers to his father's *second* burial, a custom practiced precisely in this period. A year after the first burial, after the flesh had rotted off the bones, the son would return to *rebury* the bones in a special box in a slot in the wall. This son could thus be asking for as much as a year's delay.

One of an eldest son's most basic responsibilities was his father's burial. Jesus' demand that the son place Jesus above the greatest responsibility a son could offer his father would thus have defied the social order: in Jewish tradition, honoring father and mother was one of the greatest commandments, and to follow Jesus in such a radical way would have seemed like breaking this commandment.

But while the second inquirer learned the priority of following Jesus, the third learns the *urgency* of following Jesus. One prospective disciple requests merely permission to say farewell to his family, but Jesus compares this request with looking back from plowing, which would cause one to ruin one's furrow in the field. Jesus speaks figuratively to remind his hearer of the story of Elisha's call. When Elijah found Elisha plowing, he called him to follow him, but allowed him to first bid farewell to his family (1 Kings 19:19-21). The Old Testament prophets sacrificed much to serve God's will, but Jesus' call here is more radical than that of a radical prophet! Although we must beware of others who sometimes misrepresent Jesus' message, we must be willing to pay any price that Jesus' call demands on our lives.

10. God's Friends Rejoice in Luke 15:18-32.

The religious elite were angry with Jesus for spending time with tax-gatherers and sinners; after all, Scripture warned against spending time with ungodly people (Psalm 1:1; Proverbs 13:20). The difference, of course, is that Jesus is spending time with sinners to influence them for the kingdom, not to be shaped by their ways (Luke 15:1-2).

Jesus answered the religious elite by telling them three stories: the story of the lost sheep, the lost coin, and the lost son. A hundred was roughly an average sized flock, and when one sheep strayed the shepherd would do whatever necessary to recover it. (He could leave his other sheep with fellow shepherds who would watch over their flocks together with him. Sheep would often roam together and be separated by their shepherds' distinctive calls or flutes.) When he finds what was lost, he calls his friends together to rejoice, and Jesus says it is the same way with God: those who are really his friends rejoice with him when he regains what was lost (15:3-7). The implication seems to be that the religious elite are not God's friends, or they would be rejoicing.

Jesus then turns to the story of the lost coin. If a woman had ten coins as her dowry, the money she had brought into her marriage in case of divorce or widowhood, she was a very poor woman indeed: ten coins represented about ten days' wages for the average working man. In any case, one out of ten is more than one out of a hundred, and she is desperate to find the coin! Most small, one-room Galilean homes had floors of roughly fitted stones, so coins and other objects routinely fell between the cracks and remained lost until excavated by modern archaeologists! Further, most of these homes had at most one small window and a doorway, so there was little light to help her find her coin. She thus lights a lamp, but in this period most lamps were small enough to hold in the palm of one's hand, and these did not provide much light. So she sweeps with a broom, hoping to hear the coin tinkle—and finally, she finds it! Her friends rejoice with her, just as God's friends rejoice with him—implying, again, that perhaps the religious elite are not among God's friends (15:8-10).

Jesus then turns to the story of the lost son. The younger son says to his father, "I want my share of the inheritance now." In that culture, the son was virtually declaring, "Father, I wish you were dead"—the epitome of disrespect. The father was under no obligation to divide his inheritance, but he divided it anyway; the elder brother would have received two thirds and the younger one third. Under ancient law, by dividing the inheritance the father simply was telling them which fields and items each would get after his decease; the son could not legally *spend* the estate before then. But this son does it anyway; he flees to a far country and wastes his father's years of work. In the end, however, reduced to poverty, he has to feed pigs; for Jesus' Jewish hearers, this was a fitting end for such a rebellious son, and a fitting end for the story. If the young man were involved with pigs, he would be unclean and not even be able to approach fellow Jews for help!

But the young man decides that he would rather be a servant in his father's house than starve, so he returns home to beg for mercy. His father, seeing him a long way off, runs to meet him. In that culture, it was considered undignified for older men to run, but this father discards his dignity; his son has come home! The son tries to plead that he might be a slave, but the father ignores him, instead calling for the best robe in the house—undoubtedly his own; and a ring for the young man's finger—undoubtedly a signet ring, symbolizing his reinstatement to sonship; and sandals for his feet—because most servants did not wear sandals, the father is saying, "No, I will not receive you as a servant! I will receive you *only* as my son!" The fatted calf was enough food to feed the entire village, so he throws a big party, and all his friends rejoice with him.

So far the story has paralleled the two stories that preceded it, but now Jesus goes further, challenging the religious elite more directly. Ancient literature sometimes framed an important paragraph by starting and ending on the same statement, here that his lost son has come home (15:24, 32). When the elder brother discovers that the father has welcomed home his younger brother, he has nothing to lose economically; the inheritance was already divided (15:12). The problem is that he regards as unfair his father celebrating the return of a rebellious son when he himself needed no mercy; he thought himself good enough *without* his father's mercy. He protests to his father, refusing to greet him with a title, reducing the father to coming out and begging him to come in. He is now disrespecting his father just as much as the younger brother had earlier! "I have been serving you," he protests (15:29), thereby revealing that he saw himself as a servant rather than a son—the very role the father refused to consider acceptable (15:21-22).

The religious elite despised the "sinners" who were coming to Jesus, not realizing that their hearts were no better. The sinners were like the younger brother, the religious elite like the older one. All of us need Jesus; none can be saved without God's mercy.

11. The First Gentile Christian in Acts 8:26-27

Since Samaritans were considered half-breeds (8:4-25), this African court official is the first fully Gentile convert to Christianity (though probably unknown to most of the Jerusalem church, 11:18).

The angel's instructions to go south toward Gaza (8:26) probably would have seemed strange to Philip; Samaria yielded many converts, but who would he find on a generally deserted road? Two roads led south from near Jerusalem, one through Hebron into Idumea (Edom) and the other joining the coast road before Gaza heading for Egypt, both with many Roman milestones as road-markers. Old Gaza was a deserted town whose ruins lay near the now culturally Greek cities of Askelon and New Gaza. The command to head south for a few days toward a deserted city may have seemed absurd; but God had often tested faith through seemingly absurd commands (e.g., Exodus 14:16; 1 Kings 17:3-4, 9-14; 2 Kings 5:10).

"Ethiopia" (a Greek term) figured in Mediterranean legends and mythical geography as the very end of the earth, sometimes extending from the far south (all Africa south of Egypt, the "wooly-haired Ethiopians") to the far east (the "straight-haired Ethiopians" of southern India). Greek literature often respected Africans as a people particularly beloved by the gods (the Greek historian Herodotus also calls them the most handsome of people), and some sub-Sahara Africans were known in the Roman Empire. The most commonly mentioned feature of Ethiopians in Jewish and Greco-Roman literature (also noted in the Old Testament) is their black skin, though ancient Mediterranean art also depicted other typically African features and recognized differences in skin tone. Egyptians and other peoples were sometimes called "black" by comparison with lighter Mediterranean peoples, but the further south one traveled along the Nile, the darker the complexion and more tightly coiled the hair of the people. Greeks considered the "Ethiopians" the epitome of blackness.

Here a particular African empire is in view. While we might confuse "Ethiopia" here with modern Ethiopia, that is probably not in view. That kingdom, Axum, was a powerful east African empire and converted to Christianity in the early 300s, in the same generation the Roman empire converted. The empire here, however, is most likely a particular Nubian kingdom of somewhat darker complexion, south of Egypt in what is now the Sudan. "Candace" (*kan-dak'a*) seems to have been a dynastic title of the Queen of this Nubian Empire; she is mentioned elsewhere in Greco-

Roman literature, and tradition declares that the queen-mother ruled in that land. (Ancient Greeks called all of Nubia "Ethiopia.") Her black Nubian kingdom had lasted since c. 750 BC; its main cities were Meroe and Napata. This kingdom was wealthy (giving a royal treasurer like this one much to do!) and had trade ties to the north; Rome procured peacocks and other African treasures through such African kingdoms in contact with the interior of Africa, and Roman wealth has turned up in excavations of Meroe. The trade also extended further south; a bust of Caesar has been found as far south as Tanzania. Still, the trade connection with Rome was limited, and this official and his entourage must have been among the few Nubian visitors this far north.

This Nubian court official was probably a Gentile "God-fearer." When meant literally—which was not always the case (Genesis 39:1 LXX), eunuchs referred to castrated men. Although these were preferred court officials in the East, the Jewish people opposed the practice, and Jewish law excluded eunuchs from Israel (Deuteronomy 23:1); the rules were undoubtedly instituted to prevent Israel from neutering boys (23:1). But eunuchs could certainly be accepted by God (Isaiah 56:3-5, even foreign eunuchs; Wisdom 3:14). An Ethiopian "eunuch" in the OT turns out to be one of Jeremiah's few allies and saves his life (Jeremiah 38:7-13). This African court official was the first non-Jewish Christian. Such information may be helpful in establishing that Christianity is not only not a western religion, but that after its Jewish origins it was first of all an African faith.

12. Paul preaches to Philosophers in Acts 17:22-31

Paul "contextualized" the gospel for his hearers, showing how it related to their own culture without compromising its content. (Today we often err on either one side or the other—failing to be culturally relevant, or failing to represent accurately the biblical message.) Paul speaks to two groups of philosophers present, Stoics and (probably a smaller group) Epicureans; his faith held little common ground with Epicureans, but the Stoics could agree with a number of Christian beliefs.

Paul opens by finding some common ground with his pagan audience. It was customary to begin a speech by complimenting the hearers in the opening of a speech, the *exordium.* One was not permitted to flatter the Areopagus (the leading philosophical and educational leaders of Athens), but Paul would remain free to start on a respectful note. "Religious"

Background Context Examples

meant that they were observant, not that he agreed with their religion ("superstitious," in the King James Version, does not convey the right idea).

Then Paul turns to more common ground. During a plague long before Paul's lifetime, no altars had successfully propitiated the gods; finally Athens had offered sacrifices to an unknown god, immediately staying the plague. These altars were still standing, and Paul uses this as the basis for his speech.

Paul borrows a technique from Jewish teachers who had been trying to explain the true God to Gentiles for several centuries before Paul. Non-Palestinian Jews sometimes reminded Gentiles that even they had one supreme God, and tried to show pagans that their highest religious aspirations were best met in Judaism. Stoics believed that God permeated all things and therefore was not localized in temples (see also Isa. 66:1). Stoics and Greek-speaking Judaism emphasized that God "needs nothing," using the same word Paul uses in 17:25. Jews and many Greeks alike agreed that God was creator and divider of the earth's boundaries and of seasons' boundaries (17:26). (Stoics also believed that the universe periodically dissolved back into God, but on this there was no point of contact between them and the Bible or Judaism.)

Jewish people usually spoke of God as a father specifically to his people. But Greeks, Jews scattered among Greeks, and some second-century Christian writers spoke of God as the world's "father" in the sense of creator; though Paul elsewhere uses the term more specifically, he adopts the more general sense of father as creator in this case (17:28-29). The quote from Epimenides in 17:28 appears in Jewish anthologies of proof-texts useful for showing pagans the truth about God, and Paul may have learned it there. (Greeks cited Homer and other poets as proof-texts in a manner similar to how Jewish people cited Scripture.)

But while Paul was eager to find points of contact with the best in pagan thinking for the sake of communicating the gospel, he also was clear where the gospel disagreed with paganism. Some issues might be semantic, but Paul would not ignore any real differences. Although philosophers spoke of conversion to philosophy through a change of thinking, they were unfamiliar with his Jewish and Christian doctrine of repentance towards God (17:30). Further, the Greek view of time was that it would simply continue, not that there was a future climax of history in the day of judgment, in contrast to the biblical perspective (17:31). Finally, Greeks could not conceive of a future bodily resurrection; most of them simply believed the soul survived after death. Thus Paul's preaching of the resurrection offended them most (17:31-32). But in the end, Paul was more interested in winning at least a few of these influential people to genuine faith in Christ (17:34) than in simply persuading all of them that he was harmless and shared their own views.

13. Paul Adapts Ancient Family Rules in Ephesians 5:21-6:9

Some people used Ephesians 6:5-9 alongside Greek, Roman, and Arab discussions of slavery to support the kind of slavery practiced in the Americas, but a simple knowledge of the nature of the slavery Paul addressed would have disproved their understanding of the passage. Others even more recently have used 5:22-33 to treat wives in disrespectful and demeaning ways, which also misinterprets the entire tenor of the passage.

This passage addresses an ancient sort of writing called "household codes," by which Paul's readers could try to convince their prospective persecutors that they were not subversives after all. In Paul's day, many Romans were troubled by the spread of "religions from the East" (such as Egyptian Isis worship, Judaism, and Christianity) which they thought would undermine traditional Roman family values. Members of these minority religions often tried to show their support for those values by using a standard form of exhortations developed by philosophers from Aristotle on.

From the time of Aristotle onward these exhortations instructed the male head of a household how to deal with members of his family, especially how he should rule his wife, children, and slaves. Paul borrows this form of discussion straight out of standard Greco-Roman moral writing, even following their sequence. But unlike most ancient writers, Paul changes the basic premise of these codes: the absolute authority of the male head of the house.

That Paul introduces the household codes with a command to mutual submission (5:21) is significant. In his day it was customary to call on wives, children and slaves to submit in various ways, but calling *all* members of a group (including the *pater familias,* the male head of the household) to submit to one another was unheard of.

Most ancient writers expected wives to obey their husbands, desiring in them a quiet and meek demeanor; sometimes a requirement for absolute obedience was even stated in the marriage contracts. This made sense especially to Greek thinkers, who could not conceive of wives as equals. Age differences contributed to this disparity: husbands were normally substantially older than their wives, often by over a decade in Greek culture (with men frequently marrying around 30 and women in their teens, often early teens).

In this passage, however, Paul adapts the traditional code in several ways. First, wifely submission is rooted in Christian submission in general (in Greek, 5:22 even borrows its verb "submit" from 5:21); submission is a Christian virtue, but not only for wives! Second, Paul addresses not only husbands but also wives, which most household codes did not. Third, whereas household codes told the husbands how to make their wives obey them, Paul simply tells husbands how to *love* their wives. Finally, the closest Paul comes to *defining* submission in this context is "respect" (5:33). At the same time that he relates Christianity to the standards of his culture, he actually transforms his culture's values by going so far beyond them! Paul addressed Greco-Roman culture, but few cultures today give precisely the same expressions of submission as in his culture. Today Christians reapply his principles in different ways for different cultures, but these principles still contradict many practices in many of our cultures (such as beating a wife).

No one would have disagreed with Paul's premise in 6:1-4: Jewish and Greco-Roman writers unanimously agreed that children needed to honor their parents, and, at least till they grew up, needed to obey them as well. At the same time, Greek and Roman fathers and teachers often instructed children with beatings. Paul is among the minority of ancient writers who seem to warn against being too harsh in discipline (6:4). (Greek and Roman society was even harsher on newborn children; since an infant was accepted as a legal person only when the father officially recognized it, babies could be abandoned or, if deformed, killed. Early Christians and Jews unanimously opposed both abortion and abandonment. This text, however, addresses the discipline of minors in the household, as in the household codes.) Disobedience might be permitted under some exceptional circumstances (e.g., 1 Sam. 20:32), but Paul does not qualify the traditional Roman view on children's submission as he does with wives and slaves, since the Old Testament also mandated minors' submission (Deut. 21:18-21).

Finally, Paul addresses relations between slaves and slaveholders. Roman slavery, unlike later European slavery and much of (though not all of) Arab slavery, was nonracial; the Romans were happy to enslave anyone who was available. Different forms of slavery existed in Paul's day. Banishment to slavery in the mines or gladiatorial combat was virtually a death sentence; few slaves survived long under such circumstances. Slaves who worked the fields could be beaten, but otherwise were very much like free peasants, who also were harshly oppressed and barely ever were able to advance their position socially, though they comprised the bulk of the Empire's population. Household slaves, however, lived under conditions better than those of free peasants. They could earn money on the side and often purchased their freedom; once free they could be promoted socially, and their former slaveholder owed them obligations to help them succeed socially. Many freed persons became wealthier than aristocrats. Ranking slaves in some wealthy households could wield more power than free aristocrats. Some nobles, for example, married into slavery to become slaves in Caesar's household and improve their social and economic position! Household codes addressed household slaves, and Paul writes to urban congregations, so the sort of slavery he addresses here is plainly household slavery.

Slaveholders often complained that slaves were lazy, especially when no one was looking. Paul encourages hard work, but gives the slave a new hope and a new motive for his or her labor (6:5-8). (In general, Paul believes we should submit to those in authority, when that is possible, for the sake of peace—see Rom. 12:18; 13:1-7; but that does not mean that he believes we should work to maintain such authority structures; see 1 Corinthians 7:20-23.) Paul says that slaves, like wives, should submit to the head of the household as if to Christ (6:5), but again makes clear that this is a *reciprocal* duty; slaves and slaveholders both share the same heavenly master. When Aristotle complained about a few philosophers who think that slavery is wrong, the philosophers he cited did not state matters as plainly as Paul does here. Only a very small minority of writers in the ancient world (many of them Stoics) suggested that slaves were in theory their masters' spiritual equals, but Paul goes beyond even this extreme: only Paul goes so far as to suggest that in practice masters do the same for slaves as slaves should do for them (6:9a).

Some have complained that Paul should have opposed slavery more forcefully. But in the few verses in which Paul addresses slaves, he confronts only the practical issue of how slaves can deal with their situation, not with the legal institution of slavery—the same way a minister or counselor today might help someone get free from an addiction without ever having reason to discuss the legal issues related to that addiction. The only attempts to free all slaves in the Roman Empire before him had been three massive slave wars, all of which had ended in widespread bloodshed without liberating the slaves. Christians at this point were a small persecuted minority sect whose only way to abolish slavery would be to persuade more people of their cause and transform the values of the Empire (the way the abolitionist movement spread in eighteenth and nineteenth century Britain). Further, even if this specific letter were intended as a critique of social injustice (which is not the purpose of this particular letter, though that topic arises in other biblical passages), one would not start such a critique with household slaves, but with mine slaves, and then both free peasants and agrarian slaves. A violent revolution could not have ended slavery in the Roman Empire. In any event, what Paul does say leaves no doubt where he would have stood had we put the theoretical question of slavery's abolition to him: people are equals before God (6:9), and slavery is therefore against God's will.

14. Jesus Rebukes the Self-Sufficient in Revelation 3:15-18

Laodicea became an important Phrygian city in Roman times. It was capital of the Cibryatic convention, including at least 25 towns. It was also the wealthiest city in Phrygia, and especially prosperous in this period. It was 10 miles west of Colossae and its rival city was Phrygian Antioch. The city reflected the usual paganism of the larger Mediterranean culture: Zeus was the city's patron deity, but Laodiceans also had temples for Apollo, Asclepius (the healing deity), Hades, Hera, Athena, Serapis, Dionysus, and other deities.

The church seemed to share the values of its culture, an arrogant self-sufficiency in matters including its prosperity, clothing and health, all of which Jesus challenges in 3:17-18. Laodicea was a prosperous banking center; proud of its wealth, it refused Roman disaster relief after the earthquake of AD 60, rebuilding from its own resources. It was also known for its textiles (especially black wool) and for its medical school with ear medicine and undoubtedly the highly reputed Phrygian eye salve.

Everything in which Laodicea could have confidence outwardly, her church, which reflected its culture, lacked spiritually.

The one sphere of life in which Laodiceans could not pretend to be self-sufficient was their water supply! Laodicea had to pipe in its water from elsewhere, and by the time it arrived it was full of sediment; Laodicea actually acquired a bad reputation for its water supply. Jesus comments on the temperature of the water. They were lukewarm, neither cold nor hot. This does not mean, as some have suggested, that hot water was good but cold water was bad; Jesus would not want the Laodiceans "good or bad," but only good. Cold water was preferred for drinking, and hot water for bathing (also sometimes drunk at banquets), but the natural lukewarmness of local water (in contrast with the hot water available at nearby Hierapolis or cold water of nearby mountains) was undoubtedly a standard complaint of local residents, most of whom had an otherwise comfortable lifestyle. Jesus is saying: "Were you hot (i.e., for bathing) or cold (i.e., for drinking), you would be useful; but as it is, you are simply disgusting. I feel toward you the way you feel toward your water supply—you make me sick."

Appendix 4

Examination of Jesus' Teaching Methods:

Case Study of Divorce

Some people quote only Jesus' saying that remarriage is adultery (Mark 10:11-12; Luke 16:18), but what kind of saying is this? When Jesus says that one who lusts should pluck out his eye to avoid hell (Matthew 5:28-30), should we take more literally his saying about remarriage that occurs immediately afterward (Matthew 5:31-32)? The only way to test this is to examine it in the context of all of Jesus' teachings on the subject.

First we should examine the "why" of Jesus' teaching, as best as possible. In Jesus' day the Pharisees debated among themselves as to the grounds for a husband to divorce his wife; the stricter school said a man could divorce his wife if she were unfaithful to him, but the more lenient school said he could divorce his wife if she displeased him, even if she burned his bread. In Jewish Palestine (as opposed to Roman laws), husbands could divorce their wives for almost any reason. However, wives could not divorce their husbands or prevent themselves from being divorced. Jesus was at least in part defending an innocent party from being wronged: the husband who divorces his wife and remarries commits adultery *"against her"*—against his wife (Mark 10:11). This was a sin not only against God, but also against another person innocent of the divorce (cf. also Malachi 2:14).

Second we should examine what this saying literally claims. "Adultery" in the literal sense is being unfaithful to one's marriage partner; for remarriage to be adultery against a former spouse means that, in God's sight, one is still married to one's former spouse. If we take this literally, this means that marriage cannot be dissolved, and that Christians should break up all second and third marriages. Interestingly, despite the scandal this would have caused in ancient society, we have no record of anyone breaking up later marriages in the New Testament. But is this a literal statement, or one of Jesus' deliberate overstatements meant to grab people's attention—like plucking out the eye, a camel passing through a needle's eye, or a mustard seed of faith? We can easily answer this question by examining Jesus' other sayings on the same subject.

In the same context as Mark 10:11, Jesus also says, *"What God joined together, let no one separate"* (Mark 10:9). In 10:11, marriage cannot be broken; in 10:9, it should not be and must not be, but it is breakable. The difference in meaning here is this: one says that one is always married to one's first spouse; the other says that one should remain married to one's first spouse. The one is a statement; the other is a demand. Yet marriage cannot be both unbreakable and breakable; so it is possible that 10:11 is a deliberate overstatement (hyperbole) whereas 10:9 communicates its real intention: to keep us from divorcing, not to break up new marriages.

Other sayings of Jesus help us further. For instance, Jesus himself did not take Mark 10:11 literally. He regarded the Samaritan woman as married five times, not as married once and committing only adultery thereafter (John 4:18). Further, Jesus himself allows an exception in two of the four passages where he addresses divorce. Followers of Christ must not break up their marriages but if their spouses break it up by sexual unfaithfulness, Jesus does not punish the innocent person (Matthew 32; 19:9). In that case, the marriage may be broken, but only one person is guilty of breaking it. Because both Jewish and Roman law required divorce for adultery, Mark and Luke could assume this exception without having to state it explicitly. When Paul quotes Jesus' prohibition of divorce, he tells Christians not to divorce their spouses, whether or not the spouses are Christian (1 Corinthians 7:10-14). But if the spouse leaves, the Christian is not held responsible for the spouse's behavior (1 Corinthians 7:15). His wording, *"not under bondage," "not bound"* (7:15), is the very language used in ancient Jewish divorce contracts for freedom to remarry. Paul therefore applies Jesus' teaching as a demand for faithfulness to marriage, not a statement about breaking up marriages: Christians must never break up their own marriages, but if the marriage is broken against their will, we must not punish them, either. Jesus spoke to defend an innocent spouse, not to make their condition more difficult!

But even though Jesus is not really calling Christians to break up remarriages, this does not mean we should not take seriously what he is saying. The point of a deliberate overstatement is not to let us say, "Oh, that is just overstatement; we may ignore it." The point of overstatement is to grab our attention, to force us to consider how serious is his demand. Genuine repentance (expressed in restitution) cancels past sins, but one cannot premeditate sin and expect one's repentance to be genuine. Christians are not held responsible for marriages broken against their wills, but they are responsible before God to do everything genuinely in their power to make their marriages work.

In this example, we have tried to show how we need to listen carefully to why Jesus speaks certain ways, and to examine all of his teachings to discern when he speaks literally and when he overstates his point parabolically. But overstatements are not meant to be ignored; they are meant to grip our attention all the more! We should also add two words of caution: Jesus himself uses principles like *"compassion rather than sacrifice"* (Matthew 9:13; 12:7) and looking for the heart of the message (Matthew 5:21-22; 23:23-24). But also we should be honest in grappling with what he says: proper fear of God will give us integrity in searching for truth rather than trying to justify how we want to live (see Proverbs 1:7).

Appendix 5

"The Theology of the Blood of Jesus"

a paper presented to Jos-Bukuru Theological Society
March 5, 2001 in Jos, Nigeria
by Rev. Dr. Danny McCain

"I sprinkle the blood of Jesus over this vehicle." This was a prayer that someone prayed for me recently as I was sitting in my vehicle, preparing to go on a journey. I have also heard people "sprinkle the blood of Jesus" on sick people who were seeking to be healed, on pastors before they preached, on church services as they were going on, on offerings as they were being taken and even on books as they were being launched.

The thought behind this prayer is that the blood of Jesus is the primary tool to be used by the Christian in solving any kind of problem. It can protect from any kind of accident or illness or misfortune. It can bring healing to those who have some physical disability. The blood of Jesus may also be used to cast out demons or deal with other forms of demonic activity. In fact, when one is praying about anything that is related to the occult, those in the audience will frequently started chanting together "the blood of Jesus."

The "blood of Jesus" has become perhaps the most common phrase used by many African Christians when praying about serious problems. It is that which can solve any problem. It is like a credit card. It can be pulled out and used in any situation no matter how small or how big the problem is. Just invoke the "blood of Jesus" and the problem will have to go away.

The use of the phrase "blood of Jesus" is not new. Though it probably is getting more usage now than it did in the past, it has been a very important part of our Christian tradition. This is clearly reflected in many of the hymns we sing.

> *What can wash away my sin? Nothing but the blood of Jesus.*
> *What can make me whole again? Nothing but the blood of Jesus.*
> *Oh, precious is the flow that makes me white as snow.*
> *No other fount I know, Nothing but the blood of Jesus.*[1]

The "blood of Jesus" has particularly been linked with the aspect of cleansing. The blood of Christ has special cleansing ability, particularly to cleanse away our sin.

> *There is a fountain filled with blood Drawn from Immanuel's veins;*
> *And sinners plunged beneath that flood, Lose all their guilty stains.*
> *The dying thief rejoiced to see that fountain in his day;*
> *And there may I, though vile as he, Wash all my sins away.*[2]

The blood of Jesus has also been associated with power. One of the most well-known and well-loved hymns is "There is Power in the Blood."

> *Would you be free from your burden of sin?*
> *There's power in the Blood, pow'r in the Blood.*
> *Would you o'er evil a victory win?*
> *There's wonderful pow'r in the Blood.*
> *There is pow'r, pow'r, wonder-working pow'r*
> *In the blood of the Lamb,*
> *There is pow'r, pow'r, wonder-working pow'r*
> *In the precious blood of the Lamb.*[3]

Most of these songs were written during the last one hundred years. However, the same kind of figurative language is used by older writers such as Charles Wesley who was perhaps the greatest hymn writer

---

[1] Robert Lowery, "Nothing but the Blood" in *Worship in Song Hymnal* (Kansas City, KS, USA: Lillenas Publishing Company, 1972), Hymn 130.

[2] William Cowper, "There is a Fountain," in *Worship in Song Hymnal* (Kansas City, KS, USA: Lillenas Publishing Company, 1972), Hymn 124.

[3] Lewis E. Jones, "There is Power in the Blood," in *Worship in Song Hymnal*, (Kansas City, KS, USA: Lillenas Publishing Company, 1972), Hymn 136.

throughout church history. Wesley appears to be a bit more serious and theological in the way he uses the figure of speech. Listen to this noble hymn.

> *Arise my soul, arise. Shake off thy guilty fears.*
> *The bleeding sacrifice In my behalf appears.*
> *Before the throne my Surety stands,*
> *Before the throne my Surety stands,*
> *My name is written on His hands.*
> *He ever lives above For me to intercede,*
> *His all redeeming love, His precious blood to plead.*
> *His blood atoned for all our race,*
> *His blood atoned for all our race,*
> *And sprinkles now the throne of grace.*
> *Five bleeding wounds He bears, Received on Calvary.*
> *They pour effectual prayers; They strongly plead for me.*
> *"Forgive him, oh, forgive" they cry,*
> *"Forgive him, oh, forgive," they cry,*
> *"Nor let that ransomed sinner died."*
> *The Father hears Him pray, His dear Anointed One;*
> *He cannot turn away The presence of His Son.*
> *His Spirit answers to the Blood,*
> *His Spirit answers to the Blood,*
> *And tells me I am born of God.*[4]

Some of the questions that arise when we hear such songs and such prayers are these: Is this a proper usage of the blood of Jesus? Is the blood of Jesus the primary means of protecting us from evil? How does the blood of Jesus cleanse one from sin? It is the objective of this paper to

---

[4] Charles Wesley, "Arise, My Soul, Arise," in *Worship in Song Hymnal* (Kansas City, KS, USA: Lillenas Publishing Company, 1972), Hymn 9.

answer some of those questions by examining the various phrases associated with the blood of Jesus in the New Testament.[5]

Literal Use of the Blood of Jesus

The first reference to the actual blood of Jesus occurred in the Garden of Gethsemane when Jesus was praying (Luke 22:44), *"And being in anguish, he prayed more earnestly, and his sweat was like drops of blood falling to the ground."* Whether this was actual blood or not, we do not know. Sometimes when a person is in such intense agony, the small capillaries in the skin can be damaged and blood can come out of the skin like sweat. This is called hematidrosis which is the actual mingling of sweat with blood.[6]

Jesus shed blood all throughout his last day on the earth. The scourging, which he endured, was a beating that was so severe that it would have caused much bleeding (John 19:1). There are many small blood vessels in the scalp. Therefore, when the soldiers placed the crown of thorns upon Jesus' head, this would have brought about much bleeding (Matthew 27:29). It is possible that the rough cross rubbing on Jesus' shoulders as he attempted to carry it to the place of execution would have also produced bleeding (John 19:17). When Jesus was crucified, he had nails driven through his hands and feet (Luke 24:39-40). These would have obviously produced some bleeding. In fact, the entire ordeal of Jesus' arrest, trial and crucifixion was an extremely bloody affair, far more so than typically pictured in the great paintings of Jesus' passion. Yet, interestingly, there is only one reference to the blood of Jesus during the actual crucifixion

---

[5] This study is limited to the phrases that include a direct reference to the blood of Jesus in the New Testament. It does not include other more indirect references to the "cleansing" part of the atonement. A comprehensive study of the doctrine of cleansing would need to include the sacrificial system in the Old Testament as well as studies of words like washing (from λούω and ἀπολούω), baptize (βαπτίζω), cleanse (καθαρίζω), purify (ἁγνίζω) and the related family of words associated with each.

[6] See *NIV Study Bible*, Kenneth Baker, General Editor (Grand Rapids, MI USA: Zondervan Publishing House, 1995), Note on 22:44, p. 1581.

and this was after Jesus had already died. John 19:34 says, *"Instead, one of the soldiers pierced Jesus' side with a spear, bringing a sudden flow of blood and water."* The piercing of Jesus side enabled the blood that had pooled inside Jesus' body to come out.

It is interesting to note that although the blood of Jesus is a very precious doctrine to modern Christians and was a topic that was even popular in the Epistles, the literal blood of Jesus is not emphasized in the Gospels.[7]

Metaphorical Use of the Blood of Jesus

By far the majority of the references to the blood of Jesus are in a metaphorical or figurative sense. Jesus himself refers to his blood in a metaphorical sense two times. In John 6:53-59, while in a synagogue in Capernaum, Jesus talked about eating his flesh and drinking his blood. This was in the context of the bread of life discourse. Jesus was claiming that he was the real bread of life, but then he changes the figure to eating his flesh and drinking his blood. The Jews had no idea what he was talking about. They were very confused. It is possible to interpret this in light of his teaching in the Synoptics about the Lord's Supper. However, it appears more likely that this should be interpreted in light of the metaphor Jesus used a few moments later when he said, *"I am the bread of life"* (John 6:48). What Jesus is saying is that which he provides for us is to our spiritual life what bread is to our physical bodies. Here Jesus is not talking about literal flesh and blood. He is talking about his philosophy, teachings and example. Therefore, this does not appear to be even a metaphorical reference to the blood Jesus shed on the cross.

Second, Jesus refers to his blood during the final Passover meal in which he instituted the Lord's Supper.[8] This usage of the blood of Jesus is referred to every time Holy Communion is observed in our churches. The

---

[7] W. T. Purkiser, Richard S Taylor, and Willard H. Taylor, *God, Man and Salvation*, (Kansas City, Mo USA: Beacon Hill Press, 1977), p. 401. They say, "The interest of the New Testament writers does not rest in the material blood of Christ but rather in what it stands for, namely, the provision of salvation through the death of the Son of God."

[8] See Matthew 26:28; Mark 14:24; Luke 22:20.

minister will usually say something like this, "This wine represents the blood of Jesus which was shed on the cross for our sins."

There are also two other references to blood of Jesus in a metaphorical sense in the Gospels. Matthew 27:24-25 says,

> When Pilate saw that he was getting nowhere, but that instead an uproar was starting, he took water and washed his hands in front of the crowd, "I am innocent of this man's blood," he said, "It is your responsibility!" All the people answered, "Let his blood be on us and on our children."

A similar reference is found in Acts 5:28. The Sanhedrin said to Peter and John, "You have filled Jerusalem with your teaching and are determined to make us guilty of this man's blood." These three references are simply references to the death of Christ. There is no particularly significance to the blood except as it was shed to the point of death.

These particular references give insight into the metaphorical usage of the *"blood of Jesus."* This phrase refers to the death of Christ. This is consistent with other usages of blood. Shedding of blood was a euphemism for murder. Paul says in Acts 22:20; *"And when the blood of your martyr Stephen was shed, I stood there giving my approval and guarding the clothes of those who were killing him."* Shedding of blood and killing were synonyms. In fact, the Hebrew word for murder is *damim*, which literally means "bloods."

Descriptions of the Blood of Jesus in a Metaphorical Sense

Although the phrase *"blood of Jesus"* is a very popular phrase today, it was used only two times in the New Testament. The term *"blood of Christ"* was used three times. The following is a list of the various ways Jesus' blood was used in conjunction with his passion.

- *"his blood"* – Matthew 27:25; Romans 3:25; 5:9; Ephesians 1:7; Colossians 1:14*, 20; 1 Peter 1:2; Revelation 1:5 (8)
- *"my blood"* – Matthew 26:28; Mark 14:24; Luke 22:20; 1 Corinthians 11:25 (4)
- *"blood of Christ"* – 1 Corinthians 10:16; Ephesians 2:13; Hebrews 9:14; (3)

- *"his own blood"* - Acts 20:28; Hebrews 9:12; 13:20 (3)
- *"water and blood"* – 1 John 5:6a; 5:6b; 5:8 (3)[9]
- *"blood of Jesus"* – Hebrews 10:19; 1 John 1:7; (2)
- *"blood of the Lamb"* - Revelation 7:14; 12:11 (2)
- *"this man's blood"* – Matthew 27:24 (1)
- "blood of the covenant" Hebrews 10:29; (1)
- *"blood of the Lord"* – 1 Corinthians 11:27 (1)
- *"the sprinkled blood"* – Hebrews 12:24 (?) (1)
- "the precious blood of Christ" – 1 Peter 1:19 (1)
- *"your blood"* – Revelation 5:9 (1)

Total References to the Blood of Jesus = 31[10]

*Indicates textual problem

Applications of the Blood of Jesus

There are seventeen specific applications or activities associated with the blood of Jesus in the New Testament. Most of these overlap a lot because they are metaphorical usages of the blood of Jesus. They are as follows:

1. We are *"bought with his own blood,"* Acts 20:28. This was the phrase used by Paul to the elders from Ephesus and refers to the *"church of God, which he bought with his own blood."* This is a clear reference to the doctrine of the atonement, which is the doctrine that explains how a sacrifice appeases the wrath of God and satisfies the justice of God.

2. Jesus provides *"a sacrifice of atonement, through faith in his blood,"* Romans 3:25. That is another very clear reference to the doctrine of the atonement. The context of this passage clearly states that the sacrifice of atonement was designed to satisfy the justice of God.

---

[9] Three of these are questionable; they may not directly refer to the blood of Jesus.

[10] This also includes the questionable passages and the reference with a textual problem.

Blood was the most common ingredient of the sacrifices in the Old Testament.

3. We are *"justified by his blood,"* Romans 5:9. The primary application of the doctrine of the atonement is justification, which is the release of a person from the penalty that his or her sins deserved, based upon the atonement of Christ.

4. The new covenant is provided *"in my blood,"* 1 Corinthians 11:25. The term *"new covenant"* is the corporate benefit to all of God's people today of which justification is a part. Justification is an individual thing. The new covenant includes personal justification but it also includes the promise of God to build the church and all of the other spiritual privileges which Christians have enjoyed since Pentecost (see Matthew 11:11; Acts 2:17-18; Hebrews 11:39-40).

5. We are redeemed *"through his blood,"* Ephesians 1:7; Colossians 1:14 (textual problem); 1 Peter 1:19. Redemption is a term taken from the slavery system of the first century. It teaches in a figurative sense that though we were slaves to sin, we are now free from that bondage. Redemption is one of the terms associated with the doctrine of the atonement.

6. We are *"brought near by the blood of Christ,"* Ephesians 2:13. *"Brought near"* is a figurative way of saying that the barrier between God and us has been removed. This is another description of the doctrine of justification.

7. We are able to *"make peace through his blood,"* Colossians 1:20. In the earlier part of that verse, Paul says it was through Jesus that God was able to *"reconcile to himself all things, whether things on earth or things in heaven, by making peace through his blood, shed on the cross."* This verse suggests that one of the primary purposes of the blood of Christ was to reconcile all things to God. This is not limited to personal justification because it also includes "things in heaven." One of the practical results of the blood of Jesus that provides justification is personal peace.

8. Paul declares in Romans 5:1, *"Therefore, since we have been justified through faith, we have peace with God."* Peace is one of the primary results of justification.

9. Jesus was able to *"enter the Most Holy Place once for all by his own blood, having obtained eternal redemption,"* Hebrews 9:12. This passage uses Old Testament imagery to illustrate the significance of the blood of Christ. The high priest entered the Holy of Holies once a year with the blood of animals to offer sacrifices for the sins of people. Jesus, in a similar way, has done the same thing but he offers his own blood. The value of his blood means that this sacrifice has to be made only once. This is another reference to redemption, one of the words associated with the doctrine of atonement.

10. The blood of Christ *"cleanses our consciences from acts that lead to death,"* Hebrews 9:14. This is another figurative reference to the blood of Jesus removing sin from us. Thus, it is another way of describing justification.

11. We are able to *"enter the Most Holy Place by the blood of Jesus,"* Hebrews 10:19. This passage describes the ultimate result of the blood of Jesus. It opens up opportunities for us to commune with God. The reason that this was not possible before was because of our sin. The fact that the blood of Jesus atones for our sin means that there is no longer any barrier between ourselves and God. One is justified when that barrier is removed.

12. We are made holy *"through his own blood,"* Hebrews 13:12. The complete statement is *"And so Jesus also suffered outside the city gate to make the people holy through his own blood."* Many interpreters believe the writer of Hebrews uses the word "sanctification" much like Paul uses the word "justification."[11] The application of Jesus' death should not be limited to the doctrine of justification, which is the initial and judicial removal of one's sins. The death of Christ and the power of the Holy Spirit enable the believer to move on from one degree of holiness to another. However, it is most likely that this reference to

---

[11] H. Orton Wiley, *The Epistle to the Hebrews* (Kansas City, MO USA: Beacon Hill Press, 1959), p. 92. Dr. Wiley, a theologian from the Wesleyan/Holiness movement writes, "We must understand, therefore, that the word sanctify as used here (the book of Hebrews) refers primarily to the objective work of Christ in the expiation of sin, the atonement which finds its ultimate issue in the divine declaration that 'the blood of Jesus Christ his Son cleanseth us from all sin' (1 John 1:7)."

being made holy through the blood of Jesus is another reference to the doctrine of justification.

13. God's people are *"sprinkled by his blood,"* 1 Peter 1:2. This passage clearly links the death of Christ with the Old Testament sacrificial system and thus refers to the atonement.[12] Leon Morris says about this passage, "Blood by itself might mean no more than violent death, but 'sprinkling of blood' points us to the sacrifices."[13]

14. We are purified from all sin by *"the blood of Jesus, his Son,"* 1 John 1:7. The terminology of washing or cleansing is simply a figurative way of describing the removal of sin from us. The point when sin is removed from us is when we are justified.

15. We are *"freed us from our sins by his blood,"* Revelation 1:5.[14] The point when one is freed from his sins is the point of justification. Morris says "Here the thought is that of redemption, of loosening a bond at cost ... The blood of Christ is the price which sets us free."[15]

16. The blood of Jesus *"purchased men for God from every tribe and language and people and nation,"* Revelation 5:9. The *"purchasing of men"* is another way of describing redemption, which is one of the terms associated with the doctrine of justification.

17. The people of God have *"have washed their robes and made them white in the blood of the Lamb,"* Revelation 7:14. Washing is a reference to

---

[12] The blood of sacrificial animals was sprinkled upon the altar (Exodus 24:6; 29:16, 20), in front of the curtain of the sanctuary (Leviticus 4:6), upon the mercy seat in the Holy of Holies (Leviticus 16:15), upon people (Exodus 24:8), and upon Aaron and his sons (Exodus 29:21; Leviticus 8:30). These were all related to seeking God's forgiveness for the sins of the people.

[13] Leon Morris, *The Cross in the New Testament* (Grand Rapids, MI USA: William B. Eerdmans Publishing Company, 1972), p. 321.

[14] There is a textual problem in this passage over whether the correct reading should be loose or freed from our sins ($\lambda\acute{u}\sigma\alpha\nu\tau\iota$) or washed from our sins ($\lambda o\acute{u}\sigma\alpha\nu\tau\iota$). Most modern translations follow the former reading including NASB, NIV and NLT.

[15] Morris, p. 358.

removal, which is what justification is. Man's sins are removed at the point of justification.

18. The people of God *"overcame* [the enemy] *by the blood of the Lamb and by the word of their testimony,"* Revelation 12:11. This was a statement, which John heard in heaven after witnessing the final overthrow of Satan. These *"brothers"* had apparently been able to overcome the temptation of the enemy through the blood of Jesus. Their victory obviously began at the point when they were justified. However, the implication of this passage is that the blood of Jesus also had an ability to help them overcome temptations after they were justified. The death of Christ on the cross is the basis for all spiritual benefits including the ability to overcome temptation.

When one looks carefully at these eighteen activities associated with the blood of Jesus, all of them are associated with what we might call the doctrine of the atonement. According to my way of interpreting these, three of these relate to the doctrine of the atonement in a general way; one refers to the new covenant; three refer to redemption which is one of the key words associated with atonement; nine refer to personal justification and one refers to the ability to overcome temptation. All of these references to the blood of Jesus refer directly to the doctrine of the atonement of Christ. Concepts like justification, redemption, peace, holiness, purity, victory and freedom are all a product of the atonement and are a result of the blood of Jesus.

Applications of the Blood of Jesus

No	Teaching	Verses	Number
1	Atonement	Acts 20:28; Romans 3:25; 1 Peter 1:2	3
2	New Covenant	1 Corinthians 11:25	1
3	Redemption	Ephesians 1:17; Colossians 1:14; 1 Peter 1:19; Hebrews 9:12; Revelation 5:9	3
4	Justification	Romans 5:9; Ephesians 2:13; Colossians 1:20; Hebrews 9:14; 10:19; 13:12; 1 John 1:7; Revelation 1:5; 7:14;	9
5	Victory/Overcoming	Revelation 12:11	1
	Total		17

What is absent from all of these scriptures is any reference to prosperity, protection or healing. The closest reference to any such thing is the Revelation 12:11 passage that says *"they overcame him* [the accuser of our brothers] *by the blood of the Lamb."* On the surface, one might think that this is a reference to protection of the body. However, the second part of the verse says, *"they did not love their lives so much as to shrink from death."*

The clear implication is that even though their faithfulness to Christ cost them their lives, they were willing to resist any temptation to deny Jesus. This strength and courage was all provided for them as result of what Jesus did on the cross.

Two Key Old Testament References

Though it is not the scope of this paper to treat the doctrine of blood in the Old Testament, there are two Old Testament passages related to blood worth noting.

Exodus 12

One of the most important passages related to the symbolic use of blood is found in the Passover event recorded in Exodus 12. This passage tells about the tenth plague. The angel of the Lord went through the land of Egypt and killed the firstborn male child of every person. However, the Lord informed Moses that the Hebrews were to slaughter a one-year old lamb and place the blood on the doorpost of the house. When the death angel was passing through the land to execute the others, he would pass over any house that had the blood on the doorpost.

This incident is frequently used as an example of blood being used to ward off evil and provides some kind of Biblical justification for "sprinkling the blood of Jesus" on various people and objects to keep them safe.

I will make two observations about this practice. First, the slaying of the Passover Lamb involved far more than just the blood on the doorpost. The lamb provided the Passover meal for the family inside. Specific instructions were given related to how to prepare the lamb, how to eat the meat and even what to do with the left over portions (Exodus 12:5-11). In fact, the Passover meal is the most important thing about the ceremony. This is illustrated by the fact that the killing of the lamb and the eating of the meal became a lasting ceremony throughout the history of Israel (12:17-20). The placing of the blood on the doorpost was a one-time event and was not to become a permanent part of the Passover ceremony.

Second, the blood on the doorpost was more of a symbol of faith and obedience rather than a symbol of protection. If the blood was on the doorpost, that was proof the family had believed what God had said and had killed and eaten the Passover lamb as directed by Moses. The Israelites were protected because they had obeyed the Lord, which was a demonstration of their faith. The proof of their faith and obedience was the blood on the doorpost.

Keil and Delitzsch say the key thought here is "expiation" which relates to ceremonial cleansing. This is illustrated by the fact that the blood was to be applied with the hyssop and the only other references to blood being sprinkled with the hyssop related to ceremonial cleansing.[16] John Wesley says that the typical significance of the Passover blood is its relation to our forgiveness.[17]

Although the imagery of placing blood on the doorpost for protection fits the African worldview very well, it is a misuse of this passage to use it to justify using the blood of Jesus as a protecting agent against various kinds of evil.

Leviticus 17:11

As a part of the dietary regulations, the Law did not allow a person to eat meat with blood in it. The explanation for this prohibition is found in Leviticus 17:11; *"For the life of a creature is in the blood, and I have given it to you to make atonement for yourselves on the altar; it is the blood that makes atonement for one's life."*[18] This explanation goes far beyond the dietary regulations it was intended to clarify and shows the link between blood and atoning sacrifices. When one sinned, that person deserved to die. God, in his infinite mercy, created a system whereby he would allow an animal to die in the place of that person. The explanation given here is

---

[16] C. F. Keil and F. Delitzsch, *Commentary on the Old Testament in Ten Volumes: Volume II The Pentateuch* (Grand Rapids, MI USA: William B. Eerdman's Publishing Company, reprinted 1986), pp. 13-14.

[17] John Wesley, *Notes upon The Old Testament, Volume I* (Salem, Ohio USA: Schmul Publishers, reprinted 1975), p. 232. He says, "If the blood of Christ be sprinkled upon our consciences, it will be our protection from the wrath of God, the curse of the law, and the damnation of hell."

[18] This passage is at the heart of the question of whether the blood of a sacrifice focuses on life or death. See Purkiser, Taylor and Taylor, pp. 400-401 for a balanced summary of the two positions.

that the life is in the blood and that the life blood is what God accepts as an atonement for sin.

The Old Testament sacrificial system was a divinely authorized foreshadowing of the ultimate sacrifice for sin, which would be Jesus' death on the cross. As certainly as the life of the blood of the animals in the Old Testament period in some way enabled God temporarily to overlook the sins of human beings then, the life of the blood of Jesus Christ enables God to permanently forgive the sins of all human beings today.

The entire sacrificial system was a symbolic representation of that which was to come later. And because blood was the most obvious symbol of life, the sacrificial animals had to be killed in such a way that blood was shed. Animals being sacrificed were not allowed to be strangled, drowned, or killed in any other bloodless manner. Because the sacrificial death of Jesus is built upon the theology of sacrifice of the Old Testament, it was also essential for him to die in a way that blood was shed. Though the phrase "blood of Jesus" refers primarily to death, it is also linked to the Old Testament sacrificial system, which required death by bleeding.[19]

Observations about the Blood of Jesus

1. The blood of Jesus is a symbolic reference to the death of Christ.

The many metaphorical usages of the blood of Jesus all refer to the death of Christ. The significance of the blood of Jesus is the fact that Jesus bled to the point of death. The Hebrew writer makes a very clear link between the blood of Jesus and the death of Christ. He writes (Hebrews 10:19-20), *"Therefore, brothers, since we have confidence to enter the Most Holy Place by the blood of Jesus, by a new and living way opened for us through the curtain, that is, his body . . ."* The blood of Jesus is identified in a figurative way as that

---

[19] This does not necessarily imply that Jesus literally died from loss of blood. Scholars disagree over what actually caused Jesus' heart to stop beating. However, the fact that significant blood was shed during Jesus' passion satisfies the demand that blood be shed.

which helps us pass through *"the curtain"* and, as such, is positively identified with the body of Christ.

Therefore, when we refer to the blood of Jesus, we are referring to the death of Christ. The *"blood of Jesus"* is not the only figurative reference to the death of Christ. We use the term "cross" the same way and so do the writers of the New Testament. Paul declared in 1 Corinthians 1:17-18,

> *For Christ did not send me to baptize, but to preach the gospel—not with words of human wisdom, lest the cross of Christ be emptied of its power. For the message of the cross is foolishness to those who are perishing, but to us who are being saved, it is the power of God.*[20]

Leon Morris says the symbols of the cross and the blood of Jesus "mean much the same thing."[21]

The cross has become a popular symbol in modern Christianity. We place crosses on top of our churches and hang crosses around our necks. We also sing about the cross:

> *On a hill far away stood an old rugged cross, the emblem of suffering and shame;*
> *And I love that old Cross, where the dearest and best for a world of lost sinners was slain.*
> *So I'll cherish the old rugged Cross—till my trophies at last I lay down.*
> *I will cling to the old rugged Cross—and exchange it someday for a crown.*[22]

---

[20] References to the cross as a metaphorical reference to the death of Christ are also found in Galatians 5:11, 6:12, 14; Ephesians 2:16; Philippians 3:18; Colossians 1:20, 2:14; and Hebrews 12:2.

[21] Morris, p. 217.

[22] George Bennard in *Worship in Song Hymnal* (Kansas City, MO USA: Lillenas Publishing Company, 1972), Hymn 141. There are many other popular hymns related to the cross including "At Calvary," "At the Cross," "When I Survey the Wondrous Cross," and "Lead Me to the Cross."

Other phrases like "Calvary" and "Golgotha" that were somehow connected with the death of Jesus have also been used to refer to the death of Christ.

A good question is this: Why have so many metaphors developed that are associated with the death of Jesus? There are at least two reasons. First, symbols are a very common way of communicating truth. Sports teams, political parties, businesses and other organizations are frequently identified by symbols. When referring to the government of the Federal Republic of Nigeria, people often simply refer to "Abuja" outside the country or "Aso Rock" inside the country. The fact that the blood of Jesus would become a symbol for the death of Christ is understandable because this is a common practice in society. This is a literary construction known as synecdoche, which is a part being used to refer to the whole or a whole to refer to a part.

A second reason is that we human beings often do not like to think about negative things such as death. We create euphemisms, which are words or phrases that have a more pleasant sound than the original word. For example, we frequently describe death as someone "passing away" or "falling asleep." Although the word "blood of Christ" is still a fairly graphic term, it avoids using the word "death" and is a euphemism for the death of Christ.

The death and resurrection of Christ is the central event in Christianity. Therefore, it is understandable why symbols would develop.

2. The blood of Jesus is connected with the atonement of Jesus.

The most obvious lesson we can learn from this study is the clear link between the blood of Christ and the atonement of Christ. Wayne Grudem simply says, "The blood of Christ means his death in its saving aspects."[23] This has been abundantly demonstrated above in the brief survey of the sixteen activities with which the blood of Jesus is associated. Jesus died on the cross to provide a new covenant for humanity. The most important part of that covenant is the ability to reconcile man back to God. God's

---

[23] Wayne Grudem, *Systematic Theology: An Introduction to Biblical Doctrine* (Leicester, England: Inter-Varsity Press, 1994), p. 579.

Law declares that the wages of sin is death (Romans 6:23). It is the death of Christ that pays for the sins of humanity and satisfies God's justice. By removing the penalty of sin, which is due to humanity by the death of Christ, God is able to pour out many other blessings upon us. However, all of those blessings are somehow tied to the doctrine of the atonement.

Christian soteriology is holistic. That means that salvation extends beyond just the soul of man to every part of man and, in fact, every part of the universe. Since the earth was cursed because of man's sin, and sin is dealt with by of the death of Christ, the ultimate restoration of all things including the resurrection of the body is a direct result of the blood of Jesus.

Here is a word of caution: I have heard preachers say such things as "one little drop of Jesus' blood is all that it takes to wash away your sins." That is a nice thought, but the truth of the matter is that Jesus could not have pricked his finger, squeezed out of few drops of blood and used that blood to atone for our sins. The significance of the metaphorical use of blood is the fact that Jesus bled to the point that he died. As awesome as it seems, it took God coming out of heaven, living a sinless life on the earth, and dying on the cross to provide salvation for the human race.

3. The blood of Jesus is not a magical formula to keep away evil.

In our analysis of the various references to the blood of Jesus, we did not find a single one which is associated with protection from evil or healing of sickness or providing blessings and prosperity for us. Does that mean that the blood of Jesus is not connected with protection and healing?

James says, *"Every good and perfect gift is from above, coming down from the Father of the heavenly lights,"* (James 1:17). In addition, we believe that the atonement of Christ is holistic, which means that it has benefits to our bodies, our societies, and even our earth. Therefore, in some indirect sense, the blood of Christ is associated with health, prosperity and every other good thing that we enjoy on this earth because, had it not been for the death of Christ, humanity would not even exist on the earth as it does today.

However, as a general rule the contemporary practice of invoking the blood of Jesus for health and safety is what I call "protection theology." This is popular in Africa because it is consistent with traditional African religions. One of the key elements of most African Traditional Religions is protection from all sorts of evil which people, spirits and even ancestors might want to put on them. Sometimes a cock is killed or even a bigger animal like a goat or a ram is slaughtered to appease the spirits and provide protection for oneself.

Protection theology is also illustrated in other ways. Most of the commercial vehicles bear various kinds of slogans on them. Many of these are religious in nature. One frequently sees such things as "The Lord is my Shepherd" or "There is no other King but God." Also, one finds pictures of the Virgin Mary as well as various scripture portions on vehicles. I was reared in a Catholic community and Catholics in our area used to put a stature of St. Christopher on their dashboards. It was commonly thought that this saint would provide protection for their vehicle. My father used to place a Bible on the dashboard of his vehicle whenever he traveled. On the surface one would think that those who do such things were very dedicated Christians. However, when one examines this phenomenon a bit deeper, he will see that these people are simply trying to provide protection for themselves and their vehicles. They reason that surely God will take special interest in this vehicle that is honoring God in such a prominent way. Once again, this is protection theology.

My own understanding is that the blood of Jesus is not the primary agent responsible for protecting God's children. God certainly has many ways to provide protection but perhaps the most important of these are the angels. Psalm 34:7 declares, *"The angel of the Lord encamps around those who fear him, and he delivers them."* Even Satan is aware of this. He quoted from Psalm 91:11-12 in his attempt to get Jesus to yield to his temptation. The psalm says, *"For he will command his angels concerning you to guard you in all your ways; they will lift you up in their hand, so that you will not strike your foot against a stone."*

On one occasion, the king of Syria decided that he was going to capture Elisha whom he believed was responsible for giving his battle plans to the Israelite king. One morning he surrounded Dothan where the prophet was staying. The next morning, the servant of the prophet said, *"Oh, my Lord, what shall we do?"* Elisha simply replied, *"Don't' be afraid . . . Those who are with us are more than those who are with them"* (2 Kings 6:15-16). He then prayed that the Lord would open up the eyes of the servant so he could see the real situation. *"Then the Lord opened the servant's eyes, and he looked* and saw the hills full of horses and chariots of fire all around Elisha" (6:17). Apparently this was a heavenly angelic army.

Later when Daniel was thrown into a lion's den and survived the ordeal, he explained to the king, *"O king, live for ever. My God sent His angel, and he shut the mouths of the lions"* (Daniel 6:21). The angels of the Lord are very capable of overcoming any challenge presented to them.

There is no example of one praying to an angel in the Bible. However, since it is the responsibility of angels to provide protection to us, it is certainly appropriate to pray that the Lord would send his angels to encamp around us and protect us from evil.

Conclusion

The "blood of Jesus" is a very precious Christian symbol. It is a reminder of the fact that Jesus died on the cross to provide forgiveness and deliverance from our sins and all the other benefits that God's children enjoy.

Because of that this phrase should receive highest respect and reverence among Christians. Since there are no indications that the blood of Jesus is associated with protection and since there are abundant examples and teachings that God has provided his angels to protect us, we should avoid using the blood of Jesus in our prayers for protection and rather ask God to send his angels to protect us.

Appendix 6

"Prosperity: A Biblical Perspective"

published in an earlier form in

African Journal of Biblical Studies,

Volume XV, Number 2, October 2000

"God wants you to be rich." This was a statement made to me by a University of Jos student as I was eating lunch one day on campus. The statement was a response to my complaint to the restaurant owner who had tried to overcharge me for my food, "Please charge me the normal price. I am not a rich person." In the subsequent conversation that followed, I pointed out to the young lady that Jesus had said, *"It is easier for a camel to go through the eye of a needle than for a rich man to go to heaven"* (Matthew 19:24). My young friend's reply to that was, "Oh, Jesus didn't mean that." When I also pointed out that Jesus had said that those who followed him would have to *"deny themselves and take up their cross"* (Mark 8:34) she replied once again, "Oh, Jesus didn't mean that.'

The theology reflected by this young student arises primarily from a single verse in 3 John 2 which says in the Authorized Version, *"Beloved, I wish above all things that thou mayest **prosper** and be in health, even as thy soul **prospereth**."* Because of the emphasis on prosperity, this movement has been identified as the "prosperity gospel" movement and sometimes simply called the "health and wealth gospel."

It is beyond the scope of this paper to look at the historical development of the movement. It is sufficient to say at this point that it has grown out of the Charismatic Movement, which has stressed the importance of the supernatural in the lives of all believers and particularly healing. It will be the focus of this paper to examine the Biblical foundation of the doctrine of wealth. I will do so by looking at three different perspectives on wealth as reflected in the Bible.

The Linguistic Perspective

An exhaustive examination of all words related to the concept of wealth and prosperity would be a very long paper in itself. Therefore, I have selected one Hebrew word from the Old Testament and two Greek words from the New Testament to discuss.

עשר

Perhaps the most common Hebrew word for wealth and riches in the Old Testament is the Hebrew עשר (*'ashar*). The verb form of the word in its various configurations is found 17 times and the noun form is found 37 times. It is almost always translated "rich" or "riches." Synonyms of the עשר include חון (*hon*) translated "wealth," חיל (*hayil*) translated "prosperity" or "wealth," המון (*hamon*) translated "riches," אצרר (*'otsar*) translated "treasures" and מטמון (*matmon*) also translated "treasures."

עשר is found in both a positive and negative sense in the Old Testament. The word is found in a positive sense 34 times and in a negative sense 17 times.[1] Nearly every reference to עשר in the historical books or other prose writing is positive. Wealth was normally considered a blessing from God. The negative references to wealth are found almost exclusively in poetic passages, including the prophets.

In a positive sense, עשר is thought to be a blessing from the Lord. Proverbs 10: 22 declares, *"The blessing of the Lord brings wealth (עשר) and he adds no trouble to it."*[2] In fact, wealth comes as a result of humility and the fear of the Lord. *"Humility and the fear of the Lord bring wealth and honor and life"* (Proverbs 22:4). Although wealth ultimately comes from the Lord, it also comes as a result of hard work. *"Lazy hands make a man poor, but diligent hands bring wealth"* (Proverbs 10:4). The persons most likely to enjoy wealth in the Old Testament period were the kings. Solomon is especially credited with being a wealthy man (1 Kings 10:23; 2 Chronicles 1:11-12;

---

[1] There are two references to עשר in a neutral sense and one in a figurative sense for a total of 54 references.

[2] See also 1 Samuel 2:7; Psalm 112:3; and 1 Chronicles 29:12.

9:22).³ Because the kings had wealth, they could distribute it to others. Saul promised to give great wealth, including his own daughter, to the person who defeated Goliath (1 Samuel 17:25).

On the other hand, the writers of the Old Testament recognized that there were dangers associated with wealth and riches. The Psalmist warns about trusting in one's wealth rather than God. *"Here now is the man who did not make God his stronghold but trusted in his great wealth"* (Psalm 52:7).⁴ There are many warnings in the Wisdom Literature related to riches. Proverbs 11:28 states, *"Whoever trusts in his riches will fall, but the righteous will thrive like a green leaf."* One should not overstress himself to get wealth (Proverbs 23:4). Riches often are acquired through deceit (Jeremiah 5:27) and can cause a person to be proud (Jeremiah 9:23). Unfortunately, riches do not always last (Psalm 49:16-17) and *"a good name is more desirable than great riches"* (Proverbs 22:1).

Ronald Allen states that there is a "tension between the benefits and dangers of riches"⁵ which is very well expressed in Proverbs 30:8b-9;

> Give me neither poverty nor riches, but give me only my daily bread. Otherwise, I may have too much and disown you, and say, 'Who is the Lord?' Or I may become poor and steal, and so dishonor the name of my God.

There is no clear usage of עשר in a figurative sense in the Old Testament. The closest thing is Psalm 65:9a which says, *"You care for the land and water it; you enrich it abundantly."*⁶ What this verse says is that wealth was more than silver and gold. It also included the beauties and intricacies of nature.

---

³ Jehoshaphat (2 Chronicles 17:5, 18:1), Hezekiah (2 Chronicles 32:27) and Xerxes (Esther 1:4) were also described as rich.

⁴ See also Psalm 49:6.

⁵ Ronald B. Allen, עשר in *Theological Wordbook of the Old Testament*, editor: R. Laird Harris (Chicago, IL USA: Moody Press, 1980), p.1714.

⁶ Another possible reference is Proverbs 22:4. The KJV reads, *"Humility and the fear of the Lord are riches."* However, the NIV probably more accurately reflects the true meaning of the sentence: *"Humility and the fear of the Lord bring wealth and honor and life."*

Wealth, in the Old Testament, is having more possessions that one needs to live. Since it is essential to have a certain amount of possessions to live, having more than one needs is a special blessing from God. Therefore, wealth is frequently commended and even promised in the Old Testament period. It comes from the hand of God and also is acquired through diligent work. On the other hand, wealth can lead to many temptations, which may cause one to stray from God. Thus, wealth must be handled carefully. Since there are twice as many references to wealth in a positive sense as in a negative sense, the overall attitude toward wealth was positive in the Old Testament period.

εὐοδόομαι

Third John 2 says in the KJV, "Beloved I wish above all things that thou mayest prosper and be in health, even as thy soul prospereth." The NIV translates the "prosperity" phrase, "I pray . . . that all may go well with you, even as your soul is getting along well." The word which is translated "prosper" in the KJV is the word is εὐοδόομαι (euodoomai). It is related to the name of the woman in Philippi called Euodia (Philippians 4:2). The word comes from two Greek words εὐ (eu) which means "good" and ὁδό" (hodos) which literally means "way" or "road." The word literally means to go along a good road.[7] It could refer to having a good journey. In Hausa one of the typical greetings is "Barka da hanya" (Greetings on your journey) which would be a good colloquial translation of the word.

εὐοδόομαι is found only four times in the New Testament. Two of them are found in the 3 John passage. Romans 1:10 is another passage: *"I pray that now at last by God's will **the way may be opened** for me to come to you."*[8] This is almost a literal meaning of the word. The other reference to the word is 1 Corinthians 16:2 (KJV): *"Upon the first day of the week let every one of you lay by him in store, as God hath **prospered** him, that there be no*

---

[7] William F. Arndt and F. Wilbur Gingrich, *A Greek-English Lexicon of the New Testament and Other Early Christian Literature* (Chicago, IL USA: The University of Chicago Press, 1967), p.324.

[8] The KJV says, *"Making request, if by any means now at length I might have a prosperous journey by the will of God to come unto you."*

gatherings when I come." The NIV translates the verse, **"in keeping with his income."**

Arndt and Gingrich says that the word means *"get along well, prosper, or succeed."*[9] It is a general word which describes a positive happening that leaves the recipient better than he was before. It does not exclusively refer to material blessings.

Coming at the beginning of the Epistle of 3 John, this phrase is actually a greeting. John is writing to his converts and saying something like this: *"I pray that things will go well with you, with your family, with your employment, with your health, with your community, with everything."* This is not a statement upon which one builds theology. Greetings are culturally relevant but not appropriate to create theology.

When one greets another person early in the day he or she is likely to say "Good morning." In so doing he or she is actually praying or wishing that the person will have a good morning. If two opposing football teams meet one morning, they will likely greet one another by saying "Good morning." However, in truth, they do not want each other to have a good morning. They want the other team to have a bad morning. The greeting is culturally appropriate but not a true reflection of the actual feelings of the greeter.

εὐοδόομαι is a general word referring to success in whatever one is doing. In the 3 John passage it is a greeting and not a theological statement.

πλούσιος, πλουσίως, πλουτέω, πλουτίζω, πλοῦτος

The most important family of words related to wealth in the Greek New Testament is the group of words with the πλου (plou) root. A careful analysis of these words suggests the following:

1. There are 22 negative references to wealth/riches.
2. There are 2 positive references.
3. There are 15 neutral references to wealth.

---

[9] Arndt and Gingrich, p. 324.

4. There are 11 references to wealth used in a figurative sense. Ten of them are used positively and one is used negatively.
5. There are 17 references to wealth being associated with God and/or Jesus.

I will now do some specific analysis.

As indicated above, there are fifteen references to wealth in which the wealth is not viewed in either a positive or negative sense. In Matthew 27:57, Joseph of Arimathea who claimed the body of Jesus is described as a *"rich man."* Luke records several miracles which Jesus told about rich men who had servants and who treated them in various ways (Luke 12:16; 16:1, 19; 18:23; 19:2). In these 17 cases, wealth is viewed as neither positive nor negative.

The only two positive places these words are found are both in 2 Corinthians and are associated with the offerings Paul was collecting as he was concluding the third missionary journey. In 2 Corinthians 8:1-2 he writes,

> *And now, brothers, we want you to know about the grace that God has given the Macedonian churches. Out of the most severe trial, their overflowing joy and their extreme poverty welled up in **rich generosity**.*[10]

What the verse is saying is that even though the Macedonians were suffering great trials and were poor themselves, they were able to express themselves *"richly"*—they were able to act like rich people in giving even though they did not have much.

The second reference is 2 Corinthians 9:10-11.

> *Now he who supplies seed to the sower and bread for food will also supply and increase your store of seed and will enlarge the harvest of your righteousness. You will be **made rich** in every way so that you can be generous on every occasion, and through us your generosity will result in thanksgiving to God.*

The implication of this passage is that if the Corinthians are faithful to give to others, the one who supplies all things will *"make them rich in every way."*

---

[10] The KJV translates this "unto the riches of their liberality."

"Prosperity: A Biblical Perspective" 453

However, the statement does not stop there. Paul goes on to state the purpose for which God will give them "riches—*"so that you can be generous on every occasion, and through us your generosity will result in thanksgiving to God."* The purpose of their wealth was to meet the genuine needs of others.

In the New Testament there are 22 negative references to this family of words that are translated riches and wealth.

> Matthew 13:22: *The one who received the seed that fell among the thorns is the man who hears the word, but the worries of this life and the **deceitfulness of wealth** choke it, making it unfruitful.*
>
> Matthew 19:23-24: *Then Jesus said to his disciples, 'I tell you the truth, it is hard for a **rich man** to enter the kingdom of heaven. Again I tell you, it is easier for a camel to go through the eye of a needle than for a rich man to enter the kingdom of God.'*
>
> James 5:1-6: *Now listen, you rich people, weep and wail because of the misery that is coming upon you. Your wealth has rotted, and moths have eaten your clothes. Your gold and silver are corroded. Their corrosion will testify against you and eat your flesh like fire. You have hoarded wealth in the last days. Look! The wages you failed to pay the workmen who mowed your field are crying out against you. The cries of the harvesters have reached the ears of the Lord Almighty. You have lived on earth in luxury and self-indulgence. You have fattened yourselves in the day of slaughter. You have condemned and murdered innocent men, who were not opposing you.*[11]

For every positive reference to wealth in the New Testament, there are ten negative statements about wealth. The New Testament writers recognized the dangers of wealth. It has a way of drawing a person away from God.

There are seventeen references to wealth associated with God or Jesus.

> 2 Corinthians 8:9: *For you know the grace of our Lord Jesus Christ, that though he was rich, yet for your sakes he became poor, so that you through his poverty might become **rich**.*

---

[11] There are several negative references to wealth in the Book of Revelation. A typical one is 18:3: "For all the nations have drunk the maddening wine of her adulteries. The kings of the earth committed adultery with her, and the merchants of the earth grew rich from her excessive luxuries."

> Ephesians 1:7-8: *In him we have redemption through his blood, the forgiveness of sins, in accordance with the riches **of God's grace** that he lavished on us with all wisdom and understanding.*
>
> Ephesians 2:4: *But because of his great love for us, God, who is rich **in mercy**, made us alive with Christ even when we were dead in transgressions.*
>
> 1 Timothy 6:17: *Command those who are **rich** in this present world not to be arrogant nor to put their hope in wealth, which is so uncertain, but to put their hope in **God, who richly provides us** with everything for our enjoyment.*

The point is that God is rich. He owns everything. His wealth is not limited to material things. He knows how to use wealth properly and shares it freely with humanity out of His abundance.

The New Testament refers to wealth or riches in a figurative way eleven times and ten of those are positive. For example, Paul declares in 1 Corinthians 1:5, *"For in him **you have been enriched** in every way—in all your speaking and in all your knowledge . . ."* According to this passage, a part of one's wealth is his or her ability to speak, and a part of it is his or her knowledge.

Paul gives a part of his testimony in 2 Corinthians 6:10; *"sorrowful, yet always rejoicing; poor, **yet making many rich**; having nothing; and yet possessing everything."* He was poor in material possessions but rich in spiritual blessings. He gives this exhortation in Colossians 3:16;

> Let the word of Christ dwell in you richly as you teach and admonish one another with all wisdom, and as you sing psalms, hymns and spiritual songs with gratitude in your hearts to God.

He describes those who are pleasing to God as *"rich in good deeds,"* (1 Timothy 6:18).

The only negative reference to wealth in a figurative sense is found in 1 Corinthians 4:8 where Paul is speaking sarcastically to the Corinthians about their accomplishments: *"Already you have all you want! **Already you have become rich!** You have become kings—and that without us!"*

Because wealth means an abundance or more than one needs, the word is often used in a figurative sense to describe the spiritual blessings which God has given us. This is almost always positive because God's blessings to us are positive.

As we saw in the Old Testament, wealth is viewed both positively and negatively in the New Testament. However, it is used in a negative sense far more than in a positive sense, because the New Testament writers recognized its ability to draw one away from God.

Theological Perspective[12]

One of the primary differences between the Old Testament and the New Testament is the structures through which God was working on the earth. In Genesis 12:2, God promised to make a great nation out of Abraham. Most of the rest of the Old Testament tells about the building of that nation and the subsequent blessings and difficulties of that nation. The people of Israel and the nation of Israel were God's channel of operation in that period of time. Although God would occasionally show mercy upon non-Israelite individuals, like Ruth, and cities, like Nineveh, whatever God was doing upon the earth during that time period, He was working in the context of the nation of Israel.

However, the Christian faith believes that when Jesus came, God changed the structure through which he would be working on the earth. Jesus promised, *"I will build my church, and the gates of Hades will not overcome it,"* (Matthew 16:18). As far back as the Old Testament prophet Joel, God had promised to change the "rules" related to the way one worked for and interacted with God. Joel predicted that a time would come when all people at every level of society would have access to the Holy Spirit which was only possible for the spiritual giants and leaders in the Old Testament period (Joel 2:28-32).

The basic purpose of the nation of Israel was to provide and prepare the world for the coming of the Messiah who would be the Savior of the

---

[12] A proper theology of wealth in the Old Testament would be developed by studying the development of understanding of wealth through the various periods of the Old Testament progressing through the patriarchal period, and the Mosaic period, the kingdom period under David and Solomon and the kingdom period in its declining days as reflected in the prophets.

world. The purpose of the Church is to spread the good news that the Savior has come to the world.[13]

Although both were channels of God's operation upon the earth and both share many other common characteristics, the nation of Israel and the Church have some very basic differences.

1. Israel was restricted to one geographical location. The church is not limited to one place.
2. Israel spoke one language. The church speaks many languages.
3. Israel was made up of one race of people. The church is made up of all races.
4. Israel had a capital city and "holy places." The church has no such sacred places nor any central headquarters.
5. Israel worshipped God primarily in the Temple in Jerusalem. The church worships anywhere *"in spirit and in truth."*

Because Israel was a nation, there was more of a stress on material things than there is in the church. In order for a nation to survive, there must be a certain amount of physical assets. The mark of a healthy nation is one which has many assets, including wealthy people. In order to field an army to protect its borders, a nation has to have wealth. In order to create roads and other infrastructure for its people, governments have to generate money and the more money they have, the more benefits they can provide for their citizens. Because the heart of a government is located in one central place, foreign visitors go to that place and learn something about the health of that nation by observing the kinds of property and buildings which the government has erected.

However, few if any of these things apply to the church. Although most churches have buildings today, there was no hint of such in the New Testament days. The church could meet anywhere and be successful. The church has no borders to protect and no armies to field. Although the New Testament does encourage Christians to take care of the workers who minister to them (1 Corinthians 9:7-12) and also to take care of the

---

[13] One passage of Scripture which illustrates these two points is John 20:21: *"As the Father has sent me, I am sending you."*

poor and needy (Galatians 2:10), there is far less need for money to sustain the church than for the Old Testament nation of Israel.

Because of this, the New Testament writers tend to focus on the negative aspects of wealth and not the positive ones. If wealth is not essential to develop and maintain the infrastructure of the church as Jesus instituted it, then one should use it cautiously.

Spiritual Perspective

From the linguistic analysis given above, perhaps the biggest problem with wealth is that it has a tendency to lead people away from God. Since wealth is not essential to support the infrastructure of a church, Jesus and his apostles focused more on the negative aspects of wealth and its dangers to one's spiritual life.

The Example and Teachings of Jesus

Jesus demonstrated his apathy toward wealth in his own lifestyle. He never owned a house or property and declared on one occasion, *"Foxes have holes and birds of the air have nests, but the Son of Man has no place to lay his head,"* (Matthew 8:20). Had Jesus been developing an earthly kingdom, his kingdom would have had all the trappings of other kingdoms and he would have dressed and lived in luxury accordingly. However, Jesus lived in simplicity as an example to his subsequent followers that wealth is not a prerequisite to being part of the current phase of the kingdom of God.

In addition to his example, Jesus consistently warned about wealth. Although Jesus told some stories in which wealthy men are described in a neutral way, Jesus never gives any positive teaching about wealth. For example, near the end of his ministry, Jesus warned, *"It is easier for a camel to go through the eye of a needle than for a rich man to enter the kingdom of God,"* (Matthew 19:24). In Luke's summary of the content of the Sermon on the Mount, he includes this warning, *"But woe to you who are rich, for you have already received your comfort. Woe to you who are well fed now, for you will go hungry"* (Luke 6:24-25).

A practical application of Jesus' approach to wealth is his very unique teaching about the way one should use his wealth.

> When you give a luncheon or dinner, do not invite your friends, your brother or relatives, or your rich neighbors; if you do, they may invite you back and so you will be repaid. But when you give a banquet, invite the poor, the crippled, the lame, the blind, and you will be blessed. Although they cannot repay you, you will be repaid at the resurrection of the righteous (Luke 14:12-14).

In Jesus' famous story about the rich man and Lazarus, the poor man Lazarus is the hero of the story and the rich man is the villain (Luke 16:19-31). In addition, Luke also tells the story about the rich young man who came to Jesus wanting to know how he could inherit eternal life. Jesus told him to sell all his possession and give them to the poor and he would have treasure in heaven. Luke points out that the young man was very sad *"because he was a man of great wealth"* (Luke18:23).

The one thing that rich people should be able to do better than anyone else is to give gifts to God. However, Luke also tells an amazing story about the giving of the wealthy. Once when Jesus was in the temple, he observed the various people giving their gifts. There was a stark contrast between what the rich were putting in and what a poor widow was able to give. Jesus said,

> I tell you the truth . . . this poor widow has put in more than all the others. All these people gave their gifts out of their wealth; but she out of her poverty put in all she had to live on. (Luke 21:3-4).

To Jesus, the value of one's gift was measured not in the amount that was given, but the amount that remained.

To summarize, Jesus lived a simple life by refusing to accumulate possessions and identifying with the people at the lower end of the social strata. He encouraged people to give away their possessions and warned about the accumulation and misuse of wealth. He told stories about wealthy people as a recognition that this was a normal part of society, but demanded that his followers not follow the pattern of wealth exemplified by most wealthy people.

The Example of the Early Church

There are few examples of wealth referred to in the Book of Acts. Neither of the Greek words examined earlier are found in Acts. However, there are some hints that there were some wealthy Christians in the early church. Barnabas sold a field and gave the money to the church (Acts

4:36-37). Though that act does not positively say that he was wealthy, the implication is that if a man has enough property to give a substantial portion away and continue living normally, he is wealthy.

Wealth continues to be viewed negatively in the early church. When Simon tried to make money out of the gospel, Peter rebuked him most severely (8:20-23). If there is an emphasis in the Book of Acts on wealth, it is the encouragement to distribute wealth. As indicated above, Barnabas and others gave part of their wealth away (4:34-35). In addition, the church at Antioch took up money to give to the needy in Jerusalem (11:29-30).

The Teachings of the Apostles

The ultimate commentary and application of the teachings of Jesus is given by the apostles of Jesus in the Epistles, which are written to actual persons and groups.

Paul

The Apostle Paul does not really discuss in detail riches from a traditional point of view but focuses on the figurative use of wealth. In fact, fifteen of the seventeen figurative usages of the $\pi\lambda o\hat{u}\tau o\varsigma$ family of words come from Paul's writing. Paul particularly enjoys applying the idea of wealth to God, Christ and the community.[14] To Paul, true riches included the mercy of God (Ephesians 2:4), the kindness of God (Romans 2:4), the glory of God (Romans 9:23; Ephesians 1:18; 3:16; Philippians 4:19; Colossians 1:27), the wisdom and knowledge of God (Romans 11:33), and the grace of God (Ephesians 1:7; 2:7). In addition, rather than encouraging persons to accumulate physical assets to make themselves wealthy in material things, Paul urged his readers to allow the word of God to dwell in them *"richly"* (Colossians 3:16) and *"to be rich in good deeds"* (1 Timothy 6:18)

---

[14] Friedrich Hauck and Wilheim Kasch, "$\pi\lambda o\hat{u}\tau o\varsigma$, $\pi\lambda o\acute{u}\sigma\iota o\varsigma$, $\pi\lambda o\upsilon\tau\acute{\epsilon}\omega$, $\pi\lambda o\upsilon\tau\acute{\iota}\zeta\omega$, *Theological Dictionary of the New Testament*, Editors: Gerhard Kittel and Gerhard Friedrich; translated by Geoffrey W. Bromiley, Vol. VI (Grand Rapids, MI USA: Wm. B. Eerdmans Publishing Company, 1975), p. 328.

However, like his master, Paul continued the tradition of warning about the abuses of wealth. Paul's teachings about wealth are summarized in 1 Timothy 6:9-10, 17-19.

> *People who want to get rich fall into temptation and a trap and into many foolish and harmful desires that plunge men into ruin and destruction. For the love of money is a root of all kinds of evil. Some people, eager for money, have wandered from the faith and pierced themselves with many griefs . . . Command those who are rich in this present world not to be arrogant nor to put their hope in wealth, which is so uncertain, but to put their hope in God, who richly provides us with everything for our enjoyment. Command them to do good, to be rich in good deeds, and to be generous and willing to share. In this way they will lay up treasure for themselves as a firm foundation for the coming age.*

Paul understood that wealth is a powerful temptation that many people do not have the ability to resist. Therefore, he supported the warnings of Jesus against it.

James

James was probably the first of the New Testament writer. His book contains more warnings about wealth in proportion to its size than any other New Testament book. James warns that wealth will pass away like a wild flower (1:10), and the wealthy man will do the same (1:11). In 2:1-9, James gives a stinging denunciation of the wealthy elites who had imposed a social caste system in the church, assigning good seats to the wealthy and lowly seats to the poor. He further states that one of the ways the wealthy got their wealth was through exploiting the poor (2:6). In 5:1-6, James gives his most blunt condemnation of the wealthy. They have been guilty of hoarding their wealth (5:3), failing to pay their workers (5:4), have lived in luxury and self-indulgence (5:5) and have even murdered the innocent who stood in their way of success (5:6). His advice was that they should *"weep and wail"* (5:1), no doubt a euphemism for repentance.

John

John's only references to the wealthy are in the Book of the Revelation. He reflects essentially the same attitude as Paul.[15] On the positive side, *"Worthy is the Lamb, who was slain, to receive power and wealth and wisdom and strength and honor and glory and praise"* (Revelation 5:12). All of these are good things. The Lamb is prepared to accept every good thing, including wealth. In the letter to the Church at Smyrna, Jesus recognized their *"afflictions and poverty—yet you are rich!"* (2:9). This is obviously a figurative reference to wealth. Interestingly, the opposite is said of the church of Laodicea. They thought they were *"rich"* but in reality they were *"wretched, pitiful, poor, blind and naked"* (3:17). Consistent with the other writers, John describes those who will gain their wealth through dishonest and corrupt means (Revelation 18:3, 15, 17, 19).

Summary of the Teaching of the Epistles

In summary, the Epistles teach that God is rich in many ways and that God's people should be rich in good deeds. However, they warn about the abuse of wealth, both the way it is obtained, and the way it is distributed. Christians are not forbidden to be wealthy but are expected to use their wealth to aid the needy, and avoid using it to exploit others.

Observations

The following are some general observations based upon the research given above.

1. There is no sin in wealth.

Nowhere does the Bible state that wealth itself is sin. Rather it is always either the greed for wealth or the way wealth is obtained or the way wealth is used—that is the sin of wealth.

---

[15] Friedrich Hauck and Wilheim Kasch, p. 330.

2. God is the source of wealth and gives to some and withholds from others.

The Bible consistently says that God is the ultimate owner of all things and therefore the source of all wealth. He gives to some, while withholding from others. Though this is contrary to the opinion of Job's comforters, the presence of wealth in one's life was neither an indication of God's favor or disfavor. God sometimes allows both the righteous and the unrighteous to have wealth or not to have wealth.

3. Wealth was more important to the Old Testament nation of Israel than to the Church.

Because the nation of Israel required more material possessions than the church, there was a greater stress on wealth in the Old Testament and a lesser focus on the abuses of wealth. However, Jesus and the other New Testament writers consistently warned about the abuses of wealth.

4. Wealth is a big temptation to believers to abandon God.

The biggest problem with wealth is that it causes a person to be comfortable, relaxed and, therefore, in less need of God. It also encourages pride and often leads to the abuse of others in acquiring wealth.

5. There is no evidence that wealth is related to one's faith or a special privilege for the spiritually elite.

Christianity is a religion which is independent and above the number of one's personal assets. Poor people can enjoy God's favor and blessing just as much as wealthy people. In fact, because of the many warnings against wealth in the New Testament, wealth is more of a hindrance to one's faith than an asset.

Conclusion

Poor people are greatly attracted to wealth. Those who come preaching that the gospel will make them rich automatically get the attention of the poor. However, when reality does not produce the promised prosperity, those who have experimented with that theory are often worse off than they were before.

Wealth is like a machete. It is a valuable tool in the hands of the right person but a deadly thing in the hands of the wrong person. We Christians must use wealth but not abuse it. We must control it and not allow it to control us. We must acquire possessions but not hoard them. We must serve God in wealth or in poverty. We must resist those who want to distort the message of Christianity with the message of prosperity. We must *"seek first the kingdom of God"* and be assured that all that we need will be given to us (Matthew 6:33).

Selected Bibliography

Adeyemo, Tokunboh. *Africa Bible Commentary.* Nairobi, Kenya: World Alive Publishers, 2006. Also Zondervan Corporation.

Allison, Joseph D. *Bible Study Resource Guide.* Nashville, TN USA: Thomas Nelson Publishers, 1982.

Day, A. Colin. *Roget's Thesaurus of the Bible.* Son Francisco, CA USA: Harper, 1992.

Duvall, J. Scott, and J. Daniel Hays. *Grasping God's Word.* Grand Rapids, MI USA: Zondervan, 2001.

Freeman, James M. *Manners and Customs of the Bible.* Plainfield, NJ USA: Logos International, 1972.

Froehlich, Karlfried. *Biblical Interpretation of the Early Church.* Philadelphia, PA USA: Fortress, 1984.

Grant, Robert M. and David Tracy. *A Short History of the Interpretation of the Bible,* 2nd ed. Philadelphia, PA USA: Fortress, 1984.

Grudem, Wayne. *Systematic Theology: An Introduction to Biblical Doctrine.* Leicester, England: InterVarsity, 1994.

Keener, Craig. *Matthew.* Downers-Grove, IL USA: InterVarsity Press, 1996.

Keener, Craig. *3 Crucial Questions about the Holy Spirit.* Grand Rapids, MI USA: Baker Book House, 1996.

MacGregor, Geddes. *A Literary History of the Bible.* Nashville, TN USA: Abingdon Press, 1968.

McQuilkin, J. Robertson. *Understanding and Applying the Bible.* Chicago, IL USA: Moody Press, 1992.

Metzger, Bruce. *The Text of the New Testament.* Oxford, England: Oxford University Press, 1968.

Mickelsen, A. Berkeley. *Interpreting the Bible.* Grand Rapids, IL USA: Wm. B. Eerdmans, 1963.

Ramm. Bernard. *Protestant Biblical Interpretation.* Grand Rapids, MI USA: Baker Book House, 1970.

Stein, Robert H. *Playing by the Rules.* Grand Rapids, MI USA: Baker Books, 1994.

Sterrett, T. Norton. *How to Understand Your Bible.* Downers-Grove, IL USA: InterVarsity Press.

Vanhoozer, Kevin J. *Is There a Meaning in This Text?* Leicester, England: Apollos, 1998.

Wegner, Paul D. *The Journey from Texts to Translations.* Grand Rapids, MI USA: Baker Academic, 1999.

Willmington, H. L. *Willmington's Guide to the Bible.* Wheaton, IL USA: Tyndale House Publishers, Inc., 1981.

General Index

A

African Proverbs, 292

Alliteration, 280

American Standard Version, 80, 81

Anthropomorphism, 214

Antithetic Parallelism, 276

Apocalypse of Peter, 47

Apocrypha, 44, 79, 80, 115, 168, 181

Apostrophe, 213

Application, 4, 14, 108, 329, 331, 332, 333, 334, 359, 361, 365

Atlas, 109, 110

Atonement, 438

Authority, 200

Authorized Version, 76

B

Baptism, 95, 96, 255, 338, 395

Bishop's Bible, 75

Blood of Jesus, 427, 430, 431, 432, 433, 438, 441

C

Canonization, 2, 43, 44

Chiastic Parallelism, 278

Circumcision, 336

classical liberal theory, 41

Climactic Parallelism, 277

Commands, 331, 338

Communication, 89, 90, 91, 92, 252, 253, 360

Concordance, 103, 104, 105, 180, 183, 184

Context, 147, 148, 149, 150, 151, 152, 155, 162, 163, 167, 173, 317, 369, 386, 403

Coverdale, 73, 74, 78, 87

Cultural Symbols, 255

Culture, 169

D

Dead Sea Scrolls, 16, 56, 168

Death, 271, 396

dictation theory, 41

Dictation View, 34

Dictionary, 94, 96, 97, 98, 105, 106, 115, 182, 256, 459

Didache, 47, 48

Didactic, 273, 288

Doctrine, 354, 443

Douai-Reims Version, 76

Double Parallelism, 278

Dynamic Equivalent Translation, 84

Dynamic View, 34

E

Eclectic Approach, 324

Epistle, 47, 159, 168, 181, 435, 451

Epistle of Barnabas, 47

Erasmus, 64, 65, 68

Euphemism, 214

Exegesis, 3

Exhortations, 338

F

Figurative, 177, 207, 224, 279, 302

Figures of Speech, 209, 210, 282

Futurist Approach, 324

G

Geneva Bible, 75, 87

Genre, 260, 322

Grammar, 191, 204, 302

Great Bible, 74

H

Harmony of Gospels, 110

Head covering, 344

Hebrew Idioms, 207, 215, 222

Hebrew Poetry, 18, 273, 274, 281

Hermeneutics, 1, 2, 112

Historical Psalms, 288

Hort, 60, 63, 66, 67, 68, 80, 82, 109

Hyperbole, 211

I

Idealist Approach, 323

Idiom, 222

Imprecatory Psalms, 288

Inerrancy, 29

Inspiration, 2, 28, 29, 32, 35, 37, 50, 330

Interpretation, 3, 4, 5, 6, 7, 14, 160, 224, 263, 325, 329, 332, 333, 334, 359, 361

Irony, 213

Israel, 35, 36, 37, 129, 136, 138, 152, 161, 169, 213, 217, 218, 221, 233, 234, 235, 236, 240, 241, 242, 246, 249, 250, 252, 256, 263, 269, 271, 281, 285, 286, 287, 303, 305, 306, 307, 315, 334, 352, 354, 369, 373, 381, 382, 386, 387, 400, 404, 407, 408, 416, 439, 455, 456, 457, 462

K

Kethubim, 13

King James Bible, 6, 8, 79, 83

King James Version, 72, 76, 77, 78, 79, 80, 81, 82, 86, 87, 103, 145, 184, 185, 211, 374, 417

Koine Greek, 15, 70

L

Lexicon, 181, 450

Literal Translation, 84

Litotes, 214

Liturgical, 289

Lyric, 273

M

Martin Luther, 32, 69, 72, 87, 285

Matthew Bible, 73, 74

Megilloth, 13

Messianic Psalms, 287

Metonymy, 211

General Index 469

N

National Psalms, 286

Nature Psalms, 287

Nebhiim, 13

Neo-Orthodox, 33

New International Version, 81, 86

New Living Translation, 82, 84, 86, 218

O

Observations, 85, 122, 130, 162, 222, 244, 257, 333, 441, 461

Onomatopoeia, 281

Orthodox, 15, 35

Orthodox View, 35

Over-interpretation, 8, 10, 275

P

Papyrus, 16

Parallelism, 122, 274, 275, 277, 278, 281

Paraphrases, 82, 85

Paronomasia, 281

Partial Inspiration View, 34

Penitential, 287

Personification, 212

Pleonasm, 214

Poetry, 13, 19, 259, 260, 273, 274, 282

Polyglot, 63, 64, 65

Prayers, 338

Preterist Approach, 323

Principles, 160, 172, 335, 361, 362

Progressive Revelation, 228

Prose, 18

Proverbs, 13, 19, 89, 92, 123, 148, 151, 152, 172, 220, 260, 275, 276, 277, 283, 289, 291, 294, 295, 299, 330, 335, 362, 381, 409, 412, 425, 448, 449

Psaltery, 70

Pseudepigrapha, 168

R

Relative, 215, 219

Resurrection, 34, 35, 97, 139, 143, 200, 210, 212, 300, 321, 359, 385, 386, 390, 418, 443, 444, 458

Revised Standard Version, 80, 82, 115

Revised Version, 80

Rhetorical Question, 213

Royal Psalms, 287

Ruth, 13, 234, 250, 394, 455

S

Saxon, 70

Selectivity, 135, 137, 140

Septuagint, 13, 180, 181

Shepherd of Hermas, 47

Sin, 223, 397

Sinaiticus, 63

Soteriology, 111

Study Bible, 53, 102, 107, 108, 109, 115, 430

Symbolism, 256, 322

Synecdoche, 212

Synonymous Parallelism, 275

Synthetic Parallelism, 276

T

Taverner Bible, 74

Tests of Inspiration, 49

Textual Criticism, 2

Textus Receptus, 65, 66, 67, 68, 81, 82, 109

Thecla, 47, 51

Theology, 97, 98, 106, 109, 111, 112, 175, 182, 427, 443

Torah, 13

Transcultural, 269, 362

Translations, 2, 70, 79, 82, 85

Tyndale, 71, 72, 73, 74, 84, 87

Types, 149, 273, 275, 278, 281, 282, 286, 300

V

Vaticanus, 63

Vernacular Translation, 70

Vernacular Translations, 70

W

Westcott, 60, 63, 66, 67, 68, 80, 82, 109

Western Text, 63

Wicked Bible, 79

Wycliff, 71

ACTS Publications

African Christian Theology,	Aben
AIDS is Real and it's in our Church,	Garland & Blyth
African Traditional Religion in the Light of the Bible,	Gehman
Biblical Preaching in Africa,	Janvier
Biblical Theology of Missions,	Fuller
Celebrating Life,	McCain
Christian Ethics,	Shields
Christianity and Islam,	Abashiya & Ulea
Christianity in Northern Nigeria,	Crampton (with update by Gaiya)
Christians in Politics,	Danladi Musa
Churches in Fellowship: The Story of TEKAN,	Hopkins & Gaiya
Cross-cultural Christianity,	Hassan, et al.
Culture and the Christian Home (2nd Ed),	Kore
Discipleship: a West African Perspective,	Janvier & Thaba
Essentials of Christian Religious Studies in Colleges of Ed,	Wiebe, *et al*, (3 vols.)
Every Abortion Stops a Beating Heart,	Garland & Idoko
Exposition of First Corinthians for Today,	Yamsat
Fighting Back (against HIV and AIDS),	McCain
Fundamentals of the Christian Home,	Pofi
Going to the Nations,	Fuller
Growth of the Church in Africa,	Falk
Growing Up,	Taylor/Wildman

Guide for Studying the Word of God: Esther,	Bitrus
Handbook of Bible Interpretation,	Schilling
History of EMS of ECWA,	Panya Baba
How to Write a Theological Research Thesis,	Janvier
Introduction to the Intertestamental Period,	Kafang
Journey With Jesus,	Krouse
Keys to Language Development & Bible Translation,	Crozier & Dettweiler
Leading the Church in Music & Worship,	Janvier
Legacy of Wisdom,	Bitrus
Let's Study New Testament Greek,	Preus (revised edition with Wiebe & Lillo)
Life and Teachings of Christ,	Shields
Living Messages,	McCain
Major and Minor Prophets,	Janvier/Itapson
Managing Stress, Anxiety & Burnout,	Adegboyega
Millennium Messages,	McCain
Missionary Handbook on African Traditional Religion,	Fuller
Mission Today,	Cheesman
My Brother's Keeper,	Beattie
Nigerian Harvest,	Smith
Notes on Acts of the Apostles,	McCain
Notes on New Testament Introduction,	McCain
Notes on Old Testament Introduction,	McCain
Pastor's Wife,	Gotom
Pentateuch,	Fuller
Perspectives on African Theology,	Gwamna

Philosophy of Christian Education,	Ilori
Premarital Counselling Manual,	Hogeterp
Preparation for Life and Ministry (Chapel Messages),	McCain
Principles & Methods of Teaching Christian Religious Education,	Ilori
Promoting Healthy Marriage and Family Life,	Kore
Refresh,	Wall
Religion and Politics in Nigeria,	Gwamna
Reconciliation for Africa,	C Keener & M. M. Keener
Reformed and Presbyterian Faith,	Palmer
Road to Freedom (History of Sudan United Mission),	Tett
School of Brokenness,	Abaga
Serving God Away from Home,	McCain
Story of Faith Missions,	Fiedler
Studies in Old Testament Prophecy,	Folarin
Ten Great Reasons to Say No to Sex Before Marriage,	Garland
Textbooks for Theological Education in Africa: An Annotated Bibliography,	Starcher & Anguandia
Times of Refreshing: History of Revival in Africa,	Burgess
The Battle is God's	Ferdinando
Theology of the New Testament	Palmer
Theology of the Old Testament,	Palmer
Theology of Worship,	Bartlett
Tough Tests for Top Leaders,	McCain
Train to Teach Others,	Kure
Training for Church Planters	Janvier
True Minister of God,	Onukwa
Truths for Healthy Churches,	Kore
Turn the Other Cheek,	Kadala

Two Models of Leadership,	McCain
Understanding & Applying the Scriptures,	McCain & Keener
Understanding the Bible,	Stott
Understanding Leadership,	Janvier/Thaba
We Believe: Introduction on Christian Doctrine,	McCain (2 vols.)
You Could Be a Missionary,	Adekoya

ACTS / HippoBooks / Zondervan titles

African Christian Ethics,	Kunhiyop
Guide to Interpreting Scripture,	Kyoma
My Neighbour's Faith (Islam Explained),	Azumah
Preachers of a Different Gospel,	Adeleye
The War Within,	Chukwuocha

Africa Bible Commentary Series (ACTS / HippoBooks / Zondervan)

1 & 2 Timothy and Titus,	Ngewa
Galatians,	Ngewa
Romans,	Andria
Jeremiah and Lamentations,	Katho

www.ingramcontent.com/pod-product-compliance
Lightning Source LLC
Chambersburg PA
CBHW070714160426
43192CB00009B/1180